THE ANCIENT LA[...] MESOPOTAMIA, EGY[...]

This book, derived from the acclaimed *Cambridge Encyclopedia of the World's Ancient Languages*, describes the ancient languages of Mesopotamia, Egypt, and Aksum, for the convenience of students and specialists working in that area. Each chapter of the work focuses on an individual language or, in some instances, a set of closely related varieties of a language. Providing a full descriptive presentation, each of these chapters examines the writing system(s), phonology, morphology, syntax, and lexicon of that language, and places the language within its proper linguistic and historical context. The volume brings together an international array of scholars, each a leading specialist in ancient language study. While designed primarily for scholars and students of linguistics, this work will prove invaluable to all whose studies take them into the realm of ancient language.

Roger D. Woodard is the Andrew Van Vranken Raymond Professor of the Classics at the University of Buffalo. His chief research interests lie generally within the areas of Greek and Roman myth and religion, Indo-European culture and linguistics, the origin and development of writing among the Greeks, and the interaction between Greece and the ancient Near East. His other books include *The Cambridge Companion to Greek Mythology* (2007), *Indo-European Sacred Space* (2006), *The Cambridge Encyclopedia of the World's Ancient Languages* (2004), *Ovid's Fasti* (with A. J. Boyle, 2000), *Greek Writing from Knossos to Homer: A Linguistic Interpretation of the Origins of the Greek Alphabet* (1997), and *On Interpreting Morphological Change* (1990). He has also published numerous articles and served as President of the Society for the Study of Greek and Latin Language and Linguistics from 1992 to 2001.

The Ancient Languages of Mesopotamia, Egypt, and Aksum

Edited by

ROGER D. WOODARD

CAMBRIDGE UNIVERSITY PRESS
Cambridge, New York, Melbourne, Madrid, Cape Town, Singapore, São Paulo, Delhi, Dubai, Tokyo, Mexico City

Cambridge University Press
The Edinburgh Building, Cambridge CB2 8RU, UK

Published in the United States of America by Cambridge University Press, New York

www.cambridge.org
Information on this title: www.cambridge.org/9780521684972

© Cambridge University Press 2008

This publication is in copyright. Subject to statutory exception and to the provisions of relevant collective licensing agreements, no reproduction of any part may take place without the written permission of Cambridge University Press.

Previously published in 2004 as chapters 2–3, 7–8 and 14 of Woodard, Roger D., *The Cambridge Encyclopedia of the World's Ancient Languages*
© Cambridge University Press 2004

First published 2008
Reprinted 2010

Printed in the United Kingdom at the University Press, Cambridge

A catalogue record for this publication is available from the British Library

ISBN 978-0-521-68497-2 paperback

Cambridge University Press has no responsibility for the persistence or accuracy of URLs for external or third-party internet websites referred to in this publication, and does not guarantee that any content on such websites is, or will remain, accurate or appropriate.

Contents

Figures

Tables

Map

Contributors

GENE GRAGG	University of Chicago
JOHN HUEHNERGARD	Harvard University
ANTONIO LOPRIENO	Universität Basel
PIOTR MICHALOWSKI	University of Michigan
MATTHEW W. STOLPER	University of Chicago
ROGER D. WOODARD	University of Buffalo (The State University of New York)
CHRISTOPHER WOODS	University of Chicago

Notes on numbering and cross-referencing

This volume is one of five paperbacks derived from *The Cambridge Encyclopedia of the World's Ancient Languages* (*WAL*), with the content now organized by region for the convenience of students and specialists wishing to focus on a given area of the ancient world.

Cross-references to material within this volume use its own internal chapter numbers. Any cross-references to other chapters of the original *WAL* refer to the chapter numbers in that work, and are prefixed by *WAL*. The contents list of *WAL* is reproduced at the back of this volume, as are the contents of the respective volumes of the paperback series derived from it.

Abbreviations

Any abbreviation that deviates from the form given below is noted within the text of the individual chapter or within a chapter-specific list.

Linguistic terms

abl.	ablative
abs.	absolutive
acc.	accusative
act.	active
adj.	adjective
adv.	adverb (adverbial)
all.	allative
anim.	animate
aor.	aorist
art.	article
asp.	aspirated
aux.	auxiliary (verb)
caus.	causative
cl.	clause
coll.	collective
com.	common
comp.	comparative
comt.	comitative
conj.	conjunction
conjv.	conjunctive
conn.	connective
cons.	consonant
constr.	construct (state)
cont.	continuant
cop.	copula
dat.	dative
def. art.	definite article
dem.	demonstrative
det.	determinate
detv.	determinative
dial.	dialect
dir.	directive
dir. obj.	direct object
disj.	disjunctive
du.	dual
dur.	durative
emph.-pcl.	emphatic particle
encl.	enclitic
eq.	equative
erg.	ergative
ext.	extended
fem.	feminine
final-pcl.	final-particle
fut.	future
gdve.	gerundive
gen.	genitive
ger.	gerund
impf.	imperfect
impftv.	imperfective
impv.	imperative
inan.	inanimate
inc.	inclusive
indef. art.	indefinite article
indet.	indeterminate
indic.	indicative
inf.	infinitive
instr.	instrumental
interr.	interrogative
intr.	intransitive
iter.	iterative
juss.	jussive
loc.	locative
mediopass.	mediopassive
mid.	middle

N.	noun
neg.	negative
neut.	neuter
nom.	nominative
NP	noun phrase
num.	number
obj.	object
obl.	oblique
opt.	optative
part.	participle
pass.	passive
pcl.	particle
per.	person
perf.	perfect
perfv.	perfective
perfvz.	perfectivizer
pert.	pertinentive
pl.	plural
pluperf.	pluperfect
poss. suff.	possessive suffix
postp.	postposition
PP	prepositional phrase
prec.	precative
preC.	preconsonantal
pref.	prefix
prep.	preposition
pres.	present
pret.	preterite
preV.	prevocalic
pro.	pronoun
prosp.	prospective
quot.	quotative particle
refl.	reflexive
rel. pro.	relative (pronoun)
rel./connec.	relative/connective
sg.	singular
soc.	sociative case
SOV	Subject–Object–Verb (word order)
spec.	specifier
splv.	superlative
stat.	stative
subj.	subject
subjunc.	subjunctive
subord.	subordinate/subordinator/ subordination marker
subord.-pcl.	subordinating particle
suff.	suffix
s.v.	*sub voce*
top.	topicalizer
tr.	transitive
V.	verb
var.	variant
vent.	ventive
voc.	vocative
vow.	vowel
VP	verbal phrase

Languages

Akk.	Akkadian
Ar.	Arabic
Ass.	Assyrian
Av.	Avestan
Bab.	Babylonian
Cis. Gaul.	Cisalpine Gaulish
Eg.	Egyptian (Old, Late, Earlier)
Eng.	English
Etr.	Etruscan
Gk.	Greek
Gmc.	Germanic
Go.	Gothic
Hisp.-Celt.	Hispano-Celtic
Hitt.	Hittite
IE	Indo-European
Lat.	Latin
Lep.	Lepontic
Luv.	Luvian
Lyc.	Lycian
MA	Middle Assyrian
MB	Middle Babylonian
NA	Neo-Assyrian
NB	Neo-Babylonian
OA	Old Assyrian
O. Akk.	Old Akkadian
O. Av.	Old Avestan
OB	Old Babylonian
OHG	Old High German
OP	Old Persian
PG	Proto-Greek
PGmc.	Proto-Germanic
PIE	Proto-Indo-European
PIIr.	Proto-Indo-Iranian
PIr.	Proto-Iranian
PMS	Proto-Mije-Sokean
PS	Proto-Semitic
PSo.	Proto-Sokean
SB	Standard Babylonian

Skt.	Sanskrit
Sum.	Sumerian
Y. Av.	Young Avestan

Other

abbr.	abbreviation
dict.	dictionary
intro.	introduction
lit.	literally
NA	not applicable
NS	new series
trad.	traditional
translit.	transliteration

Preface

Preliminary remarks

What makes a language ancient? The term conjures up images, often romantic, of archeologists feverishly copying hieroglyphs by torchlight in a freshly discovered burial chamber; of philologists dangling over a precipice in some remote corner of the earth, taking impressions of an inscription carved in a cliff-face; of a solitary scholar working far into the night, puzzling out some ancient secret, long forgotten by humankind, from a brittle-leafed manuscript or patina-encrusted tablet. The allure is undeniable, and the literary and film worlds have made full use of it.

An ancient language is indeed a thing of wonder – but so is every other language, all remarkable systems of conveying thoughts and ideas across time and space. And ancient languages, as far back as the very earliest attested, operate just like those to which the linguist has more immediate access, all with the same familiar elements – phonological, morphological, syntactic – and no perceptible vestiges of Neanderthal oddities. If there was a time when human language was characterized by features and strategies fundamentally unlike those we presently know, it was a time prior to the development of any attested or reconstructed language of antiquity. Perhaps, then, what makes an ancient language different is our awareness that it has outlived those for whom it was an intimate element of the psyche, not so unlike those rays of light now reaching our eyes that were emitted by their long-extinguished source when dinosaurs still roamed across the earth (or earlier) – both phantasms of energy flying to our senses from distant sources, long gone out.

That being said, and rightly enough, we must return to the question of what counts as an ancient language. As *ancient* the editor chose the upward delimitation of the fifth century AD. This *terminus ante quem* is one which is admittedly "traditional"; the fifth is the century of the fall of the western Roman Empire (AD 476), a benchmark which has been commonly (though certainly not unanimously) identified as marking the end of the historical period of *antiquity*. Any such chronological demarcation is of necessity arbitrary – far too arbitrary – as linguists accustomed to making such diachronic distinctions as *Old English, Middle English, Modern English* or *Old Hittite, Middle Hittite, Neo-Hittite* are keenly aware. Linguistic divisions of this sort are commonly based upon significant political events and clearly perceptible cultural shifts rather than upon language phenomena (though they are surely not without linguistic import as every historical linguist knows). The choice of the boundary in the present concern – the ancient-language boundary – is, likewise (as has already been confessed), not mandated by linguistic features and characteristics of the languages concerned.

However, this arbitrary choice, establishing a *terminus ante quem* of the fifth century, is somewhat buttressed by quite pragmatic linguistic considerations (themselves consequent to the whim of historical accident), namely the co-occurrence of a watershed in language documentation. Several early languages first make a significant appearance in the historical record in the fourth/fifth century: thus, Gothic (fourth century; see *WAL* Ch. 36), Ge'ez (fourth/fifth century; see Ch. 6, §1.3.1), Classical Armenian (fifth century; see *WAL* Ch. 38), Early Old Georgian (fifth century; see *WAL* Ch. 40). What newly comes into clear light in the sixth century is a bit more meager – Tocharian and perhaps the very earliest Old Kannada and Old Telegu from the end of the century. Moreover, the dating of these languages to the sixth century cannot be made precisely (not to suggest this is an especially unusual state of affairs) and it is equally possible that the earliest attestation of all three should be dated to the seventh century. Beginning with the seventh century the pace of language attestation begins to accelerate, with languages documented such as Old English, Old Khmer, and Classical Arabic (though a few earlier inscriptions preserving a "transitional" form of Arabic are known; see *WAL* Ch. 16, §1.1.1). The ensuing centuries bring an avalanche of medieval European languages and their Asian contemporaries into view. Aside from the matter of a culturally dependent analytic scheme of historical periodization, there are thus considerations of language history that motivate the upper boundary of the fifth century.

On the other hand, identifying a *terminus post quem* for the inclusion of a language in the present volume was a completely straightforward and noncontroversial procedure. The low boundary is determined by the appearance of writing in human society, a graphic means for recording human speech. A system of writing appears to have been first developed by the Sumerians of southern Mesopotamia in the late fourth millennium BC (see Ch. 2, §§1.2; 2). Not much later (beginning in about 3100 BC), a people of ancient Iran began to record their still undeciphered language of Proto-Elamite on clay tablets (see Ch. 3, §2.1). From roughly the same period, the Egyptian hieroglyphic writing system emerges in the historical record (see Ch. 5, §2). Hence, Sumerian and Egyptian are the earliest attested, understood languages and, *ipso facto*, the earliest languages treated in this volume.

It is conjectured that humans have been speaking and understanding language for at least 100,000 years. If in the great gulf of time which separates the advent of language and the appearance of Sumerian, Proto-Elamite, and Egyptian societies, there were any people giving written expression to their spoken language, all evidence of such records and the language or languages they record has fallen victim to the decay of time. Or the evidence has at least eluded the archeologists.

Format and conventions

Each chapter, with only the occasional exception, adheres to a common format. The chapter begins with an overview of the history (including prehistory) of the language, at least up to the latest stage of the language treated in the chapter, and of those peoples who spoke the language (§1, HISTORICAL AND CULTURAL CONTEXTS). Then follows a discussion of the development and use of the script(s) in which the language is recorded (§2, WRITING SYSTEMS); note that the complex Mesopotamian cuneiform script, which is utilized for several languages of the ancient Near East – Sumerian (Ch. 2), Elamite (Ch. 3), Hurrian (*WAL* Ch. 4), Urartian (*WAL* Ch. 5), Akkadian and Eblaite (Ch. 4), Hittite (*WAL* Ch. 18), Luvian (*WAL* Ch. 19) – and which provides the inspiration and graphic raw materials for others – Ugaritic (*WAL* Ch. 9) and Old Persian (*WAL* Ch. 28) – is treated in most detail in Chapter 4, §2. The next section presents a discussion of phonological elements of the language (§3, PHONOLOGY), identifying consonant and vowel phonemes, and treating matters such as allophonic and morphophonemic variation, syllable structure and phonotaxis, segmental length, accent (pitch and stress), and synchronic and diachronic phonological processes. Following next is discussion of morphological phenomena (§4, MORPHOLOGY), focusing on topics such as word structure, nominal and pronominal categories and systems, the categories and systems of finite verbs and other verbal elements (for explanation of the system of classifying Semitic verb stems – G stem, etc. – see *WAL* Ch. 6, §3.3.5.2), compounds, diachronic morphology, and the system of numerals. Treatment of syntactic matters then follows (§5, SYNTAX), presenting discussion of word order and coordinate and subordinate clause structure, and phenomena such as agreement, cliticism and various other syntactic processes, both synchronic and diachronic. The description of the grammar closes with a consideration of the lexical component (§6, LEXICON); and the chapter comes to an end with a list of references cited in the chapter and of other pertinent works (BIBLIOGRAPHY).

To a great extent, the linguistic presentations in the ensuing chapters have remained faithful to the grammatical conventions of the various language disciplines. From discipline to discipline, the most obvious variation lies in the methods of transcribing sounds. Thus, for example, the symbols *ś*, *ṣ*, and *ṭ* in the traditional orthography of Indic language scholarship represent, respectively, a voiceless palatal (palato-alveolar) fricative, a voiceless retroflex fricative, and a voiceless retroflex stop. In Semitic studies, however, the same symbols are used to denote very different phonetic realities: *ś* represents a voiceless lateral fricative while *ṣ* and *ṭ* transcribe two of the so-called emphatic consonants – the latter a voiceless stop produced with a secondary articulation (velarization, pharyngealization, or glottalization), the former either a voiceless fricative or affricate, also with a secondary articulation. Such conventional symbols are employed herein, but for any given language, the reader can readily determine phonetic values of these symbols by consulting the discussion of consonant and vowel sounds in the relevant phonology section.

Broad phonetic transcription is accomplished by means of a slightly modified form of the International Phonetic Alphabet (IPA). Most notably, the IPA symbols for the palato-alveolar fricatives and affricates, voiceless [ʃ] and [tʃ] and voiced [ʒ] and [dʒ], have been replaced by the more familiar [š], [č], [ž], and [ǰ] respectively. Similarly, [y] is used for the palatal glide rather than [j]. Long vowels are marked by either a macron or a colon.

In the phonology sections, phonemic transcription, in keeping with standard phonological practice, is placed within slashes (e.g., /p/) and phonetic transcription within square brackets (e.g., [p]; note that square brackets are also used to fill out the meaning of a gloss and are employed as an element of the transcription and transliteration conventions for certain languages, such as Elamite [Ch. 3] and Pahlavi [*WAL* Ch. 30]). The general treatment adopted in phonological discussions has been to present transcriptions as phonetic rather than phonemic, except in those instances in which explicit reference is made to the phonemic level. Outside of the phonological sections, transcriptions are usually presented using the conventional orthography of the pertinent language discipline. When potential for confusion would seem to exist, transcriptions are enclosed within angled brackets (e.g., <p>) to make clear to the reader that what is being specified is the *spelling* of a word and not its *pronunciation*.

Further acknowledgments

The enthusiastic reception of the first edition of this work – and the broad interest in the ancient languages of humankind that it demonstrates – has been and remains immensely gratifying to both editor and contributors. The editor would like to take this opportunity, on behalf of all the contributors, to express his deepest appreciation to all who have had a hand in the success of the first edition. We wish too to acknowledge our debt of gratitude to Cambridge University Press and to Dr. Kate Brett for continued support of this project and for making possible the publication of this new multivolume edition and the increased accessibility to the work that it will inevitably provide. Thanks also go to the many kind readers who have provided positive and helpful feedback since the publication of the first edition, and to the editors of *CHOICE* for bestowing upon the work the designation of Outstanding Academic Title of 2006.

Roger D. Woodard
Vernal Equinox 2007

Preface to the first edition

In the following pages, the reader will discover what is, in effect, a linguistic description of all known ancient languages. Never before in the history of language study has such a collection appeared within the covers of a single work. This volume brings to student and to scholar convenient, systematic presentations of grammars which, in the best of cases, were heretofore accessible only by consulting multiple sources, and which in all too many instances could only be retrieved from scattered, out-of-the-way, disparate treatments. For some languages, the only existing comprehensive grammatical description is to be found herein.

This work has come to fruition through the efforts and encouragement of many, to all of whom the editor wishes to express his heartfelt gratitude. To attempt to list all – colleagues, students, friends – would, however, certainly result in the unintentional and unhappy neglect of some, and so only a much more modest attempt at acknowledgments will be made. Among those to whom special thanks are due are first and foremost the contributors to this volume, scholars who have devoted their lives to the study of the languages of ancient humanity, without whose expertise and dedication this work would still be only a *desideratum*. Very special thanks also go to Dr. Kate Brett of Cambridge University Press for her professionalism, her wise and expert guidance, and her unending patience, also to her predecessor, Judith Ayling, for permitting me to persuade her of the project's importance. I cannot neglect mentioning my former colleague, Professor Bernard Comrie, now of the Max Planck Institute, for his unflagging friendship and support. Kudos to those who masterfully translated the chapters that were written in languages other than English: Karine Megardoomian for Phrygian, Dr. Margaret Whatmough for Etruscan, Professor John Huehnergard for Ancient South Arabian. Last of all, but not least of all, I wish to thank Katherine and Paul – my inspiration, my joy.

Roger D. Woodard
Christmas Eve 2002

CHAPTER 1

Language in ancient Mesopotamia, Egypt, and Aksum: an introduction

ROGER D. WOODARD

Ozymandias
I met a traveller from an antique land
Who said: "Two vast and trunkless legs of stone
Stand in the desert. Near them, on the sand,
Half sunk, a shattered visage lies, whose frown,
And wrinkled lip, and sneer of cold command,
Tell that its sculptor well those passions read
Which yet survive, stamped on these lifeless things,
The hand that mocked them and the heart that fed;
And on the pedestal these words appear:
'My name is Ozymandias, king of kings:
Look on my works, ye Mighty, and despair!'
Nothing beside remains. Round the decay
Of that colossal wreck, boundless and bare
The lone and level sands stretch far away."
Percy Bysshe Shelley

Cicero, that consummate philosopher–statesman of the late Roman Republic, wrote in his theological treatise on the nature of the gods:

A great many different opportune circumstances are found in a variety of places promoting abundant cultivation by humankind. The Nile waters Egypt – after completely inundating the place all summer long it recedes and leaves the fields soft and covered with mud, ready for sowing. Mesopotamia is made fertile by the Euphrates, each year introducing new fields, as it were . . . How great is the bountifulness of nature, teaming with so great and so pleasing a variety of sustenance . . . ! (*De natura deorum* 2.130–131)

Mesopotamia – bending with the course of both the Euphrates and the Tigris, cutting a curving swath across southwest Asia, from modern Turkey and Syria in the northwest to Iraq in the southeast – and Egypt – the tomb-studded conduit of the Nile, Ozymandias' land – trace their histories along the life-giving rivers that define them. It is in these two ancient, ancient places – Mesopotamia and Egypt – that the first evidence of human writing reveals itself and, hence, the earliest recorded words and syllables of human speech appear. In the second half of the fourth millennium BC, each place gave birth to its own form of writing – curving pictographs that would evolve into cuneiform wedges – and elaborate hieroglyphs that would survive for millennia, while spawning, even as they lived on, cursive offspring better suited for scribal alacrity. These, the first frozen forms of human language, locked in brittle paint and crumbling etch (though not the earliest human language we can recover) are little more than newcomers in the great gulf that is human linguistic history; far more ancient speech once broke upon the ears of a distant human form – peoples whose prehistorically painted symbols mark still the deep darkness of the cavernous spaces of earth, but without encoding language – their tongues were lost forever many millennia ago.

Mesopotamia and Egypt – these are places immediately familiar to many readers from the Bible – and very probably no less so from the headlines of *The Times* or the *Post*. In the Biblical books of Genesis and Exodus one reads of the patriarch Abraham who left his home in Mesopotamia (in "Ur of the Chaldeans") and journeyed, in time, into Egypt, and then out again when compelled by Pharaoh to go, and of his descendant Moses, born in Egypt, who led his Hebrew kinsmen out of Egyptian captivity, who received from God on Mt. Sinai stone tablets engraved with Ten Commandments, and who caused to be constructed for their transport to a Promised Land a chest of gilded acacia wood called the Ark of the Covenant.

But one must look to a much later book to find an account that relates the fate of those tablets and the chest that held them, a book of medieval origin. According to the Ge'ez epic *Kəbrä Nägäst* (*Glory of Kings*; see Ch. 6, §1.3), echoing and amplifying Biblical, Islamic and Classical accounts of the Queen of Sheba's visit to King Solomon of Israel, this "Queen of the South" conceived a child by Solomon – a son, Menelik, born after the queen had returned to her kingdom. When grown to be a young man, Menelik journeyed to Jerusalem to see his father; upon Menelik's departure for Ethiopia, where he would become king, Solomon sent with him a retinue composed of the oldest sons of prominent members of the Israelite community. But as this delegation left Jerusalem, they took with them the holy Ark, which, according to Ethiopian tradition, remains to this day in the ancient city of Aksum (see, *inter alia*, Ullendorff 2006).

In the early centuries AD, as the Roman Empire waned, an Aksumite Kingdom (Christian, by the early fourth century) took form and spread its realm of influence to such an extent that already in the third century the Persian teacher Mani could write that the world had four great kingdoms: Babylonian, Persian, Chinese, and Aksumite. But in comparison to the empires of Egypt and Mesopotamia, Aksum's power would be short-lived, withdrawing into the arid landscape of Ethiopia by the seventh century, as Islamic powers waxed.

Mesopotamia, Egypt, Aksum – it is to the languages of the peoples of these ancient places that this volume is dedicated. Of the three, Mesopotamia is linguistically the most diverse. Sumerian, Mesopotamia's earliest recorded (and deciphered) language, is a *language isolate*, having no known linguistic relatives among the remainder of the world's languages. Within the Mesopotamian sphere, however, Sumerian is not unique in this regard.

As a geographical entity, "Mesopotamia" has a distinctive form. According to Eratosthenes of Cyrene, the third-century BC Greek polymath who took his turn as head of the famed library in Alexandria (Egypt), Mesopotamia is "shaped like a boat" (a ὑπηρέσιον; Strabo 2.1.23, 26); since the time of the nineteenth-/twentieth-century Chicago Orientalist James Breasted, a more familiar description is that of one arcing aspect of a fertile "crescent." If the shape is distinctive, the edges of this space are somewhat vaguely delineated. Even so, along its southeastern circumference, Mesopotamia's boundary is commonly identified with the Zagros Mountains, lying within the modern political state of Iran. On the western side of the Zagros range, situated on the plains of Khuzestān, along the Shaur River, lies the ancient city of Susa, one of the chief cities of the people called the Elamites. As throughout much of their history the Elamites formed part of the cultural milieu of Mesopotamia – utilizing, for example, the Mesopotamian cuneiform script (see the Appendix at the end of Ch. 4) – often subduing or being subdued by the peoples who lived nearer the banks of the

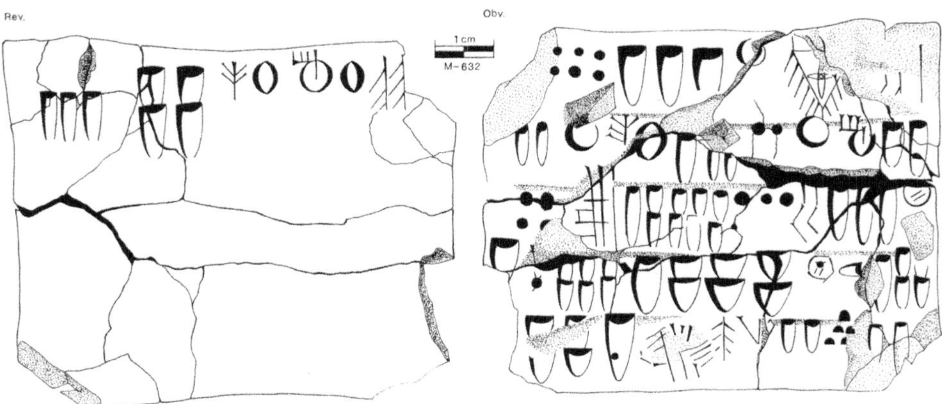

Figure 1.1 Proto-Elamite tablet

Tigris and Euphrates, Elamite will be treated herein among the "Mesopotamian languages." The boundary of the Mesopotamian and Iranian regions is, however, diffuse – now, as in antiquity – and Elam and Elamite also figure prominently in the cultural and linguistic history of Iran: thus, for example, during the period of the Achaemenid dynasty (on which, see the Introduction to *The Ancient Languages of Asia and the Americas*), Susa became a Persian royal city, and in the famous inscription of the Persian King Darius I engraved in living rock at Bīsitūn (see Ch. 3, §1.2.4.1; *WAL* Ch. 28, *passim* and especially §2.3), three languages are used for the decree – Elamite, Old Persian, and the Mesopotamian language of Babylonian.

Elamite shares with Sumerian the status of "language isolate." We should note, however, in this regard, the occurrence of two undeciphered scripts in the documentary remains of the ancient Elamite region. The earliest known of all presently undeciphered scripts (dating to the late fourth millennium BC) is that one called *Proto-Elamite* (see Fig. 1.1). Far fewer in number are inscriptions written in the script called *Linear Elamite*. For a discussion of these, see Chapter 3, §§2.1–2.2.

The majority of the several languages of ancient Mesopotamia are members of the Semitic linguistic family – specifically, the East Semitic, Akkadian languages. This group is comprised of Old Akkadian from the second half of the third millennium BC, and the subsequent Assyrian and Babylonian languages (geographically distributed in the north and south of Mesopotamia, respectively), each divided into several historical phases, beginning in about 2000 BC. The enormity of the documentary evidence for the Akkadian languages can only be described as nothing less than stunning.

In northern Syria, beyond the pale of Mesopotamia proper, lies Tell Mardikh, location of the ancient city of Ebla. It was only in the late 1960s that archeologists discovered this remarkable site, though the place name Ebla had long been known from Akkadian documents. With the discovery of the site came the addition of yet another member to the Semitic family of languages, the language dubbed *Eblaite*. At first believed to be a West Semitic language, like Hebrew, further study has revealed an apparent close kinship between Eblaite and Old Akkadian; hence Eblaite will also be treated in this volume, together with the Akkadian languages.

Among the fascinations that Egypt held for the Greek historian Herodotus, one was its proclivity for inverting the common order of things: "The Egyptians, along with having a climate of their very own and a river different in nature from any other, have established customs and habits that differ almost completely from those of all other people" (*Histories* 2.35). Herodotus then lists for his readers some of these unique practices: "Among them

Table 1.1 Characters of the Meroitic script

Character			Character		
Hieroglyphic	Cursive	Transcription	Hieroglyphic	Cursive	Transcription
𐦀	𐦠	a	𐦐	𐦬	l
𐦁	𐦡	e	𐦑	𐦭	ḫ
𐦂	𐦢	i	𐦒	𐦮	ẖ
𐦃	𐦣	o	𐦓	𐦯	s
𐦄	𐦤	y	𐦕	𐦰	se
𐦅	𐦥	w	𐦖	𐦱	k
𐦆	𐦦	b	𐦗	𐦲	q
𐦈	𐦧	p	𐦘	𐦳	t
𐦉	𐦨	m	𐦚	𐦴	te
𐦊	𐦩	n	𐦜	𐦵	to
𐦌	𐦪	ne	𐦝	𐦶	d
𐦎	𐦫	r	⁝	⁝	word-divider

[i.e. the Egyptians], the women venture into the market place and sell wares but the men stay at home and weave – and whereas other people weave by pushing the woof upward, the Egyptians push it downward." The listing goes on – eventually touching on the matter of language, if only indirectly: "While the Greeks write letters and do arithmetic computations by moving the hand from left to right, the Egyptians do it from right to left. And they use two kinds of letters – they call one 'sacred' [i.e. hieroglyphic] and the other demotic" (*Histories* 2.36).

Herodotus' two types of Egyptian "letters" (γράμματα) are, in actuality, three types: in addition to the well-known intricate hieroglyphic symbols (see the Appendix at the end of Ch. 5), the Egyptians used two cursive scripts derived from the hieroglyphic: Hieratic and, as Herodotus records, Demotic (on all three, see Ch. 5, §2.1). While ancient Egypt thus knows a diversity of writing systems, the degree of language diversity that we encountered in Mesopotamia is not replicated in the documentary record of Egypt, though distinct chronological stages of Egyptian can be identified, from Old Egyptian to Coptic, the latter giving evidence of several dialects. The notable exception to this relative linguistic homogeneity is provided by the Proto-Sinaitic inscriptions found in the Sinai Peninsula and, more recently, in Upper Egypt at Wadi el-Hol, across the Nile from ancient Thebes; these appear to preserve a Bronze Age variety of a West Semitic language (see *WAL* Ch. 12, §2.2 and the Introduction to the companion volume *The Ancient Languages of Syria-Palestine and Arabia*).

There are, nevertheless, other ancient languages attested in North Africa. The *Ancient Libyan* or *Numidian* script, or scripts, from Tunisia, Algeria, and Morocco have been interpreted as recording archaic Berber, though some scholars would regard these materials to be still undeciphered (see *WAL* Ch. 6, §1.1.3). On these scripts, see, *inter alia*, O'Connor 1996.

Between the Fifth and Sixth Cataracts of the Nile lay the ancient Nubian city of Meroë, where the Egyptian scripts must have been long known and utilized. By the third century BC, however, with the rise of the Meroitic kingdom, a native writing system appeared (having both a hieroglyphic and a cursive form), influenced by the Egyptian, and continued in use for recording Meroitic language until the fourth century AD, when Meroë collapsed under external pressures, chiefly from Aksum. The phonetic values of the symbols of the Meroitic writing system have been purportedly identified, as shown in Table 1.1. The majority of symbols have been assigned the value of a single consonant or vowel sound (i.e., the script is analyzed as fundamentally alphabetic), with a small set of syllabic CV (consonant + vowel) symbols filling out the inventory of characters (compare Ugaritic's consonantal script supplemented by three CV characters; see *WAL* Ch. 9, §2.2). While Meroitic texts can thus be given a phonetic reading, the language uttered in such a reading cannot be understood with the exception of a very few words, chiefly proper nouns. On the Meroitic script and language, see Wenig 1982, Griffith 1911, 1912.

The above mention of Aksum returns our attention to that Ethiopian kingdom, to the Aksumite epic, the *Kəbrä Nägäst*, and to the language in which the epic was composed, the language of Ge'ez – one of the focal points of this volume. Ge'ez is a Semitic language, closely related to Ancient South Arabian (see Ch. 6, §1.2; for the Ancient South Arabian language, Ch. 7 in *The Ancient Languages of Syria-Palestine and Arabia*), the latter perhaps the language of Solomon's Queen of Sheba (though the period of Solomon's reign precedes the earliest known South Arabian inscriptions by some two centuries). Ge'ez thus belongs to the same language family as the Akkadian languages of Mesopotamia – the Semitic family – but both also bear a genetic relationship to Egyptian: Semitic and Egyptian are themselves branches of the larger Afro-Asiatic language family, as is discussed in the Appendix on Afro-Asiatic found at the end of the companion volume, *The Ancient Languages of Syria-Palestine and Arabia*.

Bibliography

Daniels, P. and W. Bright (eds.). 1996. *The World's Writing Systems*. Oxford: Oxford University Press.
Englund, R. 1996. "The Proto-Elamite script." In Daniels and Bright 1996, pp. 160–164.
Griffith, F. 1911. *Karanog: The Meroitic Inscriptions of Shablul and Karanog*. Philadelphia: University Museum.
______. 1912. *Meroitic Inscriptions II*. London: Egypt Exploration Fund.
Meyers, E. (ed.). 1997. *The Oxford Encyclopedia of Archaeology in the Near East* (5 vols.). Oxford: Oxford University Press.
O'Connor, M. 1996. "The Berber Scripts." In Daniels and Bright 1996, pp. 112–116, 119.
Pittman, H. 1997. "Susa." In Meyers 1997, vol. V, pp. 107–110.
Shelley, P. 1993. *Shelley: Poems*. New York: Alfred E. Knopf.
Ullendorff. E. 2006. *Ethiopia and the Bible*. Reprint. Oxford: Oxford University Press.
Wenig, S. 1982. "Meroe, Schrift und Sprache." In W. Helck and W. Westendorf (eds.), *Lexikon der Ägyptologie*, vol. 4, pp. 104–107. Wiesbaden: Otto Harrassowitz.

CHAPTER 2

Sumerian

PIOTR MICHALOWSKI

1. HISTORICAL AND CULTURAL CONTEXTS

1.1 Introduction

Of all the extinct languages of the ancient world, Sumerian has the longest literary tradition, extending over roughly three thousand years. The time span and geographical spread of the spoken language is not known and is the subject of much speculation. Presumably it was once the major vernacular in the southern part of Mesopotamia, but it is impossible to establish if it was ever spoken outside of this enclave. In modern terms this would be the area of Iraq south of Baghdad. Estimates on the time of the demise of spoken Sumerian range from the third to the middle of the second millennium BC (see Michalowski, 2002 [2005], 2006). It seems that even in early times Sumerian speakers came into contact with Semitic languages, as evidenced by numerous loanwords from early Semitic. Some have hypothesized additional Mesopotamian substrate languages, but the evidence for this is lacking (Rubio 1999b).

The native designations for the "land of Sumer" are *kiĝir* (written *ki-en-gi*) in Sumerian and *māt šumerim* in Akkadian. Related to this are the respective language labels *eme-gir*$_{15}$ and *šumeru*, which have been the subjects of much etymological speculation. If *gir*$_{15}$ means "native," then the Sumerian terms would mean "native land" (*ki.ĝir*) and "native language" (Steinkeller 1993:112–113). The origins and meaning of the Akkadian *šumeru* – the source of modern renditions such as *Sumer* – remain unknown. Equally opaque are the native geographical concepts. We know that beginning in the middle of the third millennium BC, southern Mesopotamia was thought of as divided between the "Land of Sumer" in the south and the "Land of Akkad" to the north, but it is difficult to establish any native border between the two. A broken passage in a hymn to the main temple of the city of Nippur seems to place that city at the dividing point, but the implications of the line are unclear.

1.2 Textual evidence

The oldest Sumerian texts – perhaps even the oldest written texts known to us – are the approximately five thousand clay tablets found discarded in debris in the ceremonial center of the city of Uruk, written in an early form of the *cuneiform* script (see §2). These tablets, which are dated around 3200 BC, have been seriated, on the basis of script, format, and content, into two general groups corresponding, in theory, to archeological levels from the site: Uruk IV and III, although they were not actually found in those levels.

Close to 90 percent of these early tablets are administrative records, but there are also word lists that were used in the teaching of the writing system (about 670 of the total known

5,820 archaic texts). One composition among these has been considered by some to be a narrative literary composition; others think it is a word list. In light of later usage of such compositions in the educational system, the difference between the two categories may be less than it appears to be. While the general transactions can be understood, the texts cannot all be precisely read; even the actual number of discrete signs is disputed, with estimates ranging from just over 700 to almost 2,000. Some have argued that the system was not linked to any language or was meant to represent an unknown, pre-Sumerian tongue. The existence of phonetic glosses within certain signs, however, strongly suggests that the administrative language was indeed Sumerian. Thus the sign AMA, which is used later for Sumerian *ama*, "mother," contains within it the phonetic indicator, or gloss, am_6, to help distinguish it from similar signs and to prompt the proper identification. The latter phase of archaic cuneiform, Uruk III, is attested not only in Uruk and possibly at Larsa in the south, but also farther north at Jemdet Nasr, Uqair, and Tell Asmar, demonstrating the relatively rapid spread of the new invention.

We do not know how long this particular phase of cuneiform lasted, nor do we have any evidence for the changes that must have taken place early in the third millennium. We have to wait for about four hundred years for our next archaic texts from Ur, dated approximately 2800 BC (Wright 1969). The 375 tablets from this city are primarily administrative documents; additionally, as at Uruk, one also finds pedagogic word lists, and one possible literary mythological fragment. Although these laconic tablets are difficult to translate, the notation of a few morphological elements and phonetic glosses provides convincing evidence that the language of the texts is indeed Sumerian.

The next larger groups of texts from Sumer are the Early Dynastic III texts from Fara (ancient Shuruppak), Abu Salabikh, Nippur, and Adab from around 2500 BC. The majority of tablets found at the first two of these sites are literary, and now for the first time we have evidence for an extensive written poetic tradition. This literature was widely distributed wherever cuneiform was taught; some of the same compositions have been discovered, in slightly later copies, far to the west, during excavations of the Syrian city of Ebla. Syrian scribes used cuneiform to write a Semitic language that we call Eblaite (see Ch. 4), but they also copied Sumerian and Akkadian literary texts, including word lists, that they inherited from Sumer and from northern Babylonia. Many cities in northern Babylonia and in Syria used writing, as is documented by the roughly contemporary tablets from Ebla, Mari, Tell Beydar and Tell Brak. There are small differences in the manner in which cuneiform was used in these places, but these are only variations within a common tradition. Moreover, sometime before the middle of the third millennium, cuneiform had already been fully adapted to write Semitic languages, including Eblaite and Akkadian.

One of the characteristic peculiarities of Early Dynastic literature is the existence of a separate manner of writing that has been termed UD.GAL.NUN (UGN), from a sequence of graphemes commonly found in these texts. With a few exceptions, the signs used are the same as in "normal" Sumerian, but the values (or "readings") of these signs are clearly different. Only a small number of these have been deciphered, among them the sequence that originally gave this system its name: UD corresponds to the classifier (see §2) *dingir* "god, divine name," GAL to *en*, and NUN to lil_2. These three signs therefore spell out the name of the chief god of Sumer, Enlil, or Ellil, normally written as $^{d}en\text{-}lil_2$. This was not a local tradition, since texts of this type have been found at Nippur and Abu Salabikh as well as at Fara; its purpose and origins are simply unknown to us. This manner of writing disappears forever after this period, and remains but a reminder of the complex route that writing took from its origins, with many experiments and dead ends that have not been documented to date.

1.3 Akkadian and Sumerian

With the rise of Akkad around the year 2350 BC, the Semitic Akkadian (see Ch. 4) becomes one of the official languages of Sumer and joins the older language as a vehicle of administration and communication. Semitic had been written in the north, but was only sporadically attested in Sumer. Now certain communities limited themselves exclusively to Akkadian for written communication; others retained Sumerian for local accounts but used the other language to communicate with the central government. Very little literature has survived from this period, leaving us in the dark concerning schooling and scribal education.

Soon after the collapse of the Akkadian state, Sumer and Akkad were once again dominated by one royal house, this time centered at the old city of Ur. The Third Dynasty of Ur (*c.* 2112–2004 BC) ruled for almost exactly a century and left behind an unprecedented number of bureaucratic records. There are approximately forty thousand published administrative texts from this time, and countless more remain in museums and private collections. This documentation is almost exclusively Sumerian, but small numbers of Akkadian texts from northern sites suggest that our large sample is skewed by chance of discovery and that Sumerian was not the sole official language of the time. The documents from Puzrish-Dagan, Ur, Umma, Girsu, Eshnunna, and Nippur do indicate that the central bureaucracy preferred Sumerian as a written language, but small archives from northern places such as Ishan Mizyad indicate that Akkadian was used as well. The Ur III kings oversaw writing reforms and a drastic change in the school tradition. Most of the Early Dynastic literary legacy was discarded and new texts, many of them honoring contemporary rulers, were composed. Most of these are known only in later copies, but a sizable group of Ur III Sumerian literary tablets from Nippur awaits publication.

After the collapse of the Ur III state, Sumerian retained its status as an official language in the south, while in the north, Akkadian dialects began to take over in writing. The last Sumerian archival letter dates from the time of Lipit-Eshtar of Isin (*c.* 1873–1865 BC), and by the middle of the nineteenth century BC Sumerian was no longer used for administrative and accounting purposes. Letters, wills, and other everyday texts were written in Akkadian; Sumerian stock phrases were often employed in legal and administrative documents, but they were undoubtedly read aloud in the Semitic vernacular. Schooling, however, remained primarily in the old tongue. Indeed, this is the period that has left us the largest quantity of Sumerian literary compositions. We have a good knowledge of educational practices in southern cities such as Nippur, Isin, Uruk, and Ur. The curriculum consisted of the study of lexical lists, proverbs, and a few easy royal hymns in the early stages, after which the student graduated to the copying of a broad range of compositions, including royal and divine hymns, epics, laments, epistolary texts, as well as idealized debates, and a small number of legal, historical, and historiographic texts. Liturgical and magical texts are more common in northern and peripheral cities.

1.4 The status of Sumerian in antiquity

For inestimable years Sumerian was a living language in southern Mesopotamia. It was the first language in Western Asia that was committed to writing and this, if nothing else, assured its prestigae status for millennia to come. By the Old Babylonian period it was limited to schools and temples, and until the end of the use of cuneiform it remained a high prestige liturgical language that was studied, with various levels of success, throughout the Near East.

1.5 External affiliation

Sumerian is an isolate, like Ainu, Etruscan, Basque, or Burushaski. Over the years various unsuccessful attempts have been made to link it with a variety of languages or language families, among them Chinese, Tibetan, Hungarian, Turkish, and Indo-European. These attempts have sometimes been flavored with nationalist fervor. More recently some scholars have tried to include Sumerian within the hypothetical Nostratic proto-language of Eurasia, while others have excluded it from such reconstructions.

1.6 General characteristics

The isolate Sumerian is an agglutinating language. The word order of simple declarative sentences is strongly SOV, although this impression may be skewed by the highly formal nature and limited rhetorical scope of much of the sample. Heads and dependents are marked, nominal cases are marked with postpositions, genitives succeed the nouns they modify, adjectives follow nouns, and subordinate clauses usually, but not always, precede main ones.

Sumerian is generally characterized as an ergative language because the main participants of an action are marked according to a system that formally recognizes agents of transitive clauses as different from transitive patients and intransitive subjects. The former are marked by the ergative case, the latter by the absolutive. Few languages are fully ergative. Sumerian, like many other languages, shows various splits: while nominal marking is fully ergative, independent personal pronouns, verbal imperatives and cohortatives, as well as certain participial constructions, are nominative-accusative. Verbal concord works on a split determined by aspect: the perfective is ergative, and the imperfective is nominative-accusative. Sumerian is not alone in this respect and aspectual splits of this type are found in various unrelated Asian languages, including Georgian, Burushaski (Tibet), the Iranian Pashto, as well as in certain Indo-European languages of India. This has led some (Nichols 1993, also implied in Anderson 1985:182) to suggest that this may be an areal phenomenon.

It is usually remarked that ergativity is a strictly morphological phenomenon in Sumerian and there is no evidence that it triggers any syntactic operations (Michalowski 1980, Zólyomi 1996a), but this is a matter that requires further investigation.

1.7 The later use of Sumerian

Little is known at present about the use of Sumerian in the centuries immediately following the fall of the Old Babylonian state around 1595 BC. Akkadian was now widely used for written communication throughout the Near East, from Iran to Anatolia, the Levant, and even Egypt. Some selected Sumerian texts were transmitted to these areas and were used in the study of cuneiform, but most of the Old Babylonian compositions were discarded, and were never read again until modern times. The same holds true for subsequent Babylonian and Assyrian periods: Akkadian was the major language, and Sumerian was studied in school and used in liturgical contexts, although the old language was sometimes used in Babylonian building inscriptions in the late second and early first millennia. Sumerian prayers, laments, and incantations remained in use in rituals, indeed they were studied, edited, and reedited and new texts continued to be composed even after the conquest of Babylonia by Alexander of Macedon in 331 BC. Even as late as the third century numerous Sumerian liturgical texts were redacted and written anew in cities such as Uruk and Babylon, including large numbers of prayers and incantations. There are even a handful of tablets with Sumerian or Akkadian exercises on one side and Greek transcriptions on the other. It is difficult to date these texts, but some would claim that they might be as late as the second century AD (Geller 1997).

1.8 Sumerian dialects

Because of the official nature of written Sumerian, the study of possible dialectal distinctions is somewhat problematic. There are synchronic and diachronic variations and these have sometimes been ascribed to dialectal differences. For example, in particular places during the third millennium, a verbal prefix *i-* is written *e-* in certain contexts; in other places there is a prefix *a-* that rarely occurs elsewhere. Are such isolated isoglosses sufficient to speak of dialects? Only recently Krispijn (2002 [2005]) has attempted to define a specific Lagash-area dialect on the basis of a number of phonological and morphological features. In a literary depiction of an idealized and perhaps satirized school examination, a teacher asks a student if he knows the languages of priests, metalworkers, shepherds, and so forth (Sjöberg 1975:166). This document has been interpreted as providing information on "dialects" or, better, sociolects, but most probably it only refers to knowledge of technical terms connected with these professions that were included in word lists that were memorized and copied as part of scribal training.

1.8.1 The "main dialect" and the "women's tongue"

The main dialect distinction in Sumerian, as reflected in native terminology, is between *eme-g̃ir*$_{17}$ (EG) and *eme-sal* (ES). The former seems to be the native term for what we could call Standard Literary Sumerian. The latter is restricted to ritual texts – primarily those used by lamentation priests (*gala*) – and to the direct speech of certain goddesses and their messengers in literary texts, although these same goddesses speak fluent "Standard Sumerian" in other compositions. On the basis of false etymology, and misunderstandings of the distribution of Emesal, it has been often called a "woman's tongue," leading some to invoke unnecessary ethnographic analogies. Likewise, it has been claimed that the gala priest and the divine messengers were eunuchs (e.g., Boisson 1992:434), although there is no evidence for castration, human or divine, in ancient Sumer.

The sign SAL has three basic readings, *mi*$_2$, *munus*, and *sal*. The first represents only the phonological sequence /mi/ (with very limited distribution), the second means "woman," and the third means "thin." Thus the term *eme-sal* – and the reading is assured because of the Akkadian loan *emešallu* – refers to some sort of pronunciation, but its origins and use in living speech cannot be determined. Emesal is not attested before the Old Babylonian period. At that time Emesal texts are primarily, although not exclusively, attested in northern Babylonian cities such as Kish and Sippar, but are much less common in the school texts from Nippur, Ur, and other cities in the south. This may be attributed to differences in school curricula. It is also possible that cult texts were transmitted mainly orally in southern Babylonia, but written down in the northern area. This may have been one of the consequences of massive social and political upheavals during the last quarter of the eighteenth century BC that led to the abandonment of many southern settlements and the emigration of much of the population northwards. By the first millennium BC, the majority of Sumerian texts were liturgical Emesal compositions, aside from incantations, which continued to be copied and recited in the main dialect. Thus, most literate priests used Emesal more than the old Standard Sumerian.

Various attempts have been made to explain the origins and "dialectal" status of Emesal. Alster (1982) thought that it might be related to the UD.GAL.NUN texts of the Early Dynastic period. Others have sought its origins in regional dialects. Bobrova (1989) suggested that it was the dialect of a cultic center of the goddess Inanna, since this goddess speaks in ES in literary texts. There is no evidence at present to support this claim. Bauer (1998:436) has noted that some of the sound changes that are characteristic of ES can be sometimes found in third-millennium texts from the Lagash area; this led him to propose that Emesal was related to, if not based on, the local version of Sumerian, which was hidden from our view by the scribes who wrote in the standard version of the language.

The main distinctions between the two forms of Sumerian are phonological. Thus, EG *g̃* corresponds to ES *m* (EG *g̃ar* ~ ES *mar* "to place"), or EG *d* corresponds to ES *z* (EG *udu* ~ ES *eze* "sheep"). A small number of basic terms have unexplainable lexical alternates: EG *ereš* ~ ES *gašan* "queen, mistress," or EG *nitadam* ~ ES *mudna* "betrothed man." A full list of correspondences as well as a listing of the known ES words can be found in Schretter 1990.

1.9 The study of Sumerian

Because of a lack of known cognate tongues, and because Sumerian died out thousands of years ago, it is extremely difficult to establish a reliable grammar or lexicon of the language. Despite much progress over the years, there is still much disagreement about basic grammatical facts, and it is impossible to do justice to all the debates on the matter in a short survey. Many complex issues have had to be simplified or presented in an abbreviated fashion; because of a lack of any proper study, issues of syntax have suffered disproportionally. The following remarks represent an attempt to present the author's present opinions, tempered by a selective representation of other points of view. One should also note that despite the large number of surviving cuneiform tablets, there are severe limitations on what can be recovered. Not only was Sumerian written for thousands of years after it was no longer the vernacular, but what was written has preserved only a part of the language. The surviving texts consist primarily of highly conventionalized administrative documents, academic word lists, and poetic compositions; there is very little literary prose. As a result, one must always keep in mind that we are dealing with highly formalized forms of verbal art far removed from any putative language of the streets, constrained by certain conventions with restricted rhetorical scope.

2. WRITING SYSTEM

2.1 Cuneiform writing

Sumerian is written with a script known as *cuneiform* – impressed onto moist clay tablets, although there are also monumental texts inscribed on stone and other hard surfaces. Once dry, clay is extremely durable and therefore tens of thousands of such tablets have survived to the present day. It is impossible to quantify the available Sumerian language remains or to estimate what lies buried in museums and in the unexcavated mounds of the Near East.

Although some popular theories propose evolutionary precursors to this writing system, it seems much more probable that it was invented as a system, with all of its characteristic features intentionally bound into a comprehensive notational structure. The signs on the earliest tablets were drawn with a reed stylus (see Ch. 4, Fig. 4.2). Very soon the technique changed, and the end of the stylus was used to impress wedges to make up a grapheme, and this manner of writing persisted from that time on. The wedge-like look of the script gave us the modern name cuneiform, from Latin *cuneus* "wedge." In one Sumerian poem the signs are described as *gag*, "nail(s)." The earliest writing system, which has been variously designated as *archaic cuneiform* or *proto-cuneiform*, was designed for recording transactions, and thus the texts consist almost entirely of word and number signs.

The early history of cuneiform might be characterized as one of an uneasy adaptation of an autonomous communication system to accommodate natural language. By the middle of the third millennium the new system was capable of representing full utterances, but it was still something of a mnemonic device to the extent that no attempt was made to represent with precision all aspects of language. Only kernel elements were noted, and these were not inscribed in the order in which they were read. Thus a verb, which in later writing might have numerous affixes, would only carry one or two prefixes. The reader was expected to provide the missing elements and to unscramble the signs into their proper sequence. The graphic elements needed for fairly accurate phonological representation of Sumerian language were all in place, as was the case in contemporary Egyptian, but that was not the goal of the recording system.

2.2 Signs and conventions

The sign repertoire consists of three different types of signs: (i) *semantic classifiers* – Assyriologists refer to them as *determinatives*; (ii) *syllabograms* (also called *phonograms*) or phonetic signs; and (iii) *logograms*, or word signs. Signs have multiple values, and some can even function in all three capacities. Thus, the wedge sequence 𒀭 can be read, depending on the context, (i) as the classifier for a divine name; (ii) as the syllabogram *an*; and (iii) as the noun *an* "heavens" or as *diğir* "god."

Certain conventions are used in the transliteration of sign sequences into the Roman alphabet. Sequences of cuneiform signs that represent roots and affixes are linked in transliteration by dashes, while morphemes are separated by periods. Similar or homophonous readings have been numbered, and modern scholars represent these indices with accents and/or with subscripted numbers. For example, the Sumerian word for "house, temple" can be transliterated either as *é* or as *e_2* (the actual phonological shape was closer to /ha/). The unpronounced classifiers (determinatives) are transliterated with raised letters; for example the classifier for a divinity (*dinğir*) is abbreviated to ^{d}: for example, *^{d}en-lil$_2$* "$^{\text{(god)}}$Enlil"; *^{giš}tukul*, "$^{\text{(wooden)}}$weapon"; *uri$_5$^{ki}* "Ur$^{\text{(city)}}$." Sign names and signs with uncertain readings are represented in capital letters. The transliteration conventions are modern, but historic, and do not represent the current state of our knowledge about semiotics, morphology, or phonology. They are relicts of the decipherment of cuneiform, which has a long history going back almost two hundred years (Bottéro 1992).

2.3 Logographic writing

The early writing system is primarily logographic. Syllabograms were originally used to represent minimal grammatical information, and to assist in reading word signs by providing pronunciation glosses. Later sign usage and modern conventions of transliteration sometimes obscure this principle. For example, the Sumerian word for "ear" or "wisdom" is written with three signs and is commonly transliterated as *ğeštug$_2$*. Originally, the middle sign alone had the value *ğeštug* and the first and third signs, *ğeš* and *tug$_2$* respectively, were phonetic complements. A more accurate transliteration would thus be *^{ğeš}ğeštug$^{\text{tug}_2}$*. One could argue that this rendered the middle sign redundant, but such instances only demonstrate the consistent use of word signs and the avoidance of syllabic spellings for roots. In principle the syllabic writing of roots was reserved, from the middle of the third millennium on, for loanwords. For example, the Sumerian word for "road," *kaskal*, was written logographically with a single sign, but its synonym, borrowed from Akkadian, was written syllabically as *har-ra-an*.

The elementary indications of grammatical morphemes in Early Dynastic writing were in a sense also logographic, that is they did not always accurately represent phonological shapes but only a conventional form of a morpheme. Thus, to cite a classic example, the modal prefix *he-* (or *hV-*) is written as follows (see Civil and Biggs 1966:14):

(1)	*2500 BC*	*2400–2000 BC*	*1800 BC*
	he_2- (__/e,i,a,u/)	he_2- (__/e,i/)	he_2- (__/e,i/)
		ha- (__/a,u/)	ha- (__/a/)
			hu- (__/u/)

Around 2400 BC the signs began to be written in the order in which they were to be read, and by 2000 BC most, if not all, grammatical elements were represented in writing. The general nature of the signs remained the same, but the structure of the system changed. Logograms and syllabograms were combined according to certain principles, but this does not mean that cuneiform writing moved towards a precise phonological representation of Sumerian.

2.4 The evolution of syllabic spelling

The complex move towards the implementation of a full syllabic repertoire was probably driven by multiple motivations. The application of cuneiform to represent Semitic languages such as Akkadian and Eblaite required the development of such a syllabary, as did the need to represent Semitic personal names in Sumerian texts. Such a full syllabary is known for Eblaite as early as 2500 BC, but the first adaptation of cuneiform to Semitic must have taken place somewhat earlier. Because of the word structure of Semitic, which requires the representation of changes that take place within roots, one could not simply use the same combinatorial principles that one used to write Sumerian. The distinct structure of discontinuous Afro-Asiatic roots favored a full syllabary rather than a logographic writing system, and therefore someone applied cuneiform to these languages by exploiting the CV and VC signs of the Sumerian script.

Certain conventions helped in interpreting the written segments, such as the use of the sequence CV–VC to express the sequence CVC. Although in Syrian Semitic writings the signs were written in the proper linguistic order, the texts from Sumer still exhibit a fairly free order of signs within a case of writing.

Eventually, these syllabic practices were partially applied back to Sumerian, and in the Early Dynastic texts we find an incipient use of syllabograms for loanwords, and for limited marking of bound morphemes. Loans and other syllabically spelled words are subject to certain conventions, such as the use of CV signs for the sequence CVC, as in *li_2-ga* for *lidga* (a measure of capacity). Nominal case endings and possessive pronouns are sometimes written, sometimes omitted. Only one or two verbal affixes are provided to the reader.

The full syllabary would eventually be applied to Sumerian as well, but not in the same manner as in Semitic. Because Sumerian roots are often monosyllabic and do not take infixes, roots continued to be written with logograms. Syllabograms are used for morphological elements, but because of the nature of a syllabary, sign usage follows certain conventions and does not render linguistic units precisely. A series of graphemes that we would transliterate as *he*$_2$*-en-g̃ar* could be transcribed as *he.i.n.g̃ar* or as *he.n.g̃ar.Ø*, depending on one's view of grammar, but not as *he.en.g̃ar.*

2.5 Comparison of earlier and later systems

The differences between the nuclear early system and the fully developed second-millennium version of cuneiform can be illustrated by examples from a passage that is preserved in both versions. Here is a line from a third-millennium literary composition, followed by the manner in which the clichéd formula was written in Standard second-millennium Sumerian, a glossed version of the latter, and a translation (see Civil and Biggs 1966:12):

(2)					
	Third millennium	^{d}en-ki	isimud	gu$_3$	de$_2$
	Second millennium	^{d}en-ki-ke$_4$	isimud-ra	gu$_3$	mu-un-na-de$_2$-e
	Transcription	Enkik.e	isimud.ra	gu.Ø	mu.na.de.e
		Enkik-ERG.	Isimud-DAT.	voice-ABS.	PREF.-DAT.-pour-NOM.
		"The god Enkik says to [his vizier] Isimud"			

An unusual writing in one such early text reveals that prefixes usually not expressed in writing could occasionally surface (Civil and Biggs 1966:3):

(3)				
	Third millennium	dur$_3$	gu$_3$-di	nab-sa$_{10}$-sa$_{10}$
	Second millennium	dur$_3$	gu$_3$-di	na-ab-ta-sa$_{10}$-sa$_{10}$
	Transcription	dur	gudi.Ø	na.b.ta.sa.sa
		ass	braying-ABS.	PREF.-PRO.-ABL.-buy
		"You should not buy a braying ass"		

By the beginning of the second millennium BC, the Standard Sumerian orthography had been established that would be used, with only minor adjustments, down to the very end of cuneiform writing.

In addition to the word- and morpheme-centered manner of writing, there exists a less stable and less formalized way of writing the language syllabically. Texts of this type, which first appear in northern Babylonia and peripheral areas in Old Babylonian times, write out free morphemes by means of syllabograms rather than by means of logograms. Thus for example, the Standard Sumerian sequence *sipa* ^{d}*ur-*^{d}*namma-ke*$_4$ *mu-na-an-šum*$_2$ "he gave to the shepherd [king] Ur-Namma" is rendered as *si-pa ur-an-na-ma-ke mu-na-an-šu* in the so-called syllabic orthography. The five hundred or so texts of this type are mainly, but not exclusively, ritualistic.

3. PHONOLOGY

The phonology of the language is not well understood, and it is fair to say that it will never be fully recovered. There are many reasons for this; chief among them are the manner in which the language was encoded in writing, as well as modern misconceptions as to the nature of the script. Cuneiform was deciphered backwards, that is, it was first read in its latest incarnation, thousands of years after its origins. The Semitic Akkadian language was recovered first, and when Sumerian was discovered, it was read by means of sign values established for Akkadian. As a result, certain Sumerian phonemes that were not used in Akkadian were not initially identified. The repertoire of Sumerian phonemes currently recognized still looks suspiciously close to the Akkadian repertoire; this may be due to chance, to our inability to recognize certain sounds, or to convergence of the two systems.

3.1 Consonants

The following chart presents the conservative current view of the Sumerian consonantal inventory.

(4) Sumerian consonantal phonemes

b	d		g	
p	t		k	
	s	š		
	z			
				h
m	n		g̃	
	l	r	ṙ	

3.1.1 Stops

Ambiguities in the use of the cuneiform script to write Sumerian and Akkadian have led to many debates about the nature of Sumerian stops. Observing the behavior of certain loans from Sumerian into Akkadian, Gelb (1961:33) argued against voiced stops in Sumerian and suggested that the distinction was between voiceless aspirated stops (/p^h/, /t^h/, and /k^h/) and voiceless unaspirated stops (/p/, /t/, and /k/). Some have followed his hypothesis; Jacobsen (1957:92, n. 1) proposed that the opposition was between rounded and unrounded stops. There are serious flaws in these reconstructions, as noted by Rubio (1999a:141). For the present it seems most sensible to follow the traditional view and to argue for a voiced versus voiceless distinction. Civil (1973a:34) has observed that voiceless stops become voiced when they occur before an ending that begins with a vowel (*kalak*/*kalaga* "mighty"), although he also notes that the rule may have to be reversed.

The occurrence of a phonemic glottal stop /ʔ/ is uncertain. Spellings such as *sa-a* "cat" are commonly transcribed as *sa'a* (as if / saʔa/), but this is presently best seen as a Sumerological convention rather than a phonological claim.

3.1.2 Sonorants

Sumerian has both nasal and liquid phonemes. The evidence for phonemic glides is less straightforward.

3.1.2.1 Nasals

The writing system makes a clear distinction between /m/ and /n/. There is some uncertainty about their behavior in word-final position. Certain words ending in a nasal have a different consonant when followed by vocalic ending; thus *ezen* "festival" but *ezem-ma*. This variation may be interpreted as a change either of /n/ to /m/ before a vowel, or of /m/ to /n/ in word-final position.

The nasal /n/ also regularly becomes /l/ before /b/. This is commonly encountered in the verbal prefix chain when the prefix *nu-* is followed by *ba/i-* (written *la-ba-* or *li-bi*$_2$*-*), but also within words as in the ES *la-bar* (EG *nag̃ar*) "carpenter." An unusual change of /l/ to /n/ before /g/ is found in early syllabic writings for the word *lugal* "king" (*nu-gal*). This, however, may have to be interpreted as hypercorrection based on analogy with composites formed with *nu-* such as *nu-kiri*$_6$ "gardener" and so forth.

The identity of the phoneme commonly written *g̃* is somewhat problematic (see Krecher 1978). As Civil (1973a:61) has noted, it is regularly only found before the vowels /a/, /i/, and /e/; it has variously been described as a velar nasal, a labiovelar nasal or as a nasalised labiovelar, and has been represented phonetically by notations such as /ŋ/, /ŋm/, or /ŋg/ (Black 1990:107–108). One should not exclude the possibility that Sumerian at one point had more than one such nasal – retroflex, palatal, as well as labial – as is the case, for example, in certain Dravidian languages.

3.1.2.2 Liquids

Because of certain writing conventions, Diakonoff (1967:49) proposed a phonemic distinction between the lateral liquids /l/ and velar /ł/. This has not gained wide acceptance. The phonological status of /l/ and /r/ is difficult to determine, and there are examples of an interchange of these phonemes in final and medial position (Civil 1973c: 174).

3.1.2.3 Glides

Standard transliterations of Sumerian do not recognize the existence of glides. Third-millennium texts from Syria, however, provide spellings that suggest the existence of a labial /w/, a palatal /y/ (and possibly one or two other sonorants; see Civil 1984:80).

3.1.3 Other consonants

Because of certain writing conventions, alterations, loans, and syllabic spellings, other phonemes have been suggested over the years. Civil (1973a) has drawn attention to the alternation of [g] and [b] in certain words, concluding that these spellings represent a distinct phoneme, either the labiovelar /g^w/ or /gb/. The most widely debated extra phoneme of Sumerian has been variously notated as /dr/, /d^r/, /ř/, and, most recently as [ts^h] (Jagersma 2002 [2005]). If the last-named is correct, it was an affricate that had disappeared early on from the language, but which in certain cases was reflected in historical spellings.

3.1.4 Apocope

It is generally assumed that word-final consonants are dropped, but it is unclear if this applies in all situations. Hence most CVC signs also have a CV transliteration: for example, the sign read as *šag*$_4$ "heart" by some, is read as *ša*$_3$ by others.

3.2 Vowels

The vowels of Sumerian correspond to those found in Akkadian:

(5) Sumerian vowel phonemes

/i/				/u/
	/e/			
		/a/		

In Sumerian, however, unlike Akkadian, vowel length is not phonemic. Some have argued for the existence of a mid-back vowel /o/ (Lieberman 1979), but this has not found wide support. There is no evidence for the existence of diphthongs. In third-millennium texts from the Syrian city of Ebla, certain words are unexpectedly written with final *-n*; this may be Semiticization or an indication of nasalization of final vowels in early Sumerian (Civil 1984:79).

3.2.1 Vowel harmony

Sumerian words show a very strong tendency towards vowel harmony, both within roots and morphophonologically, but the issue has never been analyzed in detail. Thus, many bisyllabic native words in the language repeat the same vowel: *kalam* "land," *pirĝ* "lion," or *murub*$_4$ "center." Loans sometimes do conform to this tendency (e.g., *ugula* "captain, foreman" from Akkadian *waklu*), and sometimes do not (e.g., *akkil* "cry" from Akkadian *ikkilu*). Diakonoff (1983:87) thought that Sumerian had total vowel harmony, but as Boisson (1997:41) notes, no other language shows such a degree of harmony. It is probably safer to state that the language has a strong tendency towards harmony, but that the degree of the phenomenon may be masked by our transliteration system. There are many bisyllabic words with two different vowels, especially /a/ and /i/: for example, *agrig* "provider," *gisal* "oar," or *apin* "plow." There are also bisyllabic words with other vowel sequences: for example, *dedal* "ashes," *bugin* "bucket," or *ĝizbun* "banquet." Vowel harmony seems to operate strongly, but not totally, within the verbal prefix chain, but does not affect the stems, nor does it operate on nominal prefixes. Individual elements in compounds also retain their original vowels, as in *a*$_2$*-tuku* "benefit, profit."

3.3 Accent and intonation

Over the years there have been suggestions that Sumerian was a tonal language. The underlying assumption was that because the language had so many homophones, some additional distinctions were necessary, hence the tonal hypothesis. Many, but not all, Sumerian homophones are an illusion based on the system of transliteration (Parpola 1975). The only clearly identifiable prosodic feature is typologically predictable: rising phrase intonation to mark questions is sometimes expressed through the writing of additional vowels at the end of a clause.

4. MORPHOLOGY

4.1 Word formation

Sumerian distinguishes between nominal and verbal bases. The controversial category of adjectives will be discussed below; here it is assumed that most adjectives are verbs. The only recent discussions of Sumerian word formation are those of Diakonoff (1967:51–54), Kienast (1975), Schretter (1993), and Attinger (1993:155–158). This is a modified version of their analysis. One should bear in mind that the form of Sumerian words is sometimes obscured by inconsistent transliteration (on the CVC ~ CV transliteration variation, see §3.1.4).

4.1.1 Basic Word Structure

Basic words were built on the following phonotactic patterns: (i) V (e.g., a "water".) There are few such roots. Most words transliterated as simple vowels are actually CV, such as e_2

"house, temple, estate", (*/ha/*) or *a*, "father", */aya/* or */yaya/*); (ii) CV (e.g., *ki*, "earth"); (iii) VC (e.g., *ud* "day"); (iv) VCV (e.g., *ama* "mother"); (v) VCVC (e.g., *amar* "calf"); (vi) VC_1C_1VC (e.g., *addir* "river crossing, wage"); (vii) CVC (e.g., *dub* "tablet"); CVCV (e.g., *gaba* "breast"); (ix) CVCVC (*munus* "woman").

While the syllabic cuneiform script does not represent consonant clusters directly, heterogeneous clusters undoubtedly existed. In medial position one can recognize the following patterns: (i) $CV_1C_1C_2V_1C$ (e.g., *kiskil*, "young woman," written ki-sikil); (ii) $(C)V_1C_1C_2V_2C$ (e.g., *g̃eštug* "ear, wisdom"); (iii) $V_1C_1CV_2C$ (e.g., *irkab*, "bat," *adkin* "salted meat"). Initial and final clusters cannot be directly spelled out in cuneiform, but there are patterns of the type (i) C_1C_2VC (e.g., *lgud* "thick") or (ii) $CV_1CV_1C_1C_2$ (e.g., *kurušt* (*kurušda*) "ox fattener."

4.1.2 Compound forms

In addition to primary nouns and verbs, Sumerian has a rich repertoire of composite forms. For compound verbs see below §4.6. The least productive is a concatenation of two nouns. A form N_2 N_1 replaces the normal order of N_1 N_2+gen. These are found only in poetry and are archaic or archaizing: for example. *an-ša(g)* "heavens + center" for "center-of-the-heavens." Two nouns may also occur in normal order without genitive marker, as in *ereš-dingir*, "lady + god" for "priestess."

Compound nouns are also formed from a noun a verbal/adjectival root such as *dub-sar*, "tablet + write" for "scribe." In addition, nouns may be created from compound verbs without any affixes: *sa₂-dug₄*, "delivery." Finally, nouns may be formed from frozen verbal forms: *u₃-na-(a)-dug₄* "letter," literally "when you speak to him/her"; *ga-an-tuš* "tenant," literally "I want to sit"; ba-an-g̃i₄ "answer," literally "he/she answered."

4.1.3 Apophony

Apophony (or ablaut) may have played a limited role in word formation, but requires further study. At present it can be recognized in a small number of basic adjectives: for example, *gal/gul* "large/larger" (Civil 1982:12).

4.1.4 Reduplication

Reduplication plays a highly restricted role in word formation. It appears that basic color terms share reduplicated stems: for example, *babbar* < *bar₆-bar₆* "white"; *kukku* < *ku₁₀-ku₁₀* "black"; and possibly *sig₁₇-(sig₁₇)* "blue/green" (Civil 1987:155). There is also a small class of echo words, nouns created by duplication with a vowel alternation (CV_1C-CV_2V), all restricted to the semantic class of noise: for example, *dum-dam . . . za* "to clamor"; *suh₃-sah₄ . . . za* and so forth (Civil 1966). There are also isolated examples such as *nunuz* (<* *nuz-nuz*) "eggs" or of onomatopoetic words such as *zi . . . pa-an-pa-an* "to breathe." The morpheme *-didli*, which means "one by one," was originally *dil-dil* "one-one." Reduplicated nouns and adjectives mark plurality (see §4.2.3), while reduplicated verb-stems can mark imperfect aspect and plurality of absolutives (see §4.6.3).

4.2 Nominal morphology

Sumerian nominal forms consist of a base and a series of affixes, primarily suffixes. The one prefix position is occupied by derivational morphemes; all other affixes come after the stem. Nouns are marked for gender (animate and inanimate), number, and case.

Although these affixes are ordered in a strict sequence when there is only a single noun, the matter is more complex when more than one is involved. In possessive constructions only the dependent noun takes a genitive marker: for example,

(6) dumu lugal.ak
son king-GEN.
"The king's son"

When two genitives are involved, the suffixes are added cumulatively (i.e., displaced) after the last noun. For example,

(7) sa-a dumu lugal-la-ka
sa'a dumu lugal.ak.ak
cat son king-GEN.-GEN.
"The cat of the son of the king"

In more complex sequences the affixes come at the end of a noun phrase; as a result, nouns that are within the phrase receive no marking at all. Sumerian is therefore a language with case displacement and globally final NP-marking, to use Aristar's terminology (1995: 432, 445).

In schematic positional terms, the *noun chain* could be represented as follows (where PRO represents "possessive pronouns"):

(8) Sumerian noun chain

1	2	3	4	5	6	7
DERIVATIONAL MORPHEMES	N_1	N_2	GEN.	PRO.	PL.	CASE

4.2.1 Derivational morphemes (position 1)

There are two derivational prefixes. The first, *nam-*, forms abstracts (e.g., *lugal* "king," *nam-lugal* "kingship"); the second, *nig̃$_2$-*, forms nouns out of verbs (e.g., *ba* "to bestow," *nig̃$_2$-ba* "gift"). The former presents few problems; the latter is more complicated.

Originally *nig̃$_2$* was the inanimate relative pronoun. Many Sumerologists write that *nig̃$_2$* is a noun meaning "thing," but there is little to substantiate this claim. The prefix is used in ways that are not always clear to us and may have been lexicalized to some extent. It can be prefixed to certain adjectives such as *dag̃al* "broad, wide," but the difference between *dag̃al* and *nig̃$_2$-dag̃al(a)* eludes us at present. One possibility is that this forms a superlative; if this is indeed the case, it was not generalized for all adjectives. More probable is that the forms with *nig̃$_2$-* are no longer adjectives but are nouns, and therefore stand in possessive relationship with other nouns. Thus, the royal epithet *sipa gin.a* (*sipa gi-na*) means "just/true shepherd," but *sipa nig̃.gin.ak.e* (*sipa nig̃$_2$-gi-na-ke$_4$*) means "shepherd of justice." One should also note that there are a large number of *nig̃$_2$*-compounds in Sumerian in which the element has no apparent semantic role.

Attinger (1993:155) does not consider the preceding to be derivational morphemes, arguing that only the prefix *nu-* serves this role. He follows the standard opinion, based primarily on etymological grounds, that *nam-* is a substantive derived from *me* "to be" and that *nig̃$_2$* is a noun meaning "thing" that forms "concrete nouns."

It is not clear if *nu-* should be viewed as a derivational morpheme or simply as a nominal formant. It is found in a small group of nouns denoting professions such as *nu-banda$_3$* "captain" or *nu-kiri$_6$* "gardener" (Edzard 1967). It is possible that the formant is related to *lu*$_2$ "person, man." The pronunciation with /n/ is indicated by loans into Akkadian such as *nukaribbu* and *laputtu* (with change of *n* > *l* /__ *b*; see §3.1.2.1). Early texts, however, indicate that *lu*$_2$ may have been pronounced as /nu/, as evidenced by such syllabic spellings as *nu-gal* for *lugal* "king" (etymologically, or folk etymologically, from *lu*$_2$ *gal* "great man").

The formant *nam-* is also found in compound verbs (e.g., *nam . . . tar* "to decide fate"). Difficult to analyze are words such as *til* "life, to live, give health" which can function as verbs as well as nouns. These also create forms with the abstract prefix and it is difficult to distinguish the differences between *nam-til* and *til*.

4.2.2 Possession (position 4)

A noun can be followed by an adjective (*lugal gal* "great king"), or by another noun in possessive relationship (Zólyomi 1996b). In that instance the second, possessed, noun, is marked by the suffix *-ak*. Thus, *lugal kalam.ak* "king of the land." This is written as *lugal kalam-ma* in obedience to two rules: that in order to add a vocalic ending to a consonant-final root one use a CV sign, and the loss of final consonants. In rare instances there can be two or even three genitives, but no more than that. Note that the genitive *-ak* occupies a different position than the other case affixes.

There is another possessive construction in Sumerian that topicalizes the possessed noun. In the Sumerological literature this is called an *anticipatory genitive*; it is limited to literary texts and often results in tortured modern translations such as "the land – its king was." The possessed noun is fronted and carries the genitive suffix; the possessor follows and is marked with a third-person possessive pronoun. Thus, with *lugal kalam.ak* "king of the land," compare *kalam.ak lugal.bi* "the land's king."

4.2.3 Number (position 6)

Singular is unmarked, but plurality can be expressed in a number of ways. Animate plural nouns take a suffix *-ene*, but there is no equivalent plural morpheme for inanimates. Hence an unmarked inanimate noun may be plural and the number is only marked by means of plural verbal agreement. The same holds true for collective nouns, such as *eren*$_2$ "troops" which take no plural marker but can trigger plural or collective verbal agreement.

If an animate or inanimate plural noun is followed by an adjective, the latter is reduplicated (e.g., *lugal / na*$_4$ *gal gal* "great kings/stones"); this can, in some animate cases, be combined with the plural suffix as in *lugal gal gal.ene* "great kings." Plurality can also be expressed by reduplication of the stem, as in *lugal lugal* "kings." It is commonly accepted that this signifies totality (i.e., "all kings"), but this remains to be fully documented. In addition, one encounters reduplicated nominals with the ending *-ene*, as in *lugal lugal.ene* "kings," but the nuances of this formation elude us at present.

Two additional markers of plurality are usually cited: *-meš* and *-hi-a*. The ending *-meš* is the third-person plural copula, that is a form of the verb "to be"; *hi-a*, however, is not a plural marker at all, but an adjective meaning "mixed, of various sorts." Thus, *udu hi-a* means not "sheep" (pl.) but rather "various types of smaller cattle." Both have limited distribution, although the exact limits have not been studied. Since there is no formal morphological marker for inanimate plurals, the marker *-meš* may have developed from the copula to supplement the paradigm (as a sort of pseudo-morphological marker for paradigm leveling) and mimimize ambiguity. It is commonly found in administrative lists and as a marker of plurality of Sumerograms in Akkadian texts, but is much less common in Sumerian narratives.

Since Akkadian used only morphological means of marking plurality, paradigm leveling may also account for the new composite plural morpheme *-bi.ene* that begins to appear in Old Babylonian literary texts. Thus, *iri.bi.ene* does not mean that the city was considered somehow metaphysically personified; it is simply a new way of expressing "cities."

4.2.4 Case (position 7)

Sumerian has two direct and seven oblique cases. With the exception of the equative, all of these are also marked on the verb, albeit the direct cases occupy different ranks from the obliques.

(9)

Ergative	-e	
Absolutive	-Ø	
Dative	-ra	<-ar/-ir/-ur>
Comitative	-da	<-ta/-da$_5$>
Ablative/Instrumental	-ta	<-da>
Allative	-(e)še	<-še$_3$/-e$_3$/-aš/-eš/-eš$_2$/uš>
Equative	-gin	<-gin$_7$>
Locative 1	-a	
Locative 2 (terminative)	-e	

The ergative case marks the most agent-like argument of transitive clauses (corresponding to the transitive subject in English).

The absolutive case marks the patient of transitives (corresponding to English direct objects), as well as the single core argument of intransitives (corresponding to English intransitive subjects). The absolutive is also the citation form for nouns:

(10) A.

lugal.e	iri.Ø	mu.n.hul.Ø
king-ERG.	city-ABS.	PREF.-erg-destroy-ABS.

"The king destroyed the city"

B.

Lugal.Ø	i.gin.Ø
king-ABS.	PREF.-go-ABS.

"The king went"

The dative marks the beneficiary of an action (*lugal.ra* "for the king") but also functions as a locative with animates ("upon the king"), in concert with the observations of Kuryłowicz (1964) and Aristar (1996) about the typological associations of datives with animates and locatives with inanimates. It also marks the secondary agent of causative constructions.

The comitative (or proprietive) indicates accompaniment (*lugal.da* "with the king").

The ablative case is also used in an instrumental manner (*tukul.ta* "by means of a weapon") and with numbers it is used in a distributive sense (*min.ta* "two each"). The allative (usually called terminative in the literature) and the ablative denote movement towards (*iri.(e)še* "to/towards the city") and away from a goal (*iri.ta* "from the city"), respectively.

The equative denotes comparison (*tukul.gin* "like a weapon").

The locative 1 marks the inanimate place where an action takes place (*iri.a* "in the city"); while the locative 2, called locative-terminative by Sumerologists, marks propinquity (*iri.e* "next to the city"). The locative cases also mark the syntactic object of compound verbs (see §4.6.1); together with the allative they can also be used to mark the goal or object of certain verbs of affection and cognition.

There are some examples of idiomatic or verb-specific uses of certain cases with idiosyncratic meanings. In later Sumerian one sometimes encounters a redistribution of case functions under the influence of Akkadian. For example, the Akkadian preposition *ina* is both locative and instrumental, and under its influence Sumerian *-ta*, originally ablative and instrumental, acquires a locative meaning.

As is to be expected, low animacy nouns do not take ergative or dative; and high animacy nouns cannot take ablative/instrumental, allative, or locative suffixes.

In addition, Sumerian contains a set of discontinuous morphemes built by means of an initial word – often a body part – an optional bridging genitive morpheme, and a locative or directional case ending (*-a*, *-e*, (*e*)*še*, *-ta*). These can bracket nouns or nominalized clauses. Thus, for example, *bar eg-ba-ka* means "because of that ditch":

(11) bar eg.bi.ak.a
because of ditch-PRO.-GEN.-LOC.

Body parts are *bar* "exterior" ("because of"); *da* "side" ("next to"); *igi* "eye" ("before"); *eğer* "back" ("behind"); *murub*$_4$ "waist, middle" ("in the midst"); *šag*$_4$ "heart" ("inside"); *ugu* "forehead" ("before"); and *zag* "side" ("outside of"). A few other morphemes may also play this role, including *en-na*, of unknown origin ("until"); *ki* "earth" ("in, from"); *mu* "name" ("for"); and the abstract prefix *nam-* ("for the sake of"). These discontinuous morphemes allow for the spatial determination of animates, which as a rule cannot take the simple locative and allative case suffixes.

Diakonoff (1967: 56) lists *-ak.eš* as a case (he calls it causative); no other grammar does so. It is built by adding the allative to a bridging morpheme, which is the genitive. This properly belongs with the complex morphemes discussed above, as it is an abbreviation of *mu*... *–ak.(e)še* "because."

4.2.5 Gender

Sumerian had two genders, animate and inanimate. The animate class covers humans and divinities, everything else is inanimate; perhaps one should use the terms "personal" and "impersonal." Gender is not marked directly on the noun, but only surfaces in cross-reference, in pronouns, which are dominated by animates, and verbal concord.

4.3 Pronouns

As is to be expected in a head-marking language, the principal participants in an action are marked by affixes on Sumerian verbs, and therefore personal pronouns do not normally appear in sentences (Rhodes 1997). They are only used for emphasis, topicalization, and topic shift. Given the limited rhetorical range of Sumerian poetry, and the predominance of third-person narrative, it is not surprising that independent pronouns are relatively rare in the preserved texts, especially first- and second-person plural forms.

4.3.1 Personal pronouns

Unlike nouns, which show ergative case marking, independent personal pronouns can only be used as transitive and intransitive subjects, and thus have to be interpreted as nominative, albeit without any corresponding accusative form. The nominative marker is *-e*; it is possible that this is a deictic element (see Woods 2000 [2005]). In addition to nominative forms, personal pronouns have dative, terminative, comitative, and equative forms; as animates they do not take local cases. Nothing is known about the inanimate third person, although it is possible that this function was fulfilled by *ur*$_5$ (or *ur*$_5$*-bi*). As already noted, not all forms are attested. In addition to the normal forms encountered in texts, lexical texts (see §6) list compounds of singular and plural forms such as *za-e-me-en-ze*$_2$*-en* for the second person. Such forms may simply be speculative grammatical constructions, or they may indicate that Sumerian originally had an inclusive/exclusive distinction that was incomprehensible to speakers of Akkadian. The personal pronouns are presented in (12) (OB = Old Babylonian):

(12)

		Singular	*Plural*
Nominative	*1st*	ĝa$_2$-e	me-(en)-de$_3$-(en)
	2nd	za-e	me-en-ze$_2$-en
	3rd	e-ne (pre-OB a-ne)	e-ne-ne
Dative	*1st*	ĝa$_2$-a-ra/ar	
	2nd	za-a-ra/ar	
	3rd	e-ne-ra	e-ne-ne-ra
Comitative	*1st*	(a/e)-da	
	2nd	za-(a/e)-da	
	3rd	e-ne-da	e-ne-ne-da
Terminative	*1st*	ĝa$_2$-(a/e)-še$_3$	
	2nd	za-(a/e)-še$_3$	
	3rd	e-ne-še$_3$	e-ne-ne-še$_3$
Equative	*1st*	ĝa$_2$-(a/e)-gin$_7$	
	2nd	za-(a/e)-gin$_7$	
	3rd	e-ne-gin$_7$	e-ne-ne-gin$_7$

4.3.2 Possessive pronouns

Possessive pronouns affixed to nouns are etymologically related to the independent pronouns.

(13)

	Singular	*Plural*
First	-ĝu$_{10}$	-me
Second	-zu	-zu-(e)-ne-(ne)
Third animate	-a-ni	-a-ne-ne
Third inanimate	-bi	-bi-(e-ne)

4.3.3 Reflexive pronouns

Reflexive pronouns are not well attested. There is no ergative form. The base is *ni*$_2$*-*, to which can be added possessive pronouns and case endings such as the locative. The absolutive paradigm is as follows:

(14)

	Singular	*Plural*
First	ni$_2$-ĝu$_{10}$	
Second	ni$_2$-zu	
Third animate	ni$_2$-(te-a-ni)	ni$_2$-te-a-ne-ne
Third inanimate	ni$_2$-bi	ni$_2$-ba/bi-a

4.3.4 Interrogative pronouns

Unlike personal pronouns, interrogatives work on the ergative pattern (for a different view see Huber 1996:186). In these pronouns the normal marking of animate with *n* and inanimate with *b* is reversed:

(15) *Ergative* a-ba-(a) "who?"
Absolute a-ba "who?" a-na "what?"

Both pronouns can occur with suffixes. The animate form takes only the enclitic copula and personal pronouns. The inanimate form can be combined with certain postpositions, the copula, as well as possessive pronouns.

4.3.5 Relative pronouns

Sumerian uses two substantives in the function of relative pronouns. Both are related to the derivational morphemes discussed in §4.2.1. The animate pronoun is lu_2, literally "man, human," as in lu_2 e_2 du_3-*a* "who built the temple." The inanimate equivalent is *nig̃*$_2$: *nig̃*$_2$-*du*$_{11}$-*ga-ni* (*nig̃.dug.ani*) "what he/she said."

4.4 Adjectives

No proper study of adjectives exists; recent grammars contain limited information on this category (Thomsen 1984:53–65; Attinger 1993:167–168). The only preliminary study is Black (2002 [2005]). It is generally agreed that Sumerian had only a limited number of "true" adjectives and that most are uninflected verbs with the nominalizer *-a* (there is a complex debate on this issue; see, most recently, Krecher 1993, Schretter 1996). There are only a handful of adjectives that are not attested as verbal roots, and, for lack of a better analysis, one should maintain that all Sumerian adjectives are in fact verbs (Gragg 1968). In form, adjectives are bare uninflected verbal roots followed by Ø or by *-a*. This suggests that at a certain level they are simply reduced predicates. The distribution of these two forms is not clear. Most adjectives appear in one or the other, but some are attested in both forms.

Certain adjectival constructions are unclear at present. A small group of adjectives carries the derivational prefixes *nig̃*$_2$- and *nam-* (see §4.2.1). We do not know what the difference is between *dag̃al(a)* "wide, teeming" and *nig̃*$_2$-*dag̃al(a)*, or between *kas dug*$_3$ "sweet beer" and *kas nig̃*$_2$-*dug*$_3$. Since *nig̃*$_2$- usually makes nouns out of verbs, this may be construed as a nominal construction. It is also conceivable that *nig̃*$_2$- is here the inanimate relative pronoun and that this is a calque from Akkadian.

4.5 Adverbs

Sumerian adverbs are formed from nominal and verbal bases. Most commonly they are formed with a suffix *-bi* (originally probably an inanimate deictic) which can only be added to verbal ("adjectival") roots, either directly or following the nominalizing suffix *-a:* for example, *gal-bi* "greatly," *dug*$_3$-*bi* "tenderly," *gibil-bi* "anew," or *ul*$_4$-*la-bi* "rapidly." A different suffix *-(e)še*, homonymous with the allative case, created manner adverbs from nouns as well as adjectives: thus, *u*$_4$-*de-eš*$_{(2)}$ "as the day," *gal-le-eš* "grandly." In Old Babylonian texts one begins to encounter the cumulative use of both suffixes as in *gibil-bi-eš*$_3$ "anew."

In some cases, adjectives can be used as adverbs without any suffix, such as *gal* "great" but also "greatly" (Krecher 1987:74). A postulated class of adverbs in *-a* has been questioned (Attinger 1993:170).

4.5.1 Modal and temporal adverbs

The most common modal adverbs are the following: *i$_3$-gi$_4$-in-zu* "moreover, what's more"; *i$_3$-ge$_4$-en* "truly, in fact"; *a-na-aš-am$_3$*, *a$_2$-še$_3$* "how is it (that)." Temporal adverbs are as follows: *a-da-lam* (*a-da-al*, *i-da-al*) "(but) now"; *and i$_3$-ne-eš$_2$* "now."

4.5.2 Interrogative adverbs

These consist of a stem *me(n)*, complemented by directional suffixes or the enclitic copula. The most common forms are these: *me-a* "where?" *me-še$_3$* "where to?" and *me-na-am$_3$* "when?"

4.6 Verbal morphology

The analysis of verbal structure is the most controversial part of modern Sumerian grammatical study. It was also of concern to Akkadian-speaking ancients, who compiled comparative paradigms of Sumerian and Akkadian verbal forms and attempted to isolate morphological elements that they considered equivalent to ones found in their own language (Black 1984). It would be impossible to give an adequate accounting of all competing visions of the Sumerian verb in the present context; what follows is my own relatively simple analysis with selective references to competing theories. For fuller bibliographical information see Thomsen (1984), Attinger (1993), and Römer (1999).

Sumerian verbs consist of a verbal root and morphological affixes that mark certain verbal categories. The affixes mark categories such as mood, concord, and aspect. Verbs are either simple or compound. In certain verbs the base may be reduplicated to mark the imperfective, iterative action, or plurality of patient.

Compound verbs are construed with a noun and an inflected verbal base (Karahashi 2000). The noun is inanimate, indefinite, and generic; it is the semantic patient of the verb but it does not constitute a core argument of a clause, hence it is not marked by a direct case ending. The direct object of the clause is marked as oblique, usually with the locative 2 *-e*, less often with locative 1 *-a*, and with dative *-ra* on a small group of verbs, most of them verbs of emotion, and with still other cases. A good example is the verb *in-*(še$_3$) . . . *dub$_2$* "to insult" which takes the dative, although the verb takes the locative rather than the dative prefix:

(16)	ud-bi-a	gi	g̃iš-ra	in-še$_3$	mu-ni-in-dub$_2$
	ud.bi.a	gi.(e)	g̃iš.ra	in.še	mu.ni.n.dub
	day-PRO.-LOC.	reed-(ERG.)	tree-DAT.	N.-ALL.	PREF.-LOC2-ERG.-insult
	"Then (lit. 'on that day') Reed insulted Tree"				

Many compound verbs have transparent etymologies, such as *ki* "earth" + *tag* "strike, touch" = "to lay a foundation, to spread." The incorporated noun is sometimes a body part, *šu* "hand" or *ka* "mouth." Others consist of a noun and an auxiliary verbal root such as *dug$_4$* "to speak" or *ak* "to make," verbs which otherwise appear independently. Some verbs of this type may be doubly compounded with an auxiliary and it is unclear if this has any semantic consequences; thus *šu . . . bal* and *šu bal . . . ak* both mean "to overturn." A substantial group of compound verbs has no apparent etymological transparency, such as *ki . . . ağ*$_2$ "to love" (lit. "place" + "to measure out"). Small subsets allow for expansion of the noun by an adjective (e.g., *šu zi . . . ğar* "hand" + "true". . . "place" = "to bestow, grant"). One has the impression that by the time we actually observe the language, noun–verb compounding was no longer productive. A frozen set had entered the lexicon, but new verbs were not being created.

Attinger (1993) has suggested that compound verbs are an example of noun incorporation, a phenomenon attested in many languages of the Americas, Southeast Asia, and elsewhere (Mithun 1984, 1985). Some have denied this, arguing that in Sumerian this is a syntactic and not a morphological issue (Zólyomi 1996a), but this is a theoretical question that covers all of noun incorporation. Huber (1996) likewise comes out against incorporation in this language, but once again it is a definitional question. The Sumerian data suggest either what has been termed loose incorporation (Mithun 2000) or, more probably, what Miner (1986) calls "noun stripping." In such constructions the nouns are "stripped" of their affixes but remain as separate phonological entities; the nouns are backgrounded but remain as independent words.

4.6.1 Transitivity

Most Sumerian verbs are strictly transitive or intransitive. There exists a small class of labile, or ambitransitive, verbs that can be either transitive or intransitive. Examples are *gu*$_7$ "to eat ~ to feed"; *nağ* "to drink, give to drink, water"; *uš*$_2$ "to kill ~ to die"; *tuš* "to sit ~ to seat"; *kud*^{r} "to enter, bring in"; *us*$_2$ "to follow, reach, let reach." Two such verbs are semantically similar, but differ in the animacy of the subject/patient: *til* "to live, dwell, be healthy ~ to settle, give life/health" used when people are involved; and *lug* "to pasture, settle" which is used for animals. One should note, however, that *til* can be used of inanimates with the meaning "to be/make healthy."

4.6.2 Valence

Matters of valence in Sumerian have been disputed, but no consensus has been reached. It is clear that simply deleting the agent can form impersonal passives; as a consequence, this often results in a change of verbal prefixes, but there is no specific passive marker as such. The existence of other forms of valence change mechanisms, be it antipassive or causative, is difficult to ascertain at present (see, most recently, Attinger 1993:195–199, though most of his examples are actually labile verbs).

4.6.3 Aspect/Tense

Opinion is divided on whether the two forms of the Sumerian verb differ in tense or in aspect, although in recent years most scholars have come to speak of the latter rather than the former. Certain verbs utilize stem reduplication to create one of the forms, and therefore typologically it is unlikely that tense is involved (see Anderson 1985:170). For the sake of the present discussion we shall use the terms *perfective* and *imperfective* to designate these two forms; one could also designate them as *completive* and *incompletive* since the only thing that most scholars agree on is that one denotes a complete and the second an incomplete action.

Ancient lexical and grammatical texts provide us with the Akkadian names of the two basic verbal forms: *ḫamṭu* and *marû*. There has been much discussion of the exact meaning of these words as well as of whether these technical terms describe the Sumerian verbal forms or their Akkadian translations. Uncertainties aside, the terms have often been used in the modern literature in order to avoid labeling the specific aspectual or temporal qualities of the Sumerian verb. It now appears fairly certain that these Akkadian grammatical terms means simply "short" and "long" (Civil 2002: 69–100) and that the perfective (i.e., "short") form was considered the unmarked citation category. At the present time the full significance of the two forms is open to debate and the use of "perfective" and "imperfective" here is purely conventional.

4.6.3.1 *Marking of aspect*

Verbs mark these distinctions in three separate ways: through (i) agreement, (ii) stem reduplication, and (iii) suppletion. The perfective is the unmarked aspect and the perfective stem is the citation form. Reduplication and suppletion also serve to mark the plural of absolutives, that is, plural intransitive subjects and transitive objects; Sumerologists refer to this as *free reduplication*. Most verbs achieve this by means of stem reduplication, but a small class of verbs has suppletive plural forms. On rare occasions imperfective verbal roots can be tripled or even quadrupled to mark plurality of absolutives; with perfects this marks both intense action and plurality of absolutives.

There has been some disagreement concerning the marking of the two aspects. Yoshikawa (1968) in a pioneering study proposed three classes of verbs: those that formed the imperfective by affixation (*-e*); by reduplication; and by alternation of roots. It seems fairly certain, however, that there is no affixation group, and that the suffix *-e* belongs to the agreement-markers (Thomsen 1984:116).

More than half of Sumerian verbs have no overt aspectual morphology; the distinctions are expressed by means of different agreement patterns for the two aspects (e.g., *šum* "to give," *dal* "to fly"). A much smaller group of verbs utilizes partial or full stem reduplication to form the imperfective. The writing system makes it difficult to discern when a root is fully or partially reduplicated, but as a rule CV and VC roots are fully copied (e.g., *si* ~ *si-si* "to fill," *ur* ~ *ur.ur* "to drag"), while CVC roots are reduced to CV (*g̃ar* ~ *g̃a.g̃a* "to place," but cf. *gar* ~ *gar-gar*, "to pile up"), although the final consonant may resurface before a vocalic ending. Often this is not written, but forms such as *g̃a*$_2$*-g̃ar-am*$_3$ illustrate the principle well. A very small class of verbs displays root suppletion for aspect as well as number (Steinkeller 1979). As a result, one can say that there were two "regular" ways of distinguishing aspect in Sumerian: through agreement and by stem reduplication.

4.6.3.2 *Regular verbs*

Regular verbs may be represented as follows, utilizing the *šum* (written <šum$_2$>) "to give," *g̃i* (written <g̃i$_4$>) "to return," and *g̃ar* "to place":

(17) *Perfective* *Imperfective*
šum <šum$_2$> šum <šum$_2$>
g̃i <gi$_4$> g̃i.g̃i <g̃i$_4$-g̃i$_4$>

Superficially, it would seem that there was also a reduced reduplication group:

(18) *Perfective* *Imperfective*
g̃ar <g̃ar> g̃a.g̃a <g̃a$_2$-g̃a$_2$>

Although it remains to be fully demonstrated, it is most probable that all CVC verbs copied only CV in reduplication, although this is often obscured by the writing system. Thus, the reduplication of *g̃ar* is written as <g̃a$_2$-g̃a$_2$>, but the reduplication of *kin* "to seek" is written as <kin-kin>, which must be read as *ki*$_3$*-ki*$_3$.

4.6.3.3 *Suppletive verbs*

The suppletive verbs are similar in meaning to such verbs found in unrelated languages, including many North American tongues. Most of them are intransitive or labile. The complex paradigms of these verbs began to conform to the regular verbs already at the end of the third millennium, when singular roots began to replace the plural forms. For comparative purposes it is necessary to list these Sumerian verbs in full.

(19)

Verb	[Perfective]		[Imperfective]	
	Singular	Plural	Singular	Plural
"to bring"	de_6	lah_4	$tum_{2/3}$	lah_4
"to go"	*gin*	*er*	*du*	su_8-(*b*)
"to stand"	*gub*	su_8-(*g*)	*gub*	su_8-(*g*)
"to sit"	*tuš*	*durun*	dur_2	*durun*
"to speak"	dug_4	*e*	*e*	*e*
"to kill/die"	$uš_2$	$ug_{5/7}$	$ug_{5/7}$	$ug_{5/7}$
"to live, be healthy, dwell" (animate)	*til*	$še_x$(SIG_7)	*til*	$še_x$(SIG_7)
"to live, dwell, pasture" (inanimate)	*lug*	$še_x$(SIG_7)	*lug*	$še_x$(SIG_7)
"to enter, bring in"	ku_4	sun_5	ku_4-ku_4	sun_5

Three other verbs have a limited form of suppletion that consists of adding a final consonant in the imperfect: $e_3 \sim e_3$ [*d*] "to go out"; *ri* ∼ *rig* "to pour out"; *ti/e* ∼ *teĝ* "to approach." This set of three is commonly referred to as an *alternating class*, but the limited number of verbs obviates the creation of a separate fundamental category.

In the simplest terms, the Sumerian verb may be represented in the following manner:

(20) Sumerian verbal chain

1	2	3	4	5
MOOD	CONJUNCTION	FOCUS	INDIRECT OBJECT	DIMENSIONAL PREFIXES
6	7	8	9	10
AGREEMENT	ROOT	ED	AGREEMENT	NOMINALIZATION

4.6.4 Mood (position 1)

The traditional description of modes distinguishes between pairs of homophonous prefixes that differ in meaning depending on the mood. Thus *he-* is "precative" with the imperfective, but "assertative" with the perfective. As a result, translations of texts are replete with "let him/her" and "verily he/she . . . " There are reasons to reject this interpretation; certain modal prefixes are indeed usually associated with one aspect or the other, but this results from the semantics of the mode and not from any formal constraints. The following reinterpretation of the modes results in part from the author's own observations, but mainly from the work of Civil (2002 [2005]) which obviates much earlier research on the subject.

Unlike previous writers, Civil makes reference to *deontic* and *epistemic* notions of modality (Palmer 1986). To cite Chung and Timberlake (1985:246): "The epistemic mode deals with alternative worlds with respect to a given world at a given time point; the alternative worlds are those that could exist instead of a given world. The deontic mode also deals with a given world and with alternative worlds, but the alternative worlds are those that could develop out of the given worlds." In Sumerian, deontic functions are distributed over four forms, the deontic subjunctive-optative, both negative and positive, the cohortative, as well as the imperative. A variety of epistemic functions are encoded by the positive and negative epistemic subjunctive-optative markers.

4.6.4.1 *Indicative*

The normal indicative has no prefix in this position; the negative carries the prefix *nu-*. Thus, *lugal-e iri mu-un-gul* "the king destroyed the city" but *lugal-e iri nu-mu-un-gul* "the king did not destroy the city." There are also rare cases of *nu* as a predicate, as in *lu*$_2$*-še*$_3$ *lugal-g̃u*$_{10}$ *in-nu* "that man yonder is not my king."

4.6.4.2 *Deontic subjunctive-optative*

This prefix is used to make commands, give advice, or exhort someone to do the speaker's bidding, or to express the desires and wishes of the speaker. This results in phrases with counterparts to English "should," "please," or "may." The positive prefix is *he-*, written with the sign *he*$_2$, although from Old Babylonian times on the writing shows vowel harmony with what follows (written *ha* or *hu*), and the negative is *na-*.

4.6.4.3 *Epistemic subjunctive-optative*

This function expresses conditions dependent on actions from another clause or phrase, often resulting in dependent clauses or conditionals. The positive prefix is *he-*; the negative is *bara-* (written as *ba-ra-*).

The subjunctive-optative modals are treated somewhat differently in traditional grammars, which correlate four different prefixes with the two aspects of the Sumerian verb, here marked as p(erfective) and i(mperfective). Thomsen (1984:193–199) is representative. In this system *he-* is affirmative (p) or precative (i); the negative counterpart is *bara-*, which is negative affirmative (p), or vetitive (i) for first person, otherwise it is prohibitive *na-*, also with the imperfect. The prefix *na-* (see §4.6.4.6) with perfect aspect is affirmative.

4.6.4.4 *Cohortative*

The prefix *ga-* renders the intent or willful pronouncement of the speaker: for example, *ga-na-ab-dug*$_4$ (*ga.na.b.dug.Ø*) "I have decided to tell it (=*b*) to him myself." Such forms almost always use the perfect aspect, but agreement (see §4.6.10) is nominative-accusative, rather than ergative (Michalowski 1980:97). The prefix marks the accusative rather than the ergative, as is usual in the perfective. During the Old Babylonian period a first-person plural form appears, with imperfective aspect and the first-person plural ending *-enden* marking the nominative: *ga-mu-na-dur*$_2$*-ru-ne-en-de*$_3$*-en* (*ga.mu.na.durun.enden*) "We want to prostrate ourselves before him!"

4.6.4.5 *Prefix of anteriority*

The prefix *u-*, often written with the sign *u*$_3$, marks an action that precedes another action in a sequence. Such forms are usually translated as temporal clauses "when . . . "; in bilingual texts they are often rendered by imperatives. Traditionally such constructions are labeled prospective.

4.6.4.6 *Other modal prefixes*

Civil calls the prefix *na-* a marker of reported speech. In earlier treatments it is regarded as an affirmative (volitative) marker. Although it seems to be a homonym of the negative subjunctive-optative (see §4.6.4.2), it may in fact have originally had a different phonological shape. Unlike the negative prefix, this *na-* is usually combined with the perfective aspect. It is often found in contexts where traditional or mythological lore is reported, or in formulaic introductions to narratives and speeches. It is best illustrated by the standard opening formula of Sumerian letters of the late third millennium: *PN_1-ra u_3-na-(a)-dug_4 PN_2 na-(ab)-be_2*-a "When you address PN_1, this is what PN_2 says to him."

There is some evidence, however, that this prefix had other functions before the Ur III period. In third-millennium literary texts *na-* is one of the few prefixes that are regularly written before the verbal root, often with the sign *nam_2*, and it is used much more commonly than in later periods. This grapheme goes out of use in the second millennium, when it is merged, together with some other similar signs, into *$še_3$*. One could speculate that originally *na-* had a narrative foregrounding function that was lost in later Sumerian. The fact that it is apparently homophonous with the negative subjunctive-optative raises additional questions. It may be that this is a historical accident, but it is also possible that the consonants of the two prefixes were different.

Another uncertain modal prefix is *ša-* (Jacobsen 1965:73 called it "contrapunctive"). It is documented only in literary texts. As Civil notes, the distribution of this prefix is somewhat puzzling, as a third of occurrences in the middle second-millennium school curriculum are limited to four compositions. It is not perhaps accidental that one of these, *The Instructions of Shuruppak,* is attested already in Early Dynastic copies, and the second, *The Collection of Temple Hymns,* is ascribed to a princess who lived *c.* 2300 BC. It is possible that two different processes resulted in two different written forms of the same grammatical element, or even in the split of one into two: a change in meaning of *na-* and the misreading of the sign *nam_2* as *$še_3$*.

A rare modal prefix, found only in literary texts, is *nu-uš-*, charmingly named "frustrative" by Jacobsen (1965:82), and apparently means "if only, would that." Civil considers it a rhetorical interrogative particle, meaning "why not?"

4.6.4.7 Imperative

The morphology of the imperative in Sumerian is completely different from that of other moods, and is not marked by any characteristic affix. Copying the root to the front of the verbal form, which is always the perfective singular root, creates imperatives: thus *mu lugal mu-ni-in-pad_3* (*mu.ni.n.pad*) "He/she wore by the name of the king"; but *mu lugal pad_3-mu-ni-ib_2* (*pad.mu.ni.b*) "take the oath by the name of the king!" The agreement prefix *b-*, now moved after the root, in the imperative always marks the accusative, that is, the transitive object; in the corresponding indicative sentence *n-* marked the agent.

The unmarked singular second-person referent of the imperative is always nominative, that is, either transitive or intransitive subject. In early texts, this is always deleted; in the Old Babylonian times an overt plural form was created by analogy with the cohortative, resulting in forms such as *du_{11}-ga-na-ab-ze_2-en* (*dug.a.ba.b.enzen*) "you all say it!"

The nominative/accusative agreement pattern of the imperative is not surprising; this is a pragmatic universal (Michalowski 1980:97; Payne 1982:90). Note that the last form cited above has the vowel *a* after the root. This can be interpreted either as an insertion to avoid a cluster or confusion with infinitives, or as an allomorph of the conjugation prefix *i-*. The latter otherwise never occurs in imperatives. The few attested forms of the type *gar-i_3* are probably to be interpreted as *gar.(a)ni* "when he/she placed" and are not imperatives at all (Attinger 1993:299). Other examples of imperatives are *dug_4-ga-na-ab* "say it to him/her!", and *tuš-a* "sit!"

4.6.5 Conjunction (position 2)

The second rank is occupied by the conjunction prefix *inga-*, which means "as well, also, too." The rank of the prefix has been the subject of some debate; it comes after the modals, but is rarely followed by conjugation prefixes. Writings such as *nam-ga-* are probably to be analyzed as *na.(i)nga*.

4.6.6 Focus (conjugation) prefixes (position 3)

The prefixes that fall in this position constitute the most controversial part of Sumerian grammar. No two Sumerologists appear to agree fully on their form, meaning, etymology, and identity; the number of ranks that they occupy is equally disputed. It would be impossible to do justice in this short survey to the various opinions that have been expressed. I have therefore chosen to present my own working hypotheses on the subject and only mention selected previous opinions on the matter. For the numerous interpretations of these prefixes see the references offered by Thomsen (1984:182–185), with important newer discussions by Black (1986:77), Wilcke (1988), Attinger (1993:261–288), Jagersma (1993), as well as a study by Vanstiphout (1985) on foregrounding and backgrounding strategies in Sumerian.

Rather than split these prefixes into three, four, or even five separate ranks, I prefer a minimalist position according to which there are only four distinct "conjugation" prefixes: *mu-*, *ba-*, *i-* (or *V-*), and *imma-*. Gragg (1973a:93) and Civil (in Karahashi, 2002 [2005]) apparently take similar positions. I do not break these down into smaller components, as do many others. Most Sumerologists consider this position obligatory, and restore a hypothetical *i-* even in cases when it is not written. In my opinion the neutral *i-* is not marked after a modal prefix. Rather than consider the position obligatory, one should simply state that a finite verbal form cannot begin with any of the final three positions before the root.

The prefix *imma-* is most commonly considered as a compound, often etymologized as containing both *i-* and *b(a)-* as well as a locative element *a*. According to the analysis followed here, the first two are mutually exclusive and the third element does not exist. Rather than view *imma-* as a "compound" I would suggest that it represents a form of reduplication of *mu-*, in which the initial consonant is copied and the cluster is reinforced by an initial vowel.

The meanings of these prefixes are as contested as their ranking. The prefix *mu-* appears to mark focus on control over an action that is within the control and propinquity of the agent. When such control is loosened, absent – and this includes the absence of an agent in a clause – the prefix *ba-* is used. When the focus is intensified, as with verbs denoting movement towards the agent, or the agent manipulates an object, such as a tool, the prefix *imma-* is often used. When focus is not specified, the prefix is *i-*. There is a rare prefix *a-*; in Old Babylonian literary texts it is probably an allomorph of *i-*, but in earlier texts it seems to be used, in Nippur at least, to mark verbs without agents. Yoshikawa (1992) considers *ba-* to mark reduced valency, which may fit well into this scheme.

I must reiterate the contested nature of these issues. The reader should be aware that there are many graphemic and morphophonological matters that remain unresolved. For example, a sequence such as *im-ROOT* or i_3-*im-ROOT* has been interpreted as *i* followed by a "ventive" prefix that signifies "hither." I much prefer to view the *m* as a reflex of *n* (the animate third-person pronoun); it is also possible that there are other morphophonemic or even prosodic processes at play here that are represented by the extra vowel, but this is a complex issue that cannot be debated in the present work. One should also note that the writing conventions as well as the forms of these prefixes show much synchronic and diachronic variation.

4.6.7 The prefix *al-*

There exists another verbal prefix of undetermined rank, namely *al-*. The rank cannot be specified because, with rare exceptions, this morpheme cannot coexist with any other verbal affix, although such forms can be nominalized. The forms with *al-* are intransitive, and appear to correspond to Akkadian inflected verbal adjectives ("statives").

Attinger (1993: 269) and Edzard (2003: 111) deny the existence of a separate prefix and consider *al-* to be an allomorph of the vocalic prefix *a-*.

4.6.8 Indirect object (position 4)

The dative prefixes are normally classed together with the dimensional elements of the next position. For structural reasons they are set apart here in their own rank. The dimensional prefixes, when they do refer to arguments of a clause, mark adjuncts; this position, however, cross-references the beneficiary, that is, a core or core extension argument. Unlike the markers that correspond to the oblique cases of nouns (dimensional prefixes), datives have different forms for different persons:

(21)			
	First	a	me
	Second	ra	?
	Third	na	ne

The first person always follows the prefix *mu-* and together they are realized in writing as *ma-*, as in *ma-an-šum*$_2$ (*mu.a.n.šum.Ø*) "he/she gave [it] to me"; or *ma-an-dug*$_4$ (*mu.a.n.dug.Ø*) "he/she said [it] to me." The second person is also found after *mu-*; in early texts this sequence is subject to vowel harmony, and is usually, but not always, written as *ma-ra*.

4.6.9 Dimensional prefixes (position 5)

The forms and meanings of the prefixes that occupy this rank are fairly well established, due to a great extent to the work of Gragg (1973a). These prefixes are coreferential with the oblique case marking of the noun: dative, comitative, ablative-instrumental, allative, and the two locative cases. Most of them are phonologically similar or identical to those of the noun, and are presumably of the same etymological origin. As Gragg has shown, these prefixes are often connected to certain roots and are lexicalized to a degree. The dative and locatives differ in certain respects from the other prefixes and may have a different common origin. The dimensional prefixes follow one another in a set order:

(22)

	↗ Allative →	Locative 1
Comitative		
	↘ Ablative-instrumental →	Locative 2

4.6.9.1 *Comitative*

The comitative prefix is usually written as *da* (Old Sumerian *da*$_5$); sometimes as *di*, *de*$_3$, and *de*$_4$ when followed by the locative 2 (terminative). The affix can be preceded by a pronominal element: first person is either *Ø* or *e*, second is *e*, and third person is *n* or *b*, for animates and inanimates respectively. In the plural, only the third person is attested; this element, written as PI, with unknown reading, is only found in Old Sumerian documents.

Although homophonous with the equivalent nominal suffix, in most instances the verbal prefix does not copy a corresponding marker appearing on a noun. Sometimes, especially after the prefix *ba-*, *da-* must be interpreted as a writing for the ablative *ta-* (see §4.6.9.3). The comitative occurs with verbs that include the semantic notion of accompaniment, such as "to speak with" (*dug*$_4$) "to compare with" (*sa*$_2$), or "to counsel with" (*ad*... *g̃i*$_4$), as well as with verbs of emotion. Still other verbs take this prefix, including those meaning to "flee," "to escape" (*zah*$_3$). An important function of this prefix is the marking of potential – referred to as abilitative in the literature.

4.6.9.2 *Allative (terminative, directive)*

The allative prefix was originally written as *še*$_3$-, but beginning with the Ur III period it was expressed by means of the sign *ši-*. Unlike the comitative, it is closely related semantically to the nominal suffix, and denotes movement towards a goal. It is therefore frequently found on verbs of motion and often marks nuances of meaning that are connected with its basic function. It is also often found with compound verbs that denote attention; these all include body parts as the "stripped" noun (see §4.7.1). Examples are *igi*... *g̃ar/du*$_3$*/kar*$_2$, which all denote different ways of seeing and include the noun *igi* "eye"; and *g̃eštug*$_2$... *gub/g̃ar* "to pay attention to/listen" incorporating *g̃eštug*$_2$ "ear."

4.6.9.3 *Ablative-instrumental*

The primary meaning of this prefix, *ta-*, is ablative, although there are rare cases of instrumental usage. There is another prefix *ra-* that obviously also has ablative meaning and has been the subject of some debate. In Ur III documents one finds the expression *ud-ta ud x ba-zal* ~ *ba-ra-zal* ~ *ba-ta-zal* ~ *ba-ra-ta-zal*, which means "at the end of the xth day," literally "from the month the xth day having passed." This has created much confusion about the possible existence of two such prefixes, but Civil (1973b:27) ingeniously suggested that these writings all express the realization of /ta/ as /d^r/ in intervocalic position.

4.6.9.4 *Locative 1*

The locative prefix *ni-* corresponds to the nominal locative case ending *-a*. Unlike the already discussed dimensional prefixes, it primarily resumes locatives in the clause. This includes true locative adverbials as well as the logical direct objects of compound verbs and third participants of causative constructions. It is sometimes written as *in-* immediately before the root, and is thus confused with the third-person ergative marker (see §4.6.10; Attinger 1993:234).

4.6.9.5 *Locative 2 (locative-terminative)*

The second locative, which corresponds to the nominal suffix *-e*, is somewhat more difficult to isolate, and its identity as well as morphophonemic shape are disputed. Civil (1976:90) has proposed that it is a vocalic element or glide; his theory has been fully investigated, with reference to the many other theories on the subject, by Karahashi (2002 [2005]). The morphophonemic realizations in writing, following other morphemes, obscure its prototypical shape. After conjugation prefixes the main writings are *bi*$_2$- (*ba.i*), *imma-* (*imma.i*), *mu-NI-* (*mu.i*); after indirect object prefixes, *mu-e* (*mu.i*), *ri-* (*ra.i*), *ni* (*na.i*); after the comitative, *di* or *de*$_3$ (*da.i*); after "ablative" *ra-* it is *ri-*.

The function of this prefix is similar to that of locative 1: concord with locatives, and with logical direct objects of compound verbs.

4.6.10 Agreement prefixes and suffixes (positions 6 and 9)

The final position before the root is occupied by agreement prefixes (position 6), although in the plural these prefixes work cumulatively with the second suffix position (position 9). These affixes cross-reference the core arguments of the clause – ergative, absolutive, nominative, and accusative. As already noted, *perfective* verbs have *ergative* agreement, and *imperfective* verbs have *nominative-accusative* agreement. The reconstruction of the forms is somewhat complicated by morphophonemic changes. The prototypical paradigms presented here do not apply in all cases, as the agreement markers may be used for different functions with different verbs (see Yoshikawa 1977). Ergative agreement is marked by prefixes in combination with suffixes, absolutive by suffixes:

(23) Agreement affixes – perfective aspect

	Ergative agreement affixes	
	Singular	*Plural*
First	Ø/e-	(-enden)
Second	e-	(-enzen)
Third animate	n-	(-eš)
Third inanimate	b-	

	Absolutive agreement suffixes	
	Singular	*Plural*
First	-en	-enden
Second	-en	-enzen
Third	-Ø	-eš

In the imperfective aspect, the suffixes mark the nominative subject (i.e., both transitive and intransitive subjects) in the first and second person; the use of these suffixes is not obligatory with transitive verbs. However, there is a three-way split in the third person, with separate suffixed-marking of transitive and intransitive subjects, as well as distinct prefixed-marking of transitive objects (see Woods 1999).

(24) Agreement affixes – imperfective aspect

	Nominative agreement suffixes	
	Singular	*Plural*
First	-en	-enden
Second	-en	-enzen
Third (transitive subject)	-e	-ene
Third (intransitive subject)	-(e)	-eš

	Accusative agreement prefixes	
	Singular	*Plural*
First	(Ø/e-/'-/a-)	?
Second	(e-)	?
Third animate	(n-)	?
Third inanimate	(b-)	?

4.6.11 The morpheme *-ed* (position 8)

The first rank after the root is occupied by the suffix *-ed* (Edzard 1967, Steiner 1981). The form and function of this element have been much debated. Certain theories recognized a marker of the imperfective *-e*, and as a result it was unclear if the suffix was defined as *-ed*, *-d*, or *-de*. With the elimination of this imperfective marker it seems relatively certain that the form of this suffix is *-ed*, although in cuneiform writing, the consonant is dropped in final position. The meaning is less clear. This morpheme seems to refer to the future and to purpose, especially used in subordinate clauses with nonfinite verbal forms such as *iri dag̃al-e-de*$_3$ (*dag̃al.ed*) "in order to widen the city"; or *iri dag̃al-la-da* (*dag̃al.ed.a*) "the city that is/has to be widened" (Civil 1999–2000). In finite forms – which are less frequently attested – it seems to have a future function combined with a prospective obligatory modal nuance. The latter results in the incompatibility of *-ed* with modal prefixes with the exception of the indicative, although a few late literary examples of usage are attested.

More commonly this suffix is added to the bare verbal root and is followed by a vowel /e/ in final position to preserve its final consonant. This vowel is not subject to harmony; thus we have *nam tar-e-de*$_3$ "in order to/able to determine destinies"; but *šum*$_2$*-mu-de*$_3$ "in order to/to be able to give." The verb is always imperfective; this is only overtly apparent in those that have a distinct imperfective form, such as *g̃a*$_2$*-g̃a*$_2$*-de*$_3$ "to place."

4.6.12 Nominalization (position 10)

The final position of the verbal chain, after *-ed* and the pronominal suffixes, is occupied by *-a*, which creates nouns out of verbs and turns main clauses into dependent ones (Krecher 1993). Once this happens, the nominalized entity can take suffixes as if it were a noun: pronouns, as well as simple and compound and discontinuous case morphemes.

The nominalizer *-a* can be attached to both finite and nonfinite verbal forms – that is to verbs with a full set of prefixes, or to the bare root alone. With finite verbs this creates subordinate clauses dependent on another verb, on a noun, or on a relative pronoun, as in *lu*$_2$ *e*$_2$ *in-du*$_3$*-a* "the one who built the temple." The morpheme can also be attached to verbs in indirect speech clauses dependent on a limited set of verbs of speaking. Because of the restricted rhetorical range of written Sumerian, this usage is relatively rare in the preserved corpus.

With nonfinite verbal forms the suffix *-a* creates participles that are usually equivalent to English active and past participles: *kur a-ta il*$_2$*-la* "mountain rising from the waters"; *g̃eštug šum*$_2$*-ma* "given wisdom." For other uses of the nominalizer see §5.4.

4.6.13 Other suffixes

There are two other morphemes that have traditionally been assigned the same final rank as the nominalizer *-a*. Both are rarely used and both are unattested before the Old Babylonian period. Although it is difficult to prove, one might question if these are really bound morphemes or if they are independent particles. The first of these is the marker of direct speech, *-eše* and the second, *-g̃išen*, marks irrealis and seems to be equivalent to "if only" or "were it that." As Civil (2002 [2005]) has observed, *eše* is not an affix but a frozen verbal form meaning "they said."

4.6.14 The enclitic copula

The Sumerian verb *me* "to be" can be used independently, but is most commonly attested as a copula (Gragg 1968). It is intransitive, occurs only in the perfective, and takes only the pronominal endings:

(25)

	Singular	*Plural*
First	i_3-me-en	i_3-me-en-de_3-en
Second	i_3-me-en	i_3-me-en-ze_2-en
Third	i_3-me	i_3-me-eš

In its use as a copula it is morphologically identical to the forms of (25) without the prefix *i_3-* except that the third-person singular is *-am*, originally written *-am_6*, but later as *-am_3*. The final consonant of the copula is dropped in early texts; from Ur III on, this happens regularly only in the third-person singular. The copula can even be added to the conjugated form of "to be" as in the following: *pi-lu_5-da u_4-bi-ta e-me-a (e.me.am)* "these were the conventions of earlier times."

The functions of the copula are multifold. With nouns it often takes the place of an independent pronoun as a predicate: *sipa-me-en e_2 mu-du_3* "I (lit. I am) [the king,] the shepherd, have built the temple." It can function as a simple predicate, sometimes following a bridging genitive morpheme: *an-ta-sur-ra $\tilde{g}a_2$-a-kam* (*g̃a.ak.am*) "the Antasura [shrine] is mine!" It is often used pausally or emphatically after a complete sentence, appended to a finite verbal form.

The copula is also used in comparisons, much like the nominal equative ending *-gin_7*: thus, *e_2 kur gal-am_3* "the temple is akin to a large mountain."

4.7 Numerals

4.7.1 Cardinals

As a rule, Sumerian number words are written with number signs and are not spelled out syllabically; hence there is some uncertainty about the forms of the words, and not all numbers are attested. The following tentative list is based on word lists, as reconstructed by Diakonoff (1984) and Civil (1982:6–7). According to this analysis, there are five primary words that were originally compounded to create the numbers six through nine. Small numbers were counted decimally, large numbers in multiples of sixty.

(26)

1	diš, dili, aš	*9*	(y)ilimmu (ya + limmu)
2	min	*10*	hu(wu)
3	eš (written $eš_5$)	*20*	niš
4	limmu	*30*	ušu
5	ya (written ia_2)	*40*	nimin
6	aš (written $aš_3$; ya + aš)	*50*	ninnu
7	imin (ya + min)	*60*	g̃i/eš
8	ussu (ya + eš)	*360*	šar

4.7.2 Ordinals

Ordinal numbers are formed with the cardinal number word, followed by the bridging genitive morpheme and the enclitic copula *-am*: thus, *min-(a)-kam (min.ak.am)* "second."

5. SYNTAX

The syntax of Sumerian is perhaps the most neglected part of the grammar, and its complexities can only be hinted at in the limited space available here. The language is head-final; subordinate and relative clauses appear to the left of the main clause. Although Sumerian morphology is primarily ergative, it seems that ergativity plays little or no role in interclausal syntax; indeed it may very well be that the language is one of those that have no syntactic pivot (Zólyomi 1996a:106), although this is a matter that requires full investigation. Sentences are either simple or complex. The rich verbal morphology of Sumerian encodes much syntactic information, but the morphological and syntactic relationships between clauses and sentences have not been extensively studied.

5.1 Simple sentence word order

Simple sentences as a rule follow SOV order, although the object can be moved right and complements moved left for pragmatic purposes. Sentences with all three components in proper order are primarily third person:

(27) lugal-e e$_2$ mu-un-du$_3$
lugal.e e.Ø mu.n.du.Ø
king-ERG. temple-ABS. PREF.-ERG.-build-ABS.
"The king built the temple"

Unmarked first-person agents are only expressed by verbal agreement markers; pronouns are used only for emphasis or topicalization:

(28) ğa$_2$-e uri$_5^{ki}$-ma ga-na-ağ$_2$
ğa.e urim.a ga.na.ağ
PRO.-ERG. Urim-LOC. PREF.-DAT.-pay
"I want to pay him back in [the city of] Ur myself"

Agents are not obligatory; clauses without overt agents correspond to Akkadian or English impersonal passives:

(29) e$_2$ ba-du$_3$
e.Ø ba.du
temple-ABS. PREF.-build
"The temple was built"

Because Sumerian has such a complex verbal morphology, a finite verbal form can by itself constitute a well-formed sentence:

(30) bi$_2$-in-dug$_4$
ba.i.n.dug.Ø
PREF.-LOC2-ERG.-speak-ABS.
"He/she said it"

The copula can function as the predicate:

(31) dumu uri$_5^{ki}$-ma me-en
dumu urim.ak me.en
son Urim-GEN. COP.
"I am a citizen of [the city of] Ur"

A nominalized verb can be turned into a full predicate by addition of the copula:

(32) bi$_2$-in-dug$_4$-ga-gin$_7$-nam
ba.i.n.dug.a.gin.am
PREF.-LOC.-ERG.-speak-NOMINALIZER-EQUATIVE-COP.
"It was just as he had said"

5.2 Coordination

Two nouns can be seriated together to express conjunction as in *an ki* "heavens and the earth." The compound morpheme *-bi.da* (possessive pronoun and comitative case-marker) is also used to conjoin two nouns, as in *an ki-bi-da* "heavens and the earth." From the latter half of the third millennium one encounters the sporadic use of loanword u_3, presumably borrowed from Semitic *u* (originally **wa*), which is attested in both Eblaite and Old Akkadian. Simple sentences can be seriated with conjunctive, resultative, or disjunctive meaning. Again, beginning in the latter half of the third millennium, one finds the occasional use of the conjunction u_3.

(33) A.

ni$_2$	ba-da-te	su	ba-da-zi
ni.Ø	ba.da.te	su.Ø	ba.da.zi
N.-ABS.	PREF.-COMT.-fear	N.-ABS.	PREF.-COMT.-be terrified

"I was afraid, I was terrified"

B.

ĝiš	ba-gur$_4$	kuš-bi	nu-da-dar
ĝiš.Ø	ba.gur	kuš.bi	nu.da.dar
tree-ABS.	PREF.-grow	thick bark-PRO.	NEG.-COMT.-split

"The tree grew thick, [but] its bark did not split"

C.

dub-sar	me-en	na-ru$_2$-a	ab-sar-re-en
dubsar	me.en	narua.Ø	a.b.sar.en
scribe	COP.	stela-ABS.	PREF.-ACC.-write-NOM.

"I am a scribe, [therefore] I can write stele"

Seriated clauses can even have temporal or implicational relationships that are not marked by any particle or morphological marker:

(34)

a$_2$-aĝ$_2$-ĝa$_2$	lugal-ĝa$_2$-ke$_4$	i$_3$-gub-be$_2$-en	nu-dur$_2$-u$_3$-de$_3$-en	bi$_2$-dug$_4$
a'aĝa	lugal.ĝa.ak.e	i.gub.en	nu.dur.ed.en	bi.dug
orders	king-PRO.-GEN.-LOC2.	PREF.-stand-NOM.	NEG.-sit-SUFF.-NOM.	PREF.-speak

"I said: 'When acting on His Majesty's (lit."my king's") orders, I stand, I do not sit!'"

5.3 Subordination

Other complex sentences consist of a main clause preceded by a relative or other subordinate clause. The predicate of the subordinate clause is always nominalized; it may be a full verbal form (S) or, as is most often the case, a nominal form of the verb, with nominalization, but without the normal affixes (S'). Once nominalized, nominal markers such as pronouns and case endings may follow the verbs.

Full verbal forms, once nominalized, can be treated as nouns and can be bracketed by various discontinuous morphemes to create relative clauses. The first elements in these sequences include nouns (*ud* "day," *eĝer* "back") as well as particles such as *en-na* ("until") and *mu* ("because"), which do not carry meaning by themselves, but only as part of specific constructions. The nominalized verb is then followed by a locative or directional case ending, sometimes combined with the bridging genitive morpheme.

Subordinate clauses can also be introduced by conjunctions such as *tukum-bi* "if, in the event that," or by nouns such as *ud* "day." Thus *ud-da* (*ud.a* "on the day") means "when" and *ud-ba* (*ud.bi.a* "on that day") means "then."

Subordination can also be marked on the predicate with the modal prefix *he-* in its epistemic function (see §4.6.4.3). As explained by Civil (2002 [2005]), when the subordinate clause comes first, it is conditional:

(35)	u$_2$-gu	he$_2$-ni-ib-de$_2$	ki-bi	ga-mu-na-ab-g̃i$_4$
	ugu.Ø	he.ni.b.de	ki.bi	ga.mu.na.b.g̃i
	N.-ABS.	PREF.-LOC2.-ERG.-lose	place-PRO.	PREF.-PREF.-DAT.-ACC.-return

"Should it be lost, I will replace it for him"

If the *he-* clause is in final position, it marks a situation that is made possible by the main clause:

(36)	A.	u$_2$-lal-e	mu-un-du$_3$	amar-e	ha-ma-an-gu$_7$-e
		ulal.e	mu.ni.du	amar.e	ha.ma.ni.gu.e
		sweet-plant-LOC2	PREF.-LOC2.-plant	calf-LOC2	PREF.-DAT.-LOC2-eat-NOM.

"He planted the sweet-plant, so that the calf(calves) could eat them"

	B.	uri$_5^{ki}$-ma	gi	zi-bi	lal$_3$-am$_3$	ku$_6$	ha-ma-gu$_7$-e
		urim.ak	gi	zi.bi	lal.am	ku.Ø	ha.ma.gu.e
		Ur-GEN.	reed	zi-PRO.	sweet-COP.	fish-ABS.	PREF.-DAT.-eat-NOM.

"The *zi* reeds of the [the city of] Ur are sweet, and so the fish eat them"

Commonly a nominalized full verbal predicate can be followed by the ablative suffix *-ta* to create temporal clauses that mark both temporal sequence and a form of contemporaneity:

(37)	ba-tu-ud-en-na-ta	nitah	kala-ga	me-en
	ba.tud.en.a.ta	nitah	kalaga.Ø	men
	PREF.-born-NOM.-NOMINALIZER-ABL.	male	mighty-ABS.	COP.

"Ever since my birth I have been a mighty male"

More complex and varied are subordinate clauses that are construed with reduced verbal forms (S') (see Gragg 1973b:90–91; 1973c; Michalowski 1978:117; Civil 1999–2000). The simplest such predicates consist of (i) the root and the nominalizer *-a*; (ii) the root followed by the morpheme *-ed*; or (iii) the root and *-ed* + copula (obligation). The first creates simple relative clauses:

(38)	e$_2$	(lugal-e)	du$_3$-a
	e.Ø	(lugal.e)	du.a
	temple-ABS.	(king-ERG.)	build-NOMINALIZER

"The temple that the king built"

The second and third constructions differ in meaning:

(39) A.

e$_2$-a-ni	du$_3$-de$_3$	ma-an-dug$_4$
e.ani	du.ed	ma.n.dug
temple-PRO.	build-SUFF.	PREF.-ERG.-speak

"He told me to build his temple"

B.

e$_2$-a-ni	du$_3$-da	ma-an-dug$_4$
e.ani	du.ed.am	ma.n.dug
temple-PRO.	build-SUFF.-COP.	PREF.-ERG.-speak

"He told me that I had to build his temple"

Temporal clauses are often created on the patterns based on S'-*a* (i.e., the type of [38]), followed by pronouns and other endings. These create a complex paradigm with nominative/accusative rather than ergative agreement. One exception aside, only singular forms are encountered in texts. Once again the third person distinguishes between animate and inanimate forms:

(40)

	Singular	*Plural*
First	S'-a-ĝu-ne	
Second	S'-a-zu-ne	S'-ed-a-enzen
Third animate perfect	S'-(a)-ani	
Third animate imperfect	S'-ed-ani	
Third inanimate	S'-a-bi	

Examples of temporal clauses follow:

(41) A.

ka$_2$	e$_2$-gal-la-še$_3$	gub-a-ĝu$_{10}$-ne
ka	egal.ak.še	gub.a.ĝu.ne
gate	palace-GEN.-ALL.	go-NOMINALIZER-PRO.-SUFF.

"When I arrived at the gate of the palace"

B. ku$_4$-ku$_4$-da-ĝu$_{10}$-ne
ku.kud.a.ĝu.ne
enter-NOMINALIZER-PRO.-SUFF.
"When I entered"

C.

ud-bi-a	ĝiš-e	e$_2$-gal-la	ku$_4$-ku$_4$-da-ni
ud.bi.a	ĝiš.e	egal.a	ku.kud.ani
day-PRO.-LOC.	tree-ERG.	palace-LOC.	enter-PRO.

"Then, as Tree entered the palace"

The third-person forms can also occur with an addition of the ablative *-ta*: *gur-re-da-ni* "when he returns," but *gur-ru-da-ni-ta* "upon his return." According to Gragg (1973c:128), the latter indicates a time subsequent to an action, while the former relates a time at which something happened.

6. LEXICON

Although Sumerian died out millennia ago, the countless surviving cuneiform tablets preserve a rich and varied lexicon. In addition to words in narrative contexts, we also have access to an extensive native Mesopotamian lexicographical tradition in the form of ancient monolingual and multilingual lexical lists (Civil 1975). These lexical texts, which were designed for use in teaching the art of writing, have a long tradition, from the very beginnings to the very end of cuneiform use. The early versions are monolingual, but by the second millennium the entries were all provided with Akkadian translations; outside of Mesopotamia other languages were added. The longest composition of this type contains almost ten thousand entries. These lists are arranged by various criteria, graphic, semantic, etc. Some have compound words or sign combinations, and some late bilingual lists are arranged according to the Akkadian translations. The complex nature of these texts should not be underestimated. They include many terms that had long gone out of use, or were no longer properly understood. Some words were simply invented by scribes who were not native Sumerian speakers. Most important, one has to respect the organizational structure of a specific list type to properly understand the semantics of an entry.

The lexical texts contain many words that are not otherwise documented in any Sumerian texts. But the lexicon of the literary and administrative tablets must also be treated with caution. The language of written texts is often conservative and resistant to the changes taking place in the vernacular. Many if not most extant Sumerian texts were written and composed after the language was no longer spoken in the streets, and therefore one has to view diachronic developments differently than one would if this were a living tongue.

It would seem that much of the lexicon is native Sumerian, but this is difficult to gauge correctly in view of the lack of a modern dictionary, and of related languages, and because of some of the ambiguities of the script. Over the millennia, Sumerian came into direct and indirect contact with many other languages and borrowed lexical items from various donors. The majority of such loanwords come from Semitic, mostly from forms of Akkadian. Loans are often, but not always, written out syllabically. Thus, the Semitic loan *dam-ha-ra* "battle" is written with three signs, but *ugula* "overseer," likewise a Semitic loan, is written logographically with only one grapheme (*PA*). The writing of some changed over time. In early texts the Sumerian word for copper – originally a culture word that came into the language through some Semitic intermediary – is written syllabically as $a\text{-}ru_{12}\text{-}da$, then as $urudu^{a-ru_{12}-da}$ or as ${}^{a-ru_{12}-da}urudu$, and finally later on simply as *urudu*.

In the past, scholars have claimed that certain basic culture words were borrowed from one or more hypothetical substrate languages, sometimes referred to as Proto-Tigridian and Proto-Euphratic, and that one of them may even have been Indo-European. More recently Rubio (1999b) has shown that these lexemes are either native Sumerian, Semitic loans, or culture words that show up in various languages; and while one cannot discount the possibility of some substrates at some time, the current linguistic evidence does not support this in any way.

Semitic loans have a long history in Sumerian. The earliest such borrowings exclude any Semitic endings (*har-ra-an* "road" from Akkadian *harranum*); Old Akkadian period loans end in *-a* (*ugula* from Akkadian *waklum*); and second-millennium loans retain the Akkadian nominative ending and mimation ($pu\text{-}uh_2\text{-}ru\text{-}um$ "assembly" from Akkadian *puhrum*), although there are exceptions to these rules. There are also rare borrowings from Hurrian, for example, *tibira* "metal worker," although this may be a culture word, and from unknown sources, as is the case with *lams(a)r* "brewing vat." There are other "wandering words" that appear in many different languages: Sumerian $ugu_4\text{-}bi$ "monkey" belongs together with Akkadian *pagû*, as well as reflexes in Hebrew and Egyptian; $za_3\text{-}gin_2$ "lapis lazuli" compounded with *za* "stone" is of the same unknown origin as Akkadian *uqnu* or Hittite *ku(wa)nna(š)*. More complex is the matter of Sumerian *(h)urin*, *erin*, Akkadian *a/erû* "eagle." Civil (1983:3) seeks the origins of these words in a form **haran*, and points to Hittite *ḫaran-* "eagle." The root appears commonly in Indo-European, but the ultimate origin is unknown. It has been proposed that a number of Sumerian agricultural terms belong to this category, but this requires further investigation (Rubio 1999b). Borrowed words usually replace native ones, as exemplified by the Semitic loan *iri* "city," for which the original Sumerian word is not preserved; but sometimes they were used alongside the native term, as *unken* "assembly" coexisted with *pu-uh$_2$-ru-um*. There are even poetic examples of the rhetorical use of synonymic word pairs, with the native term preceded by the borrowed one, as in *har-ra-an kaskal* "road (road)." This seems to be the order encountered in most languages that have such pairs (Boeder 1991).

7. READING LIST

The most convenient place to read about Sumerian grammar is Thomsen 1984, supplemented by the important remarks of Attinger 1993, and by more recent studies listed in Römer 1999. The two classic highly influential older grammars are Poebel 1923 and Falkenstein 1959, to which one has to add the idiosyncratic but often brilliant insights of Jacobsen 1965 and 1988. Readers of Russian should not ignore the important but often overlooked contributions of Diakonoff (1967 = 1979) and of his student Kaneva (1996). Interesting insights are also found in the older sketches of Jestin (1951) and Lambert (5 fascicles, 1972–1978). The latest grammar is that of Edzard (2003). No reliable introductory primer is currently available, but there is an excellent reader that contains a selection of texts in cuneiform with a sign list, bibliography, and glossary (Volk 1997).

There is no complete modern dictionary of the language; the first volumes of the monumental *Pennsylvania Sumerian Dictionary* (Sjöberg *et al.* 1984–) are now available, but they currently only cover words beginning with the letters A and B. The web-based version of the full Dictionary, now edited by S. Tinney, is available on line at: http://psd.museum.upenn.edu/epsd.

It is impossible to list here all the published Sumerian sources; for the important word lists see Civil 1975, and for a survey of literary compositions see Michalowski 1995 with bibliography. For all types of texts and the secondary literature consult Römer 1999.

Bibliography

Alster, B. 1982. "Emesal in Early Dynastic Sumerian? What is the UD.GAL.NUN-orthography?" *Acta Sumerologica* 4:1–6.

Anderson, S. 1985. "Inflectional morphology." In T. Shopen (ed.), *Language Typology and Syntactic Description III: Grammatical Categories and the Lexicon*, pp. 150–201. Cambridge: Cambridge University Press.

Aristar, A. 1995. "Binder-anaphors and the diachrony of case displacement." In F. Plank (ed.), *Double Case: Agreement by Suffixaufnahme*, pp. 431–447. Oxford: Oxford University Press.

———. 1996. "The relationship between dative and locative: Kurytowicz's argument from a typological perspective." *Diachronica* 13:207–224.

———. 1997. "Marking and hierarchy: types and the grammaticalization of case-markers." *Studies in Language* 21:313–368.

Attinger, P. 1993. *Eléments de linguistique sumérienne. La construction de du$_{11}$/e/di «dire»* (Orbis Biblicus et Orientalis, Sonderband). Fribourg/Göttingen: Editions Universitaires/Vandenhoeck and Ruprecht.

Bauer, J. 1975. "Zum /dr-/-Phonem des Sumerischen." *Welt des Orients* 8:1–9.

———. 1998. "Der vorsargonische Abschnitt der mesopotamischen Geschichte." In J. Bauer, R. K. Englund, and M. Krebernik (eds.), *Mesopotamien. Späturuk-Zeit und Frühdynastische Zeit.*

pp. 431–585. Orbis Biblicus et Orientalis, 160/1. Fribourg/Göttingen: Editions Universitaires/Vandenhoeck and Ruprecht.

Black, J. 1984. *Sumerian Grammar in Babylonian Theory.* Studia Pohl, Series Maior 12. Rome: Biblical Institute Press.

_______. 1986. Review of Thomsen 1984. *Archiv für Orientforschung* 33:77–83.

_______. 1990. "The alleged 'extra' phonemes of Sumerian." *Revue d'Assyriologie* 84:107–118.

_______. 2000 [2005] "Some Sumerian adjectives." *Acta Sumerologica* 22:3–27.

Bobrova, L. and A. Militarëv. 1989. "Towards the reconstruction of Sumerian phonology." In *Lingvistieska rekonstrukcia i drevneiaia istoriia Vostoka*, part 1, pp. 96–105. Moscow: Nauka.

Boeder, W. 1991. "A note on synonymic parallelism and bilingualism." *Studia Linguistica* 45:97–126.

Boisson, C. 1992. "The Sumerian pronominal system in Nostratic perspective." In V. Shevoroshkin (ed.), *Nostratic, Dene-Caucasian, Austric and Amerind: Materials from the First International Interdisciplinary Symposium on Language and Prehistory, Ann Arbor, 8–12 November, 1988*, pp. 433–461. Bochum: Universittsverlag Dr. Norbert Brockmeyer.

_______. 1997. "The phonotactics of Sumerian." In I. Hegeds, P. A. Michalove, and A. Manaster Ramer (eds.), *Indo-European, Nostratic, and Beyond: Festschrift for Vitalij V. Shevoroshkin*, pp. 30–50. Journal of Indo-European Studies Monograph 12. Washington: Institute for the Study of Man.

Bottéro, J. 1992. "The 'avalanche' of decipherments in the ancient Near East between 1800 and 1930." In J. Bottéro, *Mesopotamia: Writing, Reasoning and the Gods*, pp. 55–66. Chicago: Chicago University Press.

Chung, S. and A. Timberlake. 1985. "Tense, aspect, and mood." In T. Shopen (ed.), *Language Typology and Syntactic Description III: Grammatical Categories and the Lexicon*, pp. 202–258. Cambridge: Cambridge University Press.

Civil, M. 1966. "Notes on Sumerian lexicography, I." *Journal of Cuneiform Studies* 20:119–124.

_______. 1973a. "From Enki's headaches to phonology." *Journal of Near Eastern Studies* 32:57–61.

_______. 1973b. "The Sumerian writing system: Some problems." *Orientalia* NS 42:21–34.

_______. 1973c. "Notes on Sumerian lexicography, II." *Journal of Cuneiform Studies* 25:171–177.

_______. 1975. "Lexicography." In S. Lieberman (ed.), *Sumerological Studies in Honor of Thorkild Jacobsen*, pp. 123–157. Assyriological Studies, 20. Chicago: University of Chicago Press.

_______. 1976. "The song of the plowing oxen." In B. Eichler *et al.* (eds.), *Kramer Anniversary Volume: Cuneiform Studies in Honor of Samuel Noah Kramer*, pp. 83–95. Alter Orient und Altes Testament, 25. Neukirchen-Vluyn: Neukirchener Verlag.

_______. 1982. "Studies in Early Dynastic lexicography, 1." *Oriens Antiquus* 21:1–26.

_______. 1983. "Early Dynastic spellings." *Oriens Antiquus* 22:1–5.

_______. 1984. "Bilingualism in logographically written languages: Sumerian in Ebla." In L. Cagni (ed.), *Il bilinguismo a Ebla*, pp. 75–97. Naples: Istituto Universitario Orientale.

_______. 1987. "The early history of HAR-ra: The Ebla link." In L. Cagni (ed.), *Ebla 1975–1985. Dieci anni di studi linguistici e filologici*, pp. 131–158. Naples: Istituto Universitario Orientale.

_______. 1999–2000. "Reading Gilgameš: history and stories." *Aula Orientalis* 17–18:179–189.

_______. 2000 [2005]. "Modal prefixes." *Acta Sumerologica* 22:29–42.

_______. 2002. "The Forerunners of *Marû* and *Ḫamṭu* in Old Babylonian." In T. Abusch (ed.), *Riches Hidden in Secret Place: Ancient Near Eastern Studies in Memory of Thorkild Jacobsen*, pp. 63–72. Winona Lake: Eisenbrauns.

Civil, M. and R. Biggs. 1966. "Notes sur les textes sumériens archaïques." *Revue d'Assyriologie* 60:1–16.

Cooper, J. 1996. "Mesopotamian cuneiform: Sumerian and Akkadian." In P. Daniels and W. Bright (eds.), *The World's Writing Systems*, pp. 37–57. Oxford: Oxford University Press.

Diakonoff, I. 1967. "Shumerskij iazyk." In I. Diakonoff, *Iazyki drevnei Perednei Azii*, pp. 35–84. Moscow: Nauka.

_______. 1979. "Shumerskij iazyk." In I. Diakonoff, I. M. Dunaevskaia, Iu. D. Desherier, *et al.* (eds.), *Iazyki drevnei Perednei Azii (nesemitskie): iberiisko-kavkazskie iazyki: paleoaziatskie iazyki*, pp. 7–36. Iazyki Azii i Afriki 3. Moscow: Nauka.

_______. 1983. "Some reflections on numerals in Sumerian: towards a history of mathematical speculation." *Journal of the American Oriental Society* 103:83–93.

Edzard, D. 1963. "Sumerische Komposita mit dem 'Nominalprefix' nu-." *Zeitschrift für Assyriologie* 55:91–112.

______. 1967. "Das sumerische Verlbalmorphemen /ed/ in den alt- und neusumerischen Texten." *Heidelberger Studien zum Alten Orient* 1:29–62.

Edzard, D. O. 2003. *Sumerian Grammar*. Handbuch der Orientalistik, 1.71. Leiden: Brill.

Falkenstein, A. 1959. *Das Sumerische*. Handbuch der Orientalistik. Leiden: Brill.

Gelb, I. 1961. *Old Akkadian Writing and Grammar* (2nd edition). Materials for the Assyrian Dictionary, 2. Chicago: University of Chicago Press.

Geller, M. 1997. "The first wedge." *Zeitschrift für Assyriologie* 87:43–95.

Gragg, G. 1968. "The syntax of the copula in Sumerian." In J. Verhaar (ed.), *The Verb "Be" and its Synonyms, 3: Philosophical and Grammatical Studies*, pp. 86–109. Foundations of Language, Supplementary Series, 8. Dordrecht: Reidel.

______. 1973a. *Sumerian Dimensional Infixes*. Alter Orient und Altes Testament – Sonderreihe 5. Neukirchen-Vluyn: Neukirchener Verlag.

______. 1973b. "Linguistics, method, and extinct languages: the case of Sumerian." *Orientalia* NS 42:78–96.

______. 1973c. "A class of 'when' clauses in Sumerian." *Journal of Near Eastern Studies* 32:124–134.

Huber, C. 1996, "Some notes on transitivity, verb types, and case with pronouns in Sumerian." *Wiener Zeitschrift für die Kunde des Morgenlandes* 86:177–189.

Jacobsen, T. 1957. "Early political development in Mesopotamia." *Zeitschrift für Assyriologie* 52:91–140.

______. 1965. "About the Sumerian verb". In *Studies in Honor of Benno Landsberger on his Seventy-fifth Birthday, April 21, 1965*, pp. 71–102. Assyriological Studies 16. Chicago: Chicago University Press.

______. 1988. "The Sumerian verbal core." *Zeitschrift für Assyriologie* 78:161–220.

Jagersma, B. 1993. Review of J. Hayes, *A Manual of Sumerian Grammar and Texts*. Malibu: Undena, 1990. *Bibliotheca Orientalis* 50:422–425.

______. 2000 [2005]. "Sound change in Sumerian: the so-called /dr/ phoneme." *Acta Sumerologica* 22:81–87.

Jestin, R. 1951. *Abrégé de grammaire sumérienne*. Paris: Paul Geuthner.

Kaneva, I. 1996. *Shumerskii iazyk* (The Sumerian language). St. Petersburg: Tcentr "Peterburgskoe Vostokovedenie."

Karahashi, F. 2000. "Sumerian Compound Verbs with Body-Parts." Doctoral dissertation, University of Chicago.

______. 2000 [2005]. "The locative-terminative verbal infix in Sumerian." *Acta Sumerologica* 22:113–133.

Kienast, B. 1975. "Zur Wortbildung des Sumerischen." *Zeitschrift für Assyriologie* 65:1–27.

Krecher, J. 1978. "Das sumerische Phonem g̃". In B. Hruška and G. Komoroczy (eds.), *Festschrift Lubor Matouš II*, pp. 7–73. Assyriologia, 5. Budapest: Eötvös Loránd Tudományegyetem, Ókori Történeti Tanszekek.

______. 1987. "Morphemeless syntax in Sumerian as seen on the background of word-composition in Chukchee." *Acta Sumerologica* 9:67–88.

______. 1993. "The suffix of determination -/a/". *Acta Sumerologica* 15:81–98.

Krispijn, Th. 2000 [2005]. "The change of Official Sumerian in the city state of Lagash." *Acta Sumerologica* 22:153–175.

Kuryłowicz, J. 1964. *The Inflectional Categories of Indo-European*. Heidelberg: Carl Winter.

Lambert, M. 1972–1978. *Grammaire sumérienne rédigée à l'intention des élèves de l'École du Louvre*. Five fascicles. Paris: École du Louvre.

Lieberman, S. 1979. "The phoneme /o/ in Sumerian." In M. Powell, Jr. and R. Sack (eds.), *Studies in Honor of Tom B. Jones*, pp. 21–28. Altes Orient und Altes Testament 203. Neukirchen-Vluyn: Neukirchener Verlag.

Michalowski, P. 1978. "Two Sumerian literary letters." *Journal of Cuneiform Studies* 30:114–120.

______. 1980. "Sumerian as an ergative language, part 1." *Journal of Cuneiform Studies* 32:86–103.

______. 1995. "Sumerian literary traditions: an overview." In J. Sasson, J. Baines, G. Beckman, *et al.* (eds.), *Civilizations of the Ancient Near East*, pp. 2277–2289. New York: Scribners.

_______. 2000 [2005]. "The life and death of the Sumerian language in comparative perspective." *Acta Sumerologica* 22:177–202.

_______. 2006. "The Lives of the Sumerian Language." In S. Sanders (ed.), *Margins of Writing, Origins of Culture: New Approaches to Writing and Reading in the Ancient Near East. Papers from the Symposium held February 25–26, 2005*, pp. 157–182. Chicago: The Oriental Institute.

Miner, K. 1986. "Noun stripping and loose incorporation in Zuni." *International Journal of American Linguistics* 52:242–254.

Mithun, M. 1984. "The evolution of noun incorporation." *Language* 60:847–894.

_______. 1985. "Diachronic morphologization: The circumstances surrounding the birth, growth, and decline of noun incorporation." In J. Fisiak (ed.), *Papers from the 6th Conference on Historical Linguistics*, pp. 365–394. Amsterdam: John Benjamins; Poznan: Adam Mickiewicz University Press.

_______. 2000. "Incorporation." In G. Booij, C. Lehmann, J. Mugdan, *et al.* (eds.), *Morphology: An International Handbook on Inflection and Word Formation*, pp. 916–928. Berlin: Walter de Gruyter.

Nichols, J. 1993. "Ergativity and linguistic geography." *Australian Journal of Linguistics* 13:39–89.

Palmer, F. 1986. *Mood and Modality*. Cambridge Textbooks in Linguistics. Cambridge: Cambridge University Press.

Parpola, S. 1975. "Transliteration of Sumerian: problems and prospects." *Studia Orientalia* 46:239–257.

Payne, T. 1982. "Role and reference related subject properties and ergativity in Yup'ik Eskimo and Tagalog." *Studies in Language* 6:75–106.

Poebel, A. 1923. *Gründzuge der sumerischen Grammatik*. Rostock: Selbstverlag.

Rhodes, R. 1997. "On pronominal systems." In I. Hegeds *et al.* (eds.), *Indo-European, Nostratic, and Beyond: Festschrift for Vitalij V. Shevoroshkin*, pp. 293–319. Journal of Indo-European Studies Monograph 12. Washington: Institute for the Study of Man.

Römer, W. 1999. *Die Sumerologie. Einführung in die Forschung und Bibliographie in Auswahl*. Alter Orient und Altes Testament 262. Neukirchen-Vluyn: Neukirchener Verlag.

Rubio, G. 1999a. Review of A. S. Kaye (ed.), *Phonologies of Asia and Africa*. *Language* 75:138–142.

_______. 1999b. "On the alleged 'Pre-Sumerian substratum.'" *Journal of Cuneiform Studies* 51:1–16.

Schretter, M. 1990. *Emesal-Studien: Sprach- und literaturgeschichtliche Untersuchungen zur sogenannten Frauensprache des Sumerischen*. Innsbrucker Beiträge zur Kulturwissenschaft. Sonderheft 69. Innsbruck: Institut für Sprachwissenschaft der Universität Innsbruck.

_______. 1993. "Sumerische Phonologie: Zu Konsonantenverbindungen und Silbenstruktur." *Acta Orientalia* 54:7–30.

_______. 1996. "Überlegungen zu den Wortarten des Sumerischen." *Wiener Zeitschrift für die Kunde des Morgenlandes* 86:399–412.

Sjöberg, Å. 1975. "The Old Babylonian eduba." In S. Lieberman (ed.), *Sumerological Studies in Honor of Thorkild Jacobsen*, pp. 159–179. Assyriological Studies, 20. Chicago: University of Chicago Press.

Sjöberg, Å. *et al.* (eds.). 1984–. *The Sumerian Dictionary of the University Museum of the University of Pennsylvania*. Philadelphia. Babylonian Section, University Museum.

Steiner, G. 1981. "The vocalization of the Sumerian verbal morpheme /=ED/ and its significance." *Journal of Near Eastern Studies* 40:21–41.

Steinkeller, P. 1979. "Notes on Sumerian plural verbs." *Orientalia* NS 48:54–67.

_______. 1993. "Early political development in Mesopotamia and the origins of the Sargonic Empire." In M. Liverani (ed.), *Akkad: The First World Empire*, pp. 107–129. Padua: Sargon.

Thomsen, M.-L. 1984. *The Sumerian Language: An Introduction to its History and Grammatical Structure*. Mesopotamia, 10. Copenhagen: Akademisk Forlag.

Vanstiphout, H. 1985. "On the verbal prefix /i/ in Standard Sumerian." *Revue d'Assyriologie* 79:1–15.

Volk, K. 1997. *A Sumerian Reader*. Studia Pohl, Series Maior 18. Rome: Pontifical Biblical Institute.

Wilcke, C. 1988. "Anmerkungen zum 'Kunjugationspräfix' /i/- und zur These vom «silbischen Charakter der sumerischen Morpheme» anhand neusumerischen Verbalformen beginnend mit ì-íb-, ì-im- und ì-in-." *Zeitschrift für Assyriologie* 78:1–49.

Woods, C. 2000 [2005]. "Deixis, person, and case in Sumerian." *Acta Sumerologica* 22:303–334.

Wright, H. 1969. *The Administration of Rural Production in an Early Mesopotamian Town.* Anthropological Papers, 38. Ann Arbor: University of Michigan.

Yoshikawa, M. 1968. "The *marû* and *ḫamṭu* aspects in the Sumerian verbal system." *Orientalia* NS 37:401–416.

______. 1977. "Some remarks on the Sumerian verbal infixes –n-/-b- in the preradical position." *Journal of Cuneiform Studies* 29:78–96.

______. 1992. "The valency-change system in the Sumerian verbal prefixes." *Acta Sumerologica* 14:395–402.

Zólyomi, G. 1996a. Review of Attinger 1993. *Bibliotheca Orientalis* 53:95–107.

______. 1996b. "Genitive constructions in Sumerian." *Journal of Cuneiform Studies* 48:31–47.

______. 1999. "Directive infix and oblique object in Sumerian: an account of the history of their relationship." *Orientalia* NS 68:215–253.

CHAPTER 3

Elamite

MATTHEW W. STOLPER

1. HISTORICAL AND CULTURAL CONTEXTS

1.1 Sources

Texts in Elamite come from the modern provinces of Khuzestān and Fārs, in southwestern Iran. Most are from ancient Susa and the plains of Khuzestān around it, from ancient Persepolis and Anshan (modern Tall-i Malyān) in the high valleys of Fārs, from sites on the way between Susiana and the Persepolis–Anshan area, or from the coast of Fārs. Achaemenid multilingual rock inscriptions of *c.* 520–450 BC with Elamite versions are also found in central western Iran, near Hamadān, and in eastern Turkey, near Van. Elamite texts on clay tablets from *c.* 600–550 BC have been found at the Assyrian city of Nineveh, in northeastern Iraq, at the Urartian fortress at modern Armavir Blur in Armenia, and at Old Kandahar in modern Afghanistan. The oldest dated texts are from about 2300 BC, the latest from about 350 BC. The first to come to modern attention were the inscriptions of the Achaemenid kings (*c.* 522–330 BC), whose Old Persian texts were often accompanied by Elamite and Akkadian versions, all deciphered in the 1840s. Other Elamite texts include royal display or dedicatory inscriptions written on bricks, glazed tiles or other architectural elements, or on stone or metal objects; administrative texts written on clay tablets; engravings on cylinder seals naming the owners of the seals; and a few legal texts, letters, and literary or scholarly texts on clay tablets.

1.2 History of the language and its speakers

The indigenous name for the country of Elam, *Hatamti*, is reflected in Sumerian *Elama*, Akkadian *Elamtu*, Hebrew *ʿElām*, and other forms. The indigenous name of the language is not attested. The usual modern name *Elamite* (used as early as Sayce 1874:467) corresponds to Sumerian and Akkadian usage (e.g., Sumerian *eme Elama*, "language of Elam"). Other modern names once given to the language are *Scythian* and *Median*, on the supposition that the languages of the Achaemenid royal inscriptions were those of dominant populations in the Achaemenid empire; *Susian*, in recognition of the fact that the language used beside Old Persian and Babylonian in the Achaemenid royal inscriptions was related to the language found in older texts from Susa; and *Anzanite*, on the view that the language found on texts from Susa was not original there, but was introduced by rulers from Anshan, whose location was a matter of conjecture.

Because there is some disagreement about the historical geography of ancient Iran, there is also uncertainty about the area in which Elamite was actually spoken. On the maximal view, the political and cultural area of Elam, where the Elamite language must have been commonly used, extended in the late third and early second millennia over the entire highland territory of Iran, as far northwest as Azerbaijān and as far southeast as Baluchistān. Early Elamite states conquered and held Khuzestān and promoted the use of Elamite there in a population that also spoke and wrote in Akkadian, wrote in Sumerian, and perhaps also included some speakers of Amorite and Hurrian. By the middle of the first millennium, however, after the immigration of Iranian speakers and the rise of the Achaemenid Persian state, the territory called Elam was confined to Khuzestān and the adjoining mountains of Lurestān and northwestern Fārs. The Persian rulers who made the Elamite Anshan into Persia proper continued to write inscriptions and administrative records in Elamite in much of highland Iran (e.g., Vallat 1993, 1998). Critics of this view consider the original Elamite political and language area to be much smaller, but to include Fārs, Khuzestān, and extensions of uncertain distance to the northwest and southeast. Most modern appraisals agree in considering Khuzestān, where most early Elamite texts originate, to be at the edge, not at the center, of the Elamite area, a region where Elamite language coexisted or competed with Sumerian and Akkadian.

The unsettled question of the eastern extent of the Elamite language area is connected with the hypothesis that Elamite is related to the Dravidian languages, considered in various forms since the 1850s. A comprehensive proposal of phonological, lexical, and morphological correspondences and developments, with an inference that Proto-Dravidian and an ancestor of Elamite separated from a common Proto-Elamo-Dravidian before 3000 BC, and probably in the fifth millennium BC (McAlpin 1981), has been embraced by some students of Elamite (e.g., Khačikjan 1998:3 following Diakonoff) and ignored by others. It has not been systematically criticized, and it has not yet had practical consequences for the study of Elamite grammar or lexicon (Zadok 1995:243).

The framework of Elamite history is built chiefly on texts from Mesopotamia. Sumerian, Babylonian, and Assyrian states had intermittent, sometimes intense diplomatic, political, military, and commercial connections with the intermontane valleys of Elamite Iran, rich in timber, semi-precious stones and metals, and sometimes in population. The same Mesopotamian states sometimes fought Elamite states for control of Susiana. The chronological phases into which the Elamite language proper is divided are primarily political phases. (The earliest texts from Elamite territories, however, are in undeciphered scripts called Proto-Elamite and Linear Elamite; see below, §2.1.)

1.2.1 Old Elamite (*c.* 2600–1500 BC)

Early Sumerian rulers recorded skirmishing with Elamites in southern Mesopotamia as early as *c.* 2650 BC. The Old Akkadian rulers of southern Mesopotamia (*c.* 2300–2100) recorded battles with Elamite rulers and campaigns against Elamite highland regions; they took control of Susa. When Old Akkadian power broke down, Susa fell under the control of a ruler from the interior highland, Puzur-Inšušinak of Awan, who also claimed to control other highland territories. Any political integration that lay behind this claim was short-lived, as Sumerian rulers of the Third Dynasty of Ur (*c.* 2000–1900) reestablished control over the whole of lower Mesopotamia and over Susa, and pushed into the highland districts surrounding Khuzestān with punitive military campaigns, tribute-taking, the creation of occupied provinces in nearer valley-systems, and the maintenance of active diplomacy with more distant territories. In reaction, Elamite states of the interior coalesced in an alliance that sacked Ur, destroyed the Mesopotamian state and its empire, and took its king to die in captivity in Anshan. By about 1750 BC, this alliance had reached the zenith of Elamite power, becoming the largest regional state of the time, exercising sway over smaller competing alliances in Mesopotamia and northern Syria, and sending expeditionary armies to promote its interests. A defeat at the hands of Hammurabi of Babylon removed the Elamites from Mesopotamian affairs, but the Elamite monarchy remained in place until *c.* 1500 BC.

1.2.1.1 Old Elamite texts

Elamite texts from this long interval are scarce. They include three tablets of uncertain literary or scholarly character (at least one of them excavated in southern Mesopotamia), a treaty with an Old Akkadian king, and four royal inscriptions from about 1800–1700 BC, only one of them nearly complete (Steve 1992:19; Vallat 1990). Additional evidence comes from Elamite names and words that occur in Sumerian and Akkadian texts from Elamite territories, above all in several hundred legal and administrative texts from Susa (Lackenbacher 1998; Zadok 1995:244). There are also five passages in Sumerian and Old Babylonian texts that are perhaps incantations in Elamite (van Dijk *et al.* 1985:4 and 9ff. Nos. 4, 5, and 18; Hinz and Koch 1987:1322 s.vv. Inc. 70 E–H).

1.2.2 Middle Elamite (*c.* 1500–1000 BC)

After about 1450 BC, scattered texts from sites in Khuzestān mention a series of "kings of Susa and Anshan," and after *c.* 1400 numerous inscriptions, most of them in Elamite, attest the reigns of two dynasties of "kings of Anshan and Susa" who controlled Susa and nearby sites and eventually resumed warfare with contemporary Assyria and Babylonia. These wars culminated *c.* 1150 in Elamite raids on the cities of Babylonia, from which the Elamites took trophies that include some of the ancient Mesopotamian monuments that are most celebrated in modern times, including the Victory Stele of Naram-Sin of Akkad and the stele with the Laws of Hammurabi. The wars continued with a Babylonian attack on Elam in *c.* 1120 BC. Thereafter, sources for Elamite political history fade away.

1.2.2.1 Middle Elamite texts

Texts from this period, usually considered the classical period of Elamite language and culture, include about 175 royal inscriptions on bricks, steles, reliefs, statues, and large and small votive objects. Most of them are from Susa or Choghā Zanbīl, a few from other sites in Khuzestān, a site in the valleys on the road to Fārs, a site on the Fārs coast of the Persian Gulf, and one from Anshan (Steve 1992:19–21; add van Soldt 1982:44–48; de Maaijer 1996:70–72). Among them is a single Elamite–Akkadian bilingual building inscription. Elamite administrative tablets from Anshan are attributed either to the end of this period or to the earliest phase of Neo-Elamite, as are two fragmentary legal and administrative texts from Susa (Stolper 1984:5–10; Steve 1992:21). Elamite words and titles also appear in Akkadian administrative texts from Haft Tepe, near Susa, written at the beginning of the period (Lackenbacher 1998:343; Zadok 1995:241).

1.2.3 Neo-Elamite (*c.* 1000–550 BC)

By *c.* 750 BC, when Mesopotamian sources on Elam reappear, much of central and western Iran had been populated by speakers of Iranian languages who lived among, pushed aside, or amalgamated with other ethnic and linguistic groups. The Mesopotamian texts reflect episodic conflict between the Neo-Assyrian empire, then reaching the height of its power, and Neo-Elamite kings who controlled Khuzestān. The theaters of conflict were the central Zagros valleys, where the Assyrians tried to protect the fringes of a new province, and Babylonia, where the Assyrians tried to stabilize political control against incessant resistance, while the Elamites tried to support buffers against the Assyrians in both places. In the mid-640s these encounters led to an Assyrian sack of Susa and a tour of looting and destruction around the adjoining plains of Khuzestān.

After the fall of the Assyrian Empire, 612–10 BC, successor states arose on Elamite territory, one based at Susa, another probably in the highland valleys to the north of Khuzestān, others in the valleys to the southeast, between Khuzestān and Fārs, and another in central Fārs. The rulers in Fārs were Persians who assumed the Elamite title "king of Anshan." Their descendant was Cyrus the Great (550–530 BC), who conquered Iran, Anatolia, and Mesopotamia to lay the foundations of the Achaemenid Persian Empire.

1.2.3.1 Neo-Elamite texts

Elamite texts from the first phase of this period are very scarce. Texts from after *c.* 750 BC include about thirty royal inscriptions, most on bricks and stele pieces from Susa, but also including rock inscriptions of a local ruler in eastern Khuzestān, and inscriptions of post-Assyrian local rulers on portable objects (Steve 1992:21–23, partially redated by Vallat 1996a; and add Caubet 1995, Donbaz 1996, and Vallat 1996b, Baššāš-e Kanzaq 1997:19–22; Bleibtreu 1999:21, 54; Henkelman forthcoming). An omen text and a hemerological text in Elamite are assigned to the period before 650 BC. From the period after 650 come a small group of legal texts from Susa, an archive of about 300 administrative texts, also from Susa, letters from Susa, Nineveh, and Armavir Blur in Armenia, and some unprovenienced letters and administrative texts, and Elamite inscriptions on cylinder seals from Susa and heirloom seals used at Persepolis (Steve 1992:22–23, and add Vallat 1997b and Jones in Garrison and Root 2001).

1.2.4 Achaemenid Elamite (550–330 BC)

Under the Achaemenids the region administered from Susa became the province of Elam (Old Persian *Huja*, corresponding in multilingual inscriptions to Elamite *Hatamti*, ~ *Haltamti*), and Fārs became Persia proper (Old Persian *Pārsa*, corresponding to Elamite *Parsa* ~ *Paršan* ~ *Paršaš*). Darius I (522–486 BC) and his successors built palace complexes at Susa, which became the main political center of the imperial court, and at Persepolis, not far from the old Elamite center at Anshan. They used Elamite for display and recording, but did not give the Elamite history from which they had emerged any other prominence.

1.2.4.1 Achaemenid Elamite texts

Elamite was the first language used by the Achaemenids for formal inscriptions. The Elamite version of the great inscription of Darius I at Bīsitūn (Behistān), near Kermānshāh, was the first and for a short time the only version on the rock face. In later royal inscriptions, however, the Elamite always accompanies an Old Persian text to which it usually corresponds very closely. The inscriptions are on prepared rock faces, on architectural elements, reliefs and sculpture from royal residences, on a small number of portable objects and cylinder-seals. Most Achaemenid administrative texts belong to two archives excavated at Persepolis, from about 500–450 BC, but the contemporary pieces from Susa and Old Kandahar imply wider use of Elamite recording (Steve 1992:23–24; add Garrison 1996 [Achaemenid administrative text from Susa], Scheil 1939, No. 468 [administrative text from Susa, probably Achaemenid], Helms 1982:13, 1997:101 [Elamite administrative fragments from Old Kandahār]).

1.2.5 Later Elamite

Under Hellenistic and Parthian rule, Elam continued to be a geographical and cultural entity, mostly called "Elymais" in Greek sources, but without leaving a continuing record of the Elamite language. In the tenth century AD the geographer Iṣṭaḫrī mentioned an unaffiliated language spoken in Khuzestān, called Khūzī, and Muqaddasī added that Khūzīs spoke an incomprehensible language, said by Muḥammad to be devilish, but whether a survival of Elamite lies behind these remarks is doubtful (Cameron 1948:18, n. 115; Khačikjan 1998:1).

1.3 Status of Elamite in antiquity

The Sumerian king Shulgi of Ur (*c.* 2000) claimed that he knew Elamite well enough to answer Elamite messengers in their own tongue (Civil 1985:73), but Hammurabi of Babylon (*c.* 1750) listed Elam among distant mountain lands which had languages that were "twisted" (Gadd *et al.* 1928:44–45, No. 146), a perception of outlandishness also reflected in the Old Babylonian Elamite incantations. Later Mesopotamian scholarly texts characterized plants, tools, or wagons as Elamite, correlated an Elamite calendar with the standard Sumero-Babylonian calendar, and glossed a few Elamite words, but apparently gave little attention to Elamite language.

Since the earliest Elamite texts include probable literary or scholarly pieces, Elamite may have been used more widely as a language of learning than the known sample suggests. Moreover, the writing of Elamite for display and recording may have been more widespread at an earlier date among Elamites of highland Iran than the known sample, dominated by texts from the Mesopotamian border, would indicate. In the known sample, Elamite became the preeminent language for the display inscriptions of Elamite rulers after about 1400 and for administrative and legal recording after about 1100, and by about 600 it was also used for scholarship and for international correspondence.

The hypothesis of Achaemenid "alloglottography" (Gershevitch 1979) holds that Achaemenid Elamite was a medium for transmitting texts that were conceived and dictated in Old Iranian languages, to be read out and understood as Old Iranian texts, and hence that the use of Iranian words and congruence between Elamite and Iranian morphology or syntax are not matters of borrowing or interference, but explicit notations of the underlying text. This hypothesis (which has been neither widely embraced nor rebutted) implies a literate bilingual or multilingual population who knew a living version of Elamite.

1.4 Elamite dialects

Dialects of Elamite have been postulated to account for variations in syntax (Grillot-Susini and Roche 1987:11; Grillot-Susini 1994:1; Khačikjan 1998:47 n. 129), but no dialects have been identified or described. Of the main chronological periods, most descriptive attention is given to Middle Elamite and Achaemenid Elamite. Neo-Elamite has not been systematically analyzed, although it is represented by the largest variety of text types and might allow discrimination between chronological development and dialect differences.

The frequent characterization of Elamite as "poorly understood" means in practice that sharp differences in the translation of individual Elamite texts reflect disagreements about grammar and lexicon. Behind these disagreements lies a nearly complete consensus on the identification of morphemes and paradigmatic sets of forms, as well as a general agreement that knowledge of Elamite phonology is seriously limited. The main areas of disagreement are on the meaning of particular morphemes, especially the verbal auxiliary *ma-*, the verb- and clause-suffixes *-t(a)* and *-a*; on the construction of pronouns and pronoun clusters with verbs and directional elements; on the understanding of morphological or syntactic differences between Middle and Achaemenid Elamite; and on the meanings of words.

2. WRITING SYSTEMS

2.1 Proto-Elamite

The earliest texts from the area where Elamite was spoken and written appear in scripts called *Proto-Elamite* and *Linear Elamite*. Neither script has been deciphered. It is plausible but not provable that both scripts rendered versions of Elamite language.

Proto-Elamite writing was so named at a time when "Elamite" was mostly used as a geographical term, not as the name of a language, so the name "Proto-Elamite" originally described texts without ambiguity – the first texts from Elamite territory, but not necessarily in the language that came to be called Elamite. Proto-Elamite writing was impressed or incised on clay tablets. About 1,600 texts are known, most of them from Susa, others from sites across southern and eastern Iran, as far south as Kermān and as far east as Seistān. The tablets are from archeological contexts dated *c.* 3100–2900 BC. Most of the tablets, perhaps all of them, are administrative records, having clear entries with groups of signs followed by groups of numerals, sometimes with a corresponding total on the reverse. They use sexagesimal and bisexagesimal systems that are identical with approximately contemporary Proto-Cuneiform texts from Mesopotamia. They also use a decimal system that is without a parallel in archaic Mesopotamian texts. About 5,000 attested forms of nonnumerical characters (a few clearly pictographic, most abstract patterns) probably represent about 1,000 signs or less, with paleographic variations (Brice 1962–1963; Meriggi 1971–1974; Friberg 1978–1979; Vallat 1986; Damerow and Englund 1989; Englund 1996, 1998).

2.2 Linear Elamite

This script is known from eighteen inscriptions carved on stone objects and incised on clay objects, and one inscription punched on a silver vase. Most are from Susa, one from Fārs and one from southeastern Iran. One occurs with a counterpart text in Old Akkadian (perhaps not a close translation) in the name of Puzur-Inšušinak, *c.* 2100 BC (see §1.2.1). Most or all of the texts are probably dedicatory inscriptions. Only 103 sign forms are attested, 40 of them attested only once (Hinz 1969:11–44, 1975a; Meriggi 1971–1974: I 184–220; André and Salvini 1989; Salvini 1998).

2.3 Elamite cuneiform

Readable Elamite texts are written in versions of the same cuneiform script that was developed in Mesopotamia to write Sumerian and Akkadian from the early third millennium BC on, and that was also adapted to write Eblaite, Hittite, Hurrian, and Urartian. The first progress of the nineteenth-century decipherers of cuneiform scripts came from work on inscriptions of the Achaemenid Persian kings in Old Persian, Akkadian, and Elamite. The decipherers recognized that the Akkadian and Elamite versions were written in two varieties of a single script. Hence, when the readings of the Akkadian texts were confirmed, they were also applied to Elamite cuneiform. Evidence from the Elamite versions themselves, however, did not contribute to the decipherment.

Like other versions of Mesopotamian cuneiform script, Elamite cuneiform includes several types of characters: those with syllabic values (syllabograms), those indicating words (logograms), unpronounced characters indicating semantic categories (determinatives), and numerals. Some symbols belong to more than one of these categories; some have more than one syllabic value; and some syllabic values are represented by more than one sign or sequence of signs. Regarding the last two points: in all periods, *polyphony* of signs (that is, single signs with two or more syllabic values) and *homophony* of signs (that is, two or more signs with the same syllabic value) are less common than in Mesopotamian scripts, and more often limited to writings of particular words or sequences. In Achaemenid Elamite, homophony and polyphony are almost (but not entirely) eliminated (Steve 1992).

2.3.1 Syllabograms

Syllabic symbols occur having the values V (vowel), VC (vowel + consonant), CV, and CVC (including C_1VC_1 and C_1VC_2). Almost all syllabic values of Elamite signs are the common values of the same signs in Mesopotamian cuneiform; a few are uncommon in Mesopotamia and specialized in Elamite; and a few are unique to late Elamite writing. Mesopotamian VC and CVC signs do not distinguish between voiced, voiceless, and emphatic final stops, and some CV signs do not distinguish between voiced and voiceless initial stops; the counterpart Elamite signs also do not represent a corresponding distinction between stops.

2.3.2 Logograms

As in Mesopotamian cuneiform, almost all logograms are Sumerograms, that is, historical writings of Sumerian words used to indicate words with the same meaning in Akkadian or in Elamite. The Elamite words written with Sumerograms are sometimes unknown (e.g., Sumerian DUMU, "son," Akkadian *māru*, Elamite *šak*; but Sumerian ŠE.BAR, "barley," Akkadian *uṭṭētu*, Elamite uncertain). Akkadian loanwords appear in Elamite, but Elamite cuneiform lacks Akkadograms of the kind found in Hittite cuneiform (see *WAL* Ch. 18, §2).

2.3.3 Determinatives

Most determinatives precede the words they qualify. The postpositive determinatives found in Mesopotamian cuneiform (for example, marking the preceding words as names of birds or plants) do not occur in Elamite. Some determinatives have the same value as the counterpart signs in Mesopotamian cuneiform: for example, signs that mark the following words as divine names, as personal names, as feminine personal names or words describing women, or as wooden things. Others are Mesopotamian signs used with determinative values specific to Elamite cuneiform: for example, a horizontal wedge to mark a following place name or location (commonly indicated in Mesopotamian cuneiform with different sign, postposed). The only postpositive determinative is the sign that in Mesopotamian cuneiform has the value MEŠ and marks the preceding word as a plural, but in Elamite cuneiform marks the preceding word as a logogram (this usage is also found with lower frequency in some so-called "peripheral" cuneiform writing – that is, cuneiform orthography for Akkadian in non-Akkadian speaking environments, e.g., Ugarit and Nuzi – and in Neo-Assyrian; van Soldt 1991:428–429). Postposed MEŠ also marks some pseudologograms (that is, historical spellings of Elamite words, e.g., Achaemenid Elamite *puhu* "boy," *ulhi* "house," both with nonphonemic *-h-*), and MEŠ sometimes appears after apparently ordinary syllabic spellings (e.g., *tar-mu*^{MEŠ} [a grain]). Conversely, not all logograms are followed by MEŠ (e.g., EŠŠANA = *sunki-*, "king," DUMU = *šak*, "son" are never followed by MEŠ [Vallat 1987a]).

2.3.4 Direction and division

As in Mesopotamian cuneiform and other adaptations of it, writing runs left to right, top to bottom. Word division is not ordinarily marked. Determinatives do not double as word-dividers, since most of the preposed determinatives also have common syllabic values (e.g., GIŠ [determinative for wooden objects, fruits, etc.] is used syllabically with the value *iz*), and postpositive MEŠ may be followed by signs indicating grammatical morphemes (e.g., LÚ (= *ruh*) "man" in ^{DIŠ}LÚ^{MEŠ}-*ip*, "men"). In most Elamite texts, lines of writing are not divided at word boundaries, as they are in Mesopotamian cuneiform.

2.3.5 Graphemic inventories and spelling practices

The inventory of Mesopotamian cuneiform signs and the uses of the signs were adapted for writing Elamite. Most of the adaptations were motivated by economy, few if any by specific properties of the Elamite language. In all periods, Elamite used a smaller inventory of cuneiform signs than Mesopotamian scripts; a little more than 200 signs are attested overall. For any period, only 100–140 signs are attested.

The forms of cuneiform characters found in Old Elamite, Middle Elamite, and early Neo-Elamite texts are similar in composition and general appearance to forms in contemporary Mesopotamian scripts, with very few idiosyncrasies. Forms of many signs in Neo-Elamite texts after about 650 BC and in Achaemenid Elamite inscriptions and tablets are sharply and systematically distinct from forms in contemporary Mesopotamian scripts. To a modern eye, the difference is perhaps as great as the difference between standard and *Fraktur* forms of the Roman alphabet.

Royal inscriptions, which dominate the corpus of Old and Middle Elamite texts, use few logograms. Administrative texts, numerous only in Neo-Elamite and Achaemenid Elamite, use many. Conversely, Middle Elamite and Neo-Elamite inscriptions use more syllabic signs, with more syllabic values, than Achaemenid Elamite texts. Logograms are not used to write verbs, rarely used to write adjectives (other than "big" and "small" or "male" and "female"), and never used to indicate grammatical categories (such as plurality or noun derivation).

Loss of some CV symbols made it impossible to mark a consistent distinction between two kinds of labial, palatal, and dental stops consistently (utilizing the signs that distinguished voiced from voiceless in Akkadian cuneiform). Furthermore, loss of some VC values, mostly for sonorants and fricatives (*up, us, uš, al, ar*), made it impossible to write certain CVC sequences with the unambiguous combination CV_1-V_1C. These sequences were commonly represented with "broken writings" of the type CV_1-V_2C, in which V_2 is always *i* or *u*: for example, late Neo-Elamite, Achaemenid Elamite *du-iš* versus Middle Elamite *du-uš* for *duš*, "he received." Similar broken writings were even used when not required by the inventory of syllabic signs: for example, singular *šá-lu-ur* and *šá-lu-ir* (not required); plural *šá-lu-ip* (required) "gentleman/men"; singular *li-ba-ir* (required), plural *li-ba-ap* and *li-ba-ip* (not required), "servant(s)." Some word-final variations between required broken spellings and "harmonic" spellings with different vowels, however, may represent loss of vowel distinction or presence of consonant clusters at ends of words: for example, *du-nu-iš* (required), *du-na-iš* (not required), *du-na-áš* (harmonic), "he gave" (Justeson and Stephens 1994).

Table 3.1 Middle Elamite and Early Neo-Elamite (before c. 650 BC) syllabic signs: V, CV, VC

V Symbols: a e i u, ú

CV Symbols				VC Symbols			
ba	be	bi		ap		ip	up
pa		pi	pu				
ga		gi	gu?	ak		ik	uk
ka, ka$_4$		ki	ku				
da		di	du	at		it	ut
ta	te	ti	tu, tu$_8$?				
sa		si	su	as		is	us
za		zi, zí	zu				
ša, šá	še	ši	šu	aš, áš		iš	uš
ma	me	mi	mu	am		im	um
na	ne	ni	nu	an	en	in	un
la		li	lu	al	el	il	ul
ra		ri	ru	ar		ir	ur
ha		hi	hu	Vh, Vʔ			

Table 3.2 Late Neo-Elamite (after c. 650) and Achaemenid Elamite syllabic signs: V, CV, VC (values in parentheses are not attested in Achaemenid)

V Symbols: a e i u, ú

CV Symbols				VC Symbols			
ba	be						
pa		pi	pu	ap		ip, íp	
		gi					
ka$_4$		ki	ku	ak		ik	uk
	te	ti	tu, tu$_4$	at		it	ut
da			du				
sa		si	su	as		is	(us)
za		zí					
šá, šà	še	ši	šu	áš		iš	
ma	me	mi	mu	am		im	um
na		ni	nu	an	en	in	un
la		li	lu			el?	ul
ra		ri	ru	(ar)		ir	ur
ha		hi	hu	Vh			

In Achaemenid Elamite, as in late Mesopotamian cuneiform scripts, CVC signs may be ambiguous as to vowel color (e.g., *tup-pi-ra*, *tup-pi-ip* ~ *ti-pi-ra*, *ti-pi-ip*, "scribe(s)"; *šá-tin* ~ *šá-tan*, "priest"). In Achaemenid Elamite, and sometimes earlier, as in Mesopotamian cuneiform, CVC sequences are sometimes made unambiguous by plene writings of the types CVC-VC- (e.g., *tan-an-* beside *tan-* and *da-an-*), CV-CVC (e.g., *-ri-ráš-*) or CVC-CV- (e.g., *gal-li-*, *gal-lu-* beside *gal-*; *hal-la-tam$_5$-ti* beside *hal-tam$_5$-ti*, "Elam"; see Vallat 1989).

Late Neo-Elamite and Achaemenid Elamite introduced some syllabic values not found in Mesopotamian (e.g., mak_x [KUR], tam_x [GIM]), as well as one syllabic character not found in Mesopotamian cuneiform (rak_x [from SAL+BAR]), and two determinatives: (i) the horizontal wedge (equivalent to AŠ) to mark place names, words indicating locations, and certain other words (e.g., "month" and "day"); and (ii) the signs BE and HAL, graphic variants of each other, to mark personal names and words indicating persons. Neo-Elamite and Achaemenid Elamite variants of some logograms betray misunderstanding of their Mesopotamian graphic etymologies: for example, Neo-Elamite E.GAL for historically correct É.GAL, "palace"; Achaemenid Elamite SI.KAK (once, probably erroneously) beside historically correct ŠI.KAK, "spear"; and the Sumerograms ANŠE "equid," GEŠTIN "wine," and NUMUN "seed" treated as combinations of two signs (PA+x, DIN+KAK, NU+MAN, respectively), sometimes separated by line divisions.

2.3.6 Transliteration and transcription

Elamite forms are represented below in sign-by-sign transliteration, morphological transcription, or conventional transcription. In *transliteration*, hyphens mark off syllables, logograms are in capitals, and determinatives are superscript (e.g., *hu-ud-da-an-ti*, ^{d}ITI^{MEŠ}). In *morphological transcription*, placed within square brackets herein (not within slanting brackets, as often, in order to avoid confusion with phonemic representation), hyphens mark off morphemes, and parentheses sometimes indicate vowels or doubled consonants that are inherent in syllabic writings but are apparently not morphemic (e.g., [hutta-n-t(i)]). *Conventional transcriptions* are commonly used representations that reflect underlying transliterations but do not consistently reflect inferred phonology or morphology (e.g., singular *hupirri*, plural *hupibe*, written *hu-pír-ri*, *hu-pi-be*, probably to be analyzed [hupi-r(i)], [hupi-p(e)]). Unattested or reconstructed forms are marked with *.

The following abbreviations are used: DN (divine name); GN (geographical name); PN (personal name); RN (royal name).

3. PHONOLOGY

The use of Mesopotamian cuneiform script presents obstacles to recognizing Elamite phonology. In ordinary use for writing Akkadian, the script distinguishes only three vowels consistently (*a*, *i*, *u*) and a fourth in some sequences (*e*); it does not render initial or final consonant clusters or medial clusters of more than two consonants unambiguously; it does not distinguish voicing of syllable-final stops. The simplification of the script for use with Elamite further narrowed the possibilities of expressing distinctions. Changes in Elamite phonology were not necessarily accompanied by corresponding changes in writing; thus, although *h* was probably no longer phonemic in Achaemenid Elamite, Achaemenid Elamite writing retained a complete set of hV signs, a Vh sign, and and some hVC signs, and *h* is written frequently, in some words regularly. Writing conventions for expressing phonological features peculiar to Elamite are not easily recognized or interpreted. The greatest obstacle to understanding Elamite phonology and its phonetic realization, however, is the lack of a securely identified close cognate language with a well-known phonology.

Resources for the study of Elamite phonology include transcriptions of words and names from other languages in Elamite texts (Iranian words and names in Achaemenid Elamite have been much studied (see, e.g., Hinz 1975b; Mayrhofer 1973; Tavernier 2002), but Akkadian and West Semitic words and names in Achaemenid and earlier Elamite have not);

transcriptions of Elamite words and names into other languages and scripts (words and names in Sumerian and Akkadian texts from Mesopotamia and Iran contemporary with Old Elamite and Middle Elamite have not been studied comprehensively as sources for phonology); and spelling variations within Elamite texts.

Much of this evidence, especially spelling variation, is ambiguous in that it may support either inferences about phonology or inferences about writing conventions. Conversely, where the writing does express phonemic distinctions that do not have counterparts in Mesopotamian languages, it cannot make their phonetic realizations plain.

3.1 Consonants

The consonantal inventory of Elamite is summarized in (1), though this summary is qualified below:

(1) Elamite consonants

p		t		k	
b		d		g	
		s	š		
		z			
	v/f(?)				h
m		n			
		l	r		

3.1.1 Stops

There are two series of stops, ordinarily indicated in transliteration and transcription by *p*, *k*, *t* versus *b*, *g*, *d*. Elamite syllabaries do not allow consistent distinction of all pairs in all positions. Regular geminate spellings of medial stops in some words (e.g., *hutta-* (not **hu-ta-*) "do," *-ikki* "to" versus *igi* "brother") and regular choices of initial signs in others (e.g., *pari-* (not **ba-ri-*) "go") indicate that a phonemic distinction was made. However, spelling variations within Elamite (e.g., *dumanpi*, *dumanba* but not **dumanpa*) and Elamite transcriptions of foreign words and names (e.g., Middle Elamite *pi-it* for Akkadian *bīt(u)*, "house," Achaemenid Elamite *Ba-ir-šá* (never **Pa-*) for *Pārsa* "Persepolis") indicate that the two series were not distinguished by voicing. A contrast between tense (rendered with *p*, *k*, *t*) and lax (rendered with *b*, *g*, *d*) stops, as in Dravidian, is sometimes suggested (e.g., Reiner 1969:115; Khačikjan 1995).

3.1.1.1 *Allophonic variation*

Spelling variations like *Šu-šu-ga* ~ *Šu-šu-un-ka*, "Susa (+ marker of grammatical concord)," *šu-ul-lu-me-ka* ~ *šu-ul-lu-me-en-ka* (a verbal form of uncertain meaning), *hi-nu-ka* ~ *hi-nu-un-ka* "(which) we (will) have," and perhaps *su-un-ki-ir* ~ *su-gìr* "king" (all Middle Elamite) suggest nasal allophones of the velar series. Late Neo-Elamite royal inscriptions from Khuzestān that spell a final first-person morpheme *-k* (below) with signs containing *h* suggest spirantization of the velar (Khačikjan 1995:109; Vallat 1996a:387). An affricated pronunciation of dentals may lie behind an Achaemenid Elamite spelling *zí-da-el* ~ *zí-za-el* (Hinz and Koch 1987:1288), and Akkadian writings of Elamite names of the eighteenth–seventeenth centuries BC (hence contemporary with Old Elamite) with such variations as *tempti-* ~ *šimti-* "lord," *kutir-* ~ *kušir* ~ *kusir-* "carrier" (Zadok 1984:3; Vallat 1996c:315).

3.1.2 Fricatives

At least three fricatives (sibilants), transcribed as *s*, *š*, and *z*, are expressed with signs which have common Mesopotamian values including *s*, *š* and *z* (or *ṣ*).

Variations between spellings with *s* and *š* (e.g., *Insušnak* ~ *Inšušinak* [a divine name], *mušika* ~ *muššika* ~ *musika*, "it is counted") suggest that *s* can represent an affricate. Moreover, variations between spellings with *š* and *z* (e.g., *Anšan* ~ *Anzan* [a place name], both in Elamite and in Akkadian), along with the use of signs with *z* to transcribe Iranian /č/, and the Achaemenid Elamite spellings *ku-ti-iš* and *ku-iz*, for [kutš], "he carried," suggest the existence of an Elamite phoneme /č/. However, the spellings *ku-iz-iš-da* and even *ku-iz-da-ti-iš-da* may suggest that the writers perceived a cluster /-tšt-/ to be clarified with the same graphic convention used otherwise for CVC signs (§2.3.5).

In Old and Middle Elamite, syllabic symbols with Akkadian values including *ḫ* consistently represent a phoneme transcribed as *h*. Its phonetic value is uncertain, but it was not a velar fricative like Akkadian /*ḫ*/. Spellings cease to be consistent when this /*h*/ ceases to be phonemic in late Neo-Elamite and Achaemenid Elamite, though many historical spellings with *h* and sometimes with *-hh-* occur.

A labial fricative such as /f/ or /v/, not represented unambiguously or consistently, is suggested by the spelling variations *ligawe* ~ *likame*, *suhterwe* ~ *suhterme*, and Akkadian *Ši/Ṣi-we-*, *Še-ep-* ~ Elamite *Si-me-* (in the royal name *Sim/we-palar-huhpak*); see Khačikjan 1995:107, 1998:8.

3.1.3 Sonorants

Elamite possesses nasal and liquid phonemes; the phonemic status of glides is less clear.

3.1.3.1 Nasals

Both /n/ and /m/ are unambiguously represented in Elamite spelling. Some words are regularly spelled with geminate *m* or *n*, but a phonemic distinction is uncertain.

From at least Middle Elamite on, /n/ was assimilated to following /l/ (e.g., /ullina/ < [un lina]) and perhaps to following palatal and dental consonants. In late Neo-Elamite and Achaemenid Elamite, /n/ was a labialized before a bilabial stop and written as *m* (e.g., *tahhampa* < **tahhanpa*; *sitmamba* ~ *sitmap*; *dumamba* and even *du-ma-ma* ~ *dumanba* (all plural forms on verbal stems), but also the exceptional *tah-ha-ma-am-ri*, perhaps back-formed from the plural; also in pronoun–verb phrases like *ú-um beša* "he (who) created me," *um parimanka* "I will (not) be coming there"; see Paper 1955:62; Vallat 1996a:387–388). Achaemenid Elamite spellings *hu-ut-tan-ti* ~ *hu-ut-tam*$_5$*-ti* do not indicate dissimilation, but reflect a graphic convention also found in late Mesopotamian cuneiform: *CVm* ~ *CVn* ~ *CV-Vn*.

3.1.3.2 Liquids

The liquids /l/ and /r/ are written unambiguously. The writing of Akkadian *La-gamāl* as Elamite *Lagamar* and of Elamite *Ruhuratir* as Akkadian *Lahuratil* (both divine names), as well as Achaemenid Elamite *ka-ri-ri* ~ *kar-li* "lamb," suggest a non-trilled [r] (Khačikjan 1995: 107f., 1998:8f.). The spelling variations *pi-ri-ip* ~ *pa-ri-ip* "they went to, reached," *pa-ri-iš* ~ *pa-iš* "he/they set out, went," and perhaps *mar-ri-ia* ~ *ma-ú-ri-ia* "I seized" (all Achaemenid Elamite) suggest a vocalic [r̥].

3.1.3.3 Glides

The phonemic status of [y] and [w] is unclear. The intervocalic use of the syllabograms *-i-* or *-ia-* represents a glide [y]. In contrast, word-initial *ia-*, rare except in proper nouns, represents juncture between syllables or words: thus, *ia-ak* for *a-ak* "and" in the sequence *intikka yak*; *ia-áš-pu*, a *Kulturwort* corresponding to Akkadian *ašpu* (a semi-precious stone), in the sequence *rišakki i yašpu*. Word-initial *a-a* represents two syllables separated by a glide or juncture (*a-a-ni* ~ *a-hi-in*, *a-ah-in* "family(?)," *A-a-pír* [a place-name]). In Achaemenid Elamite, the sequence *(-)ú-uC* also represents glide, syllable-boundary, or word-initial juncture (*hu-ut-ti-ú-ut* ~ *hu-ud-da-hu-ut* ~ *hu-ud-du-ud-da* "we made"; *hu-ut-ti-ip* ~ *ú-ut-ti-ip-* "makers"). But the unique Achaemenid Elamite spelling *a-áš-šá-ir-ki-* for *Manšarki* (a month name) seems to suggest some phoneme with allophones [y], [w] and perhaps [?].

3.2 Vowels

The vowels /a/, /i/, and /u/ are expressed unambiguously. The vocalic phoneme /e/ is confirmed by minimal pairs (e.g., *tetin* "beam(?)" vs. *titen-* "lying") and supported by transcriptions of foreign words (e.g., *alumelu* from Akkadian *ālum ēlum*), but it is not often expressed unambiguously by the writing system. Final [-e] and [-i] were probably not distinguished phonemically. Many spellings with final *Ci* probably indicate final [-C], especially in clusters (e.g., *hu-ud-da-an-ti* for [huttant] "you do"). Disagreement prevails concerning the existence of phonemic /o/, sometimes postulated on the basis of distinctive uses of the signs *u* and *ú* (Paper 1955:17; Khačikjan 1998:6).

Contemporary variation in spellings using signs with *u* and signs with *i* in some words (e.g., *tu*$_4$*-ru-iš* ~ *ti-ri-iš*, *mu-ši-in* ~ *mi-ši-na*, all Achaemenid Elamite) may reveal a common reduced allophone shared by /i/ and /u/. Variation in spellings of vowels in the final syllables (e.g., *dunuš* ~ *dunaš* "he gave") may indicate a reduced vowel or a final cluster with sonorant.

Spelling variations like *Hu-ban* ~ *Hu-um-ban* (a divine name), *te-em-ti* ~ *te-ep-ti* "lord," *na-ra-an-da*, *na-ra-an-te* ~ *na-ra-da*, *na-ra-te* "daily" suggest the existence of nasalized vowels.

Vowel length is not phonemic. Most long writings of vowels are susceptible to graphic explanations: for example, avoidance of one-sign spellings of open monosyllables (*a-ak* vs. *a-gi* for /ak/ "and"), or marking of final vowel versus final consonant cluster (*te-la-ak-ni-e* vs. *te-la-ak-ni* for /telakni/ not /*telakn/).

Diphthongs do not occur. In Achaemenid Elamite, some spellings with *-a-uC* appear to reflect the pronunciation of following sonorants: *mauriya* ~ *marriya* (perhaps with vocalic [r̥]) "I seized"; *zaumip* ~ *zammip* ~ *zamip* (perhaps with labial continuant; see §3.1.2) "laborers."

3.2.1 Vowel contraction

Monosyllabic pronouns in clusters, and pronouns in constructions with directional elements were often susceptible to contraction and written without word-division. The sequence *i u* does not normally occur; *u i* contracts to *u*, and *i i* to *i*: thus, [li-n-a ap u in] written *li-na-pu-un*; [pat-r ir u-r] written *pa-at-ru-ur* (Reiner 1969:99, Grillot 1983:210, Grillot-Susini and Roche 1987:9).

3.3 Accent

Neutralization of some final vowels and elision of some medial vowels suggests that stress was nonfinal, probably initial (Grillot-Susini and Roche 1987:11, 1994:15; Khačikjan 1998:10).

4. MORPHOLOGY

4.1 Word formation

Elamite is an agglutinative language. Most roots are of one or two syllables, of the types CV (*da-* "place"), VC (*ki* "one"), CVC (*nap* "god," *ruh* "man"), VCV (*igi* "brother"), CVCV (*zana* "lady"), and perhaps CVCCV (*sunki-* "king," *tingi-* "take away" [or: CVCV *su^{n}ki-*, *ti^{n}gi-* ?]). Some roots produce only nominal forms, others both nominal and verbal forms. All inflection is marked with suffixes attached to a root or to a base derived from a root with the addition of a thematic vowel, a derivational suffix, by reduplication, or by compounding. Most trisyllabic bases can be identified as composites or loanwords (Grillot-Susini 1994:1–8).

4.2 Nominal morphology

Nominal inflection affects substantives, attributes of substantives (including clauses), demonstratives and pronouns, numerals, the negative particle, and some verbal forms (derived from the bare verb-stem (gerunds or participles), and from the "nominal conjugations" formed on the verb-stem with suffixed *-k-* (Conjugation II) and suffixed *-n-* (Conjugation III)).

4.2.1 Gender, person, and number

Nominal inflection distinguishes two genders, animate and inanimate. Inflection of animates distinguishes three personal classes, corresponding to the three persons of verbal inflection. The first-person (I-class) form is sometimes called *locutive*; the second-person (you-class) *allocutive*; and the third-person (he-it-class) *delocutive*. Inflection of third-person animates distinguishes singular and plural. These suffixes mark agreement (i) between subject and verb, and (ii) between parts of possessive and attributive constructions and subordinate clauses (see below and §5.2); the gender/person/number suffixes are as follows:

(2)

Animate			
Singular	*1st*	-k	([sunki-k] "I, king")
	2nd	-t	([hutta-n-t] "you, doing" [katu-k-t] "you, living")
	3rd	-Ø	([nap] "he, god," [zana] "she, lady")
		-r	([nap-ir] "he, god," [sunki-r] "he, king")
Plural	*3rd*	-p	([nap-ip] "they, gods," [sunki-p] "they, kings")
Inanimate			
	3rd	-Ø	([hal] "town, land," [mur] "place")
		-me	([sunki-me] "kingdom, kingship")
		-n	([siya-n] "temple," [muru-n] "earth")
		-t	([hala-t] "clay, mud brick")

Third-person suffixes are derivational. The animates indicate agent nouns (*huttira* "maker, doer"), members of a class, or persons (*Babilira*, *Babilip* "Babylonian(s)"; *libar*, *libap* "servant(s)"). The inanimate *-me* indicates abstracts (*takkime* "life"). In Achaemenid Elamite, *-ta* ~ *-te* indicates generality (*marrita* "everything"). Doublets are common: thus, Achaemenid Elamite [muši-n] ~ [muši-me] "account."

In possessive and attributive constructions, the suffixes appropriate to the possessor or the determined substantive are added to the possessed or attribute. Consider the following Middle Elamite examples:

(3) A. [u PN šak PN_2-k(i) sunki-k GN-GN_2-k(a)]
"I, PN, son of PN_2, king of GN (and) GN_2"
with first-person suffixes throughout

B. [PN meni-r GN ak GN_2-r(i) šak hanik PN_2-r(i) ak PN_3-r(i)]
"he, PN, ruler(?) of GN and GN_2, beloved son of PN_2 and PN_3"
with third-person suffixes throughout

In Neo-Elamite a postposition *-na* (derived from the neutral inanimate *-n* with final "relative" *-a*), sometimes expresses possession, and in Achaemenid Elamite most possession and some attributive relationships are expressed with *-na*: Neo-Elamite [zalmu PN-na] "image of PN"; Achaemenid Elamite [halmi PN-na] "seal[ed document] of PN."

4.2.2 Case

Only personal pronouns (see §4.3.2) are marked for nominal case, distinguishing between an object-case and a subject/indirect object-case. Other spatial relationships and relationships between nouns and verbs are expressed with resumptive pronouns and with postpositions attached to nouns, to noun phrases, or to clauses.

4.2.3 Indeclinable nominals

Kinship terms in which possessive or attributive relationships are inherent (*šak* "son," *puhu* "child," *igi* "brother," *šutu* "sister," *amma* "mother," *rutu* ~ *riti* ~ *irti* "wife," *ruhušak* "sister's son") are indeclinable; that is, they do not have markers of gender and person where other nouns have such markers (Reiner 1969:88). As the possessed noun in some possessive constructions, they are marked with nominal suffixes that refer to the possessor: Neo-Elamite, Achaemenid Elamite [PN šak-r(i)], [PN riti-r(i)] (Grillot-Susini and Roche 1987:23).

4.2.4 Adjectives

Elamite adjectives do not constitute a distinct morphological class. They are marked with the personal suffixes and postpositions that express attributive and possessive constructions, including the personal marker of the modified substantive ([temti riša-r] "great lord"; [upat lansiti-p(a)] "brickwork (anim. pl.!) of gold," i.e., gilded or enameled?); and the possessive postposition *-na* ([sunki-na] "of the king," i.e., "royal"), productive in Achaemenid Elamite: e.g., GURUŠ-*na* "male"; MUNUS-*na* "female" (the Elamite words underlying the logograms are unknown); *punna*, *berna*, etc. (qualifying animals). There are no comparative or superlative forms. Superlatives are expressed with a possessive construction: Achaemenid Elamite [akka irša-r-a napi-p(e)-na] ~ [akka irša-r-a nap-b(e)-r(a)] (corresponding to Old Persian *haya maϑišta bagānām*) "[Ahuramazda] the greatest of the gods"; Middle Elamite [riša-r napi-p(i)-r(a)] "[Inšušinak], greatest of the gods."

4.3 Pronouns

Elamite has demonstrative, personal, possessive, relative, indefinite, and resumptive pronouns.

4.3.1 Demonstrative pronouns

The Middle Elamite demonstrative pronouns are *hi* ~ *i* (animate singular and inanimate) and *ap* ~ *api* (animate plural). Achaemenid Elamite distinguishes between near-deictic *hi* ~ *i* and *ap* "this, these," and far-deictic *hube* (inanimate), *hupirri* (animate singular), *hupibe* (animate plural) "that, those." The demonstrative pronouns also serve as third-person personal pronouns.

4.3.2 Personal pronouns

The personal pronouns distinguish an "unmarked" nominative/dative form for subjects or indirect objects, and a "marked" accusative form for direct objects:

(4)

	Singular		*Plural*	
	Nominative	*Accusative*	*Nominative*	*Accusative*
1st	u	un	nika ~ nuku	nukun
2nd	ni ~ nu	nun	num ~ numi	numun
3rd	i ~ hi	ir ~ in	ap ~ ap(p)i	ap(p)in
Inan.	i ~ in	i ~ in		

In Achaemenid Elamite, first-person singular accusative pronouns written *unan*, *unahan*, *unanku* ~ *uhanaunku* also occur. Analysis of them is a matter of disagreement (Paper 1955:95 and Khačikjan 1998:22). Also in Achaemenid Elamite, *ha-ap* appears once as a variant spelling of *ap*.

4.3.3 Possessive pronouns

Possessives of the personal pronouns are formed like other possessive constructions, by adding the suffixes appropriate to the possessor (see §4.2.1) or by adding the possessive post-position *-na* ~ *-ni*: Middle Elamite [napir-u-r(i)] "my god," [sunkip urip-u-p(e)] "kings, my predecessors," [takkime puhu nika-me-na ~ nika-me-me] "the live(s) of our children"; Achaemenid Elamite [ulhi nuka-me] "our house," [libar-u-r(i)] "my servant," [libar-e-r(i)] "his servant," [sunkime appi-ni] "their kingship (= rule over them)," but first-person singular with an enlarged base [libame u-ni-na] "my servitude (= servitude to me)" and first-person plural without animate/inanimate distinction [kir akkayaš nuka-me] "one colleague of ours."

In addition, there is a third-person animate singular possessive suffix *-e* that may derive from the pronoun *hi* ~ *i*, without suffix: Middle Elamite [PN ak puhu-e] "PN and her children"; Middle Elamite, Achaemenid Elamite [hiš-e] "his name." A corresponding third-person plural animate possessive is formed by adding *-e* to the demonstrative/personal pronoun: Middle Elamite [hiš(-)api-e] "their name"; Achaemenid Elamite [puhu appi-e] "their boys." Hinz and Koch 1987 diverge from Hallock 1969 and others in interpreting final *-še* in Achaemenid Elamite writings of substantives of Iranian origin as representing the Old Persian possessive *-šay*, rather than as including Elamite *-e*.

Achaemenid Elamite also has a first-person possessive suffix *-ta* (only in the construction [u atta-ta] "my father") and a second-person singular possessive suffix *-ni* (NUMUN-*ni* "your lineage," [širi-ni] "your *š*").

4.3.4 Relative pronouns

The Elamite relatives are animate *akka* "who" and inanimate *appa* "which, what." A corresponding animate plural *akkap(e)* also appears in Neo-Elamite and Achaemenid Elamite. In Achaemenid Elamite the inanimate form doubles as the accusative of the animate: *appi* 9 *sunkip appa u... mauriya* "these are the nine kings whom I captured." In Achaemenid Elamite, the relative pronouns appear as calques on the Old Persian relative pronouns and articles, *haya/hayā/taya*, connecting substantive and attribute or possessor and possessed pronouns; such calques are frequent in multilingual royal inscriptions (PN *akka Makuš* "PN the Magian," *taššup appa* PN-*na* "the troops of PN," *taššup appa unina* "my troops"); the usage also occurs in administrative texts (PN *akka* GN-*ma kurdabattiš* "PN the chief of workers at GN"). Occasional uses of the relative pronouns in expressing dates, however ([dITIMEŠ appa NN-na-ma] "in the month of NN," *bel appa* 24-*ummemana* "the 24th year"), do not have Old Persian parallels.

The inanimate substantive *mur(u)*, unmarked and undeclined, serves as the locative relative "where": Middle Elamite [muru huma-hš(i)-ta in-me durna-h] "where they took (it) I do not know"; Achaemenid Elamite [mur halmarraš hi kuši-k-a] "where this fortress is built."

4.3.5 Indefinite pronouns

An animate indefinite pronoun, "anyone," is formed from the relative *akka* with personal suffix *-r*; it occurs in negated clauses: for example, Middle Elamite [sunki-p uri-p-u-pi akka-r(a)... in-r(i) hutta-n-r(a)] "(what) former kings, any (of them) did not do," i.e., "what no former king did"; Achaemenid Elamite [appa-n-lakki-me akka-r(i) inni hutta] "I did not commit a trespass against anyone."

The inanimate indefinite *aški* "anything," also found in negated clauses, is perhaps formed with the numeral *ki* "one" (Hinz and Koch 1987:88; Khačikjan 1998:29; otherwise Hallock 1969:670).

4.3.6 Resumptive pronouns

Nominal constituents of a clause are frequently "resumed" by one or more pronouns placed immediately before the verb at the end of the clause. In Middle Elamite these resumptives are in clusters: [ap u in (written *a-pu-un*) duni-h] "to them [the gods] I gave it [the temple]." In contrast, Achaemenid Elamite normally allows only a single resumptive to precede the verb: *u* DN *un nušgišni* "I, may Ahuramazda protect me"; *u* PN *ir halpi* "I, PN, I killed him").

The element *aha* (Middle Elamite, Neo-Elamite) ~ *ah* (Neo-Elamite, Achaemenid Elamite) ~ *ha* (Achaemenid Elamite) also appears before the verb at the end of a clause, replacing or, less often, preceded by resumptive personal pronouns. In Achaemenid Elamite it is commonly transcribed as a proclitic. In Middle Elamite it sometimes takes nominal suffixes *-r*, *-n*, or *-t* to mark concord. Characterizations of this formant disagree. On a narrow interpretation, it is a locative and only a locative, indicating "here," "there," or even both "here" and "there" contrasted in a single phrase. Some contexts are susceptible only to translation with locatives: Middle Elamite [ir aha-r murta-h] "I placed him [the image of the god] in it [the temple]," expressed elsewhere [sian-r(a) ir murta-h] "his temple, I placed him" (see Grillot-Susini and Roche 1987:20–21, but cf. Grillot 1970:235 n. 40; Giovinazzo 1989:13–14). On a broad interpretation *aha* ~ *ah* ~ *ha* is a general oblique resumptive pronoun, referring to substantives of any gender and number, and indicating not only "in, at it" but also "to, for, with it" (see Hallock 1969:9, 1973:148 n. 4; Stolper 1984:25; Malbran-Labat 1995:80; cf. Khačikjan1998:25). Some contexts are susceptible only to translation with nonlocatives: thus, Middle Elamite [upat ... tepu-h ulhi i aha kuši-h] "I fashioned bricks, with them I built this house." The comparison among Achaemenid Elamite *hupimer* "then, after that," *hamer* "then," and *hami* "there" favors identifying *ha* as demonstrative and pronominal. An agnostic view identifies Achaemenid Elamite *ha-* as a prefix or particle of uncertain function and meaning (Grillot-Susini, Herrenschmidt, and Malbran-Labat 1993:51; Tucker 1998:175).

In Achaemenid Elamite administrative texts *kaš* sometimes replaces *hi* as an oblique singular resumptive pronoun (Hallock 1969:9). Vallat (1987b), accounting for this non-paradigmatic form as a ghost word arising from the misreading of an archaic form of the sign *hi*, is not supported by collation.

4.3.7 Reflexive pronouns

The reflexive *du(h)-*, perhaps related to the verb *du-*, "take, receive," occurs with possessive suffix *-e* in Middle and Neo-Elamite ([hiš duh-e] "his own name") and in Achaemenid Elamite ([halpi duh-e-ma] "by his own death" (i.e., a natural death). In Achaemenid Elamite, it also forms an animate plural (also in possessive constructions, e.g., [GUD^{MEŠ} du-p-e-ma ~ du-p(i)-ni-ma] "for their own cattle" vs. pleonastic [GUD^{MEŠ} du appi-ni-ma]), and an animate singular object-case, like the personal pronouns (e.g., [du-n nušgiš] "protect yourself").

In Achaemenid Elamite, the element *hisu* indicates emphasis of the subject of an action: *hisu* x *makiš* "he himself consumed x [grain]." It also appears with a "generalizing" inanimate suffix *-t* ([PN hisu-t(a) x du-ma-k-a] "x [grain] was received by PN himself"), but it is not marked for case or number.

4.3.8 Other pronouns

"Each, every" is expressed in Achaemenid Elamite with *unra* (referring to persons: 90 *kurtaš unra* 20-*irmaki dušda* "90 workers received a twentieth [measure of wine] each") and *lurika* (referring to animals and inanimates: UDU.NITA^{MEŠ} *lurika* x ŠE.BAR^{MEŠ} *ha-lika* "for each sheep x barley was delivered"). The form *unra* varies with *unra-na*, with the adjectival *-na* suffix.

"All" is expressed in Achaemenid Elamite by *marrida*, with the "generalizing" *-t* (*hupe marrida ... hutta* "I did all that"), also *marribepda* ~ *marbepda*, with animate plural marker ([taššup marri-p(e)-p-t(a) ~ mar-p(e)-p-t(a)] "all the people," but elsewhere *taššup marrida* (otherwise Hinz and Koch 1987, segmenting a word *marri*, plural *mar(ri)bep* from *da* "also").

4.4 Nominalized negative particle

In Middle Elamite and Neo-Elamite, and exceptionally in Achaemenid Elamite, the negative particle *in-* takes nominal suffixes (first-person singular *in-ki*, third-person *in-ri*, **in-pi*, inanimate *in-ni*, *im-me* (< **inme*)) indicating concord with the logical subject (either the subject of the verb or the subject of attention). In Achaemenid Elamite, the inanimate form *inni* is general: [taššup appa unina in-ni tiriman-p(i)] "people who do not call themselves mine."

4.5 Verbal morphology

Verb bases are simple (*ta-* "put," *dunu-* "give"), compound (*mur-ta-* "put in place"), or reduplicated. Reduplicated bases are mostly of the type $C_1V_1C_1C_2V_2$- (*beti-* > *bepti-* "rebel"), rarely of the form $C_1V_1C_1V_1$- (*li-* > *lili-* "give, deliver") or the form $C_1V_1C_1V_1C_2V_2$-(*tallu-* > *tatallu* (earlier **taltallu*) "write"). The change of meaning that reduplication conveys is not established; Steiner (1990:152–153) proposes plurality of action or patient.

4.5.1 Verb conjugations

Verbs produce three primary sets of forms labeled "conjugations": one "verbal conjugation" (*Conjugation I*) and two "nominal conjugations" (most often called *Conjugation II* and *III*, also called *participles, paraverbal forms,* or *appellatives*). Particular verbs do not belong to a single conjugation; most verbs produce forms in more than one conjugation. All three conjugations distinguish three persons and two numbers. The *nominal conjugations* are formed by adding the suffixes that mark person, gender, and number in nouns (see §4.2.1). The *verbal conjugation* is formed by adding suffixes that are specific to verbs.

4.5.1.1 Middle Elamite verbs

Conjugations I–III of Middle Elamite are presented in (5)–(7), utilizing *kulla-* "pray"; *hap(i)-* "hear"; *hutta-* "do"; *turu-* "say"; and *tahha-* "help(?)":

(5) Conjugation I (verbal conjugation) – Middle Elamite

	Singular	*Plural*
1st	[kulla-h]	[kulla-hu]
2nd	[hap-t]	[hutta-h-t]
3rd	[hutta-š]	[hutta-h-š]

(6) Conjugation II (base + -k-) – Middle Elamite

	Singular	*Plural*
1st	[*-k-k]	
2nd	[*-k-t]	
3rd animate	[hutta-k-r]	[hutta-k-p]

(7) Conjugation III (base + -n-) – Middle Elamite

	Singular	*Plural*
1st	[hutta-n-k]	
2nd	[hutta-n-t]	
3rd animate	[hutta-n-r]	[tahha-n-p]

Since the personal suffixes on nouns include no first-person plural, no first-person plural form is expected in (6)–(7). Two clear first-person plurals with a suffix *-nunk* (*turununki* "we say," *hinunka* "we get [children]") may correspond to Conjugation II first-person singulars (*hinka*, Neo-Elamite *turunka*). There is, however, disagreement on the analysis of these forms, and of a counterpart Achaemenid Elamite first-person plural on a base enlarged with auxiliary *(-)ma-*, *tiri(-)ma-nun* "we call ourselves" (summarized by Khačikjan 1998:36; Tucker 1998:188 n. 41).

4.5.1.2 Achaemenid Elamite verbs

Conjugations I–III of Achaemenid Elamite are presented in (8)–(10), illustrated with *marri-* "hold"; *hutta-* "do"; *šinnu-* "come"; *katu-* "live"; *na-* "say":

(8) **Conjugation I (verbal conjugation) – Achaemenid Elamite**

	Singular	*Plural*
1st	[marri-Ø (~ -y, -ʔ)]	[hutta-Ø-ut] (written *-hu-ut* and *-ú-ut*)
2nd	[*-t]	[*-t]
3rd	[hutta-š]	[hutta-h-š]

As a result of the loss of phonemic /h/ and inconsistency in the writing of historical *h*, singular and plural were not distinguished in the third person – at least not distinguished in writing. A juncture or syllable boundary was still pronounced at the end of first-person singular forms, however, reflected in writings of forms with suffixed *-a* as *marriya*, *pariya*, *beliya*, *tengiya*. The first-person plural form, marked with an enclitic *-ut* that also appears on nominal forms ([sunkip-ut] "we are kings"), was productive (Hallock 1973:151).

(9) **Conjugation II (base + -k-) – Achaemenid Elamite**

	Singular	*Plural*
1st	[šinnu-(k)-k-ut]	
2nd	[katu-k-t]	
3rd animate	[hutta-k-Ø]	[šinnu-Ø-p]

The third-person forms expected from the Middle Elamite paradigm occur as nouns or attributive adjectives (inanimate *katuka*, animate singular *katukra*, animate plural *katukpe*) but not clearly as predicates (Tucker 1998:171–173). The ending of the first-person singular, always written *-gi-ut*, apparently contains the same particle *-ut* found in the Conjugation I first-person plural, and on nominal forms and phrases (*sunkir appi-ni-gi-ut* "I am king of them," *titu-kur-ra-gi-ut* "I am (not) a liar"), where *-gi-ut* corresponds to Old Persian *āham* "I am" and is parallel to *ha-um*, an Elamite transcription of Old Persian *āham*.

(10) **Conjugation III (base + -n-) – Achaemenid Elamite**

	Singular	*Plural*
1st	[na-n-k]	
2nd	[na-n-t]	
3rd animate	[na-n-r]	[na-n-p]

For the first-person plural *tirimanun*, "we call ourselves," see the Achaemenid Elamite forms noted in §4.5.1.1. A similar form, *hutti-nun* has been treated as a first-person plural of *hutta-* "do," although it occurs in the phrase *hutti-nun-(h)uba*, corresponding to an Old Persian infinitive meaning "[in order] to do [battle]"; analysis of the form is disputed (summarized in Khačikjan 1998:37).

4.5.1.3 *Auxiliary and suffixed (-)*ma-

Verb phrases occur in Middle and Neo-Elamite in which an auxiliary *-ma-*, with endings of Conjugations I, II, or III, follows either (i) a bare verb base ([miši-ma-n-] "becoming dilapidated"), or (ii) Conjugation II or III stems (Neo-Elamite *pali-k-ma-n-k*, *pera-n-ma-n-k*), or (iii) verbal nouns with animate marker *-r* (*pepši-r-ma-h* "I renovated"). In Achaemenid Elamite, the element *-ma-* only follows the bare verbal-stem and precedes the personal suffixes, producing secondary sets of forms that are usually called Conjugations Im, IIm, and IIIm. Attested Achaemenid forms are presented in (11):

(11) **Achaemenid Elamite secondary conjugations**

		Singular	*Plural*
Conjugation Im	*1st*	-ma-Ø	
	3rd	-ma-š	
Conjugation IIm	*3rd*	-ma-k	-ma-p
Conjugation IIIm	*1st*	-ma-n-k	
	3rd	-ma-n-ra	-ma-n-p

Conjugation Im forms are rare, except for the verb *du-ma-* "receive." Conjugation IIm plural forms are also rare.

4.5.1.4 *Conjugation functions*

There is broad agreement on the distinctions of meaning among the conjugations, but authorities differ in emphasis on aspect, transitivity, and/or voice (perfective/imperfective, active/passive, taking one, two, or three arguments). Conjugation I is mostly active, transitive, sometimes intransitive (including verbs of motion and verbs of speaking), having neutral or absolute aspect, mostly of past tense. Conjugation II is mostly intransitive or passive, perfective in aspect hence often past. Conjugation III is transitive or intransitive, imperfective, non-past (see, among others, Hallock 1959; Grillot 1970:216–218; McAlpin 1981:71 and 80; Khačikjan 1998:33–36; see also Malbran-Labat 1990, distinguishing verbs with a single argument, with no Conjugation I, from verbs with two or three arguments in Conjugation I but fewer arguments in Conjugations II and III).

There is only partial consensus on the meaning of auxiliary *(-)ma-* (Malbran-Labat 1986): durative (Labat 1951:36); intensive or emphatic, iterative and durative (Hallock 1959:18); indicating will, intent, decision, or declaration (Grillot and Vallat 1975, Grillot-Susini and Roche 1987:36); uncertain, indicating change of state (Khačikjan 1998:36).

When Achaemenid Elamite reflects translation of an underlying Old Persian text or simply contact with Old Iranian speakers, historically original distinctions are affected by calquing on Old Iranian. Old Persian subjunctives with future meaning are regularly translated with Conjugation III forms, and Old Persian presents usually with Conjugation IIIm forms (McAlpin 1981:71; Tucker 1998:181–182).

4.5.2 Verb moods

Several modal uses of various conjugation forms can be identified.

4.5.2.1 *Precative or optative*

Forms of Conjugations I and II with the suffix *-ni* ∼ *-na* are precative or optative: Middle Elamite [tela-k-ni] "may it be dedicated(?)"; Neo-Elamite [hutta-hš-ni] "may they do"; Achaemenid Elamite [kata-k-t(i)-ni] "may you live"; [dunu-š-ni] "may he give." Achaemenid

Elamite forms in *-ni* sometimes correspond to Old Persian optatives: thus, [sura-k nima-k-ni], and [šura-k-ni], both rendering Old Persian *miϑa kariyaiš* "would do harm." The particle *-ni* may also be asseverative (Middle Elamite [hutta-h-ni] "I indeed made," [šatu-h-ni] "I will truly *š*."; see Grillot 1978:29 n. 65) and perhaps concessive (Middle Elamite [kuši-k-ni] "although(?) it was built [formerly of unbaked brick, I rebuilt it of baked brick]").

4.5.2.2 Imperative

In Middle Elamite, the second person of Conjugation I serves as the imperative (*kullak-ume hap-t(i)* "hear my prayer"). In Achaemenid Elamite, the third person of Conjugation I serves as an imperative: [mite-š . . . halpi-š] "go, defeat." In a parallel phrase the first of two imperatives, an intransitive, is rendered with the bare stem: [mite ∼ mida . . . halpi-š]. See also Vallat 1994:266, arguing for *iddu* < **in du* "he is to receive it," a bare stem used as third-person imperative or optative.

4.5.2.3 Prohibitive

Prohibitives are Conjugation III (imperfective, non-past) forms preceded by the particle *anu* ∼ *ani*: for example, Middle Elamite [par ani kutu-n] "may he not be assured of(?) progeny"; Neo-Elamite [anu i-n kuti-n-k(i)] "I must surely not support(?) him"; Achaemenid Elamite [hupe anu hutta-n-t(i)] (written *huttamti*) "do not do that"; [anu u ir turna-n-p(i)] (written *turnampi*) "lest they know me," corresponding to Old Persian *mā taya-* with a subjunctive.

4.5.3 Nonfinite verbals

The bare verbal stem used as a substantive is usually termed an "infinitive": for example, Achaemenid Elamite GN-*mar* GN_2 *laki* "a crossing from GN to GN_2," occurring at the end of the text, in a statement otherwise construed with a finite form [pari-š] "they went." The form is labeled a Conjugation I infinitive in Hallock 1965; a Participle I in Khačikjan 1998:41. Stems with animate personal markers are agent nouns: Achaemenid Elamite [lipte kuti-r-a] "bow carrier"; called Conjugation I participle in Hallock 1965. Stems with suffixed *-k* and *-n*, that is, the bases of Conjugations II and III, are passive-intransitive perfective (sometimes past) participles and active imperfective (non-past) participles, respectively. Participles in *-k* also form substantives or adjectives: [katu-k-r-a] "living"; [halpi-k-r-a] "dead"; [hutta-k hali-k] "(what is) made with effort(?)." The stem with *-n* or *-na* is also a non-past or imperfective infinitive: for example, Middle Elamite *kukkunum pittena* "[the god commanded me] to make an enclosure of (?) the *k*."; Achaemenid [tuppi talli-ma-n-a] "[I ordered] an inscription to be written." Such constructions are termed Conjugation III infinitive in Hallock 1965; verbal noun or supine in Khačikjan 1998:42. Compare, however, Achaemenid [šaparakumme hutta-ma-n-r-a] "[he came] to do battle," with a Conjugation III third-person form translating an Old Persian infinitive.

4.5.4 Other verbal morphemes

Additional suffixes can be appended to verbal forms.

4.5.4.1 The suffix -a

This suffix attaches to verbal forms of all conjugations in all periods. It is usually the final morpheme of the form (but note Achaemenid Elamite [kuši-š-t-a-p(e)] "women who have given birth" and similar forms; see §5.6). In Middle Elamite it also attaches to some nominal forms, including nominalized clauses, either replacing or following markers of gender and person: [DN GN-r-a] "DN [the god] of GN"; [siyan . . . in-me (written *imme*) kuši-hš(i)-me-a (written *kušihšima*)] "the temple which they did not build." Divergent characterizations of the function of *-a* include the following:

1. Suffixed *-a* is determinative and subordinating. It first marked determining attributes of nouns and nominal predicates of subordinate clauses, then also marked verbal predicates of subordinate clauses. In Achaemenid Elamite *-a* appears mostly on subordinate verbs. In all periods, clauses introduced with relative pronouns or conjunctions may also omit *-a* (Grillot 1970, 1973; Grillot-Susini and Roche 1987:25, 40; Steiner 1990:144, 153). In an extreme form of this interpretation, Achaemenid Elamite forms in *-a* are subordinate and only subordinate, usually with temporal implication, but also with causal and other nuances: [hutta-k-a] "which is done," hence "which has [previously] been done" (see, among others, Giovinazzo 1989; Vallat 1994:272).
2. Alternatively, *-a* is connective. It does not express subordination but coordination: thus, Achaemenid Elamite [marri-š-a (written *maurišša*) appin halpi-š] "he seized and killed them"; [marri-k-a u-ikki tengik] "he was seized and brought to me" – both corresponding to Old Persian main clauses; Middle Elamite [pepši-h-a kuši-h] "I restored and built" (see Hallock 1959:5–6, 11–12, 1973:150–151; and cf. Steiner 1990:144, comparing Elamite relative *-a* to the use of the Akkadian enclitic conjunction *-ma* in paratactic syntax to express subordination).
3. With less precision, *-a* is a semantic auxiliary expressing "non-finiteness and semantic connection . . . primarily looking forward to the finite verb." See McAlpin 1981:80 (cf. 71); in general, Khačikjan 1998:50–51.

It is probable that *-a* is determinative-relative through Middle Elamite and probably later. That *-a* is always subordinating and only subordinating in Achaemenid is less well grounded. Counterexamples for all proposals occur, notably many Achaemenid Elamite administrative texts in which all verbs are marked with *-a* (see also Tucker 1998:165, n. 2, noting Achaemenid Elamite leveling in the distribution of *-a*).

4.5.4.2 *The suffix -ti ∼ -ta*

Disagreement also prevails over the characterization of a suffix *-ti* (and *-t(i)* + *-a* > *-ta*) found on verbs of all periods. It appears mostly on third-person forms of Conjugation I (Middle Elamite [kuši-š-t-a], Achaemenid Elamite [hutta-š-t-a]), rarely on other forms (Achaemenid Elamite Conjugation II second person [huttu-k-t-a]). In Middle Elamite, forms with *-ti* ∼ *-ta* often occur in subordinate clauses; in Achaemenid royal inscriptions, they occur only in subordinate clauses; in Achaemenid administrative texts they often occur at the ends of texts.

The suffix *-ti* ∼ *-ta* is characterized by some as marking finality or completeness (Hallock 1959:6–7; McAlpin 1981:71); by others as marking past time, translatable with perfect or pluperfect tenses (Hinz and Koch 1987 *passim*), most often distant past time, anteriority with respect to another verb (Grillot-Susini and Roche 1987:33; Vallat 1994:272). Most passages can be plausibly translated with past tenses that indicate anteriority: Middle Elamite [akka kukši-š-t-a imma durna-h] "I do not know [the former kings] who had built it [the temple]"; Achaemenid Elamite [akka Makuš šari-š-t-a] "[I rebuilt the temples] which the Magian had destroyed." Khačikjan 1998:53 suggests historical development in the function of *-ti* ∼ *-ta* from a nominalizing clitic (after Labat 1951:38 and Paper 1955:49), made obsolete as the system of marking nouns for gender and person became less articulated, to a completive and/or pluperfect marker.

4.6 Adverbs

Some Achaemenid phrasal adverbs are formed with nouns and postpositions (see §5.1.1): *da'e* "other" > [daʔe-ikki] "differently"; *irša-* "big" > [irše-ikki] "much, many"; *šit-* "night," *na-* "day" > [šit-ma-na na-ma-na] "by night, by day," /nan-na/ "daily"; [hi-ma] "here," [hupe-ma] "there," [hupe-ma-mar] "from there." Dimensional elements provide the heads of other derived adverbs: Neo-Elamite [ukku-mi-na] "above"; [pat-mi-na] "below"; Achaemenid Elamite [me-ni] ~ [me-mi] "then"; [me-ša, meššì-n, me-šamerašae] "afterward." Others with a derivational suffix *-ta* have doublets without *-ta*: Achaemenid Elamite [ha-me-r ~ ha-me-r-ta] "then, after that"; [hupi-me-r ~ hupi-me-r-ta] "then, after that"; [am ~ am-ta] "now"; [šašša ~ šašša-ta] "formerly." Others are derived from nouns with various formants (Middle Elamite [šut-ki-me šat-ki-me] "by night, by day"; Achaemenid Elamite [na-zirna, na-randa] "daily"), or from participles (Achaemenid Elamite [kappa-k-a] "together"; [zilla-k-a] or [šilla-k-a] "greatly, much"). Others are simply bare stems: Achaemenid Elamite *yani* "afterwards"; *zila* "thus," but usually phrasal *hi zila* "thus."

Achaemenid Elamite distributive constructions are formed with nouns or numerals, usually paired, marked with the postposition or derivational suffix *-na*: [10 ruhip-na ak 10 ruhip-na] "[1 sheep to be received] by each group of ten"; ^{d}ITI^{MEŠ}*-na* ^{d}ITI^{MEŠ}*-na* "[one unit of wine to be received] monthly," compare [kurtaš hupipe-na unra-na ^{d}ITI^{MEŠ}-na x duš-t-a] "136 of their workers received x [barley] each per month." The suffix is usual but optional: *ruh-ra ruh-ra* ^{d}ITI^{MEŠ}*-na* ^{d}ITI^{MEŠ}*-na* "each man, per month"; 5*-ip ak* 5*-ip* . . . 5*-ip ak* 5*-ip-na* . . . 5*-ip-na ak* 5*-ip-na* . . . 5*-ip-na* (all in a single text).

4.7 Interjections

A vocative interjection *e* appears in pre-Achaemenid Elamite: for example, *e DN* "o, DN!." In Achaemenid inscriptions, Old Persian vocative cases have no corresponding formant in the Elamite version: *ruhirra*, corresponding to the Old Persian vocative *martiyā* "o, man," though perhaps *malla e*, corresponding to the Old Persian vocative *marīkā* "o, subject."

4.8 Compounds

Compound nouns are of several constructions: (i) noun plus noun (*kik-murun* "sky-earth" > "world"); (ii) participle plus participle (*huttak-halik* "done-perfected" > "handiwork, accomplishment"); (iii) infinitive plus agent noun (*paha-hutip* "protect-doers" > "protective gods"); (iv) infinitive plus infinitive (*hutta-hali* "handiwork, accomplishment"). Compound verbs consist of a noun plus verb: *mur-ta-* "place-put" > "establish"; *kur-ma-* "hand-intend(?)" > "entrust" (see Grillot 1984:190 n. 25).

4.9 Numerals

Cardinal numerals may take nominal suffixes: [ki-r] "one," 1*-ir*, 2*-ip*, 3*-ip*, and so forth; [bel ki-ma] "in one year"; [ki-r x duš] "one (man) received x (grain)"; [1-ir šalu-r] "one gentleman," but *samidakurra ki* "one *samida*-maker" (all examples from Achaemenid Elamite).

In Achaemenid Elamite, ordinal numbers are usually followed by *-ummema* ~ *-ummena* ~ *-ummemana*, probably to be analyzed as including the nominal suffix *-me* and the postpositions *-ma* and *-na* (Hallock 1969:76). Less frequent variant forms are *-umme*, *-mema*, *-mena*, and *-memana*.

In Achaemenid Elamite, fractions are formed with a suffix *-irmaki* ~ *-kurmaki* (Cameron 1948:38f; Hallock 1969:73).

5. SYNTAX

5.1 Word order and typology

The subject of attention usually occurs in sentence-initial position. In Middle and Neo-Elamite, the verbal predicate is normally at the end, indirect objects precede direct objects, attributes and clauses follow the nouns they modify, resumptive pronouns and adverbs precede verbs, so the common sentence order is:

(12) Subject (+ modifier) – Indirect object (+ modifier) – Direct object (+ modifier) – Resumptive pronoun(s) – Adverb – Verb

As partially illustrated in the following example: [sian DN-me sunki-p uri-p-u-p(e) GN in-me kuši-hš(i)-me-a u GN kuši-h] "the temple of DN which kings who were before me did not build in Susa I built (at) the acropolis."

In Achaemenid Elamite the verb is often but not always final. Free and irregular word order does not always reflect translation from Old Persian: thus, [meni sunki-me hupi-r(ri) GN-(i)p-na hutta-š] "then the kingship he of the Elamites exercised" corresponds to Old Persian *haw xšāya ϑiya abava Ūjai* "he became king in Elam"; [ap dunu-k-a ^{SAL}MUNUS^{MEŠ} appa GN hami-ma-n-p(i) gal-ma] "[grain] to them was given, women who in GN were grinding(?), as rations."

Khačikjan 1993, 1998:63–66 reviews the discussion of ergativity in Elamite (Kammenhuber 1974:204; Steiner 1979, 1990: 151, 159; Wilhelm 1978, 1982; Diakonoff 1981), concluding that Elamite was "an early nominative language [i.e., based on a fundamental opposition of subject vs. object] that had retained some features typical of ergative [i.e., based on a fundamental opposition of agent vs. patient] languages."

5.1.1 Postpositions

Elamite is chiefly postpositional, though prepositions occur as well. In Achaemenid Elamite, spatial and temporal relationships are expressed with postpositions, either enclitic (*-ma* "in, on"; *-ikki* "to"; *-mar* ~ *-ikki-mar* "from"; *-lakka* "across") or separable ([hi da-k-a] > *idaka* "with"; [hat-i-ma] > *hatima* ~*hatuma* "within, throughout"; *tubaka* "concerning"; *tibba* "before(?)"). A preposition *kuš* "to(ward), until" occurs both in Middle Elamite and in Achaemenid Elamik: [kuš Purattu ir pari-h] "I went toward the Euphrates." (see §5.5.)

In pre-Achaemenid Elamite, postpositions per se are less numerous and less frequent. Locative *-ma* "in" and possessive *-na* "of" are common in Middle Elamite. Other postpositions are occasional in Neo-Elamite: *-ikki* "to" and perhaps *-tibba* "before" (perhaps adverbial; see Grillot-Susini and Roche 1987:29). Most spatial and temporal relationships in pre-Achaemenid Elamite are indicated by "directional words" combined with pronouns in postpositional constructions. The directional words originate either as nouns (*ukku* "head" > "on"; *pat* "foot, base" > "under"; *si* "face(?)" > "before"; *me* "(?)" > "after"), or as verbs (*li-* "give" > *lina* "for"; *tuk-* "(?)" > *tikka-* "for the sake of"). Two types of postpositional constructions occur, subject to different interpretations.

One analysis distinguishes postpositional constructions as governing internally and governing externally, or as long and short constructions. The long construction, governing internally, consists of (i) the *governing* noun or an anaphoric pronoun referring to the governing noun; (ii) the directional element with a nominal suffix (see §4.2.1) referring to the governing noun; (iii) a pronoun referring to the *governed* noun plus a nominal suffix again referring to the *governing* noun:

(13) A.

[i-r	pat-r	u-r	ta-t-ni]
him-ANIM. SG.	under-ANIM. SG.	me-ANIM. SG.	place-2ND PER.-OPT.

"May you place him under me"

B.

[RN	ukku-r	i-r	murta-n]
RN	over-ANIM. SG.	it-ANIM. SG.	put in place-IMPERF.

"Establishing RN over it"

The short construction, governing externally, consists of (i) the governed noun, (ii) an anaphoric pronoun referring to the *governing* noun with a nominal suffix marking concord with the *governed* noun, and (iii) the dimensional element with a nominal suffix again referring to the *governing* noun, and usually with determinative or subordinating *-a* (see Grillot 1983; Grillot-Susini and Roche 1987:27–28):

(14)

[DN	i-r	šara-r-a	ani	uzzu-n]
DN	he-ANIM. SG.	beneath-ANIM. SG.-SUBORD.	NEG. WISH	go about-IMPERF.

"May he not go about(?) beneath the Sun God"

Another analysis distinguishes constructions in which the governed word is a *substantive* from constructions in which the governed word is a *pronoun*. In the first (corresponding to the short, external construction), (i) the relationship between the governing element and the governed substantive is unmarked, and (ii) the governed noun (*napi-r*) is followed by a resumptive pronoun referring to the governing element ($i = zalmu$) and by (iii) a dimensional element with nominal suffix referring to the governing element:

(15)

[zalmu . . .	DN	napi-r	u-r(i)	i	sima-Ø	ta-h]
statue	DN	god-ANIM. SG.	me-ANIM. SG.	it	before-INAN.	place-1ST PER.

"The statue, I placed it before my god, DN"

In the second (corresponding to the long, internal construction), (i) the governing noun or an anaphoric pronoun referring to it is followed by (ii) the directional element with a nominal suffix referring to the governing noun and (iii) a personal pronoun indicating the governed noun (Khačikjan 1998:45–47):

(16)

[peti-p	pat-p	u	p-rabba-k-na]
be hostile-ANIM. PL.	under-ANIM. PL.	me	ANIM. PL.-bind-PERFV.-OPT.

"May enemies be bound beneath me"

These same constructions sometimes appear in Achaemenid Elamite:

(17) A. [sunki-r murun hi ukku-r(i)]
king-ANIM. SG. earth this on-ANIM. SG.
"King on this earth"

B. [PN... me-r(i) i-r ta-k-a sa-k]
PN after-ANIM. SG. he-ANIM. SG. put-PERF.-REL./CONNEC. go-PERF.
"He got under way(?) after PN"

Note the phrasal adverb [i-n tukki-me], a long construction corresponding to the Middle Elamite short construction [i-n-tikka], both "for the sake of it, therefore."

5.2 Agreement

A distinctive feature of Elamite syntax is "bracketing" (Bork 1933–1934), in which nominal suffixes that identify gender and person mark the constituents of possessive and attributive constructions and subordinate clauses (see §4.2.1).

In possessive and attributive constructions, the suffixes appropriate to the possessor or the determined substantive are added to the possessed or attribute; consider the following Middle Elamite examples:

(18) A. [u PN šak PN_2-k(i) sunki-k GN-GN_2-k-a]
"I, PN, son of PN_2, king of GN (and) GN_2"
with first-person suffixes throughout

B. [PN meni-r GN-r ak GN_2-r(i) šak-Ø hanik-Ø PN_2-r(i) ak PN_3-r(i)]
"He, PN, ruler(?) of GN and GN_2 beloved son of PN_2 and PN_3"
with third-person suffixes throughout

The last noun in a sequence is always marked, but not all elements in the series are necessarily marked (in [18B] [hani-k], Conjugation II participle, not *[hani-k-r]). The suffix on the final element is sometimes doubled, without apparent change of meaning: [u PN šak PN_2-**ki-k** liba-k hanik-Ø DN-**ki-k**]; see Grillot 1978:6, suggesting that the final *-k* marks the end of the clause, Grillot-Susini and Roche 1987:24, suggesting that the first suffix marks agreement and the second marks determinacy.

A single noun may govern more than one possessor: thus, [puhu kuši-k u-p(e) ak PN-p(e)] "children born of me and PN."

5.2.1 Other possessive and attributive constructions

For kinship terms in possessive and attributive constructions see §4.2.3. In Neo-Elamite and Achaemenid Elamite, kinship expressions sometimes invert the word order that is usual in Middle Elamite inscriptions: [^{f}PN PN_2 riti-r(i)], "^{f}PN, PN_2's wife"; [PN PN_2 šak-r(i)], "PN, PN_2's son." Since the inverted construction is already occasional in Middle Elamite ([lika-me riša-r(i)] "enlarger of the realm"), its later use is probably not a calque on Old Persian. The construction may reflect the syncopation of a resumptive pronoun: [šak (i)-r], [riti (i)-r] (Hallock 1962:54, Grillot-Susini and Roche 1987:23).

In Neo-Elamite, descent is also expressed PN *šak* PN_2*-na*. The postposition *-na* (probably to be analyzed as the neutral inanimate *-n* + *-a*), sometimes expresses possession or other qualification in Middle Elamite: *erentum-na* ~ *erentum-ma* ~ *erentum-ia* "[made] of baked brick." In Achaemenid Elamite most possession and some attributive relationships are expressed by the (so-called) genitive *-na*: Neo-Elamite *zalmu* PN-*na* "image of PN"; Achaemenid Elamite *halmi* PN-*na* "seal[ed document] of PN." Occasional inversion of the word order in Achaemenid Elamite is probably a calque on Old Iranian: PN-*na miyatukka* "viaticum of (= issued by) PN"; [hupirri-na gal-ma] "as his rations."

5.3 Resumptive pronoun-verb constructions

Verbs of Conjugation I are often preceded by one, two, or three resumptive pronouns that refer to the arguments of the verb. In Middle Elamite, pronouns that refer to logical indirect object, subject, and/or direct object of the clause regularly appear in that order; they may be contracted in writing, and some or all pronouns may be omitted: [ap u in (written *a-pu-un*) duni-h] "to them I gave it," with variant [ap u (written *a-pu ú*) duni-h] "to them I gave" (see Grillot 1978:31; Grillot-Susini and Roche 1987:18, 39). In Achaemenid Elamite, pairs or groups of resumptive pronouns do not occur before Conjugation I verbs. Single resumptive pronouns refer to subjects or objects: PN... *sunkime hupirri marriš* "PN, he seized the kingship"; *u* PN... *ir halpi* "I, PN, him I killed"; *u* DN *un nuškišni* "I–may DN protect me."

Verb forms of Conjugation II and Conjugation III are often but not always preceded by resumptive pronouns: (V)*n* for the first and second persons, (V)*r* and (V)*p* for third-person animates. The same pronominal forms that mark the objects of transitive Conjugation I verbs thus mark the agents of Conjugation II and III forms (in a typically ergatival fashion): Neo-Elamite [anu i n (written *in*) kuti-n-k(i)] "I will truly not support(?) him"; Middle Elamite [nu u n (written *un*) tahha-n-t-a] "[O DN] you command[?] me"; [u r (written *ur*) tahha-n-r-a] "he [DN] commands(?) me"; Neo-Elamite [u ip tahha-n-p-a] "they [DN and DN_2] command(?) me"; Achaemenid Elamite [GN-ikki ir pari-k] "he arrived at GN," but [anu u ir (not *ip) turna-n-p(i)] "lest they(!) know me"; [hi zila ap (i)r titu-k-a] "thus he lied to them," but [hi zila titu-k-a] "thus he lied" (see Khačikjan 1998:35 and 65, Grillot-Susini and Roche 1987:35; cf. Malbran-Labat 1990 and Grillot 1978:19, 25. Grillot (1978:20–21), however, demurs, taking (V)*r*- and (V)*p*- as vestigial elements referring to the agent, but (V)*n* as marking the logical object).

In Achaemenid Elamite, indirect objects of verbs of all conjugations are regularly expressed with resumptive pronouns (Hallock 1969:9).

5.4 Coordination

The conjunction *ak* (usually spelled *a-ak*, sometimes *a-gi*, *ia-ak*), meaning both "and" and "or," connects (i) words or (ii) clauses. Consider the following Middle Elamite examples:

(19) A. [siyan DN ak DN_2-me]
"Temple of DN and DN_2"

B. [sunki-r peti-r ak tari-r akka melka-n-r-a... ak lansit-e du-n-r-a ak hiš RN sukuš a-ak (written *su-ku-ša-ak*) i-m-e-ni aha-r ta-n-r-a]
"A king, enemy or ally, who destroys [the temple] or takes its gold or erases the name of RN and puts his own there"

In Achaemenid Elamite inscriptions, it also introduces a new paragraph: [ak RN sunki-r na-n-r] "and RN the king declares," where the Old Persian and Akkadian versions have no conjunction.

Another conjunction, *kudda* "and" occurs in Achaemenid Elamite, sometimes coupled with *ak*: *kudda Paršip ak kudda Madabe ak kudda dayauš appa dae* "Persia and Media and the other countries." A possible Neo-Elamite occurrence of *kudda* raises doubt about the suggestion that *kudda* is not an Elamite word but a graphic device meant to indicate that "and," written in Elamite as *ak*, was to be read out in Old Persian as *utā* (Gershevitch 1979:132; Zadok 1995:243). In one inscription Elamite *utta* transcribes Old Persian *utā* "and."

Coordinate clauses are thus connected with *ak*; in Achaemenid Elamite also with *kudda*; or asyndetically. In pairs of closely coordinated verbs, suffixes on the second verb may apply to both verbs (without a conjunction): thus, Middle Elamite [e DN hutta-t u-n duni-t-ni] "O, DN, may you do [and] give me"; and so with participles, [hutta-k hali-k-u-me] "what I made and finished(?)."

5.5 Subordination

Achaemenid Elamite uses subordinating conjunctions, including (i) simple conjunctions (*anka* "if, when"; *kuš* "until" (also prepositional "to(ward)"); *sap* "as, when"); (ii) phrasal conjunctions (*sap innu* "as long as"; *meni sap anka* "after"); and (iii) phrasal conjuctions with the relative *appa*, perhaps calques on Old Persian conjunctions compounded with relative *taya* (*appa anka* "as"; *sap appa* "when"). In pre-Achaemenid Elamite, *anka* appears once at the head of a clause ([anka ruri-n-a ak miši-ma-n-a] "if [the temple] . . . -s and becomes dilapidated"), and *kuš* appears only as a preposition.

Most subordinate clauses precede the verb of the main clause. In Achaemenid Elamite, purpose clauses governed by *šera*, "order," are formed with infinitives of Conjugation III with auxiliary *-ma-* and follow the governing verb: *meni u šera* DUB^{MEŠ} *tallimana* "then I ordered an inscription to be written" (Grillot 1973:155–162; Grillot and Vallat 1975:215; Grillot-Susini and Roche 1987:41).

Since Achaemenid Elamite verb forms marked with *-ta* are often final, a correlate of the view that *-ta* marks anteriority is the supposition that temporal clauses referring to anterior action often follow the clauses that refer to prior action: [du-š-a . . . hutta-š-t-a] "(barley) which he received, because he had previously done . . . " (see Vallat 1994:272–273).

5.6 Relative clauses

Elamite relative clauses may be introduced by the relative pronouns *akka* "who" or *appa* "which." The clause may follow its antecedent (e.g., Middle Elamite [sunki-r akka ta-š-t-a] [lit. "king-ANIM. SG. who he-has put"] "the king who set up [the stele]"), or the relative clause may occur without an expressed antecedent (e.g., Middle Elamite [akka ulhi i melka-n-r-a] [lit. "who house this he-destroys"] "he who destroys this house").

There is a another way, predominant in Middle Elamite, in which Elamite forms relative clauses. Attributive relative clauses may also be marked like other attributes, by adding nominal suffixes to the verb at the end of the clause. In Middle Elamite *-a* is often attached to the nominal suffix ([sian . . . in-me kuši-hš(i)-me-a] "the temple that they had not built"), but the presence of *-a* is optional ([lika-me i-r hani-š-r(i)] "whose realm DN loves," Grillot 1978:11). In Neo- and Achaemenid Elamite examples, *-a* attaches to the verb form before the nominal suffix: Neo-Elamite [6-(i)p ANŠE.KUR.RA^{MEŠ} tukka-š-t-a-p(e)] "six people who fed(?) horses"; Achaemenid Elamite [6 MUNUS^{MEŠ}-na kuši-š-t-a-p(e)] "six [women] who gave birth to girls"). In Middle Elamite, a relative pronoun can optionally (pleonastically) occur at the head of such clauses ([sian appa (variant omits *appa*) kuši-h-me-a] "the temple that I built"); no Neo-Elamite or Achaemenid Elamite examples combine this construction with a relative pronoun. See Grillot 1978:8–15; Grillot-Susini and Roche 1987:24, 41;

Khačikjan 1998:59–60; Hallock 1969:37, 1978:115, 1973:149 (the last-mentioned demurs on Middle Elamite examples).

The occurrence of these two types of relative constructions varies over time. In Achaemenid Elamite, use of the relative pronoun is regular, but it is uncommon in Middle Elamite. Conversely, the nominal construction of relative clauses (with *-a*) is common in Middle Elamite but rare in Achaemenid (and Neo-) Elamite.

5.7 Direct discourse

The close of a quoted statement is indicated by a form of *ma-*, probably identical with the verbal auxiliary *ma-*, with suffixes in agreement with the speaker: *manka* (Conjugation III first-person singular), *mara* ~ *mar* and *mapa* (animate singular and plural agent nouns) and *maka* (passive participle, impersonal).

In Achaemenid Elamite, a verb that indicates speaking (*turu-* ~ *tiri-* "tell, speak"; *na-* "say") usually introduces the quoted statement:

(20) A. [hi zila ap tiriya mite-š . . . halpi-š ma-n-k-a]
"I told them thus, 'Go, defeat (the enemy)' "
B. [na-n-ri PN šera-š ma-r-a]
"He said 'PN gave the order' "

In Neo-Elamite, verbs of speaking sometimes follow the quoted statement plus *ma-*:

(21) A. [ir unsa-h-a mara tiri-n-r-a]
"[PN] who says 'I made an exchange(?) with him' "
B. [akka zalmu . . . in-k(i) in-dunu-n-k(u) mar turu-n-r-a]
"He who says 'I will not give the statue' "

The verb of speaking in such constructions may, however, be omitted.

Neo-Elamite and Achaemenid Elamite letters begin with verbs of speaking, introducing the body of the letter as quoted matter to be spoken to the addressee:

(22) [PN turu-š PN_2 na-n turu-š]
"Tell PN [the addressee], PN_2 [the sender] speaks, saying"

Mara and *mapa* are not added at the end of the letter, where the end of direct speech is self-identifying (but cf. *u nun turriya nanki . . . hupirri mušin huttanra manka* "I spoke to you, saying ' . . . He will do the accounting,' " apparently quoting from a previous letter).

6. LEXICON

Without a body of bilingual texts, an indigenous scholarly tradition, or a well-known language that is closely related to Elamite, few pre-Achaemenid Elamite words can be translated with precision and many can be translated only with guesses. The geographical and chronological distribution of the lexicon has not yet been analyzed. A comprehensive collection of parsed forms, useful for problems in Elamite grammar, has not been made (Zadok 1995:243).

Elamite words in Akkadian texts from southwestern Iran, where Elamite was also spoken and where it was often the language of the rulers, include titles of officials, names of professions, and words for realia (in legal and administrative texts), and architectural terms and titles or kinship terms (in dedicatory inscriptions). Elamite words in Akkadian texts from

Mesopotamia include titles and terms describing people in or from Elam and a small number of common nouns that may be actual loanwords. A few other Elamite nouns are identified and glossed in Mesopotamian lexical texts (Zadok 1995:244–245; Vallat 1998; Stolper 1978). Elamite words appear in personal names, often of people identified as Elamites, in Sumerian and Akkadian texts of many periods (Zadok 1984, 1991). *Kam/bnaskires*, the name or sobriquet of rulers in Parthian Elymais, is probably the survival of an Elamite title, *kapnuškir*, "treasurer" (Alram 1986:139–153, Stolper 2000:287).

Akkadian words in pre-Achaemenid Elamite building inscriptions are mostly proper nouns, including names of places and buildings (*alumelu* ~ *alimeli* "acropolis," *abul mišari* "gate of justice"), epithets of gods and rulers (*melki ilani* "king(s) of the gods"), and names of votive objects (*nur kibrati* "light of the world"). Possible Sumerian or Akkadian words for materials or objects in administrative texts may be *Kulturwörter* or Akkadograms (written as Akkadian but read as Elamite): Middle or Neo-Elamite *zabar* "copper or bronze," *anaku* "tin," *kušuru* "beam," Achaemenid Elamite *paru* "mule," *basbas* "duck" (Stolper 1984:21–22).

Achaemenid Elamite inscriptions contain transcriptions of Old Iranian words, not always representing forms identical to those used in the corresponding Old Persian texts: for example, Elamite *miššadanašpena*, transcribing Old Persian **visadanānām*, where the Old Persian text has the non-Persian form *vispazanānām*, "of all kinds" (genitive plural). Transcribed Iranian words include terms with specific cultural nuance (*irdama* corresponding to Old Persian *artāvā* "blessed [in death]"), and occasional common words and particles (enclitic *-aham*, *-me* corresponding to Old Persian *āham* "I was," *-mai* "my"). Achaemenid Elamite administrative texts include transcriptions of hundreds of Iranian words, many unattested in Old Iranian (e.g., *miyatukka* < Iranian **viyātika-* "authorization, viaticum"), some also found as loanwords in Achaemenid texts in other languages (*kanzabarra* < Iranian **ganzabara-* "treasurer," Akkadian *ganzabaru*, Aramaic *gzbr* and *gnzbr*, etc.; see Hinz 1975b). The Elamite transcriptions represent both Persian and non-Persian Iranian forms (*misapušša*, *miššaputra* corresponding to Persian **viϑapuça-*, non-Persian **visapuϑra-*, "prince"). For those who hold that Achaemenid Elamite texts are not translations, but Elamographic transcriptions of texts that are dictated in Iranian and read out in Iranian, these forms are not foreign words or loanwords but explicit writings of the underlying text (Gershevitch 1979).

7. READING LIST

Hinz and Koch 1987:133–168 offers comprehensive bibliography of works on Elamite texts, language, and history published between 1711 and 1986, arranged chronologically. Later items are listed in the journals *Abstracta Iranica*, *Archiv für Orientforschung*, and *Orientalia*.

Potts 1999 surveys current knowledge of the archeology and history of Elam from prehistory to the Islamic conquest. A short current survey of Elamite history is Vallat 1997a (but many contemporary historians of the ancient Near East will hesitate over the geographical framework). An encyclopedic survey of Susa in Elamite and Iranian history is Steve *et al.* 2002. Longer surveys, including Cameron 1936, Hinz 1965, 1972–1973, and Carter and Stolper 1984, are out of date.

A current survey of Elamite grammar is Khačikjan 1998. Among earlier surveys, Labat 1951, Reiner 1969, and Grillot-Susini and Roche 1987 represent successive generations of a school that gives greatest prominence to Middle Elamite evidence; Paper 1955 and Hallock 1959, 1965, 1969:8–10 are explicitly confined to Achaemenid Elamite; McAlpin 1981:63–83 includes separate parallel treatments of Achaemenid and Middle Elamite as a basis for systematic comparison with Proto-Dravidian.

The lexicon Hinz and Koch 1987 covers texts of all periods, including proper names and Elamite words in non-Elamite texts, and includes a survey of published treatments of many entries. Hallock 1969:664–776 is a nearly complete glossary of Achaemenid Elamite. Elamite personal names are collected in Zadok 1984, Elamite place names in Vallat 1993.

Useful transcriptions and editions of most pre-Achaemenid Elamite royal inscriptions are in König 1965. Other collections of Elamite inscriptions are Steve 1967 (Middle Elamite texts from Chogha Zanbil), 1987 (pre-Achaemenid and Achaemenid inscriptions from Susa), and Malbran-Labat 1995 (pre-Achaemenid building inscriptions from Susa).

The synoptic edition of Achaemenid Elamite multilingual texts of Weissbach 1911 is dated but not replaced. A recent edition of the longest Achaemenid Elamite royal inscription, at the monument of Darius I at Bisitun, is Grillot-Susini, Herrenschmidt, and Malbran-Labat 1993. A compendium of the Elamite versions of the Achaemenid inscriptions is to appear in the *Corpus Inscriptionum Iranicarum*. Editions of Achaemenid Elamite administrative texts from Persepolis are Cameron 1948 and Hallock 1969, 1978. All translations of Elamite texts merit reading with some reservation.

Bibliography

Alram, M. 1986. *Nomina Propria Iranica in Nummis*. Iranisches Personennamenbuch, IV. Vienna: Österreichische Akademie der Wissenschaften.

André, B. and M. Salvini. 1989. "Réflexions sur Puzur-Šušinak." *Iranica Antiqua* 24:53–72.

Baššāš-e Kanzaq, R. 1997. "Šarḥ-e čahār mōred az katībehā-ye manqūr bar ašiyā-ye ğār-e Kalmākare." In *Yādnāme-ye gerdehamāʾēīye bāstān-šenāsī–Šūš*, vol. I, pp. 13–22. Tehran: Sāzmān-e Mīrāš-e Farhangī-ye Kešvar (National Organization of Cultural Heritage).

Bleibtreu, E. 1999. "Ein vergoldeter Silberbecher Assurbanipals (668–627)." In W. Seipel (ed.), *Schätze des Orients. Meisterwerke aus dem Miho Museum. Kunsthistorisches Museum Wien, 22 Juni–31 Okt. 1999*, pp. 21–30, 54–56. Vienna(?): SKIRA.

Bork, F. 1925. "Elam, B. Sprache." In M. Ebert (ed.), *Reallexikon der Vorgeschichte*, vol. III, pp. 70–83. Berlin: Walter de Gruyter.

———. 1933–1934. "Die elamische Klammer." *Archiv für Orientforschung* 9:292–300.

Brice, W. 1962–1963. "The writing system of the Proto-Elamite account tablets of Susa". *Bulletin of the John Rylands Library* 45:15–39.

Cameron, G. 1936. *History of Early Iran*. Chicago: University of Chicago Press.

———. 1948. *Persepolis Treasury Tablets*. Oriental Institute Publications 65. Chicago: University of Chicago Press.

Carter, E. and M. Stolper. 1984. *Elam: Surveys of Political History and Archaeology*. Near Eastern Studies 25. Berkeley/Los Angeles: University of California Press.

Caubet, A. 1995. "Acquisitions: Moyen orient ancien, Musée du Louvre, Département des Antiquités Orientales, 1: Gobelet." *Revue du Louvre* 4:81.

Civil, M. 1985. "Sur les 'livres d'écolier' à l'époque paléo-babylonienne." In J.-M. Durand and J.-R. Kupper (eds.), *Miscellanea babylonica, mélanges offerts à Maurice Birot*, pp. 67–78. Paris: Editions Recherche sur les Civilisations.

Damerow, P. and R. Englund. 1989. *The Proto-Elamite Texts from Tepe Yahya*. American School of Prehistoric Research, Bulletin 39. Cambridge, MA: Peabody Museum of Archaeology and Ethnology.

De Maaijer, R. 1996. "Recently acquired cuneiform texts." *Oudheidkundige Mededelingen uit het Rijksmuseum van Oudheden te Leiden* 76:69–84.

Diakonoff, I. 1973. "Bemerkungen zu einer neuen Darstellung altkleinasiatischer Sprachen." *Orientalistische Literaturzeitung* 68:14–16.

———. 1981. "Ist das Elamische eine Ergativsprache?" *Archäologische Mitteilungen aus Iran* NS 14:7–8.

Dijk, J. van, A. Goetze, and M. Hussey. 1985. *Early Mesopotamian Incantations and Rituals.* Yale Oriental Series, Babylonian Texts 11. New Haven/London: Yale University Press.
Donbaz, V. 1996. "A median (?) votive inscription on silver vessel." *Nouvelles Assyriologiques Brèves et Utilitaires* 1996, no. 43.
Englund, R. 1996. "The Proto-Elamite script." In P. Daniels and W. Bright (eds.), *The World's Writing Systems*, pp. 160–164. Oxford and New York: Oxford University Press.
_______. 1998. "Elam, iii. Proto-Elamite." In *Encyclopaedia Iranica*, vol. VIII, fascicle 3, pp. 325–330. Costa Mesa, CA: Mazda.
Friberg, J. 1978–1979. *The Third Millennium Roots of Babylonian Mathematics, I. A Method for the Decipherment, through Mathematical and Metrological Analysis, of Proto-Sumerian and Proto-Elamite Semi-Pictographic Inscriptions.* Göteborg, Sweden: Chalmers University of Technology and University of Göteborg.
Gadd, C., L. Legrain, S. Smith, *et al.* 1928. *Royal Inscriptions.* Ur Excavations, Texts, 1. Publications of the Joint Expedition of the British Museum and of the Museum of the University of Pennsylvania to Mesopotamia. London: British Museum.
Garrison, M. 1996. "A Persepolis Fortification seal on the tablet MDP 11 308 (Louvre Sb 13078)." *Journal of Near Eastern Studies* 55:15–35.
Garrison, M. and M. Root. 2001. *Seals on the Persepolrs Fortification Tablets*, I: *Images of Heroic Encounter.* Oriental Institute Publications 117. Chicago: Oriental Institute.
Gershevitch, I. 1979. "The alloglottography of Old Persian." *Transactions of the Philological Society of London*, pp. 114–190.
Giovinazzo, G. 1989. "L'expresssion '*ha duš ha duka*' dans les textes de Persépolis." *Akkadica* 63:12–26.
Grillot, F. 1970. "A propos de la notion de subordination dans la syntaxe élamite." *Journal Asiatique* 258:213–241.
_______. 1973. "La postposition génitive *-na* en élamite." *Cahiers de la Délégation Archéologique Française en Iran* 3:113–169.
_______. 1974. "A propos du verbe moyen élamite." *Journal Asiatique* 262:31–35.
_______. 1978. "Les affixes nominaux et les pronoms indépendants de la langue élamite." *Journal Asiatique* 266:1–35.
_______. 1983. "Le mécanisme des groupes nominaux en élamite." *Journal Asiatique* 271:207–218.
_______. 1984. "Trinôme de la royauté en Élam." *Studia Iranica* 13:185–191.
Grillot, F. and F. Vallat. 1975. "Le semi-auxiliaire *ma-* en élamite." *Journal Asiatique* 263:211–217.
Grillot-Susini (= Grillot), F. 1994. "Une nouvelle approche de la morphologie élamite: racines, bases et familles de mots." *Journal Asiatique* 282:1–18.
_______. 1998. "Elam, v. Elamite language." In *Encyclopaedia Iranica*, vol. VIII, fascicle 3, pp. 332–335. Costa Mesa, CA: Mazda.
Grillot-Susini, F. and C. Roche. 1987. *Éléments de grammaire élamite.* Paris: Editions Recherche sur les Civilisations.
Grillot-Susini, F., C. Herrenschmidt, and F. Malbran-Labat. 1993. "La version élamite de la trilingue de Behistun: une nouvelle lecture." *Journal Asiatique* 281:19–59.
Hallock, R. 1958. "Notes on Achaemenid Elamite." *Journal of Near Eastern Studies* 17:256–262.
_______. 1959. "The finite verb in Achaemenid Elamite." *Journal of Near Eastern Studies* 18:1–19.
_______. 1962. "The pronominal suffixes in Achaemenid Elamite." *Journal of Near Eastern Studies* 21:53–56.
_______. 1965. "The verbal nouns in Achaemenid Elamite." In *Studies in Honor of Benno Landsberger on his Seventy-Fifth Birthday, April 21, 1965*, pp. 121–125. Assyriological Studies 16. Chicago: University of Chicago Press.
_______. 1969. *Persepolis Fortification Tablets.* Oriental Institute Publications 92. Chicago: University of Chicago Press.
_______. 1973. "On the Middle Elamite verb." *Journal of Near Eastern Studies* 32:148–151.
_______. 1978. "Selected fortification texts." *Cahiers de la Délégation Archéologique Française en Iran* 8:109–136.
Helms, S. 1982. "Excavations at 'The city and the famous fortress of Kandahar, the foremost place in all of Asia'." *Afghan Studies* 3–4:1–24.
_______. 1997. *Excavations at Old Kandahar in Afghanistan 1976–1978.* Society for South Asian Studies Monograph 2. BAR International Series 686. Oxford: Archaeopress.

Henkelman, W. Forthcoming. "Persians, Medes and Elamites, Acculturation in the Neo-Elamite Period." In G. Lanfranchi (ed.), *Continuity of Empire: Assyria, Media, Persia.*

Hinz, W. 1965. *Das Reich Elam.* Stuttgart: Kohlhammer.

———. 1969. *Altiranische Funde und Forschungen.* Berlin: Walter de Gruyter.

———. 1972–1973. *The Lost World of Elam.* Translated by Jennifer Barnes. London: Sidgwick and Jackson, 1972; New York: New York University Press, 1973 (= translation of Hinz 1965).

———. 1975a. "Problems of Linear Elamite." *Journal of the Royal Asiatic Society* 2:105–115.

———. 1975b. *Altiranisches Sprachgut der Nebenüberlieferungen.* Göttinger Orientforschung, III. Reihe (Iranica) 3. Wiesbaden: Otto Harrassowitz.

Hinz, W. and H. Koch. 1987. *Elamisches Wörterbuch.* Archäologische Mitteilungen aus Iran, Ergänzungsband 17. Berlin: Dietrich Reimer.

Justeson, J. and L. Stephens. 1994. "Variation and change in symbol systems: case studies in Elamite cuneiform." In C. Renfrew and E. Zubrow (eds.), *The Ancient Mind, Elements of Cognitive Archaeology*, pp. 167–175. Cambridge: Cambridge University Press.

Kammenhuber, A. 1974. "Historisch-geographische Nachrichten aus der althurrischen Überlieferung, dem Altelamischen und den Inschriften der Königen von Akkad für die Zeit vor dem Einfall der Gutäer (ca. 2200/2136)." *Acta Antiqua Academiae Scientiarum Hungaricae* 22:157–248.

Khačikjan, M. 1993. "To the typological characteristics of the Elamite language." In J. Zablocka and S. Zawadski (eds.), *Šulmu IV: Everday Life in the Ancient Near East*, pp. 143–150. Adam Mickiewicz University, Seria Historia 182. Poznan.

———. 1995. "Notes on the Elamite phonology." *Studi micenei ed egeo-anatolici* 35:105–109.

———. 1998. *The Elamite Language.* Documenta Asiana 4. Rome: Istituto per gli studi micenei ed egeo-anatolici.

König, F. 1965. *Die elamischen Königsinschriften.* Archiv für Orientforschung Beiheft 16. Graz.

Labat, R. 1951. "Structure de la langue élamite (état présent de la question)." *Conférences de l'Institut de Linguistique de Paris* 9:23–42.

Lackenbacher, S. 1998. "Elam, vii. Non-Elamite Texts in Elam." In *Encyclopaedia Iranica*, vol. VIII, fascicle 4, pp. 342–344. Costa Mesa, CA: Mazda.

Malbran-Labat, F. 1986. "Le «semi-auxiliaire» élamite *-ma*. Une nouvelle approche: essai de définition d'un champ sémantique." *Bulletin de la Société de Linguistique de Paris* 81:253–273.

———. 1990. "Système pronominale et système verbal en élamite achéménide." *Bulletin de la Société de Linguistique de Paris* 85:61–90.

———. 1995. *Les inscriptions royales de Suse.* Paris: Editions de la Réunion des musées nationaux.

Mayrhofer, M. 1973. *Onomastica Persepolitana. Das altiranische Namengut der Persepolis-Täfelchen.* Vienna: Österreichische Akademie der Wissenschaften.

McAlpin, D. 1981. *Proto-Elamo-Dravidian: The Evidence and its Implications* (= *Transactions of the American Philosophical Society* 71, part 3).

Meriggi, P. 1971–1974. *La scrittura proto-elamica* (I: *La scrittura e il contenuto dei testi*, 1971. II: *Catalogo dei segni*, 1974. III: *Testi*, 1974). Rome: Accademia Nazionale dei Lincei.

Paper, H. 1955. *The Phonology and Morphology of Royal Achaemenid Elamite.* Ann Arbor, MI: University of Michigan Press.

Potts, D. 1999. *The Archaeology of Elam: Formation and Transformation of an Ancient Iranian State.* Cambridge World Archaeology. Cambridge: Cambridge University Press.

Reiner, E. 1960. "Calques sur le vieux-perse en élamite." *Bulletin de la Société de Linguistique de Paris* 55:222–227.

———. 1969. "The Elamite language." In B. Spuler (ed.), *Altkleinasiatische Sprache.* pp. 54–118. Handbuch der Orientalistik, Leiden/Köln: E. J. Brill.

———. 1992. "Elamite." In W. Bright (ed.), *International Encyclopedia of Linguistics*, pp. 406–409. Oxford: Oxford University Press.

Salvini, M. 1998. "Elam, iv. Linear Elamite." In *Encyclopaedia Iranica*, vol. VIII, fascicle 3, pp. 330–332. Costa Mesa, CA: Mazda.

Sayce, A. 1874. "The languages of the cuneiform inscriptions of Elam and Media." *Transactions of the Society of Biblical Archaeology* 3:465–485.

Scheil, V. 1939. *Mélanges épigraphiques. Mémoires de la mission archéologique de Perse*, 28. Paris: Ernest Leroux.

Steiner, G. 1979. "The intransitive-passival conception of the verb in the languages of the ancient Near East." In F. Plank (ed.), *Ergativity: Towards a Theory of Grammatical Relations*, pp. 185–216. London: Academic Press.

_______. 1990. "Sumerisch und Elamisch: typologische parallelen." *Acta Sumerologica* 12:143–176.

Steve, M.-J. 1967. *Textes élamites et accadiens de Tchoga Zanbil*. Tchoga Zanbil, III. Mémoires de la Délégation Archéologique en Iran 41. Paris: Paul Geuthner.

_______. 1987. *Nouveaux mélanges épigraphiques, inscriptions royales de Suse et de la Susiane*. Ville Royale de Suse 7. Mémoires de la Délégation Archéologique en Iran 53. Nice: Editions Serre.

_______. 1992. *Syllabaire élamite: histoire et paléographie*. Civilisations du Proche-Orient, Série II: Philologie, 1. Paris/Neuchâtel: Recherches et Publications.

Steve, M.-J. F. Vallat, and H. Gasche. 2002. "Suse." *Supplément au Dictionnaire de la Bible*. Paris: Letouzey & Are. Fasc. 78: 359–511.

Stolper, M. 1978. "Šarnuppu." *Zeitschrift für Assyriologie* 68: 261–269.

_______. 1984. *Texts from Tall-i Malyan 1: Elamite Administrative Texts (1972–1974)*. Occasional Publications of the Babylonian Fund 6. Philadelphia: University Museum.

_______. 2000. "Ganzabara." *Encyclopaedia Iranica* vol X, fasc. 3, pp. 286–288. Costa Mesa, CA: Mazda.

Tavernier, J. 2002. "Iranica in de Achaemenidische Periode." Ph.D. dissertation, Katholicke Universiteit Leuven, Dept. Oosterse en Stavische Studies.

Tucker, E. 1998. "The 'nominal conjugations' in Achaemenid Elamite." In M. Brosius and A. Kuhrt (eds.), *Studies in Persian History: Essays in Memory of David M. Lewis*, pp. 165–194. Achaemenid History 11. Leiden: Nederlands Instituut voor het Nabije Oosten.

Vallat, F. 1986. "The most ancient scripts of Iran: the current situation." *World Archaeology* 17:335–347.

_______. 1987a. "L'expression *da-ma da-ak* en élamite." *Nouvelles Assyriologiques Brèves et Utilitaires* 1987, no. 6.

_______. 1987b. "Le pseudo pronom personnel **kaš* en élamite achéménide." *Nouvelles Assyriologiques Brèves et Utilitaires* 1987, no. 114.

_______. 1989. "Les compléments phonétiques ou graphiques en élamite achéménide." *Annali* (Istituto Universitario Orientale di Napoli) 49:219–222.

_______. 1990. "Deux inscriptions royales en élamite de l'époque des Epartides (sukkalmah)." *Nouvelles Assyriologiques Brèves et Utilitaires* 1990, no. 137.

_______. 1993. *Les noms géographiques des sources suso-élamites*. Répertoire Géographique des Textes Cunéiformes, 11. Beiheft zum Tübinger Atlas des Vorderen Orients, Reihe B, Nr. 7/11. Wiesbaden: Dr. Ludwig Reichert.

_______. 1994. "Deux tablettes élamites de l'Université de Fribourg." *Journal of Near Eastern Studies* 53:263–274.

_______. 1996a. "Nouvelle analyse des inscriptions néo-élamites." In H. Gasche and B. Hrouda (eds.), *Collectanea orientalia: histoire, arts de l'espace et industrie de la terre, études offertes en hommage à Agnès Spycket*, pp. 385–395.

_______. 1996b. "Le royaume élamite de SAMATI." *Nouvelles Assyriologiques Brèves et Utilitaires* 1996, no. 31.

_______. 1996c. "L'Élam à l'époque paléo-babylonienne et ses relations avec la Mésopotamie." In *Amurru, 1: Mari, Ebla et les Hourrites*, pp. 297–319. Paris: Editions Recherche sur les Civilisations.

_______. 1997a. "Elam, I. The History of Elam." In *Encyclopaedia Iranica*, vol. VIII, fascicle 3, pp. 301–312. Costa Mesa, CA: Mazda.

_______. 1997b. "La lettre élamite d'Arménie." *Zeitschrift für Assyriologie* 87:258–270.

_______. 1998. "*hašša* et *kiparu*, deux termes élamites dans les textes accadiens de Suse." *Nouvelles Assyriologiques Brèves et Utilitaires* 1998, no. 127.

Van Soldt, W. 1982. "The cuneiform texts in the Rijksmuseum van Oudheden, Leiden (I)." *Ouheidkundige Mededelingen uit het Rijksmuseum van Oudheden te Leiden* 63:43–59.

_______. 1991. *Studies in the Akkadian of Ugarit: Dating and Grammar*. Alter Orient und Altes Testament 40. Kevelaer: Butzon and Bercker; Neukirchen-Vluyn: Neukirchener Verlag.

Weissbach, F. 1911. *Die Keilinschriften der Achämeniden*. Vorederasiatische Bibliothek 3. Leipzig: Hinrichs.

Wilhelm, G. 1978. "Ist das Elamische eine Ergativsprache?" *Archäologische Mitteilungen aus Iran* NS 11:7–12.

———. 1982. "Noch einmal zur behaupteten Ergativität des Elamischen." *Archäologische Mitteilungen aus Iran* NS 15: 7–8.

Zadok, R. 1984. *The Elamite Onomasticon* = Suppl. 40 to *Annali* (Istituto Universitario Orientale di Napoli) 44.

———. 1991. "Elamite onomastics." *Studi epigrafici e linguistici sul vicino oriente antico* 8:225–237.

———. 1995. "On the current state of Elamite lexicography." In *The Lexicography of the Ancient Near Eastern Languages* = *Studi epigrafici e linguistici sul vicino oriente antico* 12:241–252.

CHAPTER 4

Akkadian and Eblaite

JOHN HUEHNERGARD AND CHRISTOPHER WOODS

1. HISTORICAL AND CULTURAL CONTEXTS

1.1 Classification and dialects

Akkadian, the language of the ancient Babylonians and Assyrians, is the oldest known Semitic language and the most widely attested member of the eastern branch of the Semitic family – the other member being the closely related Eblaite, which is considered by many Assyriologists to be a dialect or subbranch of Akkadian. The name Akkadian (*akkadû*), used by the Babylonians and Assyrians themselves for their language, derives from the northern Babylonian city of *Akkad(e)*, the capital city built by Sargon in about 2300 BC. While it is not known when speakers of Akkadian, or of its linguistic predecessor(s), first arrived in Mesopotamia, Akkadian personal names first appear in Sumerian texts dated to about 2600 BC. Connected Akkadian texts appear *c.* 2350 and continue more or less uninterrupted for the next two and a half millennia, with the major text genres attested for most periods. Akkadian probably died as a spoken language in the middle of the first millennium BC when it was gradually replaced by Aramaic. However, Akkadian continued in use as a liturgical and learned language until the beginning of the current era; the latest positively dated Akkadian text comes from the first century AD. To date, nearly one million texts have been excavated, and with ongoing excavations in Iraq, Syria, and Turkey this number steadily increases. The majority of these texts remain unpublished.

As may be expected from the remarkably long life and wide distribution of Akkadian, numerous dialects and geographical variations can be identified. Traditionally, Assyriologists acknowledge eight major subphases or dialects which roughly correspond to the major political periods. However, within these often arbitrary divisions, further geographical and chronological distinctions can be delineated. The earliest such major subphase, *Old Akkadian*, the language spoken by the Sargonic kings, refers collectively to the texts from the earliest attestation of Akkadian (mid-third millennium) to the beginning of the second millennium. Owing to the relatively small size of the Old Akkadian corpus, many grammatical forms are thus far still unattested.

Contemporaneous with the date of Old Akkadian materials, *c.* 2400 BC, are the thousands of texts excavated at Ebla in northwest Syria. Although the majority of these texts were written in Sumerian, many were written in a Semitic language, referred to as *Eblaite*, which has striking similarities to Old Akkadian. Eblaite is attested in bilingual (Sumero-Eblaite) lexical texts, administrative documents, treaties, incantations, and several literary texts, some of which have parallel versions from the Mesopotamian sites of Abū Ṣalābīkh and Fara (Šuruppak). Eblaite is attested only for a few generations during the middle of the third millennium; thus, the historical development of the language cannot be traced.

The beginning of the second millennium marks a watershed in the development of Akkadian, after which the language is characterized by two broad geographical dialects, *Babylonian* in southern Mesopotamia and *Assyrian* in the north. The two are distinguished by several phonological differences, by minor morphological variations, and, to a limited extent, by lexicon. Significantly, some of the characteristic features (in the areas of phonology and morphology) of both the Assyrian and Babylonian dialects cannot be derived directly from the attested forms of Old Akkadian. Within the broad geographical dialects of Babylonian and Assyrian, chronological divisions of approximately five hundred years, labeled Old, Middle, and Neo-, are recognized for each:

(1)	Old Babylonian (OB)	2000–1500 BC	Old Assyrian (OA)
	Middle Babylonian (MB)	1500–1000 BC	Middle Assyrian (MA)
	Neo-Babylonian (NB)	1000–600 BC	Neo-Assyrian (NA)
	Late Babylonian (LB)	600 BC–AD 100	

Throughout the parallel development of Babylonian and Assyrian, the latter was always the more restricted dialect, limited primarily to Assyria proper. Even the Old Assyrian materials, which hail for the most part from eastern Anatolia (particularly from the site of Kaneš, modern Kültepe), represent primarily the business transactions of native Assyrian merchants residing in far-flung outposts in Anatolia. Babylonian was the more cosmopolitan of the two, reflecting Babylonia's perennial ascendancy in matters of culture, and it was not uncommon for even the Assyrian kings to adopt the Babylonian dialect when recording their inscriptions and annals.

Middle Assyrian is more sparsely attested than Old Assyrian, although it displays a variety of genres, including royal inscriptions, legal and economic texts, and an important collection of laws, the so-called Middle Assyrian laws. Neo-Assyrian is very well-preserved and was the language of Assyria under the important Sargonid dynasty until its fall in the latter half of the seventh century BC.

Old Babylonian is often considered by modern scholars as the classical phase of Akkadian, not only because of the remarkable uniformity of its grammar, but also because literature and scholarship flourished during this period. Old Babylonian is extremly well-preserved, and nearly all major text genres (discussed below) are attested for it. Indeed, the scribes of subsequent periods, in both Babylonia and Assyria, evidently regarded Old Babylonian as a classical language as well, as witnessed by the rise of *Standard Babylonian* (or *Jungbabylonisch*) – a contrived, nonspoken dialect of the first millennium which was based on archaic Old Babylonian features and used for the composition and transmission of literary works such as *Gilgameš* and *Enūma Eliš* as well as for many Assyrian and Babylonian royal inscriptions.

Middle Babylonian is much more sparsely attested than Old Babylonian and is known primarily from letters, economic texts, and a few royal inscriptions. Neo-Babylonian is well-preserved, especially in letters and economic texts written during the time of the short-lived Chaldean dynasty (625–539 BC) and the subsequent Persian occupation. Late Babylonian was written during the late Persian period and subsequent Seleucid occupation of Babylonia; it is heavily influenced by Aramaic, the spoken language of the time.

During the time of Middle Babylonian (particularly *c.* 1500–1200), Akkadian was used as a lingua franca throughout the ancient Near East. An archive of some 350 letters unearthed at Tell el-Amarna in Egypt records the diplomatic exchanges of the independent states of the ancient Near East, including Babylon, Assyria, Mittani, Hatti, Cyprus, and Egypt. Additionally, Akkadian archives have been found at Alalakh, Ugarit, and Emar in Syria, and

Hattuša in Anatolia, among other sites. The language of these texts, which were written by scribes who were not native Akkadian speakers, is frequently termed *Peripheral Akkadian* because of the heavy influence of the scribes' native tongues and its variance with normative Akkadian grammar.

The grammatical sketch of Akkadian presented here will be largely based on Old Babylonian, although important dialectal variations and diachronic developments will be noted.

1.2 Text genres

Akkadian is represented by an extremely wide variety of genres including both personal and court letters, royal inscriptions, annals, treaties, legal texts, law collections, such as the Old Babylonian Laws of Hammurabi, as well as many administrative and economic dockets such as purchase, loan, and rental agreements, and marriage, divorce, and adoption contracts. Additionally, an array of scholarly works are preserved, including historical and chronographical texts, mathematical and medical texts, literary commentaries, and grammatical and lexical compendia. There is also a large number of magical and divinatory texts, as well as ritual and religious texts, particularly for the later periods. Literary works, such as myths and epics, are largely preserved in the archaizing literary language of Standard Babylonian (about 40,000 lines of text are preserved) and, to a lesser degree, in Old Babylonia.

1.3 Sumerian and Akkadian

As demonstrated by early Sumerian texts bearing Akkadian personal names, particularly those from the southern Mesopotamian site of Abū Ṣalābīkh, the Sumerian and Akkadian populations commingled and interacted, at least on the border regions between northern and southern Babylonia, from at least the dawn of attested Akkadian, *c*. 2600 BC, until the death of Sumerian as a spoken language. During the course of this long period of integration, Akkadian was greatly influenced by Sumerian at every level – phonologically, morphologically, syntactically, and lexically. Most of these developments were already underway, if not completed, by the time of the Sargonic kings and the first connected Akkadian texts *c*. 2350 BC. Thus, while the Akkadian at our disposal may be described as morphologically and syntactically conservative, a form of the language not subject to Sumerian interference has not survived. Significantly, the level of Sumerian influence, especially with regard to lexicon, is markedly greater in Babylonian than in Assyrian.

2. WRITING SYSTEM

2.1 Description and development

Akkadian and Eblaite used the cuneiform system of writing which the Sumerians devised during the fourth millennium to write their language. The system consists of wedge-shaped graphs (hence *cuneiform*, from Latin *cuneus* "wedge") which were usually impressed into wet clay with a reed stylus. Other media were also employed, including wax, metal, and particularly stone for the recording of monumental inscriptions.

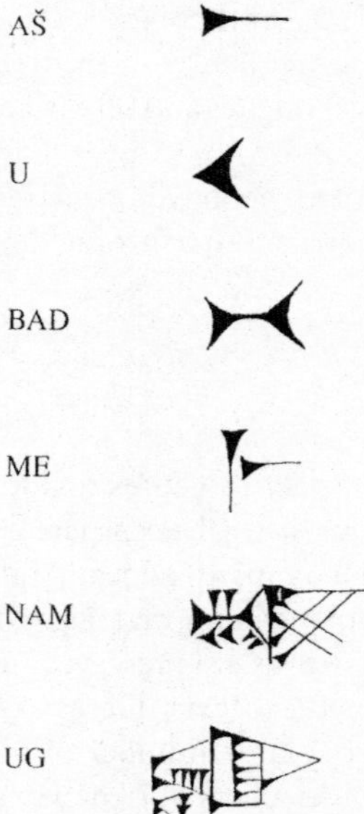

Figure 4.1 Sample of Old Babylonian lapidary signs

As the forms in Figure 4.1 reveal, individual signs may consist of one or several wedges. Akkadian script is read from left to right with the notable exception of the Code of Hammurabi, which was read from top to bottom, representing a purposefully archaizing attempt to mimic the Sumerian writing of the early third millennium. Except for the inconsistent use of a word-divider mark in Old Assyrian texts, there are no punctuation marks; often there is not even a dividing space between words.

The earliest Sumerian writing was fundamentally logographic in that a given graph represented a word, or a range of semantically related words. In many cases, but by no means all, the earliest graphs shared a pictographic relationship with their referents, being realistic, albeit stylized and highly conventionalized, depictions of the items represented. But already by the middle of the third millennium BC the graphs were largely stylized and thus unrecognizable as the objects they originally depicted. One of the main motivations for this change was the producing of the signs as a series of impressed wedges, rather than as curvilinear incised lines – a development that greatly facilitated the physical act of writing on wet clay. Very early in the development of the script, *c.* 3000 BC, the logographic signs of early Sumerian began to be assigned purely phonetic values. This was accomplished with the invention of rebus writings whereby a word symbol (logogram; see §2.3.20) such as A (Sumerian words are conventionally transcribed by Roman capitals), the Sumerian word meaning "water," could be used more generally to represent the syllable [a]. The graph A could thereby be used, for example, to express the Sumerian locative case-marker which also happened to be pronounced [a], solving the problem of how "in-ness" might be expressed pictographically.

Thus, by the Old Akkadian period, when Akkadian is first attested in connected texts, the script was largely phonetic, in part logographic, and graphically stylized in comparison with the earliest signs. As spoken Akkadian evolved along parallel Assyrian and Babylonian courses, the Assyrian and Babylonian scripts, too, developed somewhat independently of

Sign and Meaning	Archaic Sumerian Pictograms c. 3000 BCE	OAKK		OB/OA	MB/MA	NB/NA
KA "mouth"			Bab.			
			Ass.			
KIRI$_6$ "garden"			Bab.			
			Ass.			
GUD "ox"			Bab.			
			Ass.			
MUŠEN "bird"			Bab.			
			Ass.			
KU$_6$ "fish"			Bab.			
			Ass.			

Figure 4.2 Comparison of Sumerian, Babylonian, and Assyrian cursive cuneiform signs

one another. Additionally, there was considerable difference between the shape of the signs used for lapidary inscriptions and those used on clay.

Modern sign lists recognize nearly 600 signs, although there is great variation in the number and even the types of signs attested for various dialects. For the most part, the number of commonly used signs for a given dialect was often considerably less; Old Babylonian, for example, used about 150 frequent signs.

2.2 Recovery and modern decipherment

After the last Akkadian texts were written at the beginning of this era, *c.* AD 100, Akkadian and the cuneiform writing system faded into oblivion. Unlike the situation in Egypt where a form of the language, namely Coptic, lingered on until modern times, even if only as a liturgical language, knowledge of Akkadian and the cuneiform writing system was completely lost. Aside from the isolated reports of travelers during the late Middle Ages, it was not until the seventeenth century that clay artifacts with "certain unknown characters" were brought back to Europe. The eighteenth century witnessed the first organized missions to collect information and artifacts concerning the ancient Near East. The first and most notable of these was sponsored by the Danish crown in 1761 under the direction of mathematician Karsten Niebuhr. Soon thereafter, philologists began the decipherment of the cuneiform languages. The publication of a long trilingual inscription (Akkadian–Old Persian–Elamite), which Darius engraved high on the rock of Behistun in western Iran, the so-called Rosetta stone of Assyriology, greatly aided attempts at deciphering Akkadian. Once the simpler script of Old Persian was deciphered, it was then possible to begin decoding the Akkadian version. The efforts of three men should be noted, as they contributed most significantly to the decipherment effort – Edward Hincks, Jules Oppert, and Sir Henry Creswicke Rawlinson. In 1857 the Royal Asiatic Society invited these three men, along with the mathematician W. H. Fox Talbot, to prepare independent translations of an unpublished Middle Assyrian text. When the four translations were compared and found to be reasonably close, the decipherment of the Akkadian was officially validated. Since that time a great deal of scholarship has been devoted to the publication of texts, the clarification of the grammar, and the preparation of dictionaries. Akkadian is considered to be well understood at the present time, although it still has a few dark corners.

In 1968 an Italian excavation identified the Syrian site of Tell Mardikh with the ancient city of Ebla, and with the thousands of texts found at that site came the discovery of the Eblaite language. Initially, Eblaite was thought to be an early form of West Semitic because of the location of the site in northwest Syria, well outside Mesopotamia proper. However, at this time there is a general agreement among Assyriologists that Eblaite represents a form of East Semitic and, possibly, even an early dialect of Akkadian. The numerous problems encountered in Eblaite orthography have greatly hampered the decipherment effort, and thus an understanding of the Eblaite language remains very much in its infancy.

2.3 Signs

Akkadian is expressed using three types of signs: logograms, phonetic signs, and determinatives. The three types are formally indistinguishable from one another, and certain signs may be used in all three roles in different contexts.

2.3.1 Phonetic signs

As noted above, the cuneiform script used by Akkadian is partly syllabic and partly logographic. For all dialects, and for most genres, the use of syllabic writings dominates. Syllables or parts of syllables are expressed by phonetic signs, or *syllabograms*, which may represent a vowel alone (V) or a sequence of a vowel and consonant(s), such as VC, CV, CVC; individual consonants cannot be written. The assignment of VCV or CVCV values to certain signs reflects the application of morphological or morphophonemic rules to the writing system (Reiner 1966:28).

When providing a sign-by-sign rendering of the cuneiform (i.e., a *transliteration*; see §2.4), phonetic signs are given in italics and connected by hyphens: for example, *a-wi-lum* "man"; *e-ka-al-lum* "palac."

2.3.2 Logograms

Word signs, or logograms, are Sumerian words or phrases that must be read with the corresponding Akkadian value. Thus, logograms, often referred to as *Sumerograms*, may be said to have Sumerian graphic etymologies, but represent Akkadian phonic material (Reiner 1966:26). For example, in the sentence LUGAL *a-na a-lim ik-šu-ud* "the king arrived at the city," the logogram LUGAL, representing the Sumerian word for "king," is to be read as *šarrum*, the Akkadian equivalent. Most words may be written either syllabically or logographically; often the scribal conventions of a given dialect or genre dictate the preferred writing, but otherwise the choice is one of scribal whim.

As the above example illustrates, logograms are traditionally transcribed in (nonitalicized) capital letters according to their Sumerian pronunciation. The individual components of a *compound logogram* are separated by a period: for example, DUMU.MUNUS, literally "child.female," for Akkadian *mārtum* "daughter" (on an additional conventional use of transcription with capitals, see §2.5.2).

Logograms are often followed by phonetic signs, known as *phonetic complements*, which usually serve to clarify the Akkadian reading of the logogram by specifying the pronunciation of the last part of the word. The use of a phonetic complement may limit the interpretation of a logogram to one Akkadian word from among several possible readings: thus, KUR-*tum* for *mātum* "country," versus KUR-*ú-um* for *šadûm* "mountain," where the words for "country" and "mountain" are homonymous in Sumerian. In other cases a phonetic complement may indicate part of the morphological shape of a given Akkadian word, such as (i) the appropriate case ending, as in A.ŠÀ-*lum* (= *eqlum*, nom.) "field," A.ŠÀ-*lam* (= *eqlam*, acc.), A.ŠÀ-*lim* (= *eqlim*, gen.); or (ii) a possessive pronominal suffix, as in A.ŠÀ-*šu* (= *eqelšu*, nom./acc., or *eqlīšu*, gen.) "his field."

2.3.3 Determinatives

Akkadian writing borrowed from Sumerian a subset of logograms used to specify the semantic class to which a given word belongs. Determinatives were a feature only of the writing system and had no phonological value. In transliterations of Akkadian, determinatives are indicated in superscript either before or after the word they modify, according to their placement in the cuneiform text. Although very common with certain words, determinatives were optional and not a mandatory part of the writing of any word. There are roughly nineteen commonly used determinatives; examples include: GIŠ (= *iṣum*) "wood," often used before objects made of wood (e.g., ^{giš}GU.ZA = *kussûm* "throne"); KI (= *erṣetum*) "place, land, district," used after city and country names (e.g., KÁ.DINGIR.RA^{ki} = *Bābil* "Babylon"); DINGIR (= *ilum*) "god" (abbreviated ^{d} in transliteration when used as a determinative), used before god names (e.g., ^{d}EN.LÍL [= *Enlil* or *Ellil*] "(the god) Enlil").

2.4 Transliteration and transcription

Akkadian is rendered into Latin characters in two distinct forms. A sign-by-sign rendering, or *transliteration*, attempts accurately to reflect the signs expressed in the cuneiform text; as noted above, phonetic signs belonging to a single word are connected with hyphens, while logograms are written in capital letters and are connected with periods. A *transcription*, or *normalization*, attempts to reflect the actual pronunciation, indicating vocalic and consonantal length (i.e., consonantal doubling). The phonetic signs of a given word are connected without their distinguishing diacritic marks (see §2.5.1), and logograms are written with their corresponding Akkadian equivalents. Transliteration and transcription are illustrated in (2) with a portion of Law §150 from the Code of Hammurabi.

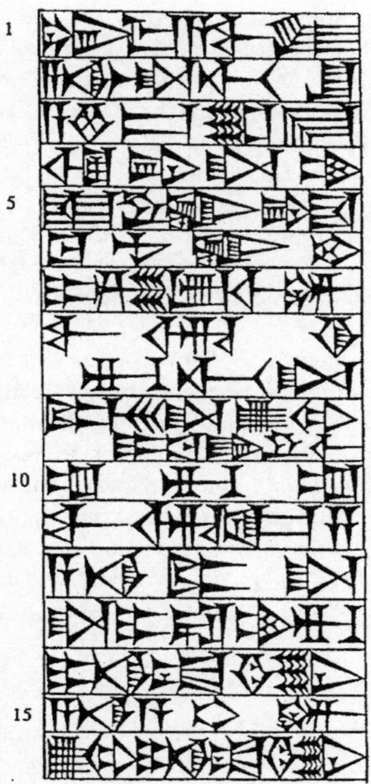

Figure 4.3 Law (§150) from the Code of Hammurabi (turned 90°) with Transliteration, Transcription, and Translation. (Autographed text after Harper, 1904)

(2)

Transliteration	*Transcription*	*Translation*
[1]*šum-ma a-wi-lum*	*šumma awīlum*	If a man
[2]*a-na aš-ša-ti-šu*	*ana aššatīšu*	to his wife
[3]A.ŠÀ ^{giš}KIRI$_6$ É	*eqlam kiriam bītam*	a field, orchard, house
[4]*ù bi-ša-am*	*ū bīšam*	or movable property
[5]*iš-ru-uk-šim*	*išrukšim*	gave to her, (and)
[6]*ku-nu-uk-kam*	*kunukkam*	"a sealed document"
[7]*i-zi-ib-ši-im*	*īzibšim*	made out for her,
[8]*wa-ar-ki*	*warki*	after
mu-ti-ša	*mutīša*	her husband (has died),
[9]DUMU.MEŠ-*ša ú-ul*	*mārūša ul*	her children will not
i-ba-qá-ru-ši	*ibaqqarūši*	bring a claim against her;
[10]*um-mu-um*	*ummum*	the mother
[11]*wa-ar-ka-sà*	*warkassa*	her estate
[12]*a-na* DUMU-*ša*	*ana mārīša*	to her child
[13]*ša i-ra-am-mu*	*ša irammu*	whom she loves
[14]*i-na-ad-di-in*	*inaddin*	will give,
[15]*a-na a-ḫi-im*	*ana aḫîm*	to an outsider
[16]*ú-ul u-na-ad-di-in*	*ul inaddin*	she will not give (it).

"If a man gave to his wife a field, orchard, house, or movable property, and made out a sealed document (i.e., contract) for her, after her husband's death, her children will not bring a claim against her; the mother will give her estate to the child whom she loves – she will not give it to an outsider."

2.5 Characteristics and problems of Akkadian orthography

The cuneiform writing system, in its earliest manifestation, was in essence a type of mnemonic device or *aide-mémoire* that was only loosely tied to the spoken language; it was in this sense an incomplete system in which only the core elements of speech were represented, the decoder or reader of a text having to depend on his knowledge of the language and the context of the message to restore most morphological markers and grammatical elements. Even as Sumerian writing evolved, becoming more closely tied to the spoken language, it was possible to omit certain, more or less predictable, elements from the writing that were presumably present in the utterance. Thus, at no time did the orthography strive to render an exact phonemic representation of the language. This fundamental weakness of the writing system was greatly exacerbated when the script was applied secondarily to express Akkadian; for as poorly as the script represented the phonemes of Sumerian, it expressed to an even lesser degree the phonemic inventory of Akkadian, which was genetically unrelated to Sumerian. The preservation of many Sumerian values along with the addition of new Akkadian values served to complicate the system even more. Consequently, cases of both over-differentiation and under-differentiation of Akkadian phonemes occur within the writing system. Although, during the evolution of the script, scribes attempted to alleviate these problems with the development of new signs and with the secondary differentiations of old ones, these attempts complicated the system still further. Moreover, the structure of Akkadian was less suited to the cuneiform writing system than that of Sumerian, as the agglutinative nature of Sumerian lent itself to the syllabic script more readily than did the inflecting morphology of Akkadian. Some of the more important complications associated with the writing system will be taken up in the following sections.

2.5.1 Homophony

Indicative of the over-differentiation of Akkadian phonemes in the writing system is the common existence of two or more signs with the same phonological value. These homophonous signs are distinguished in transliteration by a convention of diacritical marks. The most frequent sign for a given value is unmarked, the second most frequent is marked with an acute accent over the vowel, the third with a grave accent, while the fourth and following signs are marked with subscript index numbers: for example, *gi*, *gí*, *gì*, gi_4, gi_5 … gi_{27}. Paradoxically, the presence of exceptionally high index numbers such as gi_{27} or $še_{29}$ does not indicate that homophony played an unduly important role in the Akkadian syllabary. Rather, the system of diacritical marks accounts for the entire time-span of attested Akkadian, including not only the Assyrian and Babylonian dialects, but the peripheral dialects as well. For a given corpus, defined both temporally and geographically, the extent of homophony is much more limited, with at most two or three signs expressing a given value. In many cases the presence of homophonous signs is conditioned by scribal habits; for example, during the Old Babylonian period the Ù sign is restricted to writing the conjunctions *u* "and" and *ū* "or," whereas the Ú sign is used for most other occurrences of /u/ (use of the U sign, "*u*-one," was uncommon during this period).

2.5.2 Polyphony

Many signs may have more than one phonetic value; for example, the logogram UD also has the phonetic values *tam*, *ṭám*, *pir*, and *par*, among others. The correct value for a given sign must be determined by context. As with homophony, the role of polyphony in Akkadian is limited by dialectal considerations. Note that by Assyriological convention capital letters are used to indicate a given sign, such as UD, without specifying the phonological value with which it is to be read.

2.5.3 Distribution of signs

The failure of the writing system to distinguish many phonemes (i.e., phonemic under-differentiation) manifested itself in the distribution of certain signs. For instance, the writing system did not contrast voiced, voiceless, or emphatic consonants (see §3.1.1) at the end of a syllable, presumably because such distinctions were not significant in Sumerian. In Akkadian, however, the opposition of voiced, voiceless, and emphatic consonants is phonemic. Thus, an Akkadian scribe had to content himself with using, for example, the UD sign to express /ut/ and /uṭ/ as well as /ud/, the AG sign to express /ak/ and /aq/ as well as /ag/, and so on for all VC signs. The same holds true not only for the final consonant of CVC signs, but also for the initial consonant of certain CVC signs: thus, variant readings are possible such as *d/tan, d/t/ṭal, d/t/ṭim, b/pan*, and so forth. For CV signs, voice is often distinguished (although not in Old Akkadian or Old Assyrian); for example, there are different signs for the syllables /ba/ and /pa/, /bi/ and /pi/. However, this distinction is not always made as, for example, there is only one sign for the pair /bu/ and /pu/. Emphatic consonants were almost never distinguished in the early periods: for example, the ZA sign represented both /za/ and /ṣa/, the DI sign represented /di/ and /ṭi/. Only in the later dialects were emphatics commonly distinguished with certain signs: for example, the KIN sign was used for /qi/ and /qe/ (as opposed to the KI sign for their expression in earlier dialects); KUM for /qu/, and GÍN for /ṭu/. The lack of these distinctions in the writing system clearly increased the degree of polyphony in the syllabary.

Several other features regarding the distribution of signs should be noted. Signs that contain /e/ are often not distinguished from those with /i/. For instance, while there are different signs for the respective syllable pairs /te/, /ti/; /me/, /mi/; /en/, /in/; and /eš/, /iš/, there is only one sign for the syllable pair /ge/ and /gi/, and only one for /ke/ and /ki/. Moreover, certain signs do not distinguish either between /e/ and /i/ or among voiced, voiceless, and emphatic consonants; thus, IG represents the syllables /eg/, /ek/, /eq/ and /ig/, /ik/, /iq/; IB, the syllables /eb/, /ep/ and /ib/, /ip/.

Only for the post-Old Babylonian dialects is there a specific sign for writing the glottal stop ʾ(/ʔ/). In the earlier dialects there were various conventions for expressing this consonant: (i) use of the *ḫ*-signs (ḪA, ḪI, ḪU for syllable-intial /ʔ/, AḪ for syllable-closing /ʔ/, as in *i-na*-AḪ-ḪI-*id* for *inaʾʾid* "s/he will heed"); (ii) writing of the appropriate vowel sign (e.g., *le-ú-um* for *leʾûm* "to be able"); or (iii) broken writings (see §2.5.4). The sign ʾA that appeared in later periods represents a graphic variant of the AḪ sign.

For each of the two glides, /w/ and /y/, there is only one sign used regardless of the accompanying vowel: the PI sign has the values /wa/, /we/, /wi/, /wu/ (and /aw/, /ew/, /iw/, /uw/); IA, the values /ya/, /yi/, /yu/ (and /ay/).

It has been proposed that the distribution of vowel signs in Old Akkadian distinguishes three degrees of consonantal onset in the representation of the glottal stops (Gelb 1961:24–28). According to this proposal, the Old Akkadian vowel signs, which are purely vocalic in Old Babylonian and later dialects, were used to express consonantal onset when a syllable began or, less often, closed with the reflex of one of the five Proto-Semitic guttural consonants *ʾ(*/ʔ/), **h*, **ḥ*(*/ħ/), *ʿ(*/ʕ/), **ǵ*(*/γ/) or the two Proto-Semitic glides **w* and **y* (referred to as $ʾ_1$–$ʾ_5$ and $ʾ_6$–$ʾ_7$ respectively by Assyriologists). According to this scheme – which, it must be noted, is not strictly adhered to in Old Akkadian orthography – the signs A, E, I, and Ú represent onset (not indicated in the transliteration); the signs Á, È, Ì, and Ù are used to express stronger onset; the É sign is used with the value ʾà to express the strongest onset, which is identified with the Proto-Semitic sequences *ḥa- and *ha-. Further, it is proposed that the signs BÍ, MÁ, RÍ, LÍ, and LÚ are used either for morphologically long vowels (marked by a macron), or for vowels followed by the reflex of one of the Proto-Semitic gutturals or glides.

2.5.4 Spelling conventions and sequences of signs

Akkadian words are always written according to their syllabification (see §3.4); in other words, signs are chosen so that the syllable boundaries are clear. For example, the word *šarrum* "king" may be written syllabically in the following ways: *šar-rum, ša-ar-rum, šar-ru-um, ša-ar-ru-um*, or *ša-rum*, but not as ***šar-um* (however, see below for exceptional Old Akkadian writings of this type). The choice of a C_1V-VC_2 sequence rather than a single C_1VC_2 sign is largely a matter of scribal preference, although CVC signs do not exist for all CVC combinations: for example, the sequence [paz] must be written *pa-az* since a specific *paz* sign does not exist in the syllabary. Additionally, the historical development of the syllabary may determine the choice, since C_1VC_2 signs are relatively uncommon (except for CV*m* signs) before the Middle Assyrian and Middle Babylonian periods.

Writings of the type (C)VC-V(C), the so-called "broken writings," do not conform to the syllabification of the language and thus are generally not tolerated. However, for the early periods, when the glottal stop was not distinguished by a specific sign, broken writings could be used to express it after another consonant. For the Old Akkadian period, such broken spellings additionally indicate the following: (i) a lexical base and a morphological ending (e.g., *i-šar-um* (nom. case ending *-um*) for [išarum] "straight"); (ii) a doubled consonant (e.g., *qar-ad* for [qarrād] (bound form) "strong"); or (iii) a combination of the two (as in *šar-um* for [šarrum] "king").

Vowel length is, as a general rule, not indicated in Old Akkadian and Old Assyrian, although it is contrastive in the language. Vowel length can only be determined either by the surrounding grammar or by the context. For the Old Babylonian and later dialects, vowel length is similarly left unexpressed in most environments; a notable exception is Middle Assyrian where long vowels are often expressed with an extra vowel sign (so-called *plene writings* of the type CV+V). In the other dialects exceptional indications of vowel length occur when long vowels are derived from roots in which either the second or third consonant was "weak" (see §4.2). With the former, a morphologically long vowel in the middle of the word may occasionally be written with an extra vowel sign: for example, *kīn* "it (masc.) is firm" (< √*kwn*) may be written *ki-in* or *ki-i-in* with no difference in pronunciation. With the latter, a long vowel at the end of a word, resulting from the contraction of two vowels, is often indicated with an extra vowel sign: for example, *ib-nu-ú* for *ibnû* "they (masc.) built" (< *ibni* + *ū*).

Similarly, consonantal length (i.e., consonant gemination), although contrastive, may or may not be indicated in the writing. For Old Akkadian and Old Assyrian, again, length is, as a general rule, not expressed; for the later dialects, the expression of consonantal length is mainly a matter of scribal whim (the exception again being Middle Assyrian, as well as the letters from Hammurabi's chancellery, which often express double consonants). Thus, for example, the word *inaddiššum* "s/he will give to him" may be written in any of the four following forms in Old Babylonian: *i-na-di-šum, i-na-ad-di-šum, i-na-di-iš-šum, i-na-ad-di-iš-šum*. Similarly, morphologically contrastive word pairs such as *ipparras* "it will be cut" and *iparras* "it will cut" may both be written as *i-pa-ra-as*; only the context can distinguish the two. With the exception of relatively rare writings of the type *i-din-nam* for *iddinam* "he gave to me" (see §2.5.5), expressly written double consonants always reflect long consonants in speech.

2.5.5 Morphographemic writings

Certain morphophonemic processes were reflected inconsistently in the orthography. *Morphographemic* writings reveal the constituent morphemes rather than the phonetic character of a given word. For example, /awāssu/ "his word" (representing the lexical base *awāt-* "word" and the 3rd masc. sg. suffix *-šu*) may be written with the partial morphographemic writing *a-wa-at-su* (beside the regular phonetic spelling *a-wa-as-su*). Although morphographemic writings of this type are occasionally encountered in the early periods, they are more frequent in the later dialects. However, Old Akkadian (and frozen Old Babylonian) writings of the type *šar-um* /šarrum/ and *i-din-nam* /yiddinam/, where the writing reflects a lexical base and a suffixed morphological ending, may also be considered morphographemic (see §2.5.4).

2.6 Eblaite orthography

The Eblaite orthographic tradition was quite similar to that of Old Akkadian, and, like the latter, Eblaite did not express vocalic or consonantal length. Likewise, the writing system did not distinguish among voiced, voiceless, emphatic, or otherwise similarly articulated consonants. Most syllabograms, therefore, represent a class or group of Proto-Semitic reflexes, some of which may or may not have merged. However, in the case of Old Akkadian, the existence of later dialects with different writing conventions allows, at least in part, for the disentanglement of true phonological mergings from the semblance of mergings suggested by the writing system. Thus, the existence of a single orthographic tradition for Eblaite, as well as Eblaite's uncertain relationship to Akkadian, does not allow us to comment on possible mergings, or lack thereof, beyond what is suggested by the writing.

Unique to Eblaite are several other orthographic features, essentially archaic in nature, which serve further to obscure the phonology, morphology, and syntax. Foremost among these features is the fact that logograms, which do not reproduce the grammatical forms dictated by context, comprise the vast majority of writings; by some estimates, no less than 90 percent of the Eblaite corpus consists of logograms. Logograms may express any part of speech, including prepositions and verbs. Even pluralization may be expressed by logographic reduplication: for example, KALAM-*tim*.KALAM-*tim* "the lands" (gen. pl.); UDU.UDU "all the sheep." Furthermore, in what may possibly represent a transition between logographic and phonetic spellings, syllabograms may function logographically, masking the expected grammatical form of a word. Specifically, orthographic conventions allow for the nominative singular to be written instead of the expected case or form dictated by context: for example, *il-tum* for expected /ʔilātim/ (fem. gen. pl.) or /ʔilī/ (masc. gen. pl.) "(of) the god(desse)s." Similarly, syllabograms functioning logographically may also be reduplicated to indicate the plural: for example, NA.SE$_{11}$.NA.SE$_{11}$ for /nišī/ or /našī/ "people" (gen. pl.).

Also peculiar to Eblaite are both (i) the frequent omission of certain speech elements, particularly prepositions and possessive suffixes (as in *an-da* ŠEŠ *ù an-na* ŠEŠ "you are [my] brother and I am [your] brother"); and (ii) the combination of Sumerian verbal forms with Eblaite pronominal suffixes (as in Ì.NA.SUM-*kum* "he has given to you"). When words are expressed syllabically, the lack of certain syllabograms in the Eblaite syllabary often results in the graphic omission of phonemes in certain environments: for example, in the verbal form *a-za-mi-ga* /ʔaṣ(am)mid-ka/ "I bound you" or "I bind you," the /d/ phoneme of the syllable /mid/ is not expressed in the writing because of the lack of a VC syllabogram, *id*, in the syllabary; while the fact that *a-za* could represent two open syllables, /ʔaṣa/, or one closed syllable, /ʔaṣ/, means that the writing system could not even indicate the intended syllabic structure unambiguously.

Table 4.1 The consonantal phonemes of Akkadian (post-Old Akkadian period)

Manner of articulation	Place of articulation						
	Bilabial	Dental/ Alveolar	Palato-alveolar	Palatal	Velar	Uvular	Glottal
Stop							
Voiceless	p	t			k		ʾ(/ʔ/)
Voiced	b	d			g		
Emphatic		ṭ(/t'/)			q (/k'/)		
Fricative							
Voiceless			š (/š/ / /s/)		ḫ(/x/)		
Voiced					r (/γ/)	~ r (/ʁ/)	
Affricate							
Voiceless		s (/^{t}s/)					
Voiced		z (/^{d}z/)					
Emphatic		ṣ (/^{t}s'/)					
Approximant							
Voiced	w			y			
Lateral approximant							
Voiced		l					
Nasal							
Voiced	m	n					

3. PHONOLOGY

3.1 Phonemic inventory

3.1.1 Akkadian consonants

The classification of Akkadian phonemes is based largely on the phonemic inventories of other Semitic languages and that postulated for reconstructed Proto-Semitic. To a much lesser degree, it also relies secondarily on the Greek transcriptions of Late Babylonian lexical texts – the so-called *Graeco-Babyloniaca*, as well as on Aramaic transcriptions of Akkadian words and Akkadian glosses of Egyptian. Naturally, the phonetic character of these phonemes is impossible to recover, given that Akkadian is a dead language.

Akkadian distinguishes twenty consonant phonemes – a marked reduction from the original twenty-nine posited for Proto-Semitic. It is commonly assumed that much of this reduction, particularly with regard to the Proto-Semitic *gutturals* (i.e., glottals *ʾ(*/ʔ/) and *h; pharyngeals *ḥ (*/ħ/) and *ʿ (*/ʕ/), and voiced velar fricative *ġ (*/γ/)), is due to extensive and long-term contact with Sumerian, for which these consonants are not attested. As a result, Akkadian underwent a more radical development of its phonological system than any other Semitic language before modern times. In Table 4.1 Akkadian consonantal phonemes are presented using their conventional representations; probable or possible phonetic values follow in parentheses where conventional transcription differs from common phonetic transcription. It must be noted, however, that the places of articulation, and hence the phonetic renderings given here, are approximate – the significance of the chart lies in the phonemic contrasts.

As Table 4.1 indicates, Akkadian possessed four voiceless stops, /p, t, k, ʔ/, three voiced stops, /b, d, g/, and two stops, *ṭ* and *q*, known in Semitic linguistics as *emphatics*, which were probably characterized by glottalic coarticulation (i.e., /t’/ and /k’/ respectively). Similarly, there was a triad of affricates, voiced /^{d}z/ (<z>), voiceless /^{t}s/ (<s>), and emphatic /^{t}s’/ (<ṣ>). These became fricatives in later dialects; the voiceless member of this later, fricative set was pronounced [s] in Babylonian, but [š] in Assyrian, while the reflex of Proto-Semitic **š*, which was probably simple [s] originally, continued to be pronounced as such in Assyrian, but as [š] in Babylonian. The only other fricative was the velar /x/ (<ḫ>). There were six sonorants, the glides /w/ and /y/, the nasals /m/ and /n/, the liquid /l/, and, finally, /r/; as the last-mentioned often patterned with *ḫ*, it was probably realized phonetically as a voiced fricative, either velar ([γ]) or uvular ([ʁ]).

3.1.2 Eblaite consonants

As noted above, our understanding of the phonemic character of Eblaite is restricted by the limits imposed by the writing system; that is, the syllabic orthography did not distinguish single phonemes, but rather individual syllabograms representing groups of similarly articulated phonemes. It cannot be determined with any certainty which, if any, of these orthographically identical consonants actually merged phonologically. Generally, the phonology of Eblaite appears to be quite similar to that of Old Akkadian, and both languages seem to have maintained reflexes of at least some of the Proto-Semitic gutturals. Eblaite deviates most significantly from Akkadian in the treatment of the liquids /l, r/ (see §3.8.1, **8**) and in the distinction between Proto-Semitic **ð* and **z* (see §3.8.1, **1**).

Only the reflexes of the Proto-Semitic consonants **ḫ*, **m*, and **n* are expressed unambiguously in Eblaite orthography (i.e., with distinctive *ḫ*V- (-V*ḫ*), *m*V- (-V*m*), and *n*V- (-V*n*) signs, respectively). The reflexes of each of the following Proto-Semitic consonants are expressed ambiguously (i.e., the consonants of each group are represented by a common group of signs): (i) **b* and **p* (with *b*V- and -V*b* signs); (ii) **d*, **t*, and **ṭ* (*d*V-, -V*d*, *t*V-); (iii) **g*, **k*, and **q* (*g*V-, -V*g*); (iv) **ś* and **š* (*s*V-, -V*š*); (v) **ð* and **θ* (*š*V-, -V*š*); (vi) **z*, **s*, **ṣ*, **ṣ́*, and **θ̣* (*z*V-, -V*š*). The reflex of **l* is written with distinctive *l*-signs (*l*V-, -V*l*), while the reflex of **r* is written with *r*-signs (*r*V-, -V*r*). Significantly, however, the reflex of **r* may also be written with the set of *l*-signs (for examples of this phenomenon see §3.8.1, 8). The converse phenomenon, writing the reflex of **l* with *r*-signs, does not occur.

As in Old Akkadian, the reflexes of the Proto-Semitic gutturals *ʾ, *ʿ, **h*, **ḥ*, and **ǵ* are evidenced in certain spellings, although the writing system was incapable of representing them properly or of distinguishing separate reflexes fully. However, there appears to have been an attempt, at least in part, to distinguish these reflexes by assigning one group of vowel signs to express *ʾand *ʿ (i.e., *a*/ʾa_x(NI), *ì*, *ù*/u_x(NI)) and another set to indicate **h* and **ḥ* (i.e., ʾ*à*(É)/*a*/ʾa_x(NI), *i*/*ì*, u_9(EZENxAN)). The reflex of **ǵ* is attested in a single word, [ǵāribu(m)] "raven," written with both *ga*- and *ḫa*-. As in Akkadian, **w* and **y* were preserved only in certain environments (see §3.8.1, **5**, **6**). The sequence *w*V was written with the PI sign (as in Old Akkadian). There was no sign in the syllabary for reflex of **y*; instead, where **y* is expected at the beginning of words and between vowels the following signs were used: *a* for /(y)a/, *i* for /(y)i/, u_9(EZENxAN) for /(y)u/.

3.1.3 Akkadian and Eblaite vowels

Akkadian and Eblaite distinguish three primary vowel phonemes, /a/, /i/, and /u/, reflecting the original stock of Proto-Semitic vowels, and a fourth, /e/, which is secondary, derived from either /a/ or /i/:

(3) **Akkadian and Eblaite vowel phonemes**

/i(:)/ /u(:)/
/e(:)/
/a(:)/

Vowels may be either long or short; short vowels are transcribed unmarked while two types of long vowels are distinguished in transcription: morphologically long vowels, marked with a macron, *ā*, *ē*, *ī*, *ū*, and long vowels which result from vowel contraction, marked with a circumflex, *â*, *ê*, *î*, and *û*.

3.1.3.1 *The phoneme /e/*

As noted above, the vowel /e/ was a secondary development in Akkadian. The Proto-Semitic gutturals **ḥ*, *ʿ, **ǵ* had the effect of coloring neighboring */a/ vowels to [e] before being lost (see §3.8.1, **4**). Only in the Babylonian dialects did the loss of these consonants additionally cause */ā/ > [ē]. As these gutturals, or their reflexes, appear to have been retained in Old Akkadian and Eblaite and the change of */a/ > [e] does not occur consistently in their presence (see §3.8.1, **4**), [e] was simply an allophone of /a/ in these dialects. In other Old Akkadian environments /i/ had an allophone [e], as in the third-person prefix of verbs I-ʾ: for example, *i-mu-ru* [yiʔmurū] beside *e-mu-ru* [yeʔmurū] "they saw." It appears, then, that for Old Akkadian, and probably Eblaite, *e* was not phonemic. However, with the merging and loss of the Proto-Semitic gutturals, *e* achieved phonemic status in the Old Babylonian period as evidenced by minimal pairs such as *pelûm* "egg" versus *palûm* "reign"; *šērum* "morning" versus *šārum* "wind"; *elīšu* "on it" versus *ilīšu* "his gods" (gen.-acc.); *rēmum* "pity" versus *rīmum* "wild bull," although the writing system remained unable to reflect the distinction between /e/ and /i/ in many cases.

A vowel [e] also occurred in the post-Old Akkadian dialects as the result of various phonological changes:

1. In Babylonian, [a] and [e] were incompatible in the same word, with the result that long or short [a] was assimilated to [e], a process called *Babylonian vowel harmony*: thus, Bab. *epēšum* versus Ass. *epāšum* "to make"; Bab. *bēlētum* versus Ass. *bēlātum* (nom.) "ladies." The change is conditioned even by an [e] subsequently lost by vowel contraction: for example *leqûm* < **leqēum* < **laqēum* < **laqēḥum* < **laqāḥum* "to take." Babylonian vowel harmony did not take place across all morpheme boundaries; in addition, a secondary [e] (derived from /i/ or arising by vowel contraction) does not normally condition the change. However, the [a] of the prefixes *a-* and *ta-* often assimilates to [e] in verbs containing that vowel: for example, *ešme* beside *ašme* "I heard"; Bab. *teleqqe* versus Ass. *talaqqe* "you (masc. sg.) take." The rule of Babylonian vowel harmony was not applicable to Old Akkadian or the Assyrian dialects.
2. The phoneme /a/ became /e/ in words that contained Proto-Semitic *ʾ and a Proto-Semitic sonorant **m*, **n*, **r*, or **l*, as in **ʾarṣatum* > (ʾ)*erṣatum* > *erṣetum* "earth"; **śaʾnum* > **šeʾnum* > *šēnum* "sandal."
3. The phoneme /i/ had an allophone [e], which occurred immediately before /ḫ/ ([x]) or /r/: for example, *laberum* "old," *meḫrum* "copy, reply."
4. Additionally, the loss of mimation (*-m* occurring in final position) caused [i] of the original word-final sequence [-im] to shift to [e] in Assyrian. Thus, the final vowel of the genitive singular, the accusative-genitive plural of feminine nouns and adjectives, the ventive for the plural, and the second and third feminine singular dative suffixes are pronounced [e] in Middle and Neo-Assyrian: for example, Old Assyrian

šarritim > Middle and Neo-Assyrian *šarrete* "queens"; Old Assyrian *illikūnim* > Middle and Neo-Assyrian *illikūne* "they came here"; Old Assyrian *išpuršim* > Middle and Neo-Assyrian *išpurše* "he sent to her."

5. In Middle Babylonian, Standard Babylonian and Neo-Babylonian the [a] of the second syllable of the preterites, perfects, and precatives of D and Š stems often underwent partial assimilation to the [i] or [e] of the following syllable and appeared as [e]: for example, *ubenni* beside *ubanni* "he built"; *ušeknis* beside *ušaknis* "he subjugated."

3.1.3.2 Akkadian /o/

The phoneme /o/ has been suggested for Akkadian primarily on the basis of the distribution of *u*-signs in certain Old Babylonian lexical texts from the city of Nippur, as well as of Greek transcriptions of Late Babylonian texts (Westenholz 1991). The evidence from the lexical texts suggests that the signs U and U_4 are used to express [ô], while Ú represents [u, ū]. The U and U_4 signs are consistently used to represent the contraction of [ă] + [ŭ] (or [ĕ] (<[ă]) + [ŭ]; i.e., where [ē] is derived secondarily from [ā]), as evidenced by such writings as, for example, *na-du-u_4* "to throw" (*nadā + u*); *tap-pu-u* "companion" (*tappā + u*); *lā e-el-qú-u-ma* "I did not take [oath]" (*elqe + ū + ma*). The Ú sign is used in other environments, as (i) in the reflex of [i] + [u] and [u] + [u] (e.g., *ra-bu-ú* "great" (< *rabi + u*), *zu-uk-ku-ú* "to cleanse" (< *zukku + u*); (ii) in plene writings of [ū] (e.g., *du-lu-ú-tum* "hoisting device" (*dulūtum*)); and (iii) for short [u] (e.g., *im-du-ú* "support" (*imdu*), *ba-a-a-ú* "to walk, pass along" (*bâ'u*). These writings are in agreement with later Greek transcriptions such as *βιλλοδω[ζ]* < *billuda-ū-šu*. The Greek evidence also suggests that Proto-Semitic (PS) **aw* > [ō]: for example, ω "day" = *ōw* < **yawm-*. It is also proposed that the choice of U-signs in spellings such as *u_4-ru-ḫu* "hair on the head" (*uruḫḫu*) and *u_4-ḫu-li* "suds" (*uḫūlum*) may indicate /u/ → [o]/_{/r/, /ḫ/}. Further, the possible minimal pairs *nadôm* "to throw" (< *nadā + um*) and *nadûm* "thrown" (< *nadi + um*) may demonstrate that *ô* was phonemically distinct from *û*. However, given the limited evidence for an /o/ phoneme and given that the writing system did not distinguish *u* from *o* outside of the lexical materials, the phonological significance of these data remains uncertain. Moreover, the possibility exists that the scribal differentiation of *u*-signs in these lexical texts reflects the superimposition of the Sumerian phonological system (for which an /o/ phoneme has been similarly proposed), rather than a phonemic distinction within Akkadian (Lieberman 1979).

3.2 Possible allophones

In the Assyriological literature other variations in the pronunciation of various vowels and consonants have been pointed out; among these are the so-called vocalic consonants (syllabic allophones of /l, r, n, m/), a palatal nasal [ɲ], a voiced emphatic [g], spirantized variants of the nonemphatic stops (*b̲, p̲, t̲, d̲, k̲, g̲*), and the secondary vowels [ȯ] and [ü]. Although some of these consonants and vowels may have existed in certain dialects of Akkadian, probably none of them attained phonemic status. In at least several cases, the evidence upon which these alleged allophones rests can be reinterpreted if varying scribal practices and dialectal syllabaries are taken into account.

3.3 Length

As noted above, both vocalic and consonantal length are phonemic in Akkadian, although neither is regularly expressed in the script (see §2.5.4). Long vowels are considered to be of two types, morphologically long vowels, marked in transcription with a macron, and long vowels resulting from vowel contraction, marked with a circumflex. However, despite such apparent minimal pairs as *imlāšu* "he filled it" and *imlâšu* "they (fem.) filled it"; *pānū* "face" and *pānû* "first," the distinction between the two types of long vowels is not considered to be phonemic by most Assyriologists.

3.4 Syllable structure

The syllabification of Akkadian is based on three fundamental rules: (i) every syllable has only one vowel (thus vocalic clusters are divided by a syllable boundary); (ii) no syllable may begin with a vowel (with two exceptions – a word-initial vowel, and the second of two successive vowels); (iii) no syllable may begin or end with two consonants.

3.5 Stress

In Akkadian the stress of a given word is predictable in terms of the quantity of its constituent syllables. The fact that the position of word stress is determined by the phonological environment, and the lack of minimal pairs distinguished by stress show that word stress was nonphonemic. The rule for determining stress may be stated as follows: stress falls on the ultimate syllable if it is closed and has a long vowel (either macron or circumflex) or if it is open and has a circumflex vowel: for example, [i'dūk] "s/he killed"; [ib'nû] "they built." Otherwise, the stress falls on the rightmost nonfinal syllable either closed with a consonant or open with long vowel (macron or circumflex): for example, [i'parras] "s/he will cut"; ['mārum] "son." If neither condition is met, the stress falls on the first syllable: for example, ['nadin] "is given"; ['ilū] "gods."

3.6 Intonation

Lexical or grammatical tones are not attested for any Semitic language, modern or ancient. However, suprasegmental intonation no doubt conveyed important synactic information in Akkadian, although its role is scarcely known. Occasionally, a plene writing of the type CV+V is used to express intonation. The rising pitch of a yes-or-no question may be indicated by a plene writing of the final syllable: for example, *in-na-ak-su-ú* ([innak'sú]) "Are they cut?"; *ga-me-e-er* ([ga'mér]) "Is it complete?" With penultimate syllables, a plene writing often indicates intonation of emphasis: for example, *te-e-er-ra* ['tèrra] "Return (pl.) it!!"; *ne-e-si* (['nèsi]) "It is (indeed) distant!"

3.7 Phonotactics

According to some scholars, Akkadian exhibits free variation between [V:C] and [VC:], for example *ḫiṭṭu* and *ḫīṭu* "fault," except with I- and II-weak verbs where the place of length is functional and serves to distinguish two morphs – thus, *ippuš* "he makes" against *īpuš* "he made"; *ikūnū* "they (masc. pl.) became firm" against *ikunnū* "they (masc. pl.) will become firm" (Reiner 1966:45). However, the occurrence of minimal pairs such as *mārum* "son" versus *marrum* "shovel," and *šārum* "wind" versus *šarrum* "king" suggests that the distinction between /V:C/ and /VC:/ is in fact contrastive. Variations such as *ḫīṭu* and *ḫiṭṭu* "fault" probably reflect dialectal resolutions of the contact of glottalized (emphatic) consonants and a glottal stop: *ḫiṭ'um = [xit'-ʔum] > [xīt'um] or [xitt'um].

Clusters of three or more consonants are not permissible in Akkadian. Any vowel or consonant except [y] may occur in word-initial position, while consonant clusters (including long consonants of the type C_1C_1) and vocalic clusters are not permissible in word-initial position. Loanwords with initial consonantal clusters are resolved with the insertion of anaptyctic vowels. A glottal stop may have been permissible in word-initial position, but the ambiguous rendering of this consonant prevents certainty in this matter. The glide [w] was only retained in word-initial position in the Old Akkadian, Old Babylonian, and Old Assyrian periods; (see §3.8.1, **5**, **6**). In word-medial position any vowel, long or short, or cluster of no more than two consonants (of either the C_1C_1 or the C_1C_2 variety) is allowed. The nonoccurrence of certain consonant clusters of the type C_1C_2 limits the possible combinations of this type. In word-final position, any vowel or consonant may occur; however, consonant clusters (both C_1C_1 and C_1C_2) and glides are not permitted in word-final position. When consonant clusters arise from morphological processes, they are resolved with anaptyctic vowels or, in the case of long consonants (C_1C_1), they may be shortened.

3.8 Diachronic developments in Akkadian and Eblaite

3.8.1 Consonantal changes

As noted above, Akkadian exhibits a significant reduction in the number of Proto-Semitic consonants. The following outline illustrates these mergers and losses along with other significant diachronic developments:

3.8.1.1 Mergers

1. Proto-Semitic **ð* and **z* merged as *z*: for example, **ðakārum* > *zakārum* "to remember"; *'*uðnun* > *uznum* "ear"; **zamārum* > *zamārum* "to make music"; **ʿazābum* > *ezēbum* "to leave." However, in Eblaite the syllabary indicates that these phonemes remained distinct (see **3**).

2. Proto-Semitic **ṣ*, **ṣ́*, and **θ̣* merged as *ṣ*: for example, **ṣarāḫum* > *ṣarāḫum* "to cry out"; **ṣ́amādum* > *ṣamādum* "to bind"; **naθ̣ārum* > *naṣārum* "to watch." These phonemes were expressed with the same set of signs in Eblaite (see **3**).

3. Proto-Semitic **ś*, **š* and **θ* merged as *š*: for example, **śapatum* > *šaptum* "lip"; **šakānum* > *šakānum* "to place"; **θalāθum* > *šalāšum* "three". However, during the Old Akkadian period the reflex of **θ* was still distinct from the merged **ś/š* phoneme; this is clearly demonstrated by the choice of orthographic signs used to express each phoneme. Note that the Old Akkadian phonemes represented in (4) below (and throughout this chapter) as *θ* and *š* are usually represented as *š* and *ś* respectively by Assyriologists (according to scholarly convention, though the phonetic particulars of both are actually unknown):

(4) The sibilants of Old Akkadian and Old Babylonian

Proto-Semitic		*Old Akkadian*		*Old Babylonian*	
		Phoneme	*Graphemes*	*Phoneme*	*Graphemes*
*θ	→	θ	ŠA, ŠI, ŠU	š	ŠA, ŠI, ŠU
*ś, *š	→	š	SA, SI, SU	š	ŠA, ŠI, ŠU
*s	→	s		s	SA, SI, SU
*ð, *z	→	z	ZA, ZI, ZU	z	ZA, ZI, ZU
*ṣ́, *ṣ, *θ̣	→	ṣ		ṣ	ZA, ZI, ZU

Thus, for the Old Akkadian period one encounters, for example, the spelling *ú-ša-ab* for /yuθθab/ "he dwells," *sa-ap-ta-su* for /šaptā-šū/ "his lips (dual)," and *su-mu* from √**šm* "name." The Proto-Semitic sibilants *s and *ð/z, while remaining distinct in Akkadian, were written with the same signs in the Old Akkadian period (e.g., *zi-ku-ru-um* < **sukkūrum* "bolt"; *zi-kà(ga)-ar* < **ðikar* "male"; *i-za-mar* < **yazammar* "he sings"), and were only distinguished graphically beginning in the Old Babylonian period.

In Eblaite PS *ð and *z remained distinct and did not merge as they did in Akkadian. Rather, the reflexes of PS *ð and *θ were written with the same set of signs; however, as discussed above, this indicates only a possible merger:

(5) The sibilants of Eblaite

Proto-Semitic	*Eblaite graphemes*
*ð	ŠA, ŠÈ, ŠU
*θ	ŠA, ŠÈ, ŠU
*ś, *š	SA, SI, SU
*z, *s	ZA, ZI, ZU
*ṣ, *ṣ́, *θ̣	ZA, ZI, ZU

4. As noted above, the five Proto-Semitic guttural consonants *ʾ, *h, *ḥ, *ʿ, *ǵ (ʾ$_1$–ʾ$_5$) merged as /ʔ/ and were then lost in most environments. Directly before or after consonants, the loss of /ʔ/ resulted in the compensatory lengthening of the preceding vowel: for example, **milʾum* > *mīlum* "flood"; **marʾum* > *mārum* "son"; **nahrum* > *nārum* "river". If the lost guttural was at the beginning or end of a word, it was lost with no further change to the word: for example, **ʾamārum* > *amārum* "to see"; **halākum* > *alākum* "to go"; **imlaʾ* > *imla* "he filled." When ʾ$_1$–ʾ$_5$ originally stood between vowels, its loss left those vowels contiguous and subject to the rules of vowel contraction for that particular dialect (see §3.8.2.4).

Three of the gutturals, *ḥ, *ʿ, *ǵ (ʾ$_3$–ʾ$_5$), also colored neighboring *a* vowels to *e* before they were lost (only in Babylonian did the loss of these consonants additionally change *ā* to *ē*): for example, **ʾaḥpuš* > *ēpuš* "I did"; **taḥpušā* > *tēpušā* "you (pl.) did"; **ḥarāθum* > Ass. *erāšum*, Bab. *erēšum* "to plow"; **ʿazābum* > Ass. *ezābum*, Bab. *ezēbum* "to leave"; **ǵaθāyum* > *ešûm* "to confuse" (see §3.1.3, **1** for Babylonian vowel harmony). However, the orthographic practices of the Old Akkadian period seem to indicate that the gutturals ʾ$_1$–ʾ$_5$, or at least the reflex of ʾ$_3$–ʾ$_5$, were maintained in most environments and the shift *a* > *e* did not occur consistently: for example, Old Akkadian *u-śa-rí-ib* /yušaʕrib/ "s/he brought in," as opposed to Old Babylonian *ú-še-ri-ib* /ušērib/; *a-lí-tám* /ʕalītam/ "upper" (OB /elītam/). Similarly, in Eblaite *a* was usually retained in the vicinity of the preserved reflexes of *ʿ, *ḥ, and *ǵ: for example, *maʿmadu(m)* "support"; *ǵāribu(m)* "raven."

3.8.1.2 Segmental loss

5. Proto-Semitic *w (ʾ$_6$) was lost at the end of syllables, unless followed by another *w. The loss of *w resulted in the compensatory lengthening of the preceding vowel: for example, **šuwrid* > *šūrid* "send down (masc. sg.)!"; but *nuwwurum* "to brighten."

Initial *w was retained in the early dialects of Akkadian, but was lost by the end of the Old Babylonian period: for example, OB *warḫum* > SB/MB/NB *arḫu* "month." However, in Middle Assyrian, and subsequently in Neo-Assyrian, initial **wa* became *u*: for example, OA *wardum*, MA/NA *urdu* "slave" (however, in Middle Assyrian/Neo-Assyrian initial *wā* shifts to *ā*: OA *wāšibum* > MA/NA *āšibu* "inhabitant").

In the Middle Babylonian period, intervocalic *w* was written as <m> (<VmV> = /VwV/): for example, SB/MB/NB *a-me/mi-lu* for /awīlu/ "man" (see **18** below). On analogy with <VmV> in verbal forms such as MB *ú-ma-aš-šar* /uwaššar/ "he releases," forms of the verb that originally had initial *w* (i.e., the imperative, the infinitive, and the verbal adjective) are written with initial <m> and do not show the expected loss of *w* (e.g., MB *mu-uš-šu-ru* /wuššuru/ "to release"). In Middle Assyrian, however, the sequence *VwV often appears as VʾV, as in *aʾīlu* < *awīlum* "man." In Neo-Assyrian, if an intervocalic <m> is secondary, that is, originating from an etymological *w*, then it often shifts to written <b>: for example, OA *awātum*, NA *abutu* "word" (with *Assyrian vowel harmony*; see §3.8.2.3).

In Eblaite **w* was preserved word-initially, as in the early dialects of Akkadian: for example, *wa-ba-lu* /wabālu(m)/ "to bring." Although **w* appears also to be preserved intervocalically (e.g., *ma-wu* /mawū/ "water"), some writings may indicate a loss of **w* in that position: thus, *ga-nu-um* beside *ga-nu-wu* for /ganu(w)u(m)/ "reed."

6. Proto-Semitic **y* (*ʾ7*) was also lost at the end of syllables, unless – as was the case with **w* – followed by another **y*. Similarly, the loss of **y* resulted in the compensatory lengthening of the preceding vowel: for example, **yupaḫḫar* > *upaḫḫar* "he gathers"; **rabiytum* > *rabītum* "great"; but *dayyānum* "judge."

Initial **y* was also lost, but only after the change of **#ya-* to **#yi-* (probably preserved in Old Akkadian, in view of plene-writings of the type *i-ik-mi* /yikmi/ "he captured"): for example, **yaprus* > (OAkk.) *yiprus* > (OB/OA) *iprus* "he cut." A single intervocalic **y* is preserved only in the possessive suffix *-ya* (e.g., *bēlīya* [gen.] "my lord"), but after long vowels the *y* of the possessive suffix is often written as <ʾ> (e.g., *bēlū-ʾa* "my lords" [nom.]; *šēpē-ʾa* "my feet" [acc.-gen.]).

In Eblaite, word-initial **ya* often shifted to *y(i)* as in Akkadian: for example, *i-sa-lum* < **yašarum* "straight." But note the apparent biforms *i-me-tum* and *a-me-tum* < **yamintum* "right (side)" (fem. sg.). As the writing system had no direct means of expressing /y/, little else can be said concerning its behavior in other environments; thus, for intervocalic *y* note the spelling *ba-ga-um* for /bakā(y)um/ "to weep."

7. Beginning with the late Old Babylonian and Old Assyrian periods, *mimation* (the occurrence of *-m*) was lost when word final (retained only when followed by *-ma* and the pronominal suffixes). However, often the spelling does not reflect this change; as a result some CV*m* signs assume CV values; thus, OB *šarrātum* "queens" (nom. pl.), written <šar-ra-tum>, becomes MB *šarrātu*, but is still written as in Old Babylonian, as a historical spelling. To reflect the sound change in transliteration, the final sign may be read *tu*$_4$, thus *šar-ra-tu*$_4$.

8. In Eblaite, *l* and *r* are apparently lost in the spellings of some words: for example, *la-i-mu* and *a-i-mu* for /laħimu(m)/? < √**lḥm* "to press together"; *sa-ʾà-lum* and *sa-ʾà-a-um* for /śah(a)rum/ "new moon"?; *ba-a-ḫu-um* for /palāxum/ "to fear." These spellings possibly suggest that *l* and *r* may be weakened to ʾ, *y*, or perhaps Ø. As the second set of examples indicates, *r* may be written with the set of syllabograms for <l->: for example, *ba-ga-lum* /bakʾ(a)rum/ "cow"; *bu-ga-ru*$_{12}$ and *bu-ga-lu* for /buk(a)ru(m)/ "first-born." However, the converse – writing *l* with <r-> signs – is not attested (see §3.1.2).

3.8.1.3 Dissimilation

9. By *Barth's Law of Dissimilation*, initial **m* (except for **#mu-*) dissimilated to *n* in forms containing the other labials, namely, *p*, *b*, *m*: for example, **markabtum* > *narkabtum* "chariot"; **mamṣarum* > *namṣarum* "sword."

In Eblaite, however, Barth's Law does not appear to apply: thus, *má-ma-du* /maʕmadu(m)/ = Akk. *nēmedum* "support."

10. By *Geers' Law of Dissimilation*, in roots originally containing two Proto-Semitic emphatic consonants, one of the emphatics dissimilated to its nonemphatic, voiceless counterpart: (i) **ṭ* became *t* in forms that also contained *q* or *ṣ* (< PS **ṣ*, **ṣ́*, or **θ̣*): for example, **qaṭārum* > *qatārum* "to smoke"; **ṣabāṭum* > *ṣabātum* "to seize"; (ii) in forms with both *q* and *ṣ*, the first dissimilated,

(6) {q, ṣ} > {k, s} / _ (X) {ṣ, q}

for example, **qaṣārum* > *kaṣārum* "to knot"; **ṣayāqum* > *siāqum* "to be narrow."

11. The first member of a voiced geminate cluster, particularly in the case of dentals, often undergoes nasalization. This phenomenon is characteristic of the post-Old Babylonian periods, but is occasionally attested for some Old Babylonian dialects and sporadically for Old Akkadian. Examples are *ambi* beside *abbi* (< **anbi*) "I called"; *inandin* and *inamdin* beside *inaddin* "s/he will give"; *inanziq* and *inamziq* beside *inazziq* "he becomes vexed"; *nangāru* and *namgāru* beside *naggāru* "carpenter." In Middle Babylonian and later, the assimilatory change *dn* > *nn* often took place in forms of the verb *nadānu* "to give."

3.8.1.4 Assimilation

12. Proto-Semitic **n* assimilated to a following consonant: for example, **tanθur* > *taṣṣur* "you (masc. sg.) guarded"; **libintum* > *libittum* "brick." Exceptions occur when **n* is the second root consonant: **ʿanzum* > *enzum* "female goat."

In Eblaite, **n* assimilates to the feminine ending: for example, *li-bí/ba-tu* /lib{i,a}ttum/ < √**lbn* "a kind of brick." In other environments, however, it remains unchanged. Additionally, **m* may also assimilate to a following consonant: for example, *si-tum* /šittum/ (Akk. *šimtu*) "sign, color"; *ti-da-ḫu-ru₁₂* probably /tittaxrū/ < **timtaḫrū* "they approached."

13. The dentals *d* and *ṭ* assimilate completely to the feminine ending *-t*: for example, **paqidtum* > *paqittum* "entrusted"; **baliṭtum* > *balittum* "alive." The sibilants *s*, *ṣ*, and *z* become *š* before the feminine ending *-t*: for example, **paristum* > *parištum* "separated"; **maruṣtum* > *maruštum* "sick." Beginning with the Middle Babylonian and Middle Assyrian periods, this *š* becomes *l*, not only before the feminine ending *-t*, but regularly before dentals *d*, *t*, *ṭ* and sibilants *s*, *ṣ*, *z* as well (i.e., *š* + {*D*, *Z*} > *l* + {*D*, *Z*}): for example, OB *mazzaztum* > *mazzaltu* "place"; OB *aštapar* > *altapar* "I have sent"; OB *ušziz* > *ulziz* "he caused to stand." One notable exception to this change is found in the Middle Assyrian preposition *ištu* "from" (cf. Middle Babylonian *ultu*). In Neo-Assyrian the *lt* that originates from *št* often changes to *ss*: for example, MA/MB *altakan* > NA *assakan* "I have placed." Occasionally, *lt* becomes *ss* even when *lt* was not originally *št*: for example, OA *ilteqe* > NA *isseqe* "he has taken." Rarely, *d* assimilates to an immediately following *š*, as in *eššu* "new" < **edšu*.

In Eblaite, as in the later Akkadian dialects, sibilants may shift to *l* before dentals: for example, *dal-da-i-bù* /taltaḫḫibu(m)/ < */taštaḫḫibu(m)/, from the verb *šaḥābu(m)* (cf. Arabic *saḥaba* "to withdraw, take away").

14. The infixed *-t-* of the Perfect and of the Gt and Dt stems assimilated completely when immediately before or after the dentals, *d* and *ṭ*, and the sibilants, *s*, *ṣ*, *z*; and when immediately before *š*, but not when after *š* (i.e., {*D*, *Z*} + *t* > {*DD*, *ZZ*}; while *t* + {*D*, *Z*, *š*} > {*DD*, *ZZ*, *šš*}): for example, **idtamiq* > *iddamiq* "it has improved"; **ḫitdulum* > *ḫiddulum* "to become knotted"; **istaḫur* > *issaḫur* "he has turned"; **pitšušum* > *piššušum* "to anoint oneself"; but note *ištakan* "he has placed." The infixed *-t-* became *d* when immediately after *g*: **igtamar* > *igdamar* "he has finished." In the Middle Assyrian and Neo-Assyrian periods, the infix *-t-* became *ṭ* after *q*: for example, *iqtibi* > *iqṭibi* "he has said."

15. The sequence of stem-final dental or sibilant (*d*, *t*, *ṭ*, *s*, *ṣ*, *z*, *š*) plus the *š* of the third-person pronominal suffixes yielded *ss* (i.e., {*D*, *Z*, *š*} + *š* > *ss*): for example, **ikšud-šu* > *ikšussu* "he reached him (masc.)"; **ikkis-šu* > *ikkissu* "he cut it (masc.) off." However, there are qualifications to this assimilatory change for the Old Akkadian and Old Assyrian periods regarding stem-final *š* (< PS **ś*, **š*, **θ*). In the Old Akkadian period, when the reflexes of PS **ś/š* and PS **θ* were still distinguished, the result of a stem-final *θ* or *š* plus the *š* of the pronominal suffix was *šš*: for example, Old Akkadian *iqīššum* < *iqīš-šum* "he gave to him";

erēššunu < *erēθ-śunu* "their cultivation." Similarly, in Old Assyrian, after the merger of PS **ś/š* and PS **θ* > *š*, the sequence *šš* was preserved: for example, Old Assyrian *lubūššunu* < **lubūš-šunu* "their clothing"; Old Assyrian *epuššum* < **epuš-šum* "do for him!"

16. In Middle Assyrian and Neo-Assyrian, *š* before *b* and *p* shifted to *s* (i.e., *š* > *s* / _ [bilabial stop]): for example, OA, OB *wašbat* > MA *usbat* (MB *ašbat*), NA *usbat*/*uspat* (for *wa* > *u* see **5** above).

17. The bilabial stops *b* and *p* assimilated to the labial nasal *m* at morpheme boundary (i.e., {*p*, *b*} + *m* > *mm*). Aside from relatively rare sandhi writings of the type *ḫiṣimmātim* < *ḫiṣib mātim* "abundance of the land," these phonemes are only juxtaposed when the enclitic particle *-ma* follows the morpheme boundary: for example, *irkamma* < *irkab-ma* "he rode and . . ." In Neo-Assyrian, *b* sometimes devoices after *s* (i.e., *b* > *p* / *s* _): for example, *uspākūni* beside *usbākūni* versus Babylonian *wašbāku* "(where) I dwell."

18. From Middle Babylonian on (and sporadically already in Old Babylonian), intervocalic *m* was pronounced [w], as in [šawaš] for the god *Šamaš*, so that etymological *m* and etymological *w* were indistinguishable intervocalically (e.g., OB *awātum* "word" and *amātum* "female slaves" were in MB both pronounced [awātu]); as a result of this development, signs for *m* + vowel came to be used to write both *m* and *w* (see **5** above). In Middle Babylonian, Standard Babylonian, and Neo-Babylonian *m* and the infix *-t-* usually yield the sequence *nd* (less frequently *md*), showing a reciprocal assimilation in voicing and place of articulation: *m* + *t* > *nd*, as in *imtala* > *indala* "he has become full." Just as OB *wuššurum* is analogously replaced by MB/SB *muššuru* (see **5** above), the Old Babylonian perfect *ūtaššer*, "he has released," is replaced by *umtaššer*, appearing as MB/SB/NB *undaššer* or *undeššer* (see §3.1.3.1).

From the Middle Babylonian period onwards, *m* that is part of the root may also shift to *n* before the other dentals, *d* and *ṭ*, as well as before *š*, *ṣ*, *q*, *k*, as in *anši* < *amši* "I forgot"; *enqu* < *emqu* "wise." In Neo-Assyrian this secondary *n* completely assimilated to the following consonant: for example, *attaḫar* < **antaḫar* < *amtaḫar* "I received." Moreover, in Neo-Assyrian an etymological intervocalic *m* was often written as <'> or deleted from the script entirely: for example, <da'iq>, <dêq> for earlier *damiq* "it is good" (< √*dmq*).

19. The final *m* of the ventive suffix (*-am*, *-nim*, *-m*) and of the locative adverbial *-um* assimilated completely to the consonant of a following pronominal suffix: for example, *ašpurakkum* < **ašpuram-kum* "I sent to you (masc.)"; *šēpuššu* < **šēpum-šu* "at his foot."

20. The assimilation of *l* and *r* to a following consonant is rare but attested: for example, *kilattān* < **kilaltān* (fem.) "both"; *qarnum*/*qannum* "horn." In Neo-Babylonian and Late Babylonian, *r* very often becomes *š* before *t* and *k*: for example, *lištappud* < *lirtappud* "may he always run"; *šipištu* < *šipirtu* "message."

21. In the Middle Babylonian and Neo-Babylonian periods the voiceless velar *k* often becomes voiced when immediately following the nasals *m* and *n* (i.e., *k* > *g* /{*m*, *n*} _): for example, *kankum* > *kangu* "sealed document"; *ṭēmka* > *ṭēnga* "your report" (for *m* > *n* see **18** above).

3.8.1.5 Metathesis

22. Metathesis of consonants occurs in unprefixed verbal forms (i.e., infinitive, imperative, verbal adjective) with an infixed *-t-*, specifically, in forms of the Gt, Gtn, and adjectives of the form *pitrās*, when the first radical is *z*, *s*, *ṣ*, *d* (and in Old Assyrian *š* as well); in other words, {Z, D} + Vt > tV{Z, D}: for example, *tiṣbutum* (Gt inf.) < **ṣitbutum* "to grasp one another"; *tizqārum* (*pitrās* adj.) < **zitqārum* "prominent"; Old Assyrian *tišammeā* alongside *šitammeā* (Gtn pl. imperative) "listen continually!"

3.8.2 Vocalic changes

The Proto-Semitic vowels **a*, **i*, and **u* were subject to various developments in Akkadian (for secondary /e/, including Babylonian vowel harmony, see §3.1.3.1; for possible /o/, see §3.1.3.2).

3.8.2.1 Loss of final vowels and resolution of consonant clusters

In Akkadian, short final PS **a* and **u* were lost; final **i* was retained in Old Akkadian, but was also lost thereafter. Exceptions to this change are the prepositions *ana* "to," *ina* "in," and the subordination marker *u*. The final consonant clusters created by the loss of these vowels were resolved by the insertion of an anaptyctic vowel. In Babylonian this vowel was of the same quality as the preceding vowel, while in Assyrian an *a* was always inserted, regardless of the preceding vowel: for example, in the bound forms of *rigmum* "noise," singular nominative **rigmu*, accusative **rigma* both > **rigm* > Ass. *rigam*, Bab. *rigim*; compare the bound form singular genitive *rigmi* (in Old Akkadian) > **rigm* (post-Old Akkadian) > Ass. *rigam*, Bab. *rigim* as well.

3.8.2.2 Vowel syncope

In all dialects of Akkadian, the last of two or more non-final short vowels in open syllables was syncopated. Before the consonants *l* and *r* vowel syncope was optional: thus, **rapašatum* > *rapaštum* (fem. sg.) "wide"; **ʾakalum* > *akalum* beside *aklum* "food." Syncope did not take place at the end of a word (where two successive open syllables were allowed), before vowels, before certain pronominal suffixes, or in some Sumerian loanwords.

3.8.2.3 Assyrian vowel harmony

In the Assyrian dialects a short *a* vowel in an open, unaccented syllable assimilated to the vowel in the following syllable: for example, OA *šarritim* (gen.) versus OB *šarratim* "queen"; Ass. *iṣbutū* versus Bab. *iṣbatū* "they (masc.) seized." Old Assyrian was characterized by an additional rule which stipulated that in the N stem (see §4.2.2), preterite *i* of the second syllable (which resulted from regular Assyrian vowel harmony) remained even though the influencing vowel was syncopated: for example, OA *iššiknū* < **iššikinū* versus MA *iššaknū* "they were placed." This rule was not applicable to the Gt stem: for example, OA *ētitiq* "he marched away" beside OA *ētatqū* "they (masc.) marched away." In Neo-Assyrian, vowel harmony sometimes took place across two consonants (e.g., *idubbub* < *idabbub* "he is speaking") or when the influencing vowel was lost (e.g., *ittuqtū* < **imtaqutū* "they (masc.) have fallen"). For Babylonian vowel harmony see §3.1.3.1, **1**.

3.8.2.4 Vowel contraction

In Old Akkadian and during most of the history of Assyrian, vowels that became contiguous with the loss of the Proto-Semitic gutturals **ʾ*, **h*, **ḥ*, **ʿ*, **ġ* or the glides **w* and **y* did not contract. In Babylonian, however, these contiguous vowels contracted to an ultralong vowel (marked in transcription by a circumflex) of the quality of the original second vowel. There are two exceptions to this rule: (i) the regular contraction *ā* + *ĭ* > *ê* for all Babylonian dialects; and (ii) the sequences *ĭ* + *ă* and *ĕ* + *ă* do not contract in Babylonian until the end of the Old Babylonian period (except in the northern Old Babylonian dialect exemplified by the many texts from the site of Mari, in which {*i*, *e*} + *ă* > *ê*): for example, Ass. *ibniū* = Bab. *ibnû* "they (masc.) built" (< **ibniyū*); Ass. *banāim* = Bab. *banêm* (gen.) "to build" (< **banāyim*); Ass. *zakuim* = Bab. *zakîm* "clear" (masc. gen.) (< **zakuwim*); Ass. *kalaum* = Bab. *kalûm* "entirety, whole" (< **kalaʾum*). Only in the Neo-Assyrian period does Assyrian contract adjacent vowels: *a* + {*i*, *e*} > *ê*; *ia*, *iu* and *ua* do not contract at the end of a word; however, if one or more syllables follow, with the exception of *ia*, contraction usually takes place (*ia* and *ua* do not contract in verbs II-ʾ).

3.8.2.5 *Contraction of diphthongs*

Before a consonant, the Proto-Semitic diphthong **aw* contracted to *ū* (for a possible **aw* > *ō*, see §3.1.3.2), while **ay* contracted to *ī* in Babylonian and *ē* in Assyrian: for example, **mawtum* > *mūtum* "death"; **baytum* > Bab. *bītum*, Ass. *bētum* "house." Note that in the case of the sequences **aww* and **ayy* (in effect, when a geminated glide occurs), contraction did not take place (cf. §3.8.1.2, **5**, **6**); however, in middle weak verbs (i.e., verbs in which the second radical was originally **w*, **y*, or one of the five Proto-Semitic guttural consonants *ʾ, **h*, **ḥ*, *ʿ, **ġ*) the following developments may have occurred: **yadayyan* > **yadīyan* > *idīan* "he judges"; **yadawwak* > **yadūwak* > Ass. *idū(w)ak*, Bab. *idâk* "he kills."

In Eblaite, the Proto-Semitic diphthongs **aw* and **ay* are normally preserved, although the writing system has no means of representing them directly. The diphthong *aw* is expressed with either *-a* or *-a-wa*: for example, *a-mu* and *a-wa-mu* for /yawmū/ "days." The diphthong *ay* is sometimes written with an extra A sign, possibly in an attempt to express the second element: for example, *ʾa*$_x$(NI)*-a-la-nu* for /ʔaylānu(m)/ a kind of tree; but more often no attempt is made to express the *-y* of the diphthong: for example, *ʾa*$_x$(NI)*-la-nu-um*; *ba-du* for /baytu(m)/ "house"; *ba-nu* for /baynu(m)/ "tamarisk."

3.8.2.6 *Simplification of triphthongs*

Akkadian simplified the Proto-Semitic triphthongs **awi* and **ayi* to *ī* in Babylonian and *ē* in Assyrian: for example, **kawin* > Bab. *kīn*, Ass. *kēn* "he is true"; **šayim* > Bab. *šīm*, Ass. *šēm* "it is established." Similarly, **áya* (and **áwa*?) was reduced to *ā*, for example, **ṭáyab* > *ṭāb* "he is good."

4. MORPHOLOGY

As with the other Semitic languages, Akkadian is characterized by a fusional or inflecting morphology based, with the exception of primitive nouns and the pronominal system, on a consonantal root structure of three consonants or *radicals* ($C_1C_2C_3$ or PRS, after the paradigmatic verb *parāsum* "to cut"). Morphological information is conveyed by vowel patterns, various affixes, and other modifications such as consonant doubling. As noted above, Akkadian morphology is historically quite conservative.

Although Eblaite morphology has not been studied extensively (and the problems encountered in the writing system may prevent such a study), it appears to be remarkably close to that of Akkadian. The only major morphological deviations appear to be the presence of infinitives with prefixed *t-*, which represent an innovation within Eblaite, and third masculine plural verbal forms with *ti-* prefix (see §4.2.1, §4.2.11.3).

4.1 Nominal morphology

The Akkadian noun is morphologically marked for case (nominative, accusative, and genitive), gender (masculine and feminine), and number (singular, dual, and plural). There is no dative case for Akkadian nominals; instead indirect objects are expressed by nouns in the genitive governed by prepositions. Certain transitive verbs, however, may govern two accusative nouns or pronouns, one of which represents the indirect object. The accusative case may also be used to fulfill a wide range of adverbial functions. The dual is only productive for the Old Akkadian period, after which it is generally confined to nouns referring to parts of the body and other natural pairs. Additionally, the Akkadian nominal can assume four possible forms or "states": (i) the free form or *declined* state; (ii) the *construct* or bound form; (iii) the *absolute* form or state; and (iv) the *predicative* form or the predicative construction (also referred to as the stative in some grammars).

4.1.1 Declined form

Below, the Old Babylonian paradigm for the declined form is given for the noun *ilum* "god" (*iltum* "goddess"):

(7) Akkadian noun declension (Old Babylonian)

		Masculine	*Feminine*
Singular	*Nominative*	ilum	iltum
	Genitive	ilim	iltim
	Accusative	ilam	iltam
Dual	*Nominative*	ilān	iltān
	Genitive-accusative	ilīn	iltīn
Plural	*Nominative*	ilū	ilātum
	Genitive-accusative	ilī	ilātim

The short vowels *u*, *i*, and *a*, which mark the nominative, genitive, and accusative, respectively, are inherited from the Proto-Semitic case system. In the dual and plural, the genitive and accusative forms collapse into a single form marked with *i*, often referred to as the oblique case. The masculine singular and the feminine singular and plural forms exhibit a final *-m*, mimation, which, as noted above (see §3.8.1.2, **7**), disappeared after the Old Babylonian and Old Assyrian periods (in Assyrian the loss of mimation resulted in forms with a final *i* changing to *e*; see §3.1.3.1). Dual forms exhibit a final *-n*, *nunation*, which is similarly lost after the Old Babylonian and Old Assyrian periods.

In the later dialects of Akkadian the distinctions in the case system were blurred. The loss of mimation (and nunation) in the Middle Babylonian and Middle Assyrian dialects served to obscure the case and number of many nouns, given that the writing system did not generally distinguish vowel length. Moreover, in the Neo-Babylonian, Neo-Assyrian, and Standard Babylonian dialects, both the nominative and accusative cases are written with *-u* (for example, the nom./acc. sg. *šarru*). And in the Standard Babylonian and Neo-Assyrian dialects, *-ī/ē* is used not only for the oblique plural, but for the nominative as well. In Late Babylonian and to a lesser degree in Neo-Babylonian, the loss of final short vowels often resulted in case endings being dropped completely.

The nominal declension of Eblaite is identical to that of Akkadian. As with the early dialects of Akkadian, Eblaite exhibits mimation although it is not regularly indicated in the script.

There is no definite or indefinite article in Akkadian or Eblaite. Thus, a word such as *šarrum* (Akk.) may represent "king," "a king," or "the king" depending on context.

4.1.1.1 Gender

Most unmarked substantives are masculine. However, perhaps 15 percent are either feminine (e.g., *ḫarrānum* "road") or both masculine and feminine (e.g., *urḫum* "road"). Additionally, a significant number of substantives (perhaps 30 percent) are masculine in the singular, but are either feminine in the plural (e.g., *eqlum* "field," pl. *eqlētum*) or have both masculine and feminine plurals (e.g., *kunukkum* "seal," pl. *kunukkū* or *kunukkātum*). Feminine singular substantives are marked with the allomorphs *-t* and *-at*, the occurrence of which is based solely on phonological grounds: *-at* is employed when the base ends in two consonants, as in *šarratum* (nom.) "queen"; otherwise *-t* is employed, as in *bēltum* "lady" (< *bēlum* "lord"). Feminine plural nouns are universally marked with *-āt*.

4.1.1.2 Number

As the above paradigm indicates, external plurals are standard for Akkadian. However, there may be remnants of internal plurals in the language as exemplified by a relatively small number of nouns: for example, *ṣuḫārû* "boys, servants" (<**ṣuḫarā'u*); plurals with double middle radical, as in *abbū* "fathers" (sg. *abum*); *aḫḫū* "brothers" (sg. *aḫum*); *aḫḫātum* "sisters" (sg. *aḫātum*); *iṣṣū* "trees" (sg. *iṣum*); note also *arrakūtum*, possibly a plural of *arkum* "long."

4.1.1.3 The terminative and locative endings

In addition to the nominative, genitive, and accusative case endings, nouns may take two other endings. The ending *-iš* has a terminative or locative function, as in *iliš* "for the god," *qātiššu* "to his hand" (*qātum* "hand"); *-um* (identical to the nominative case) is used with a locative function: for example, *libbum* "in the heart"; *šaptukki* "on your (fem.) lips" (< *šaptum* + *ki*). Both endings are productive only in Old Akkadian, after which they are restricted to certain nouns and compounds, particularly in the Old Babylonian literary and Standard Babylonian dialects. However, *-iš* and *-um* continue to be used in the formation of adverbs: for example, *rabîš* "greatly"; *apputtum* "please" (see §4.3.2). It is not clear whether the terminative and the locative represent vestigial case markers or adverbial formatives. Eblaite also displays the terminative ending *-iš* and the locative ending *-um*: for example, *ga-tum-ma ga-ti-iš* /k'ātum-ma k'ātiš/ "from hand to hand."

4.1.1.4 The particularizing suffix -ān

The particularizing suffix *-ān* may appear directly after the root and immediately before the case endings. It serves to identify a particular individual or object from among a general group or class: for example, *nādinānum* "the seller in question, the particular seller"; *šarrāqānum* "the thief in question, that particular thief." In some instances it may acquire a specific meaning: for example, *rabiānum* "mayor" (lit. "the particular great man"). With plural substantives it indicates a specific group: for example, *ilānū* "(a certain group of) gods"; *šarrānū* "(a certain group of) kings." In the post-Old Babylonian and Old Assyrian dialects (but attested already in the Old Babylonian and Old Assyrian periods) the words *ālum* "city," *ilum* "god," and *šarrum* "king" regularly exhibit the particularizing suffix in their plurals – in such cases, the particularizing meaning of *-ān* has been lost.

4.1.1.5 The abstract suffix -ūt

The suffix *-ūt* (Ass. *-utt*) is added to the bases of nouns to form abstracts. The suffix precedes the expected case ending (with feminine forms the marker *-(a)t* is usually dropped): for example, *šarrūtum* "kingship" (< *šarrum* "king"); *ilūtum* "divinity" (< *ilum* "god"); *awīlūtum* "humanity" (< *awīlum* "man"); *dannūtum* "strength" (< *dannum* "strong"); *aššūtum* "wifehood" (< *aššatum* "wife"). Although the Babylonian suffix *-ūt* is identical to the masculine plural ending of adjectives, nouns formed with this suffix are grammatically feminine singular.

4.1.1.6 *Noun forms*

As in the other Semitic languages, many Akkadian nouns are derived from verbal bases. Nouns that are not associated with verbal bases are referred to as *isolated*. Many such nouns inherited from Proto-Semitic display fixed bases in the singular consisting of two or three consonants with one or two intervening vowels: for example, **ʿayn-* "eye"; **kalb-* "dog," **šinn-* "tooth"; **paraš-* "horse"; **ʿiṣ́-* "wood"; **ʾil-* "god." However, most native Akkadian nouns are derived from verbal bases, and some – though not most – are classifiable with regard to a predictable pattern and associated meaning. The following list of noun patterns is not in any way exhaustive, but merely illustrates the phenomenon (verbal noun and adjective patterns are not included); the root *p-r-s* (< *parāsum* "to cut") is used here to represent $C_1C_2C_3$, following the traditional presentation of the Akkadian root.

1. *parrās nouns.* Often designate professions: for example, *dayyālum* "spy" (< *dâlum* "to wander"); *errēšum* "farmer" (< *erēšum* "to plow"); *šarrāqum* "thief" (< *šarāqum* "to steal").
2. *mapras(t) nouns.* Denote place, time, or instrument (such as tools and vehicles): for example, *maškanum* "threshing floor" (< *šakānum* "to place"); *mūšabum* "dwelling" (< *wašābum* "to dwell"); *narkabtum* "chariot" (< *rakābum* "to ride"; for *ma-* > *na-* see §3.8.1.3, **9**, Barth's Law).
3. *purussāʾ nouns.* Often denote legal activities: for example, *purussûm* "legal decision" (< *parāsum* "to cut, to decide"); *rugummûm* "legal claim" (< *ragāmum* "to complain"); *uzubbûm* "divorce(-payment)" (< *ezēbum* "to leave").
4. *pirs (fem. pirist) nouns.* Often associated with a passive nuance: for example, *isiḫtum* "assignment" (< *esēḫum* "to assign"); *šiprum* "message, mission" (< *šapārum* "to send"); *šiṭrum* "(piece of) writing" (< *šaṭārum* "to write").
   An *ipris* form is attested, a less common variant of *pirs*: for example, *ikribum* "prayer" (< *karābum* "to pray"); *ipṭerū* "ransom" (< *paṭārum* "to loosen, to remove").
5. *purs (fem. purust) nouns.* Often abstracts of adjectival roots: for example, *šulmum* "well-being" (< *šalāmum* "to be well/whole"); *rupšum* "width" (< *rapāšum* "to be wide").
6. *taprās nouns.* Associated with the Gt stem (see §4.2.5): for example, *tamḫārum* "battle" (< *mitḫurum* "to oppose one another"); *tāḫāzum* "battle, combat" (< *atḫuzum* "to seize one another").
7. *taprīs and taprist nouns.* Associated with the D stem (see §4.2.3): for example, *talmīdum* "student" (< *lummudum* "to teach"); *tarbītum* "offspring" (< *rubbûm* "to rear").
8. *Forms with a reduplicated radical.* Especially associated with insect names: for example, *zuqaqīpum* "scorpion"; *kulbābum* "bee"; *adammūmum* "wasp."

4.1.2 The bound form

Genitival relationships are most commonly expressed by juxtaposing the governing and governed noun. In such constructions, the former occurs in the bound form and the governed noun in the genitive case. The bound form is also used for nouns that syntactically govern pronominal suffixes and, less often, introduce relative clauses (see §5.12.1): for example, *bīt awīlim* "the house of the man" (< *bītum* "house"); *šarrat mātim* "queen of the land" (< *šarratum* "queen"); *kalabšu* "his dog" (nom./acc.).

The bound form of a given noun may be described as the shortest form of the noun phonetically possible. As such, the bound form lacks mimation/nunation and case vowels – with the exception of the final *i* of the genitive singular and oblique feminine plural forms which was retained during the Old Akkadian period, but lost thereafter (see §3.8.2.1). However, the bound form in all dialects retained, and probably lengthened, the genitive singular *i* when it occurred before pronominal suffixes: for example, *bēlīšu* "his lord (gen.)" versus *bēlšu* (nom.-acc.). Similarly, plural and dual forms retained their case vowels before pronominal suffixes: for example, *mārūka* "your (masc.) sons (nom.)"; *uznāšu* "his (two) ears (nom.)." The loss of case vowels in all other instances, that is, all forms before nouns, and nominative and accusative singular forms before suffixes, often resulted in an impermissible word-final consonant cluster (see §3.7). Such impermissible clusters were resolved in a variety of ways according to the morphological shape of the base (see §3.8.2.1). One-syllable nouns ending in -C_1C_1 either added a short *-i* (e.g., *libbi* < *libbum* "heart") or dropped the second consonant (e.g., *ekal* < *ekallum* "palace"). Bases ending in -C_1C_2, where $C_2 \neq t$, insert an anatyptic vowel of the same quality as that of the preceding syllable (in Assyrian, *a* is inserted regardless of the preceding vowel): for example, *puḫur* (Ass. *puḫar*) < *puḫrum* "assembly." Bases ending in -C*t* either insert an *a*-vowel (e.g., *mārat* < *mārtum* "daughter") or add an *-i* (e.g., *qīšti* < *qīštum* "gift"). Two-syllable nouns ending in -C*t* exhibit bound forms with an additional *i* vowel: thus, *napišti* < *napištum* "life" (exceptions being feminine participles, which insert *a*: *māḫirat* < *māḫirtum* "rival"). Before suffixes, singular bases ending in -C_1C_2 universally insert *a* before the suffix in the nominative and accusative; as noted above, in the genitive the *i* case vowel is maintained before suffixes: for example, *napištaka* "your (fem.) life" (nom.-acc.) versus *napištīka* (gen.). The syntax of the genitive construction is discussed in section 5.4.

The morphological shape of the bound form in Eblaite cannot be determined with any certainty given the ambiguities posed by the writing system. For example, there are writings with and without final vowel (often *-u*, perhaps representing the nominative case): for example, *ḫa-za-nu* GN "mayor of GN"; *ma-lik* GN "king of GN," where Akkadian would omit the final vowel in both cases. Additionally, in what may represent fixed or logographic writings (see §2.6), there are forms such as *ma-za-lum-sù* where the reading may be either /maθ̣θ̣ārŭ̄šu/ or /maθ̣θ̣āršu/ "his guard."

4.1.3 The predicative form

Substantives and adjectives may enter into a predicative construction whereby a specific set of pronominal suffixes are added directly to the indeclinable base. The resulting construction constitutes a verbless clause, and as such, predicative forms are not marked for tense. The pronominal suffix serves as the subject, and the substantive or adjective as the predicate: *marṣāku* "I (*-āku*) am sick (*marṣ-*)"; *rabiānu* (post-Old Babylonian *rabânu*) "we (*-ānu*) are great (*rabi-*)"; *bēlū* 'they (*-ū*, masc.) are lords (*bēl-*)." The third masculine singular of the predicative form is marked with -Ø: *šar* "He (-Ø) is king (*šar-*)." The nonfinal *a*-vowels of the other endings are subject to Babylonian vowel harmony whereby *a* shifts to an *e* vowel when there is an *e* elsewhere in the word (see §3.1.3.1, **1**). Substantives may appear in the predicative construction only when not followed by any modifiers, including adjectives, genitive nouns, pronominal suffixes, relative clauses, and the emphatic particle *-ma*.

The Old Babylonian paradigm of the predicative construction for the substantive *šarrum* (for example, *šarrāku* "I am/was/will be king") and the adjective *ezbum* (for example, *ezbēku* "I am/was/will be abandoned") appears below:

(8) Old Babylonian predicative form paradigm

		Suffix	*šarrum*	*ezbum*
Singular	*1st com.*	-āku	šarrāku	ezbēku
	2nd masc.	-āta	šarrāta	ezbēta
	2nd fem.	-āti	šarrāti	ezbēti
	3rd masc.	-Ø	šar	ezib
	3rd fem.	-at	šarrat	ezbet
Plural	*1st com.*	-ānu	šarrānu	ezbēnu
	2nd masc.	-ātunu	šarrātunu	ezbētunu
	2nd fem.	-ātina	šarrātina	ezbētina
	3rd masc.	-ū	šarrū	ezbū
	3rd fem.	-ā	šarrā	ezbā

Note the following developments for the enclitic subject pronominal suffixes: (i) in Assyrian the first common plural subject marker is *-āni*; (ii) in Old Assyrian the second masculine singular subject is *-āti*; (iii) in Neo-Assyrian and Neo-Babylonian the first common singular is *-āk(a)* (< *-āku*). Only in Old Akkadian and Old Assyrian is there a third masculine dual form attested, with subject marker *-ā*: for example, *šarrā* "the two are kings"; Old Akkadian also attests a third feminine dual form with the enclitic subject marker *-tā*: for example, *šalimtā* "you two are well."

The predicative form appears to be ancient, given the appearance of a similar construction in Old Egyptian. In other Semitic languages, however, the form has become an active, perfective verb: for example, Hebrew *ʿāzəbû* "they have abandoned" versus Akkadian *ezbū* "they are abandoned."

The predicative form is also attested for Eblaite, as evidenced by forms such as *na-im* /naʕim/ "he/it is good"; *da-nu-nu* /dannunū/ "they (masc.) are strengthened"; *ʾa*$_5$(NI)*-bù-ḫa* /ʔabbuxā/ "they (fem.) are girded." Additionally, both Eblaite and Old Akkadian (as well as Amorite) attest an archaic third masculine singular predicative form ending in *-a*. This form is no longer productive by the time of the first attested texts and is limited primarily to personal names: for example, the Eblaite name *Na-ma-Da-mu* "Damu is pleasant"; and the Old Akkadian name *Šu-be-la* "he is a lord."

4.1.4 The absolute form

The absolute form of the noun is an indeclinable form, without mimation or case ending, and resembles the third masculine singular of the predicative form (see §4.1.3); in fact, the absolute form may represent in origin an embedded predication. Although the absolute form is not fully understood, several functions are clear: (i) for certain frozen adverbial expressions (e.g., *zikar sinniš* "male (and) female," *ṣeḫer rabi* "small (and) great"); (ii) to express the vocative (e.g., *bēlet* "lady!", *šar* "king!"); (iii) often for cardinal numbers (e.g., *ištēn* "one," *šinā* "two"); (iv) in expressions of mass and quantity, where both the number and the unit of measurement appear in the absolute (e.g., *sebe uṭṭet (kaspum)* "seven grains (of silver)"); and (v) in distributive expressions or in expressions in which the substantive is unmistakably singular (e.g., *ina ellat ellat* "with every caravan," *šanat* "a single year").

The absolute form is sparsely attested in Eblaite where it is used to express: (i) divine names (e.g., ^{d}*Ga-mi-iš*, ^{d}*Ra-sa-ap*); (ii) geographical names (e.g., *A-da-bí-ik*^{ki}, *A-da-ti-ik*^{ki}); and (iii) month names (e.g., ITI *za-ʾà-na-at*).

4.1.5 Adjectives

4.1.5.1 Attributive adjectives

In addition to predicative adjectives (see §4.1.3), Akkadian displays attributive adjectives which follow their head nouns and agree with their antecedents in case, gender, and number. For the most part, attributive adjectives are declined like substantives (see [7]), with the exception of the masculine plural endings *-ūtum* (nom.), *-ūtim* (obl.), which are distinctive. Eblaite likewise exhibits these plural forms: for example, *a(-wa)-mu ʾà-mu-tum* /yawmū ḫammūtum/ (= Akk. *ūmū emmūtum*) "hot days."

Most Akkadian adjectives are derived from verbal roots, and as such, have the form *parVs*, where the second vowel is *i* for active roots (both transitive and intransitive), but unpredictable for adjectival/stative roots (*a*, *i*, or *u*). However, the distinctive vowel of the second syllable is syncopated in all forms except for the attributive feminine singular (see §3.8.2.2) and the predicative form with third masculine singular subject.

Verbal adjectives denote the condition or state resulting from the action of the verb from which it is derived: (i) for transitive verbs, the verbal adjective is passive (e.g., *ṣabtum* "captured" < *ṣabātum* "to capture"); (ii) for active-intransitive verbs, the verbal adjective is resultative and perfective (e.g., *maqtum* "fallen, having fallen" < *maqātum* "to fall"); (iii) for stative/adjectival verbs, the verbal adjective is descriptive (e.g., *damqum* "good" < *damāqum* "to be good"). Old Babylonian and Old Akkadian declensions of *šarrum* "king," *šarratum* "queen," and the modifying attributive adjective *damqum* "good" are presented in (9):

(9) Akkadian adjective declension (Old Babylonian and Old Akkadian)

	Masculine	*Feminine*
Singular		
Nominative	šarrum damqum	šarratum damiqtum
Genitive	šarrim damqim	šarratim damiqtim
Accusative	šarram damqam	šarratam damiqtam
Dual		
Nominative	šarrān damqūtum	šarratān damqātum
	šarrān damqān (OAkk.)	šarratān damqatān (OAkk.)
Genitive-accusative	šarrīn damqūtim	šarratīn damqātum
	šarrīn damqīn (OAkk.)	šarratīn damqatīn (OAkk.)
Plural		
Nominative	šarr(ān)ū damqūtum	šarrātum damqātum
Genitive-accusative	šarr(ān)ī damqūtim	šarrātim damqātim

An adjective modifying more than one noun appears in the plural; compound, mixed gender antecedents are modified by masculine plural adjectives. Dual adjectives are only attested for the Old Akkadian period, after which dual nouns are modified by plural adjectives.

Any adjective may be used substantively: for example, the masculine singular adjective *ṣabtum* "seized" (< *ṣabātum* "to seize") may also be used to express the masculine singular substantive "captive." Frequently, the feminine singular of an adjective is used substantively to denote an abstract noun: for example, *damiqtum* "good(ness), luck, fame" (cf. masc. sg. *damqum* "good" < *damāqum* "to be good").

4.1.5.2 *Comparatives and superlatives*

Akkadian did not possess distinct forms for expressing the comparative and superlative; instead, either the attributive or the predicative adjective was used. The preposition *eli* was used in comparative expressions: for example, *awīlam ša elīšu rabû imḫaṣ* "he struck a man who is greater than he." The superlative is expressed by the bound form of the adjective: for example, *Ištar rabīt ilātim* "Ištar is the greatest of the goddesses." Additionally, the Š stem (see §4.2.4) verbal adjective is often used as a superlative: for example, *šurbûm* "very great, greatest" (< *rabûm* "great").

4.1.5.3 *Denominative adjectives*

The addition of the ending *-ī* to the base of a noun, followed by the adjectival case ending, forms an adjective with the meaning "pertaining to, related to (the noun in question)." Common denominative adjectives include *maḫrûm* "former, earlier" (< *maḫrī-um*; cf. *maḫrum* "front"); *elûm* "upper" (< *elī-um*; cf. *elum* "top"); *šaplûm* "lower" (< *šaplī-um*; cf. *šaplum* "bottom"). Gentilic adjectives are formed by adding the denominative *-ī* to place names: for example, *Akkadûm* (< *Akkad* + *ī* + *um*) "Akkadian" (masc. nom.).

4.1.5.4 *Independent possessive adjectives*

Possession may be expressed by a set of possessive adjectives (as well as with pronominal suffixes; see §4.1.6.2), particularly for the Old Assyrian and Old Babylonian periods (although even for these periods, possession is usually expressed by the pronominal suffixes). The possessive adjectives agree with their antecedent nouns in case, gender, and number; they do not agree with the gender of the possessor. These adjectives may be used attributively (e.g., *kaspam yâm* "my silver" [acc.]) or, more commonly, as predicates (e.g., *bītum šū yûm* "that house is mine"; *šūrūtum yā'ū* "the black [textiles] are mine" [masc. pl.]). The nominative forms of the attested possessive adjectives are presented in (10); attested Assyrian forms appear in parentheses:

(10) Nominative forms of the possessive adjectives

	SINGULAR		PLURAL	
	Masculine	*Feminine*	*Masculine*	*Feminine*
Singular				
1st	yûm (yā'um)	yattu^{m}/n	yût(t)u^{m}/n	yât(t)u^{m}/n
2nd	kûm (kuā'um)	kattum (kuātum)	kûttu^{m}/n	kâttu^{m}/n
3rd	šûm (šuā'um)	šattu^{m}/n (šuātum)	šûttu^{m}/n	—
Plural				
1st	nûm (niā'um)	niattu^{m}/n	nûttu^{m}/n	—
2nd	kunûm	(kunūtum)	(ku(w)ā'ūtum)	—
3rd	šunûm	šunūtum	—	—

The unusual nunation (rather than expected mimation) that often accompanies feminine and plural forms of these adjectives, as well as feminine and plural forms of the demonstrative *annûm* "this" (see §4.1.5.5; for example, fem. sg. *annītun*, masc. pl. *annûtun*), is probably the result of partial assimilation to the preceding *t* of such forms.

In the Middle Babylonian period the possessive pronoun *attu-* replaced the possessive adjectives discussed above. It was always combined with the possessive suffixes (see §4.1.6.2): for example, *ḫarrāna attū'a* "my caravan (acc.)"; *šibšu attūšu* "his lease."

4.1.5.5 Demonstrative adjectives and pronouns

The most common near demonstrative ("this," "these") in Akkadian is *annûm* (base *anni-*), feminine *annītum*; in Neo-Babylonian, *agû*, feminine *agātu* largely replaces *annûm*. Far demonstratives ("that," "those") are represented by *ullûm*, feminine *ullītum*, in Babylonian, and *ammiu(m)*, feminine *ammītu(m)*, in Assyrian. All of the preceding are inflected with adjectival case endings. For the Old Babylonian, Middle Babylonian, and Standard Babylonian periods particularly, the third-person independent personal pronouns (see §4.1.6.1) are used to express the far demonstrative. This pronoun also serves as an anaphoric pronoun, expressing "the aforementioned": for example, *alpam šuāti išriq* "he stole the aforementioned ox."

4.1.6 Pronouns

4.1.6.1 Independent personal pronouns

Akkadian distinguishes a nominative, dative, and common genitive-accusative case for the independent personal pronoun. As noted above, the third-person nominative and genitive-accusative forms are also used for the anaphoric pronoun. The genitive-accusative forms are marked with *-ti*, the dative with *-ši(m)*. The dative form represents an innovation within Akkadian – and Eblaite, which also attests these pronouns – and is not found in the other Semitic languages; it is most often found after the preposition *ana* "to": for example, *ana kâšim taklāku* "I trust you" (fem. sg.). Dative forms are attested primarily in Old Babylonian and in the post-Old Babylonian periods; in Old Assyrian the genitive-accusative forms were usually employed for the dative (i.e., after the preposition *ana*). Nominative personal pronouns are often found in verbless clauses, or for emphasis or clarification in verbal clauses, since the pronominal subject is always included in the verb; the genitive-accusative and dative pronouns are used principally for emphasis. Only for the Old Akkadian period is a dual independent personal pronoun attested, third common *šunīti* (gen.-acc.); however, the presence of dual suffixed pronouns (see §4.1.6.2) in both Old Akkadian and Eblaite may suggest that both languages had a full set of yet-unattested, dual independent personal pronouns. The Old Babylonian paradigm for the most common forms of the independent personal pronouns is set out in (11); Old Assyrian forms (when different from the Old Babylonian) are placed in parentheses, and attested Eblaite forms in brackets:

(11)

	Nominative	*Genitive-accusative*	*Dative*
Singular			
1st com.	anāku [ʾana]	yâti	yâši(m)
2nd masc.	attā [ʾanta]	kâti/a (ku(w)āti) [kuwāti]	kâši(m) [kuwāši(m)]
2nd fem.	attī	kâti (ku(w)āti)	kâši(m)
3rd masc.	šū (šūt) [šuwa]	šuāti/u [šuwāti]	šuāši(m) [šuwāši(m)]
3rd fem.	šī (šīt) [šiya]	šiāti	šiāši(m)
Plural			
1st com.	nīnu (nēnu)	niāti	niaši(m)
2nd masc.	attunu [ʾantanu]	kunūti	kunūši(m)
2nd fem.	attina	kināti	kināši(m)
3rd masc.	šunu [šunū]	šunūti	šunūši(m)
3rd fem.	šina	šināti	šināši(m)

4.1.6.2 Pronominal suffixes

The pronominal suffixes are attached to both nouns and verbs: (i) the genitive or possessive suffixes are appended to the bound form of the noun (including nonfinite forms of the verb), (ii) while the accusative and dative suffixes, which refer to direct and indirect objects, respectively, may only be appended to finite verbs (predicative adjectives may accept dative suffixes as well): for example, *bītni* "our house" (nom., acc.); *iṣbatniāti* "he seized us"; *alikniāšim* "Come (masc. sg.) to us!" In later dialects the accusative and dative suffixes are no longer carefully distinguished. The ventive morpheme (see §4.2.9) may precede the accusative and dative suffixes; when both an accusative and a dative suffix are attached to a given verb the order is Verb–(Ventive)–Dative–Accusative: for example, *aṭrud(ak)kuššu* (< *aṭrud(+am)+kum+šu*) "I sent him to you." The pronominal suffixes for the Old Babylonian period are given in (12); Old Assyrian forms (when different from the Old Babylonian) are placed in parentheses, and attested Eblaite forms in brackets:

(12)

	Possessive (genitive)	*Accusative*	*Dative*
Singular			
1st com.	-ī, -(y)a [-ī]	-anni/-nni/-ninni [-ni]	-am/-m/-nim
2nd masc.	-ka [-ka]	-ka	-kum [-kum]
2nd fem.	-ki [-ki]	-ki	-kim
3rd masc.	-šu [-šu]	-šu [-šu]	-šum [-šum]
3rd fem.	-ša [-ša]	-ši	-šim
Plural			
1st com.	-ni [-ni]	-niāti [-ni]	-niāšim (-niāti)
2nd masc.	-kunu	-kunūti (-kunu)	-kunūšim (-kunūti)
2nd fem.	-kina	-kināti (-kina)	-kināšim (-kināti)
3rd masc.	-šunu [-šunu]	-šunūti (-šunu)	-šunūšim (-šunūti)
3rd fem.	-šina [-šina]	-šināti (-šina) [-šināt]	-šināšim (-šināti)

Only for Old Akkadian and Eblaite are dual pronominal suffixes attested: second common dual *-kunī* [*-kumayn*] (gen.),*-kunīšim* [*-kumay(n)*] (dat.), *-kunīt(i)* (acc.); third common dual *-šunī* [*-šumay(n)*] (gen.), *-šunīti* [*-šumay(n)*] (acc.), *-šunīšim* (dat.). As noted above, the third person is expressed with *š* in Old Akkadian, prior to the merger of **ś/š* with **θ*. The first common singular possessive suffix has the allomorphs *-ī*, *-(y)a*, the choice of which depends on the morphological shape of the preceding noun: *-ī* is used after singular nouns in the nominative or accusative (e.g., *mārtī* "my daughter," *epēšī* "my doing"); otherwise, *-(y)a* is used, including after the case-vowel of singular nouns and adjectives in the genitive (e.g., *ināya* "my eyes" [dual], *itti abīya* "with my father"); after *-ū* (and sometimes *-ā*), *-(y)a* is often written as *-a* (i.e., written with the A sign; e.g., *mārū'a* "my sons," *epšētū'a* "my deeds").

The first common singular dative suffix is identical to the ventive morpheme (see §4.2.9), and the choice of allomorph *-am/-m/-nim* is dependent on morphological considerations (namely, the person and number of the verb on which it appears): *-am* is attached to forms without a vocalic ending (i.e., 3rd com. sg., 2nd masc. sg, 1st com. sg., and 1st com. pl.); *-m* is attached to the form ending in *ī* (i.e., the 2nd fem. sg.); *-nim* is attached to forms ending in *-ū* (i.e., 3rd masc. pl.) and in *-ā* (i.e., 3rd fem. pl. and 2nd com. pl.).

The allomorphs of the accusative suffix, *-anni/-nni/-ninni*, are derived from the ventive/dative suffix + *-ni*, where the *m* assimilates to the following *n*; the distribution of the accusative forms is identical to that of the corresponding ventive/dative suffix. The second- and third-person genitive pronominal suffixes may be apocopated in poetic texts, the singular forms usually following the appropriate case-vowel: for example, *libbuš* "her heart" (nom.; for *libbaša*). In Old Assyrian, after a short *-a*, bisyllabic suffixes are shortened: for example, *ṭuppašnu* "their tablet" (< *ṭuppašunu*); *libbaknu* "your (pl.) heart" (< *libbakunu*).

4.1.6.3 *Reflexive pronouns*

The noun *ramānum* (Ass. *ramunum*) "self, oneself" is used with pronominal suffixes as a reflexive pronoun: for example, *ana ramānīya* "for myself." The nouns *pagrum* "body, corpse" and *napištum* "life" may also be used as reflexive pronouns when pronominal suffixes are attached: for example, *pagarka uṣur* "guard yourself!"

4.1.6.4 *Determinative-relative pronoun*

The determinative-relative pronoun was fully declined in Old Akkadian and Eblaite. Because of the ambiguity of the writing system, it is not certain whether the initial consonant of the Eblaite form was *θ* as in Old Akkadian or *ð* as in West Semitic. The paradigm of the Old Akkadian determinative-relative pronoun is given in (13); the signs used to represent the attested Eblaite forms appear in brackets:

(13)

	SINGULAR		PLURAL	
	Masculine	*Feminine*	*Masculine*	*Feminine*
Nominative	θū [θU]	θât [θU-DU]	θût	θât [θU-DU]
Genitive	θī [θI]	θâti [θU-TI]	θûti [θU-TI]	*θâti [θU–TI]
Accusative	θā [θA]	θât	θût	θât

The determinative-relative pronoun for all subsequent periods, *ša* (< *θā*, the Old Akkadian accusative masculine sing. form), was indeclinable, although declined forms of the pronoun still remained in several frozen expressions: for example, *šūt rēši* "the ones (masc. pl.) of the head," that is, "courtiers." As a determinative pronoun, *ša* represents "the one of": for example, *ša Bābilim* "the one of Babylon"; usually, however, it stands in apposition to a preceding noun, and is translated "of." Nouns that follow *ša* are always in the genitive case: for example, *šarrum ša mātim* "the king, the one of the country," that is, "the king of the country." As a relative pronoun, *ša* is translated "which, who, etc." and serves to introduce relative clauses (see §5.12.1).

The relative pronouns in Eblaite are often expressed by the logogram LÚ, Sumerian "man," which was normally used in Sumerian to introduce relative clauses with male animate antecedents. In Eblaite, however, it is used with animates and inanimates, both male and female.

4.1.6.5 *Interrogative/Indefinite pronouns and adjectives*

The personal interrogative pronoun in Akkadian and Eblaite is *mannum* "who?," which is declined for case, but has no special feminine or plural forms. The impersonal interrogative pronoun *mīnum*, or *minûm*, "what?," is similarly declined for case and likewise is without special feminine or plural forms; note also the phrase *ana mīnim* "for what?" that is, "why?." Additionally, there is an interrogative adjective *ayyum* "which?," that agrees with its antecedent in case, number, and gender: for example, *ayyītum iltum* "which goddess?"; *ayyum*, unlike most adjectives, may precede the noun it modifies.

The indefinite pronouns are formed either by the reduplication of the bases of the interrogative pronouns, or by appending the particle *-ma* to the latter. The personal indefinite pronoun is *mamma(n)* (< **manman*) "anyone, someone," with the negative adverb *lā*, "not any, no." The impersonal indefinite pronoun is *mimma* (< *mīnum* "what?") "anything, something, all," with negative adverb *lā*, "nothing." Both *mamma(n)* and *mimma* are indeclinable and both may be used as generalizing relative pronouns, especially in late texts. Additionally, the adjectival *ayyumma* "whichever, any, some," based on the interrogative adjective, *ayyum* "which?," agrees with its noun in case, number, and gender.

4.2 Verbal morphology

As in other Semitic languages, the verbal morphology of Akkadian is complex. The verbal root usually consists of three consonants; however, Akkadian displays many so-called *weak verbs* – verbs in which one or more of the original root consonants disappeared altogether or were susceptible to certain phonological changes in specific environments. Additionally, roots of four radicals, referred to as *quadriradical* verbs, are attested as well. Akkadian exhibits four finite forms (tenses or aspects): durative, preterite, perfect, and imperative. As in other Semitic languages, Akkadian derives verbs by means of prefixes and modifications of the verbal roots. These set patterns, better known as *stems*, have characteristic meanings and functions; the range of meanings of a verb for a given derived stem can be more or less extrapolated from the basic stem. Each stem has three nonfinite forms: infinitive, participle, and verbal adjective. For reasons of economy, the outline of the Akkadian verbal morphology presented below is based solely on the strong verb, although it should be kept in mind that many of the most basic and frequent verbs in the language are weak.

Knowledge of Eblaite verbal morphology is greatly limited by the paucity of syllabically spelled verbs. However, it is clear that Eblaite exhibits both the preterite and the durative forms. Verbs with infixed *-t-* (see below) may indicate either G perfects, or Gt or Gtn preterites. Other stems attested for Eblaite are the D, Š, Št, N, Ntn, and ŠD (?), although examples for many of these are scarce. The stem-vowel of the various stems and tenses behaves as it does in Akkadian. The West Semitic fientive *qatala* form cannot be confirmed for Eblaite; rather, such forms most likely represent an archaic predicative form (see §4.1.3).

4.2.1 G stem

The basic verbal stem is the G stem (*Grundstamm*, sometimes referred to as the B stem for *basic*). Finite forms of the G stem exhibit a *thematic vowel* between the second and third radical which is lexical and unpredictable. In most cases, the vowel is the same for both the durative and the preterite (the perfect shares its theme vowel with the durative, while the imperative shares its theme vowel with the preterite) – *a*, *i*, or *u*. However, the largest class of verbs, the *ablaut class*, displays an *a* in the durative (and perfect) and *u* in the preterite (and imperative). As evidenced throughout Semitic, the various semantic categories may be roughly associated with the different theme-vowel classes: (i) the ablaut class (*a-u*) contains predominantly transitive verbs; (ii) the relatively small *a*-class similarly contains mostly transitive verbs; (iii) the large *i*-class (which represents the confluence of the Proto-Semitic *a-i* and *i-a* classes) is associated with many stative verbs, but active transitive and intransitive verbs appear in this class as well; and (iv) the large *u*-class is associated with many intransitive verbs.

Person, number, and gender are indicated by prefixes and suffixes; the durative, preterite, and perfect of the G stem (and N stem as well, discussed below) share the same set of affixes. Old Babylonian forms are given below:

(14)

	Singular		*Plural*		
3rd com.	i-		*3rd masc.*	i-	-ū
			3rd fem.	i-	-ā
2nd masc.	ta-		*2nd com.*	ta-	-ā
2nd fem.	ta-	-ī			
1st com.	a-		*1st com.*	ni-	

For the Assyrian dialects, Old Akkadian, and the Old Babylonian literary dialect, there was a distinct third feminine singular form marked with the prefix *ta-*. In Eblaite the third feminine singular prefix was regularly *ta-* (with a biform *ti-*): for example, *taqīś*, *tiqīś* "she presented." Furthermore, Eblaite exhibits a third masculine plural form with prefixed *ti-* (*tiprusū*): for example, *ti-da-ḫa-ru*$_{12}$ /tittaxrū/(?) "(the gods) approached"(?) (cf. Akk. *mitḫurum*); *ti-na-ḫu-uš* /tiʔnaxū-š/(?) "(the gods) got tired of it"(?) (cf. Akk. *anāḫum*), which is also encountered in Old Akkadian texts from Mari (and in Middle Babylonian-period peripheral texts from Amarna and Ugarit). For Old Akkadian, Old Assyrian, and Eblaite a third common dual form is attested, marked by the prefix *i-* (Ebl. *yi-*) and the suffix *-ā*.

As noted above, the prefix *i-* derives from PS **ya* (see §3.8.1.2, **6**) and/or **yi*; only in Old Akkadian and Eblaite is the *y* of the prefix preserved. The prefixes *a-* and *ta-* become *e-* and *te-* when used with verbs containing *e* in Babylonian (see §3.1.3.1, **1**): for example, Bab. *telqe*, Ass. *talqe* "you (masc. sg.) took"; or with I-*e* verbs in Babylonian and Assyrian: for example, *ēpuš* "I did." With I-*w* verbs, *u* replaces the *a-* and *i-*vowels of the prefixes: for example, *urid* "I/he descended," *turid* "you descended."

4.2.1.1 Durative (parrVs)

The durative of the strong verb is characterized by the doubling of the middle radical; the vowel between C_1 and C_2 is invariably *a* (except where *a* > *e* by Babylonian vowel harmony, see §3.1.3.1, **1**) and the vowel between C_2 and C_3 is, as noted above, the theme vowel. Note the G durative paradigm for the verb *parāsum* (*a-u* class) "to cut":

(15)

	Singular		*Plural*
3rd com.	iparras	*3rd masc.*	iparrasū
		3rd fem.	iparrasā
2nd masc.	taparras	*2nd com.*	taparrasā
2nd fem.	taparrasī		
1st com.	aparras	*1st com.*	niparras

The durative describes action that is nonpunctual or imperfective; most often it corresponds to the English present or future. As its name implies, the durative may also be used to describe any durative, nonpunctual action, past, present, or future: for example, *ikannak* may also be used with the meanings "he was sealing, he is sealing, he will be sealing." However, the durative may be used to describe habitual or customary action – *išakkan* "he used to place, he (continually) places, he will place (regularly)" – as well as potential or probable action: for example, *iṣabbat* "he may/might/could/can/should/would seize." The precise nuance of the durative can only be determined from the surrounding context. The durative form was inherited from Proto-Semitic, and like forms are found in Ethiopian and modern South Arabian; however, the form was lost in the Central Semitic languages (for example, Arabic, Hebrew, and Aramaic).

4.2.1.2 Perfect (ptarVs)

The perfect is characterized by an infixed *-ta-* immediately after the first consonant. With the addition of the plural suffixes (*-ū*, *-ā*, *ī*), subordination marker (*-u*), or ventive morpheme (*-am*), the theme vowel between C_2 and C_3 is lost according to the vowel syncope rule (see §3.8.2.2). The infixed *-t-* assimilates completely to the first consonant when that consonant is a dental or sibilant (except *š*) (see §3.8.1.4, **14**). Below is the G perfect paradigm for *parāsum*:

(16)

	Singular		*Plural*
3rd com.	iptaras	*3rd masc.*	iptarsū
		3rd fem.	iptarsā
2nd masc.	taptaras	*2nd com.*	taptarsā
2nd fem.	taptarsī		
1st com.	aptaras	*1st com.*	niptaras

The perfect roughly corresponds to the English present perfect, for example, *nimtaqut* "we have fallen," and represents actions that have been completed but affect the present. However, the perfect has many other nuances and functions that are dialect- and genre-specific. In Old Akkadian the perfect is only sparsely attested. For the Old Babylonian period, however, the perfect is quite common, especially in letters and in the conditional clauses that comprise the various law codes, including the Code of Hammurabi. In these genres, the perfect has a focusing nuance, denoting the central event in a sequence of events. In the letters of the Old Babylonian period the perfect is used with this nuance in conjunction with the adverbs *inanna* "now" or *anumma* "now, herewith, hereby" to emphasize the immediacy or current relevance of the event, the so-called epistolary or announcement perfect: for example, *inanna wardam ana maḫrīka aṭṭardam* "I have now sent the servant to you." Because of its emphatic character, the perfect rarely occurs in questions or relative clauses.

After the Old Babylonian and Old Assyrian periods, the perfect replaced the preterite as the main form used to express the past, the preterite having become restricted to negative main clauses and subordinate clauses. This distribution of forms is exactly parallel to that of certain pairs of forms in some modern Ethio-Semitic languages (Hetzron 1968); to borrow the terminology used in reference to the marked member of the Ethiopic forms, we may say that the *t* of the Middle Babylonian and Middle Assyrian perfect functions as a main verb marker.

4.2.1.3 *Preterite (prVs)*

The preterite denotes a punctual, completed action as seen by the speaker or writer: for example, *iddin* "he gave." It is most often translated by the simple past tense in English. Below is the paradigm of the G preterite for *parāsum* (*a-u*):

(17)

	Singular		*Plural*
3rd com.	iprus	*3rd masc.*	iprusū
		3rd fem.	iprusā
2nd masc.	taprus	*2nd com.*	taprusā
2nd fem.	taprusī		
1st com.	aprus	*1st com.*	niprus

The preterite form is found in secondary uses in other Semitic languages, having been replaced as the past tense by a suffix-pronoun conjugation.

4.2.1.4 *Imperative and precative*

The imperative occurs only in the second person; in form, the imperative is the preterite without prefix. The resulting initial consonant cluster is generally resolved by inserting the preterite theme-vowel between C_1 and C_2: for example, *ṣabat* "seize! (masc. sg.)." In the feminine singular and common plural forms, the addition of the respective *-ī* and *-ā* suffixes causes the vowel between C_2 and C_3 to be lost according to the rule of vowel syncope (see §3.8.2.2).

The imperative is complemented by the precative, which is used to express wishes and indirect commands in the first and third person. Like the imperative, the precative is based on the preterite. The Babylonian precative is formed by replacing the first-person singular prefixes with *lu-* and third-person prefixes with *li-*; the first common plural precative consists of an unattached short *i* before the preterite: for example, *lukšud* "may I arrive, let me arrive"; *i niškun* "let us place, may we place." In Assyrian the precative has the form of the preterite plus a prefixed *l-* (except in the first common plural and third feminine singular, where the particle *lū* appears before the preterite). In Old Akkadian, the precative is identical to the Babylonian form, with the exception of the third feminine singular, which follows the Assyrian model: for example, *lū tamḫur* "may she receive." Additionally, Old Akkadian attests a third common dual precative: for example, *lilqutā* "may they (dual) gather." Note the suppletive injunctive (imperative plus precative) paradigm for *parāsum* (*a-u*); Assyrian forms are in parentheses:

(18)

	Singular		*Plural*
3rd com.	liprus	*3rd masc.*	liprusū
(*3rd fem.*	lū taprus)	*3rd fem.*	liprusā
2nd masc.	purus	*2nd com.*	pursā
2nd fem.	pursī		
1st com.	luprus	*1st com.*	i niprus
	(laprus)		(lū niprus)

Neither the imperative nor the precative is used with a negative adverb; rather, the prohibitive and the vetitive are used to express negative commands and wishes.

4.2.1.5 *Prohibitive and vetitive*

The negative counterpart of the imperative is the prohibitive, used to express negative commands and prohibitions. The form consists of the negative adverb *lā* followed by the durative: for example, *lā tašappar* "do not send, you may not send (masc. sg.)"; *lā ipallaḫā* "they (fem.) may not/ shall not fear." The vetitive, used to express negative wishes, is formed by prefixing *ayy-* to forms of the preterite that have an initial vowel, and *ē-* to forms with an initial consonant (in Assyrian the prefix is *ē-* in all cases): for example, *ē-taškunā* "may you (pl.) not place, you should not place"; *ayy-ašpur* "may I not send, I do not wish to send." In the Neo-Assyrian dialect the distinction between the prohibitive and the vetitive is blurred, and often the two are used interchangeably.

4.2.2 N stem

The N stem is characterized by a prefixed *n* before the root; in forms in which *n* stands directly before a consonant, it assimilates completely to that consonant (see §3.8.1.4, **12**). The N stem, being based on the G stem, shares the same set of personal affixes, and, as in the G, the middle radical is doubled in the N durative and the theme vowel of the N perfect is that of the durative. However, the N differs from the G in its organization of vowel classes: verbs of the *a-u* and *a* classes in the G are collapsed into an *a-i* class in the N; G *i* class verbs are unchanged in the N. G *u* class verbs, which are rare in the N, sometimes remain *u*-class and sometimes join the dominant *a-i* pattern. When vocalic suffixes are added to the preterite, the vowel between C_2 and C_3 is lost because of syncope (see §3.8.2.2). Note the following singular and plural forms for the verb *parāsum* "to cut":

(19) Third person and imperative forms of the N stem

Durative (3rd com. sg./3rd fem. pl.)	ipparras/ipparrasā
Perfect (3rd com. sg./3rd fem. pl.)	ittapras/ittaprasā
Preterite (3rd com. sg./3rd fem. pl.)	ipparis/ipparsā
Imperative (fem. sg./com. pl.)	naprisī/naprisā

The N stem serves as the passive of active-transitive G verbs: for example, *ipparis* "it was separated"; *ṭuppum iššebir* "the tablet was broken." Stative verbs, although rarely attested in the N, assume an ingressive nuance: for example, *šumšu immassik* "his name will become bad" (cf. *maskum* "bad" [G verbal adj.]). Several verbs have a reflexive meaning in the N: for example, *ittalbaš* "he has clothed himself" (< *labāšum* "to put on clothing"). A few verbs have N rather than G as their basic form (i.e., lexical N verbs): for example, *ippalis* "he looked" (< *palāsum* "to see," rare in G).

4.2.3 D stem

The D stem (*Doppelungsstamm*) is distinguished by a double middle radical in all finite and nonfinite forms. The personal prefixes of the D (and Š, see below) all have *u* where the G and N stems have *a* or *i*; thus, the first-person and third-person singular are formally identical: for example, *udammiq* "I/she/he made good." The distribution of U-signs suggests that in Old Akkadian there was a difference in the pronunciations of the first- and third-person prefixes, i.e., the U-sign is used fairly consistently for the third-person prefix (probably representing *yu-*), whereas the first person is usually written with the Ú- and Ù-signs (probably for *'u-*). All D verbs belong to the *a-i* class (as do Š verbs; see below), regardless of their vowel classes in the G or N; significantly, the theme-vowel of the perfect follows the preterite and not the durative, as in the G and N. Hence, the theme-vowel of all D duratives is *a*; the theme-vowel of all preterites, perfects, and imperatives is *i*. The Assyrian D and Š imperatives, as well as the other prefixless forms, i.e., the verbal adjective and infinitive, differ from their Babylonian counterparts in exhibiting *a* between C_1 and C_2 rather than *u*. Below is a sample of singular and plural forms in the D stem (Assyrian forms are in parentheses):

(20) Second person and imperative forms of the D stem

Durative (2nd masc. sg./2nd com. pl.)	tuparras/tuparrasā
Perfect (2nd masc. sg./2nd com. pl.)	tuptarris/tuparrisā
Preterite (2nd masc. sg./2nd com. pl.)	tuparris/tuparrisā
Imperative (masc. sg./com. pl.)	purris/purrisā (parris/parrisā)

A recent study concludes that "the basic function of the D stem is that of underlining an increase in transitivity vis-à-vis the corresponding G stem" (Kouwenberg 1997:445). For intransitive G verbs the D normally has a factitive function, as in *mātam urappiš* "he widened the land" (cf. G *mātum irpiš* "the land became wide"), whereas for transitive G verbs the D connotes "plurality and salience, mostly plurality of the direct object and the action itself" (Kouwenberg 1997:445), as in *nārātim upetti* "I opened canals" (cf. G *nāram epte* "I opened a canal"). The D may denote an activity performed on plural objects: for example, *ušebber ṭuppātim* "he broke many tablets" (cf. G *išber ṭuppam* "he broke the tablet"). The D also serves to form denominative verbs: for example, *ruggubum* "to roof something" (< *rugbum* "roof"). Additionally, there are some lexical verbs for which the D is the basic stem: for example, *kullumum* "to show."

4.2.4 Š stem

The Š stem is characterized by a prefixed *š(a)-* before the verbal root. The vowel class and the personal prefixes correspond precisely to those of the D; in other words, all verbs belong to the *a-i* class and *u* replaces the *a* and *i* vowels of the G (and N) prefixes. As noted under the D stem, prefixless forms of the Š stem (i.e., the imperative, verbal adjective, and infinitive) have *a* in the first syllable in Assyrian and *u* in Babylonian. Note the following forms (Assyrian forms are in parentheses):

(21) First person and imperative forms of the Š stem

Durative (1st com. sg./1st com. pl.)	ušapras/nušapras
Perfect (1st com. sg./1st com. pl.)	uštapris/nuštapris
Preterite (1st com. sg./1st com. pl.)	ušapris/nušapris
Imperative (fem. sg./com. pl.)	šuprisī/šuprisā (šaprisī/šaprisā)

The main function of the Š stem is to form the causative of G verbs, particularly active-intransitive verbs: for example, *ušamqit* "I/she/he caused (someone, something) to fall" (cf. G *imqut* "she/he fell"). For some adjectival verbs, the Š rather than the D serves as the factitive stem: for example, *tušamriṣā* "you (pl.) made sick, caused trouble" (cf. *nimraṣ* "we became sick"). As with the other derived stems, some verbs occur only in the Š and have no G counterpart: for example, *šuklulum* "to complete."

4.2.5 Infixed *-ta-* stems

For each of the stems presented above there is an infixed *-ta-* sub-stem: Gt, (Nt), Dt, $\check{S}t_1$, and $\check{S}t_2$. The theme-vowels of the *-ta-* stems are those of the corresponding basic stems (however, G *a-u* verbs are *a* class verbs in the Gt). The infixed *-ta-* is inserted after the first radical in the G and D, or after the characteristic preformative of Š (and N) stems. The preterites of the *-ta-* infixed stems are formally indistinguishable from the G, D, N, and Š perfects, so that the two can be distinguished only by context; the perfect of the *-ta-* stem infixes *-tat(a)-*.

The Gt stem denotes (i) a reciprocal meaning (e.g., *mitḫuṣum* "to strike one another," *qitrubum* "to draw close to one another"); (ii) a reflexive nuance (e.g., *piššušum* (< **pitšušum*) "to anoint oneself"); or (iii) a separative sense with verbs of motion (e.g., *atlukum* "to go away"). While the first two functions of the Gt are known from elsewhere in Semitic, the last-named, the separative sense, represents an innovation within Akkadian.

The Dt and $\check{S}t_1$ stems serve principally as the passive of their respective stems: for example, *uštalpit* "he was destroyed" (cf. *ušalpit* "he destroyed"). The $\check{S}t_2$ stem, which is distinguished from the $\check{S}t_1$ stem only in the durative (by a characteristic doubled middle radical, e.g., $\check{S}t_1$ *uštapras*, $\check{S}t_2$ *uštaparras*), has a variety of functions, including reflexive and passive of the Š, causative of the Gt and N, and denominative (Streck 1994).

The Nt stem is exceptionally rare and its existence may very well be questioned, especially given that attested forms are identical to the Ntn (see §4.2.6). Where it does seem to appear, it has a reciprocal or separative nuance.

4.2.6 Infixed *-tan-* stems

Similarly, each of the main stems has an infixed *-tan-* stem associated with it – Gtn, Ntn, Dtn, and Štn; the theme-vowel is that of the corresponding *-ta-* stem. As with the

-ta- stems, the *-tan-* morpheme is inserted immediately after the first consonant in the G and D, or, in the N and Š, after the characteristic preformative. Only in the durative is the *-tan-* morpheme completely preserved: for example, Gtn *iptanarras*, Ntn *ittanapras*, Dtn *uptanarras*, Štn *uštanapras*. In all other forms, the *n* either assimilates to the following consonant (in the Gtn), or is dropped (in the Ntn, Dtn, and Štn), as in the following preterite forms: Gtn *iptarras*, Ntn *ittapras*, Dtn *uptarris*, Štn *uštapris*. Therefore, with the exception of the durative, the Ntn, Dtn, and Štn forms are identical to their *-ta-* counterparts. For all stems, the *-tan-* infix serves as an iterative to the meaning of the corresponding main stem: for example, *aštanappar* "I am continually sending word" (cf. *ašappar* "I am sending word"); *ištatakkan* "he has placed repeatedly."

4.2.7 Rare stems

In addition to the stems described above, several other stems of rare or restricted occurrence are also attested. The ŠD stem – which combines the double middle radical of the D stem and the *š-* preformative of the Š stem (e.g., *ušpazzer* "he saved") – is used for poetic effect and is limited to Standard Babylonian and the Old Babylonian literary dialect where it may replace either the D or the Š stem. The very rare R and Rt stems, which are characterized by reduplication of the third radical (e.g., *iprassas* 3rd com. sg. durative), denote intensification of the verbal root and are, therefore, similar to the D. The Dtt stem (e.g., *uptatarras* 3rd com. sg. durative) is attested only in Neo-Assyrian where it acts as the passive of the D stem (the expected Dt stem probably does not occur in Neo-Assyrian). Additional stems have been suggested, but such forms are so sparsely attested that they may very well represent scribal errors.

4.2.8 Quadriradical verbs

As noted above, a few roots have four radicals; for some the fourth radical is weak. The vast majority of these verbs are not attested in the G stem, but instead have the N as their basic stem. Causatives are formed with the Š, and iterative Ntn and Štn are attested as well: for example, *nabalkutum* N (*a*) "to jump, rebel"; *šubalkutum* Š causative. Most quadriradical verbs have *l* or *r* as the second radical.

4.2.9 The ventive morpheme

The ventive morpheme is closely related to the first common singular dative suffix; in fact, the two are identical in terms of morphological shape, *-am*, *-m*, and *-nim*, and distribution (see §4.1.6.2). The ventive is a directional element that denotes motion or activity in the direction of the speaker or writer; it is most frequently found with verbs of movement and of sending. The element may be suffixed to any finite verbal form including the imperative: for example, *nillikam* "we came here" (< *alākum* "to go"); *šūbilam* "send (it) here!" (< Š *wabālum* "to carry"). As with the separative sense of the Gt stem, the ventive seems to represent an innovation within Akkadian; note the opposition created by the two with the verb *alākum* "to go": *atlak* "go away!" (Gt) against *alkam* "come here!" (G + ventive).

4.2.10 Subordination markers

The morpheme *-u* is suffixed to all verbal forms that occur in subordinate clauses, provided that the verb does not have an ending that is part of the subject marker (2nd fem. sg. *-ī*, pl. *-ū* and *-ā*) or the ventive morpheme. In Babylonian, verbs that have one of these endings are unmarked in subordinate clauses. In Old Assyrian, *-ni* is attached to forms that cannot take *-u*. In Middle Assyrian and Neo-Assyrian *-ni* is attached even to those forms which are already marked with *-u*; in these dialects a pronominal suffix may intervene between the *-u* and the *-ni* subordination markers. The variations in the form of the subordination marker may be summarized as follows (after Huehnergard 1997:284; *iprus* = 3rd masc. sg. preterite of *parāsum* "to cut"):

(22) Forms of the subordination markers

	MAIN CLAUSE	*SUBORDINATE CLAUSE*		
	Bab./Old Ass.	*Old Bab.*	*Old Ass.*	*Mid/Neo-Ass.*
Pret. 3rd masc. sg.	iprus	ša iprusu	ša iprusu	ša iprusū-ni
+*Ventive*	iprusam	ša iprusam	ša iprusan-ni	ša iprusan-ni
+*3rd masc. sg. suff.*	iprussu	ša iprusūšu	ša iprusūšu	ša iprusūšū-ni
+*Vent.*+*suff.*	iprusaššu	ša iprusaššu	ša iprusaššū-ni	ša iprusaššū-ni
Vbl. Adj.+*3rd fem. sg.*	parsat	ša parsat	ša parsat-ni	ša parsatū-ni

In Old Akkadian the normal subordination marker is *-u*; however, in addition to *-u*, sometimes the suffix *-ni* (or *-na*) is used as in Assyrian. In Old Akkadian texts from the Diyala region a unique subordination suffix *-a* is attested. For the syntax of subordinate clauses see §5.12.

4.2.11 Nonfinite verbal forms

Akkadian exhibits three nonfinite forms: infinitive, participle, and verbal adjective, all of which are attested for the G, N, D, Š and their respective *-ta-* and *-tan-* stems.

4.2.11.1 Verbal adjective

The functions of the verbal adjective and its G form have already been discussed above (see §4.1.5.1). The verbal adjective for the derived stems can similarly be used attributively or predicatively. The morphological shape of the verbal adjective is formally identical to the infinitive for all derived stems: Gt *pitrus-* (Ass. *pitars-*); Gtn *pitarrus-*; N *naprus-*; Ntn *itaprus-* (with loss of initial *n*); D *purrus-* (Ass. *parrus-*); Dt, Dtn *putarrus-*; Š *šuprus-* (Ass. *šaprus-*); $\check{S}t_{1-2}$, Štn *šutaprus-*.

4.2.11.2 Participle

The participle is a declined adjective that is very often substantivized. The shape of the participle in the G is *pāris-*; for the other derived stems the participle is characterized by the prefix *mu-*: Gt *muptaris-*; Gtn *muptarris-*; N *mupparis-*; Ntn *muttapris-*; D *muparris-*; Dt, Dtn *muptarris-*; Š *mušapris-*; $\check{S}t_{1-2}$, Štn *muštapris-*. The participle is active in voice for transitive verbs while the verbal adjective is passive: for example, *ṣābitum* "captor" versus *ṣabtum* "captive." For active intransitive verbs the participle is characterized by an imperfective aspect, while the verbal adjective imparts a perfective nuance: for example, *wāšibum* "sitting down" versus *wašbum* "having sat down, seated." Participles of stative verbs do not occur. As a substantive, the participle is most often found in the bound form with a dependent genitive: for example, *pāris purussê* "the one who decides decisions"; *wāšib ālim* "the one who dwells in the city, city-dweller."

4.2.11.3 *Infinitive*

The Akkadian infinitive is a verbal noun and is always masculine and singular. The shape of the infinitive in the G stem is *parās-*. For the derived stems the morphological shape of the infinitive is identical to that of the verbal adjective (see §4.2.11.1).

In Eblaite, the D and Š stem infinitives have the same form as in Assyrian Akkadian, namely, D *parrus* and Š *šaprus*. (The forms *purrus* and *šuprus* are also attested in copies of one recension of a large Sumerian–Eblaite vocabulary text; see Conti 1996. It is likely that this recension reflects the influence of a contemporary dialect of Old Akkadian.) In addition to these forms, Eblaite attests infinitives of *t*-stems that, in addition to an infixed *-t-*, also exhibit a prefixed *t-*: G iterative /tartappidum/ (cf. G /rapādum/ "to run"); D iterative(?) /tuðtaqqinum/ (cf. G /ðaqānum/ "to be bearded," D /ðaqqunum/); Š iterative /tušta?kilum/ (cf. Akkadian G *akālum* "to eat," Š *šūkulum* "to feed"). Such forms are otherwise unknown in Semitic.

For the syntax of the infinitive see §5.5.

4.3 Particles

Prepositions, adverbs, and the particle *lū* are treated below; for the conjunctions and enclitic particles see Syntax.

4.3.1 Prepositions

Common prepositions in Akkadian are the following: *ina* "in"; *ana* "to, toward"; *ištu*, Middle Babylonian *ultu*, Neo-Assyrian *issu* "from, out of," temporal "since, after" (from Proto-Semitic **wišṭu(m)* "in(side)"); *adi* "up to"; *kī*, *kīma* "like, as"; *lāma* "before" (temporal) (from *lā* "not" + enclitic *-ma* [see §5.7]); *aššu(m)*, Old Assyrian *aššumi* "on account of, for the sake of" (from *ana šum(i)* "for the name (= sake) of"); *ašar* "where" (originally the bound form of a noun *ašrum* "place," i.e., "(in the) place of"); *mala* "as many as, as much as" (originally the bound form of the infinitive *malûm* < **malā'um* "to become full," i.e., "fullness of"). The prepositions *itti* "with" and *eli* "upon, over, against" regularly take possessive suffixes: for example, *elīya* "upon me"; *ittīšu* "with him." Nouns governed by prepositions are always in the genitive case.

Of the above-mentioned prepositions, Eblaite shares the prepositions *in* "in" (Akk. *ina*), *'a*$_5$(NI)*-na* "to" (Akk. *ana*), which are not found elsewhere in Semitic outside of these two languages. Eblaite also attests a preposition *'aštā* or *'aštī* "with, from" (corresponding to the Old Akkadian preposition *ištē/ištī*), *'aštu(m)* (OAkk. *ištum*) "from, after," and *bali* "without, without the knowledge/consent of" (Akk. *balu(m)*). Additionally, Eblaite contains the prepositions *si-in* "to, for the sake of" (not attested in Akkadian, but found in South Arabian *s*$_1$*n*); *min* "in, at" (not attested in Akkadian, but cf. Hebrew *min-* "from"); *mi-nu* "from, to"; *si-gi* "with"; GABA "before" (probably for *maḫar* as in Akk.; construct of *maḫrum* "front (part)"); *iš-ki* "in favor of" (which has been compared with Ethiopic *'əska* "until"); and *al* "on" found elsewhere in Semitic (Akk. *eli*). Significantly, Eblaite, like Akkadian, does not display the common West Semitic proclitic prepositions **bi-* "in" and **la-* "to."

4.3.2 Adverbs

It was noted above that the locative ending *-um* and terminative ending *-iš* remained productive after the Old Akkadian period in the formation of adverbs (see §4.1.1.3): for example, *elēnum* "above, in addition"; *mādiš* "much, greatly." When followed by the morpheme *-am*, possibly the accusative case, the terminative often assumes a distributive force: for example, *ūmišam* "daily"; *warḫišam* "monthly." Additional adverbial endings include *-i* (e.g., *ali* "where") and -Ø (i.e., the absolute form [see §4.1.4]; e.g., *zamar* "quickly, suddenly").

The accusative case may be used in a wide range of adverbial functions: (i) accusative of place (e.g., *šumēlam* "on the left"); (ii) accusative of time (e.g., *urram* "tomorrow"); (iii) ablative accusative (e.g., *nilqēšunūti* "we took from them"); (iv) accusative of respect, manner, or means (e.g., *ḫamuttam alkam* "Come quickly!").

An adverbial use of the accusative is attested for Eblaite as well: for example, (i) accusative of place (e.g., *zi-il* NE-*na-áš*^{ki} *mu*-DU É *ma-tim* "at the junction of N., we will enter into the mausoleum"; cf. var.: *zi-il* NE-*na-áš*^{ki} *mu*-DU *si-in* É *ma-tim*); (ii) accusative of time (e.g., 5 UD GIBIL... [TUŠ] "on the fifth day... they sat"); (iii) accusative of respect (e.g., *wa-a* PAD *ma-lik-tum ba-na-sa* "she veiled the face of the queen"; lit.: "she veiled the queen with respect to her face"; *ma-lik-tum* represents a fixed logographic writing for /māliktam/ (see §2.6 and §4.1.2)).

There are two negative adverbs in Akkadian, *ul* and *lā*. The former also has the form *ula* in early Old Babylonian and Old Assyrian. The particle *ul* is used to negate independent declarative sentences and clauses, both verbal and verbless. It is also used to negate interrogative sentences in which no interrogative pronoun or adverb occurs. Elsewhere *lā* is used to negate: all subordinate clauses; injunctions, both verbal and verbless (see §§4.2.1.5, 4.3.3); interrogative nouns and pronouns; and individual words, including infinitives and adjectives: for example, *ṭēmum lā damqum* "an unfavorable report"; *dabāb lā kittim* "untrue speech."

Although some adverbs may stand at the beginning of their sentence, their regular position is directly before the verb (in verbless clauses, the negative adverb *ul* stands likewise before the predicate).

4.3.3 The particle *lū*

This particle has three functions in Akkadian: (i) to express alternatives (e.g., *abum lū aḫum lū aššatum* "father, brother, or wife"); (ii) to denote injunctions in verbless clauses (e.g., *lū awīlāta* "be (masc. sg.) a man"; negative injunctions are formed with *lā*: e.g., *lā ina ekallim šina* "they (fem.) must not be in the palace!"); and (iii) as an asseverative particle (e.g., *lū ēpuš* "I verily built").

4.4 Compounding

As with the other Semitic languages, Akkadian is characterized by a poverty of real word compounds. However, certain compound noun phrases are expressed by a bound form governing a genitive: for example, *mār(i) šiprim* "messenger" (lit. "son of the message"); *bēl ḫubullim* "creditor" (lit. "lord of the debt"). Only occasionally are these expressions treated as a morphological unit; in other words, their plurals are most often formed by pluralization of the governing noun (e.g., *mārū šiprim* (nom.) "messengers"), rather than by marking the end of the phrase (e.g., *mār šiprī*). Rarely, however, a bound form with accompanying genitive evolved into a type of word compound, especially when the final consonant of the bound form was an *n* and was therefore susceptible to assimilation to the first consonant of the following genitive: for example, *būn pānī* (lit. "features of the face") > *buppānu* "face"; *šaman šammim* (lit. "oil of the plant") > *šamaššammum* "sesame seed oil"; *mūr nisqim* (lit. "foal of choice quality") > *murnisqum* "(select) horse or donkey."

4.5 Numerals

Cardinal and ordinal numbers are usually expressed logographically in Akkadian. Thus, the pronunciation and construction of many numbers are unknown.

4.5.1 Cardinal numbers

The cardinal numbers from 1 to 10, except for 2, occur in the absolute and, less often, free forms. There was no "zero" in the Akkadian numerical system. The numbers from 11 to 19 occur only in the absolute state. Below are the Old Babylonian forms for numbers 1 through 10:

(23) The old Babylonian cardinal numbers (1–10)

	DECLINED STATE		ABSOLUTE STATE	
	Masculine	*Feminine*	*Masculine*	*Feminine*
1	(ištēnum)	(ištētum)	ištēn	išteat, ištēt
2	šinā	šittā	—	—
3	šalāšum	šalāštum	šalāš	šalāšat
4	erbûm	erbettum	erbe/erba	erbet(ti)
5	ḫamšum	ḫamištum	ḫamiš	ḫamšat
6	šeššum	šedištum	šediš?	šeššet
7	sebûm	sebettum	sebe	sebet(ti)
8	samānûm	samāntum	samāne	samānat
9	tišûm	tišītum	tiše	tišīt
10	eš(e)rum	ešertum	ešer	eš(e)ret

The cardinals 20 through 50 are expressed in the feminine plural of the absolute form; they may modify masculine or feminine nouns: *ešrā* "20"; *šalāšā* "30"; *erbeā/erbâ* "40"; *ḫamšā* "50". In compound numbers, higher-order components precede lower ones.

The numerical system, as inherited from Sumerian, was based on both the sexagesimal and the decimal systems. Higher numbers are expressed in both systems; the following forms modify both masculine and feminine nouns:

(24) Higher-ordered Old Babylonian cardinal numbers: sexagesimal and decimal systems

SEXAGESIMALS			DECIMALS		
	Absolute	*Free*		*Absolute*	*Free*
60	šūš(i)	šūšum	*100*	meat	(meatum)
600	nēr	nērum	*1,000*	līm(i)	līmum
3,600	šār	šārum			

4.5.1.1 *Agreement with cardinal numbers*

The numbers 1 and 2 agree in gender with the item counted; however, the numbers 3 through 19 are subject to the phenomenon of chiastic concord encountered elsewhere in Semitic, whereby the gender of these numbers is the opposite of that of the item counted: for example, *ištēn wardum* "one male slave," *ištēt amtum* "one female slave," but *šalāšat wardū* "three male slaves"; *šalāš amātum* "three female slaves." While numbers are usually expressed in the absolute case as noted above, the item counted or measured is usually in the free form, its case determined by the context.

4.5.2 Ordinal numbers

The ordinal numbers are adjectives which always agree with the gender of the modified noun (i.e., chiastic concord is not observed; see §4.5.1.1). The base of the cardinal numbers in Babylonian is *parus-*, in Assyrian *paris-*. There are several terms for "first"; additionally, "first" is the only ordinal regularly to precede its noun. Note the following Old Babylonian forms:

(25) The old Babylonian ordinal numbers (1–10)

	Masculine	*Feminine*
First	pānûm	pānītum
	maḫrûm	maḫrītum
	(ištīʾum)	(ištītum)
	ištēn	išteat
Second	šanûm	šanītum
Third	šalšum	šaluštum
Fourth	rebûm	rebūtum
Fifth	ḫamšum	ḫamuštum
Sixth	šeššum	šeduštum
Seventh	sebûm	sebūtum
Eighth	samnum	samuntum
Ninth	tešûm	tešūtum
Tenth	ešrum	ešurtum

5. SYNTAX

To date there have been no comprehensive studies concerning the historical development of Akkadian syntax; thus, the description given below is based largely on Old Babylonian, the most thoroughly studied dialect. However, even a fairly cursory review of the other dialects reveals that Akkadian is remarkably conservative not only in its morphology, but also in its syntax, despite the fact that the written language in all probability lagged behind the spoken language.

Beyond the brief comments made below regarding word order and use of the conjunction *wa*, almost nothing can be stated with certainty regarding the syntax of Eblaite. Note: In the word-for-word renderings of Eblaite, the verb forms are given simply as bare lexical forms, such as "go," "dwell," since the logograms used to write them do not specify person or tense.

5.1 Word order

One of the most significant innovations within Akkadian is the adoption of an SOV (Subject–Object–Verb) word order, under Sumerian influence, for both main and subordinate clauses. This development is in sharp contrast to the VSO order of most other Semitic languages, with the notable exception of modern Ethiopic, which similarly adopted an SOV order under Cushitic influence. In literary genres, however, Akkadian word order was much less restricted, the verb often preceding the object, or even the subject, for poetic effect.

Word order in Eblaite appears to be much freer than in Akkadian. In addition to the SOV order encountered in Akkadian and Sumerian, SVO order is frequently attested as well, as in other Semitic languages.

5.2 Agreement

As noted above, the Akkadian and Eblaite verbs agree with their subject in gender and number; attributive adjectives follow their head nouns and must agree with them in gender, number, and case. The predicative construction is not subject to the same rules of agreement as the attributive form; the base is indeclinable and not marked for gender, number, or case, while the enclitic subject pronoun has a clearly defined gender (except for the first person), number, and case, which is invariably nominative. For example, *šarr-āku* means both "I am king" and "I am queen" (i.e., a feminine form ***šarrat-āku* does not exist); similarly, *šarr-ānu* literally means both "we are king" and "we are kings."

5.3 Apposition

Nouns and phrases are very frequently found in apposition, particularly with titles and epithets. Nouns in apposition agree in number and in case with their antecedent: for example, *ana Marduk, bēlim rabîm, rubêm maḫrîm* "for Marduk, the great lord, the foremost prince," where all substantives and modifying adjectives are governed by the preposition *ana*, and are thus in the genitive case.

5.4 Genitive constructions

In Akkadian the genitive may be expressed either with or without the determinative pronoun, with no ascertainable difference in meaning. The determinative pronoun *ša* (see §4.1.6.4) is placed in apposition to the preceding governing noun; the governed noun appears after *ša* and is in the genitive case (26A). Occasionally *ša* appears before its antecedent, in which case the governed noun is re-expressed with a resumptive possessive pronoun (26B–C):

(26) A. šarrum ša mātim
king, the one of land-GEN.
"The king of the land"

B. ša bēlim kussīšu
the one of lord-GEN. his throne
"The throne of the lord"

C. ša PN aštakan dabdâšu
the one of PN-GEN. I brought about his defeat
"I brought about the defeat of PN"

The latter construction, often referred to as the *anticipatory genitive*, is used for poetic effect and is most often found in literary texts.

However, the use of the bound form (see §4.1.2) directly before a dependent noun is the more common construction for expressing the genitive. The determinative pronoun is deleted and the governing noun appears in the bound form, juxtaposed to the governed noun in the genitive: for example, *qaqqad awīlim* "the head of the man." The resulting construction, the so-called *genitive chain*, represents an inseparable unit. Adjectives modifying the governing noun occur after the chain in the appropriate case (27A–B). Only the negative adverb *lā* may intervene between the bound form and its genitive (27C–D):

(27) A. mār awīlim ṣeḫrum
son-of man.GEN. young
"The young son of a man"

B. mār bīte rabû
son-of house.GEN. great
"The oldest son of the house" (Middle Assyrian)

C. erṣet lā târi
land-of not return.GEN.
"Land of no return"

D. bēl lā ilim.
owner-of not god.GEN.
"Owner of no god" (i.e., "irreligious person")

Normally, only one genitive noun can be dependent on a governing noun; an exception occurs when two genitives form a logical unit: for example, *bēl šamê u erṣetim* "lord of heaven and earth." It is impossible for more than one bound form to govern a single genitive; in instances of multiple governing nouns *ša* must be used:

(28) ina eqlim kirîm ū bītim ša ilkīšu
in field.GEN. orchard.GEN. or house.GEN the one of his service obligation-GEN.
"Among a field, orchard, or house belonging to his service obligation"

When chains of more than two elements occur, all but the last element appear in the bound form:

(29) A. qurun šalmāt ummānātīšu
pile-of corpses-of his troops.GEN.
"The pile of corpses of his troops"

B. ina qāt mār awīlim
from hand-of son-of man.GEN.
"From the hand of the son of a man"

5.5 Syntax of the infinitive

The syntax of the Akkadian infinitive is very complex, and only the basic aspects can be mentioned here; for details see Aro 1961. The infinitive, as a verbal noun, may occur in any case. As the subject or direct object of its clause, it appears in the nominative and accusative cases, respectively: for example, *erēšum qerub* "planting is near"; *erēbam ul iddiššim* "he did not allow her to enter" (lit. "entering he did not give to her"). When governed by a preposition or bound noun, the infinitive appears in the genitive: for example, *ašar lā amārim* "a place that cannot be found" (lit. "a place of not finding"). When governed by certain prepositions, particulary *ina* "in," the resulting prepositional phrase is often equivalent to a temporal clause: for example, *ina kašādim* "when arriving, upon arrival"; *itti zikarim šanîm ina utūlim lā ittaṣbat* "(if) she has not been caught while lying with another man." With other prepositions, particularly *ana* "to," the construction may express purpose: for example, *ana lā enê* "so that it cannot be changed" (Neo-Babylonian/Late Babylonian); *ana amār bēlīya šarik* "it was donated so that my lord sees it" (lit. "for the seeing of my lord"; Middle Babylonian). Many other prepositions may be construed with the infinitive, resulting in a wide range of meanings and nuances: for example, *aššum elêm aštaprakkum* "I have written to you (masc. sg.) about coming up"; *kīma lā ragāmim epuš* "act (masc. sg.) so that there be no legal contest" (lit. "act according to not contesting"). Additionally, as a noun, the infinitive may take possessive suffixes: for example, *ṭēmka ina šemêya* "upon my hearing your report"; *adi târīšu šibā* "stay (pl.) until his return."

The infinitive may also be construed as a verb, taking a subject or object: for example, with a pronominal suffix serving as the logical subject:

(30) ṭuppam ina šemêka
tablet in hear.INF.=your
"When you hear the tablet"

With the infinitive taking both a subject and an object (rare), one finds, for example:

(31) dannum enšam ana lā ḫabālim
strong weak to NEG. oppress.INF.
"So that the strong do not oppress the weak"

The subject or object of an infinitive may be expressed in the genitive if it follows a preposition:

(32) A. ana šemê bēlīya ašpuram
to hear.INF.-of lord=my I=wrote=VENT.
"I have written so that my lord hears it"
B. ana awâtīšu kašādim ēgurakka
to words=his achieve.INF. he=hired=VENT.=you
"Has he hired you in order to achieve his goals?"

As verbs, infinitives may also govern prepositional phrases and adverbial complements:

(33) A. ina Kaniš ina erābīšu
in Kaniš in enter.INF.=his
"When he entered into Kaniš" (Old Assyrian)
B. lā alāka iqbīšu
NEG. go.INF. he=spoke=him
"He ordered him not to go" (Neo-Assyrian)

Infinitives may also enter into paranomastic constructions which serve to intensify the verbal form; in such constructions, the infinitive takes the locative-adverbial *-um* (§4.1.1.3) and often *-ma* (§§5.7, 5.9): for example, *šapārum-ma ašpur* "I have certainly sent."

In a construction unique to Eblaite, infinitives placed in apposition to their objects may accept dative pronominal suffixes, which in Akkadian are restricted to finite verbal forms:

(34) A. 1 DUG Ì ^{giš}GAB.LIŠ.ME na-ba-ba-šum (for /napāp-šum/)
1 vessel oil G... sprinkle.INF.=to-him
"A vessel of G.-oil, to be sprinkled on him"
B. ḫa-sa-nu BAR_6:KÙG sa-ḫa-da-šum (for /šaḫād-šum/)
Ḫ. silver give.INF.=to-him
"An Ḫ. of silver, to be given to him"

5.6 Verbless clauses

There is no verb "to be" in Akkadian; instead, equational and existential clauses are verbless, expressed by juxtaposing the subject and the predicate. The tense of verbless clauses can only be determined from context. In Old Babylonian, when the subject of a verbless clause is a noun, it precedes the predicate:

(35)

Ḫammurapi	šarrum	ša	Bābilim
Hammurapi	king	the one of	Babylon

"Hammurapi [is/was] king of Babylon"

If the subject is a pronoun, it follows the predicate:

(36)

šarrum	ša	Bābilim	šū
king	the one of	Babylon	he

"He [is/was] king of Babylon"

In other dialects, such as Old Assyrian (37A–B), and in Eblaite (37C) these rules of word order are not in force:

(37) A.

nēnu	lā	awīl	gimillim
we	NEG.	man-of	compliance

"We [are] not compliant people"

B.

gāmer	awâtim	nēnu
concluder-of	matters	we

"We are the concluder(s) of the legal matters"

C.

an-da	ŠEŠ	ù	an-na	ŠEŠ
you	brother	and	I	brother

"You [are my] brother, I [am your] brother"(?)

In Akkadian, clauses of the type *Adverb (Phrase)–Noun (Phrase)* occur occasionally. Most often this construction is used for existential clauses; for example:

(38)

ina	imitti	ḫašîm	šēpum	ina	šumēl	ḫašîm	piṭrum
in	right-of	lung	foot	in	left-of	lung	fissure

"on the right of the lung [there] was a 'foot,' on the left [there] was a fissure"

Verbless clauses may also express simple possession when a noun phrase governed by *ša* (see §5.4) constitutes the predicate, as in:

(39)

kaspum	u	ḫurāṣum	ša	ālim
silver	and	gold	that of	town

"The silver and gold belong to the town"

5.7 Topicalization

In the writing of Akkadian there are two methods of emphasizing a nonpredicate constituent: (i) left dislocation, and (ii) the addition of the emphatic particle *-ma*. With the former, the dislocated noun or noun phrase is placed at the beginning of the clause in the nominative case (sometimes referred to as the *nominative absolute* or *casus pendens*). Such clauses appear to have two subjects; however, the dislocated element is not part of the clause grammar. The noun or noun phrase that is dislocated is replaced in the clause by a corresponding pronominal suffix; for example:

(40) A.

šumma	awīlum	ḫubullum	elīšu	ibaššī-ma
if	man.NOM.	debt.NOM.	against=him	it=is-present=CONJ.

"If a man – a debt is lodged against him . . . "

B.

šumma	awīlum	šārassu	. . . ṣalmat
if	man.NOM.	hair-NOM.=his	. . . is black

"If a man – his hair is black"

With B compare:

C.

šumma	šārat	awīlim	. . . ṣalmat
if	hair-of	man.GEN.	. . . is black

"If the hair of a man is black"

The enclitic particle *-ma* serves to mark the logical predicate of a clause (Rainey 1976); translation into English is usually facilitated by a cleft sentence, as in:

(41) A.

aššum	mārī	Yā'ilānim	ša	maḫrīka,	tuša	warkānum
concerning	sons-of	Y.	REL.	before=you	perhaps	later

salīmum	ibbaššī-ma	ina	qātim	kullašunu	aqbi.
peace	it=becomes-present=CONJ.	in	hand	hold.INF.=them	I=said

inanna	mimma	salīmum	itti	Yā'ilānim	ul	ibašši,	ša
now	anything	peace	with	Y.	NEG.	it=is-present	REL.

ṣabātīšū-ma	adabbub
seize.INF.=him=TOP.	I=speak

"As for the Yā'ilānum tribesmen who are with you, I had said to hold them just in case peace should be established later. Now, there is no peace with Yā'ilānum; it is to seize them that I am planning"

B.

Gimillum	šū,	dūršu	nuḫatimmum;	watriššu	ana	rēdîm
G.	that	status=his	cook	superfluously	to	r.-soldier

iššaṭer.	inanna	Gimillum	šū,	ina	nuḫatimmī-ma	illak!
he=was-written	now	G.	that	in	cooks=TOP.	he=goes

pūḫšu,	šani'am-ma	ana	rēdî	mulli
replacement=his	other=TOP.	to	r.-soldiers	assign.IMPV.

"As for this Gimillum, his permanent status is that of cook; he was registered as a rēdû-soldier superfluously. Now, as for this Gimillum, it is with the cooks that he will serve! In place of him, it is someone else that you must assign"

5.8 Cliticism

In addition to the emphatic particle *-ma* and the subordinate marker *-ni* in Assyrian (and *-na* in Old Akkadian), Akkadian possesses two other enclitics: *-mi* and *-man* (Old Assyrian *-min*). The particle *-mi* is used to indicate direct speech; it may be attached to one or more words within the speech:

(42)

šāpirī	iqbiam	kīda	šunū-mi	lībalū-mi
overseer=my	he=said=VENT.	outside	they=QUOT.	may=they=dry=QUOT.

"My overseer said to me, 'Those should be dried outside'"

The relatively infrequent irrealis particle, *-man/-min*, is appended to *šumma* "if" to form unreal clauses: for example, *šumma-min mētāku* "if I had died."

Akkadian does not possess any true proclitics; however, in some dialects, the prepositions *ina* "in," *ana* "to," and *eli* "upon" may lose their final vowels and become proclitic, with assimilation of the consonant to the first consonant of the following word. Often the resultant consonantal doubling is not indicated in the script: for example, *a-pa-ni-ia* for *ap-pānīya* "towards me" (< *ana pānīya*); *i-li-bi-ša* for *il-libbīša* "within it (fem.)" (< *ina libbīša*); *e-ni-ši-i* for *en-nišī* "above the people" (< *eli nišī*).

5.9 Coordination

There are two independent coordinators in Akkadian, *u* and *ū* (*lū*), in addition to the enclitic *-ma*, which, besides its function as an emphasizing particle, is frequently used as a coordinator (Patterson 1970; Kraus 1987). The conjunction *u* (< **wa*) is used to connect both noun phrases and sentences. Clauses that are connected with *u* are of equal semantic stress and are reversible (i.e., a change in the order of the clauses does not affect their relationship or meaning): for example, ... *bītam inaṣṣarū u ṣeḫrūtim urabbû* "... they may keep the house and raise the children."

The coordinating conjunction *-ma* is suffixed to verbs and is used only to connect clauses. Unlike *u*, clauses connected by *-ma* are logically or temporally related to one another and are therefore irreversible. Usually the first clause provides the conditions for the action expressed in the second clause; thus, *-ma* serves syntactically or logically to subordinate the first clause to the second. The following example demonstrates the various interpretations of clauses connected with *-ma*:

(43)

ina	nār	GN	mû	maṭû-ma	eqel	biltīni
in	river-of	GN	water.PL.	diminished-are=CONJ.	field-of	tax=our

ul	ikaššadū
NEG.	they=reach

"In the canal of GN the waters are (too) low and so they do not reach our taxable field"

"Because/ When/ If the waters are (too) low they will not reach our taxable field"

Akkadian did not possess a separate word for "but"; rather, both *u* and *-ma* can be used in this sense, especially when one of the clauses contains a negative, as, for example, in the following:

(44)

BÙR.30.IKU	šītāt	eqlim	šuāti	bēlni	ana	ŠU.ḪA.MEŠ
BUR=30(-DETV.)	remainder-of	field	that	lord=our	to	fishermen

UD.DA	nadānam-ma	ipiršunu	lā	šūṣâm	iqbi
collective	give.INF.ACC.=and	ration=their	NEG.	release.INF.ACC.	he=said

"Our lord said to give the remaining 30 BUR of that field to the fisherman's collective but not to release their rations"

The conjunction "or" is expressed by *ū* (< **ʾaw*) or *ū lū*. The conjunctions *u* and *ū* are identical in the writing system and, in the absence of *lū*, the two can only be distinguished by context.

Clauses may also be joined asyndetically, with the deletion of any of the conjunctions described above:

(45)

Purattu ...	miqtīša	usuḫ	ḫamīša	šutbi
Euphrates ...	silt.PL.=its	remove.IMPV.	litter.PL.=its	cause-to-arise.IMPV.

šutēšerši
cause-to-be-in-order.IMPV.=it

"... as for the Euphrates, ... dredge its silt, remove its litter (and) set it in order!"

The conjunctions *wa* (Akk. *u*) and *-ma* are attested for Eblaite as well, although little is known of their syntactic ranges. In at least some instances *-ma* behaves as it does in Akkadian, connecting logically related clauses, for example:

(46) ^{d}EN.KI . . . LUGAL iš$_{11}$-gur-ma MAḪ(?) il-tum ^{d}EN.LÍL
Ea . . . king he=summoned=CONJ. exalted(?) gods Enlil
ʾa$_5$(NI)-na ^{d}EN.KI INIM.DI
to Ea spoke
"he summoned Ea, . . . , the king, and then the exalted one(?) of the gods, Enlil, spoke to Ea"

The conjunction *wa* is much more frequent in Eblaite than in Akkadian; and, as in Akkadian, it is often used to connect clauses and noun pairs. As in West Semitic, *wa* is often used to introduce clauses and sentences (and is presumably to be left untranslated):

(47) A. wa Ì.NA.SUM-kum É in ba-da-a ša 2 li-im
CONJ. give=to-you house in B. REL. 2 thousand
"I am (herewith) giving you property in Baytān, (populated) by 2,000 (people)"
B. wa iš$_{11}$-da-ga-sù 1 SUD MAŠKIM.E.GI$_4$-ma si-in
CONJ. he=established(?)=him 1 star representative=TOP. toward
I-li-lu A.MU DINGIR.DINGIR.DINGIR
Enlil father gods
"The star established(?) him as representative to Illil, the father of the gods"
C. wa ÍL IGI.IGI EN wa NAM.KU$_5$
CONJ. lift eyes lord CONJ. swear
"The lord lifted (his) eyes and swore"

Such a use of *u* in Akkadian is very rare. Eblaite also attests the conjunctions *šumma* (see §5.11); *ʾap* "and then, but then," which occurs in Ugaritic and Hebrew, but not in Akkadian; and *ù-ma* (a compound of *u* [< *wa*] and *-ma*) "and then, and also, even."

5.10 Sequence of tenses (*consecutio temporum*)

For Old Babylonian and Old Assyrian (i.e., those periods in which the perfect is used with a focusing nuance; see §4.2.1.2), past actions performed in sequence are often expressed by one or more preterites followed by a final perfect. This sequence of tenses is used to emphasize the final clause, the crucial event upon which the action in the subsequent clauses is based. Often the coordinator *-ma* connects the clause(s) containing preterite(s) to the following perfect clause; for example:

(48) A. kaspam aknukam-ma uštābilakkum
silver I=sealed=VENT.=CONJ. I=have caused-to-carry=VENT.=to-you
"I sealed the silver and have sent it to you"
B. inanna mīlum illikam-ma nār Irnina ana dūr
now flood it=went=VENT.=CONJ. river-of I. to wall-of
kārim issaniq (< *istaniq; see §3.8.1.4, **14**)
quay it=has-reached
"Now, the flood has come, and the Irnina Canal has reached up to the wall of the quay"

C.

ana	Ilī-imguranni	ṭuppam	ušābil-ma	meḫer	ṭuppi
to	I.	tablet	I=caused-to-carry=CONJ.	copy-of	tablet

ušābilam-ma	uštābilakkum
he=caused-to-carry=VENT.=CONJ.	I=have-caused-to-carry=VENT.=to-you

"I sent a letter to Ilī-imguranni, and he sent a response to me, and I have sent (it) to you"

5.11 Conditional sentences

Akkadian exhibits both marked and unmarked conditional sentences. Unmarked clauses (with no word for "if") are characterized by the conjunctive *-ma*, which serves to connect the protasis and the apodosis. The verbs of both clauses are usually in the durative: for example, *taša"al-ma iqabbâkku* (Middle Babylonian) "If you ask, he will tell you." Sometimes the protasis has instead the preterite or precative; thus

(49)

mārī	šanûtim	liršû-ma	PN	aḫūšunu	rabûm
sons	other	may=they=acquire.PREC.=CONJ.	PN	brother=their	big

"Even if they acquire (adopt) other children, PN will be their older brother"
lit. "Let them acquire other children . . . "

Marked conditional sentences, those introduced with *šumma* "if," are more frequently attested. With such sentences, there is no conjunction between the protasis and apodosis; the two clauses are simply juxtaposed (with no intervening word for "then"). In *šumma* clauses, the negative adverb in the protasis is *lā*, whereas in the apodosis it is *ul*. Mesopotamian omens and laws are invariably expressed with marked conditional clauses, as in the following:

(50) A.

šumma	ina	birīt	martim	šīlum	šakin –	šarram	ina
if	in	midst-of	gall-bladder	depression	situated-is	king	in

pānī	pilšim	idukkūšu
front-of	breach	they=kill=him

"If a depression is situated in the middle of the gall-bladder – they will kill the king in front of a breach"

B.

šumma	mārum	abāšu	imtaḫaṣ –	rittašu	inakkisū
if	son	father=his	he=has-struck	hand=his	they=cut-off

"If a son strikes his father – they will cut off his hand"

Possibly under Sumerian influence, the subordination marker is not used with marked or unmarked conditional sentences.

Eblaite also exhibits both marked and unmarked conditional clauses. Marked clauses are likewise introduced by *šumma*; however, *wa* often serves to connect the protasis and apodosis (whereas in Akkadian they are normally joined asyndetically):

(51)

su-ma	INIM	ḪUL	al	PN	PN_2	DUG_4	wa	NAM.KU_5
if	word	evil	against	PN	PN_2	speak	CONJ.	swear

"If PN_2 utters an evil word against PN, then he will swear . . . "

With an unmarked clause, *-ma* may or may not be used to connect the protasis and apodosis; for example:

(52) si-a-ma MÍ.DUG$_4$.GA áš-da DUMU.NITA DUMU.NITA AL.TUŠ ap
she=TOP. want with son son dwell also
NU.MÍ.DUG$_4$.GA É EN AL.TUŠ
NEG.=want house lord dwell
"If she wants, she will live with her two sons; but if she does not want to, she will live in the house of the lord"

5.12 Subordinate clauses

Akkadian subordinate clauses are traditionally grouped into three categories: (i) relative clauses; (ii) temporal clauses; and (iii) other types of clauses, including local, causal, and object clauses. In all cases, where permissible, the verb is marked with the subordination marker (see §4.2.10). The negative adverb for all subordinate clauses is *lā*.

5.12.1 Relative clauses

For all Assyrian and Babylonian dialects the indeclinable determinative-relative pronoun (rel.), *ša*, is used to introduce relative clauses. Only for Old Akkadian and Eblaite is the pronoun fully declinable (see §4.1.6.4); for later periods the original accusative masculine nominative form (i.e., *ša*) is used, regardless of the environment.

The relative pronoun *ša* may occur without an antecedent, in which case the clause beginning with *ša* is syntactically equivalent to a noun and thus may serve as the subject (52A), direct object (52B), or indirect object of a main clause verb:

(53) A. ša iṣṣabtū-ma ilikšu ittalku
REL. he=has-taken=SUBORD.=CONJ. service=his he=has-gone=SUBORD.
šū-ma illak
he=TOP. he=goes
"the one who has taken possession and performed his service obligation shall be the one to continue to perform the obligation"
B. ša īn-ka maḫru ana PN idin
REL. eye=your receives=SUBORD. to PN give.IMPV.
"that which seems just to you, give to PN"
lit. "That which your eye receives, . . . "

Most often, however, *ša* is preceded by an antecedent, as in the following:

(54) A. kaspum ša PN ilqe'ūni
silver REL. PN he=took.SUBORD.
"The silver that PN took" (Old Assyrian)
B. ana mārīša ša irammu
for son=her REL. she=loves.SUBORD.
"For her son whom she loves"

Since the relative pronoun must follow its antecedent noun directly, it may not be preceded by a preposition. When *ša* expresses the genitive (55A) or dative (55B), it must be resumed by the appropriate pronominal suffix:

(55) A. šarrūtum ša išdā-ša šuršudā
kingship REL. foundations=its firm-are
"A kingship whose foundations are firm"

B. mannum	awīlum	ša	ṭuppaka	ana maḫrīšu	tašpuru
who	man	REL.	tablet=your	toward=him	you=sent=SUBORD.

"Who is the man to whom you sent your tablet?"

When *ša* represents the direct object of a verb, the pronominal suffix is optional; for example, compare (56A) and (56B):

(56) A.

ṣēnū	ša	šarrum	iddinu
flocks	REL.	king	he=gave=SUBORD.

"The flocks (sheep and goats) that the king gave"

B.

ana	^{kur}Uišidiš	ša	Ursa	ēkimu-š(u)	aqṭirib
to	U.	REL.	U.	he=conquered=SUBORD.=it	I=have-approached

"I approached the land of Uišdiš, which Ursa had conquered" (Standard Babylonian)

As with the genitive construction, *ša* may be deleted, the antecedent noun then appearing in the bound form (§4.1.2): for example, *awât niqabbû ul išemme* "he does not listen to the words we say" (= *awâtim ša niqabbû ul išemme*). Such constructions, inherited from Common Semitic, are already comparatively rare in Old Akkadian and Old Babylonian, and are virtually unknown in Old Assyrian and in the late Assyrian and Babylonian dialects, with the exception of certain literary texts in Babylonian.

Relative clauses may also be verbless; in Assyrian texts the particle-*ni* is suffixed to the predicate, as in the following Old Assyrian example:

(57)

ṭuppam	ša	kaspum	kaspī-ni	ukâl
tablet	REL.	silver	silver=my=SUBORD.	I=have

"I have a tablet (that proves) that the silver [is] my silver"

The indefinite pronouns *mamman* "whoever," *mimma* "whatever," as well as *mala*, Ass. *(am)mar* (bound form of *malûm* < **malāʾum* "to become full") "as much/many as" may all be used as relative pronouns with the omission of *ša:* for example, *âm mala ērišūki idnīm* "Give (fem. sg.) me as much grain as I requested of you."

In Eblaite, relative clauses may be either introduced by the declineable pronoun *θa* or simply juxtaposed to their main clauses; in the latter case the morphological shape of the preceding noun (i.e., whether or not it assumes the bound form as in Akkadian) cannot be determined because of the ambiguity of the writing system:

(58)

^{giš}GIGIR-sum	ša-ti	U_5	^{d}Ku-ra	wa	^{d}Ba-ra-ma
chariot=his	REL.	ride	K.	CONJ.	B.

"(Concerning) the chariot upon which K. and B. rode"

(cf. variant ^{giš}GIGIR-sum U_5 ^{d}Ku-ra ù ^{d}Ba-ra-ma).

5.12.2 Temporal clauses

Akkadian temporal clauses are introduced by a number of subordinating conjunctions. Frequently encountered conjunctions include: *inūma* (*inu*) "when"; *ūm* "on the day that, when"; *ištu* (Standard Babylonian *ultu*) "after, as soon as, since"; *kīma* (Middle Babylonian *kī*) "as soon as, when"; *warka/i* "after"; *adi* "until, as long as, while"; *lāma* "before"; and *adi (. . .) lā* "before." Temporal clauses usually precede their main clause; the tenses of both the main and the temporal clause verbs are determined by fairly predictable patterns. For example, with many of the conjunctions (specifically, *inūma*, *ūm*, *ištu*, *kīma*, *warka/i*, and *adi*), when the main clause action is completed in the past (i.e., with a verb in the preterite or perfect), the temporal clause, if verbal, stands in the preterite:

(59)	mārum	šū	warki	abūšu	imūtu	irgum
	son	that	after	father=his	he=died.PRET.=SUBORD.	he=brought-suit.PRET.

"That son brought suit after his father died"

If the main clause action is completed in the present or future (i.e., with a verb in the durative, imperative, precative, prohibitive, or verbless clause), the temporal clause, if verbal, stands in the perfect or durative. The perfect is used to mark the anteriority of the action of the temporal clause when compared to that of the main clause; for example:

(60)	inūma	âm	taštāmu	alkam
	when	grain	you=have-bought.PERF.=SUBORD.	go.IMPV.=VENT.

"When you have bought the grain, come here"

The durative is used either when the anteriority of the temporal clause is unmarked or to express the coincidence of the two actions; thus:

(61)	inūma	âm	tašammu	alkam
	when	grain	you=buy.DUR.=SUBORD.	go.IMPV.=VENT.

"When you buy the grain, come here"

In Middle Babylonian the conjunction *kī* (< *kīma*) "as soon as, when, after" is particularly common. When the verb of the temporal clause is in the preterite and the main clause verb is in the perfect (or preterite with negative clauses, see 4.2.1.2 and 4.2.1.3), *kī* is positioned immediately before the verb rather than at the beginning of the clause:

(62)	šēpīšu	kī	unakkisu	itūšu
	feet=his	when	he=cut-off.PRET.=SUBORD.	beside=him
	iktalāšu			
	he=has-detained.PERF.=him			

"After he cut (the enemy's) feet off, he kept him prisoner"

Several *kī* clauses may stand next to one another asyndetically, as in the following:

(63)	ṭēm	murṣīša	kī	iš'alūši	riksa
	report-of	illness=her	when	he=asked.PRET.=SUBORD.=her	bandaging
	kī	ēsiḫu	urakkasūši		
	when	he=obtained.PRET.=SUBORD.	they=bind.DUR.=her		

"After he has inquired about the report of her illness (and) obtained material for bandages, they bind her"

When the temporal clause verb is in the perfect and the main clause verb is in the present, imperative, or precative, *kī* does not necessarily stand immediately before the verb. In such clauses, the perfect is used to mark anteriority or temporal clause action in the future; often *kī* is translated as "as soon as":

(64) A.	kī	PN	DUMU	šiprīya	iktaldakku
	when	PN	son-of	message=my	he=has-reached.PERF.=VENT.=to-you
	gišGIGIR.MEŠ	liššâm-ma			
	wagons	may=he=carry.PREC.=VENT.=CONJ.			

"as soon as PN, my messenger, has come to you, let him deliver the wagons"

B. PN ana pānīka kī altaprakku
PN to front-of=you when I=have-sent.PERF.=VENT.=to-you
šitālšū-ma liqbâkku
ask.IMPV.=him=CONJ. may=he=say.PREC.=VENT.=to-you
"As soon as I have sent PN to you, ask him so that he may tell you"

C. ana mê mūti kī taktalda
to water.PL-of death when you=have-reached.PERF.=VENT.
teppuš mīnu
you=do.DUR. what?
"When you have reached the waters of death, what will you do then?"

When no such marking is intended, the temporal clause verb is in the present; similarly, *kī* may stand either before the verb or at the beginning of the temporal clause; thus:

(65) kī DUMU šiprīya u DUMU šiprīka
when son-of message=my CONJ. son-of message=your
illaka itti aḫāmiš lilqûni
he=goes.DUR.=VENT. with each-other may=they=take.PREC.=VENT.
"If my messenger and your messenger are coming, may they deliver (it) together"

In Eblaite, temporal and main clauses may be juxtaposed without a conjunction, as in the following:

(66) A. ^{d}A-NI-ru$_{12}$ U$_{5}$ GABA ^{d}Ku-ra DU si-in NE-na-áš^{ki}
A. ride front-of K. go toward N.
"The god A. rides before K. (when) they go to N."

B. BA$_{4}$.TI ^{d}Ku-ra ù ^{d}Ba-ra-ma si-in É ma-dím MU.DU
arrive K. CONJ. B. toward house-of death go
^{d}Ku-ra ù ^{d}Ba-ra-ma si-in DURU$_{5}$:É^{ki}
K. CONJ. B. toward chamber
"(When) K. and B. arrive at the mausoleum, K. and B. enter into [their] chamber"

Alternatively, the conjuction *wa* may connect a temporal clause to a main clause, as in

(67) ZÀ.ME UD sa-ba-da-su-ma wa PAD.TÚG ba-na-a ^{d}Ku-ra wa ^{d}Ba-ra-ma
rite(s) day seven=his=TOP. CONJ. veil(verb) faces-of K. CONJ. B.
"(When) their rites which last seven days are carried out, the faces of K. and B. are veiled"

Additionally, Eblaite attests several temporal conjunctions: *a-ti* "until" (cf. Akk. *adi*); *in* UD "when" (cf. Akk. *in(a) ūm*); *ù-lu(-um)* "after" (cf. the Akk. demonstrative *ullûm* "that, distant" < **ʾullay-*): for example, NU TÚG-ZI:ZI *a-ti-ma* MU.DU É ^{d}*Ku-ra* "She did not put on (the ceremonial garments) when she entered the temple of K."; 4 NITA:UDU SIKIL.SIKIL... *ma-lik-tum* NÍDBA *in* UD BA$_{4}$.TI É ^{d}*Ku-ra* "Four pure male sheep... the queen offered in sacrifice, when she arrived at the temple of K."; *ù-lu* BA$_{4}$.TI EN *ù ma-lik-tum*... *A-ma-za-ù* NÍDBA "After the king and queen arrived... A. offered a sacrifice."

5.12.3 Other subordinate clauses

The remaining subordinate clause types likewise precede the main clause; however, unlike the instance of the temporal clauses, there are no predictable patterns for the use of tenses. The perfect, however, generally does not occur. Local clauses are usually expressed with the conjunction *ašar* (bound form of *ašrum* "place") or *ēm(a)* "where(ever)": for example, *imtasi ašar iwwaldu* "He forgot where he was born" (Standard Babylonian); *ēm tammarūšu ṣabassu* "Wherever you see him, seize him!" Causal clauses often use the conjunctions *aššum* "because," *ana ša* "because (of the fact that)," or *ištu* "because, since":

(68) A. ana ša / lā / ḫabbulākūšunnī-ma / kaspam
because (to+REL.) / NEG. / indebted=I=to-him=SUBORD.=CONJ. / silver
ilqe'u / ṣabtāšu
he=took=SUBORD. / seize.IMPV.=him
"Because I am not indebted to him and he took the silver, seize him!" (Old Assyrian)

B. ištū-ma / dīnam / ušāḫizūkā-ma . . . / lā
because / judgment / I=caused-to-take=SUBORD.=you=CONJ. . . . / NEG.
tešmû / ul / wašrāta
you=heard=SUBORD. / NEG. / obedient=you
"Because I have uttered the judgment and . . . you have not listened, you are disobedient"

The conjunction *kīma*, in addition to its temporal use, often introduces object clauses (i.e., "that, the fact that" clauses); for example:

(69) šāpirum / kīma / immerī / nēmettaka / ana / ekallim / lā
overseer / that / sheep / tax=your / to / palace / NEG.
tublam / ulammidanni
you=brought=VENT. / he=informed=VENT.=me
"The overseer informed me that you had not brought the sheep, your tax, to the palace"

In Middle Babylonian the conjunction *kī* serves a variety of functions. Its position in its clause is semantically significant: in causal or object clauses it stands first, like other conjunctions, as in *kī annīta amāta iqbûni* "because they told me this matter." Temporal clauses, however, are marked by the placement of *kī* immediately before the verb, as in *ana muššurīni kī illika* "when PN came to release us."

6. LEXICON

The majority of the Akkadian lexicon is inherited from Proto-Semitic; however, there is also a great deal of Sumerian lexical interference in Akkadian as well. Although there are no comprehensive treatments of the lexical integration of Sumerian loanwords into Akkadian, recent statistical analyses suggest that one-tenth of the lexicon is borrowed from Sumerian; most of the words are nouns covering a wide semantic range. It must be noted, however, that this figure reflects the total percentage of lexical entries for the nearly three millennia of attested Akkadian and not the frequency of use or the degree of lexical integration for particular dialects. For Old Akkadian the number of Sumerian loanwords in Akkadian is quite small. A study of Sumerian loanwords in Old Babylonian Akkadian has found 529 loanwords, of which, however, 102 are found only in lexical lists (i.e., learned texts containing Akkadian words and their Sumerian counterparts) and were therefore probably not part of the spoken language. Only four of the Old Babylonian Sumerian loanwords are also attested for Old Akkadian (Edzard 1970:157, n. 2; Lieberman 1977:7).

Early Sumerian loanwords are characterized by voiceless consonants where the original Sumerian word has what, in later Sumerian at least, seems to have been a voiced consonant: for example, *ikkarum* "farmer" (< ENGAR); *laputtûm* "captain" (< NU.BANDA); *parakkum* "dais" (< BARAG); *asûm* "physician" (< A.ZU). This shift is due no doubt to the differences in the Sumerian and Akkadian phonological systems and, consequently, the way in which Akkadian speakers heard Sumerian phonemes. Late Sumerian loanwords, borrowed most likely after the death of Sumerian as a spoken language in the Old Babylonian period, display a one-to-one correspondence between Sumerian and Akkadian voiced and voiceless consonants: for example, *guzalû* "throne bearer" (< GU.ZA.LÁ); *agubbû* "basin for holy water" (< A.GÚB.BA); *bandudû* "bucket" (< BA.AN.DU_8.DU_8).

During the long period in which Akkadian is attested, Mesopotamians came into contact with many peoples, through either the filtration of various semi-nomadic groups into the region, trade and diplomacy with neighboring areas, or the conquests of the imperial periods. Thus, within the lexicon of Akkadian, loanwords and foreign phrases are attested in various periods and dialects from such diverse languages as Amorite, Egyptian, Elamite, Greek, Hittite, Hurrian, Kassite, Persian, Subarian, Urartian, as well as various West Semitic languages. With the rise of Aramaic during the first millennium and the beginning of its eventual eclipse of Akkadian as the spoken language of Mesopotamia, many Aramaic loanwords filtered into Akkadian as well.

Eblaite, similarly, derives a great deal of its lexicon from Proto-Semitic, such as the following words, here grouped semantically:

1. *Body parts*: for example, /ʔammatum/ "forearm," /ʕaθ'mum/ "bone"
2. *Kinship terms*: for example, /ʔumm-um/ "mother," /kallatum/ "wife"
3. *Clothing*: for example, /kusītum/ "garment," /śaʔnā(n)/ "pair of sandals"
4. *Building*: for example, /baytum/ "house," /libittum/ "brick"
5. *Tools and techniques*: for example, /magazzu(m)/ "blade for shearing," /t'aħānum/ "to grind"
6. *Social organization*: for example, /maliktum/ "queen," /mayšarum/ "justice"

However, Eblaite also shares many lexical isoglosses with Akkadian which find no parallel in the other Semitic languages: for example, /zaʔ$_x$ārum/ "to hate" (Akk. *zêrum*), /ramānum/ "self" (Akk. *ramānum*). Eblaite also attests many isoglosses with West Semitic that are not encountered in Akkadian: for example, /bak'aru(m)/, Hebrew and Arabic *baqar* "cow"; /mabt'aħ-/, Hebrew *mibṭāḥ* "confidence"; /ʔarzatum/, Hebrew, Aramaic, and Arabic *'arz* "cedar."

Eblaite also contains a number of Sumerian loanwords, which may have made their way into Eblaite by way of Akkadian: for example, /malāxum/ (Sum. MÁ.$LAḪ_4$, Akk. *malāḫu*) "sailor"; /melammu/ (Sum. ME.LÁM, Akk. *melammu*) "divine radiance," as well as numerous words and names from unknown language(s).

7. READING LIST

The standard reference grammar of Akkadian is von Soden 1995 (3rd edition, *GAG*). A more concise, but nonetheless excellent, overview of Akkadian is Ungnad 1992 (English translation). Dialect-specific treatments include Aro 1955 (Middle Babylonian), Deller 1959 (Neo-Assyrian), Gelb 1961 (Old Akkadian), Hecker 1968 (Old Assyrian), Hueter 1996 (Late Babylonian), Mayer 1971 (Middle Assyrian), von Soden 1931, 1933 (Standard

Babylonian), Streck 1995 (Late Babylonian), de Vaan 1995 (Neo-Babylonian), Woodington 1982 (Neo-Babylonian).

A recent teaching grammar of (Old Babylonian) Akkadian is Huehnergard 1997. Riemschneider's grammar of Akkadian (1974, English translation) includes useful chapters outlining the distinguishing characteristics of the various dialects. Other introductory texts covering the essential grammar include Caplice 1988 and Marcus 1978; Miller and Shipp 1996 includes a useful sign list and glossary, as well as paradigms for introductory study.

Major studies of the various peripheral dialects include Adler 1976 (Mitanni), Huehnergard 1989 (Ugarit), Izre'el 1991 (Amurru), Labat 1932 (Boghaz-köi), and Wilhelm 1970 (Nuzi). Linguistically oriented treatments of Akkadian include Buccellati 1996, Gelb 1969, Groneberg 1987 (Standard Babylonian), and Reiner 1966.

There are two extensive dictionaries for Akkadian, von Soden's three-volume *Akkadisches Handwörterbuch* (1965–1981; *AHw*), which includes many attestations for each entry, but without extensive citation or translation, and *The Assyrian Dictionary of the University of Chicago* (also referred to as the *Chicago Assyrian Dictionary*, or *CAD*), an encylopedic reference work nearing completion (to date, seventeen of the twenty-one volumes have been published).

There are three standard sign lists in common use. Labat's *Manuel d'épigraphie akkadienne* (1988, *MEA*) illustrates the diachronic development of the individual sign forms and provides their phonetic and logographic values. Borger's *Assyrisch-babylonische Zeichenliste* (1988, *ABZ*) presents the same information, although there is greater concentration on sign values and less on the evolution of the individual sign forms. Von Soden and Röllig's *Das akkadische Syllabar* (1991, *AS*) is the authoritative reference for phonetic sign values; however, logographic values and the sign forms for the individual dialects are not given.

Editions of Akkadian (and Sumerian) texts published through 1973, with cross-references to subsequent commentaries, can be found in Borger's three-volume *Handbuch der Keilschriftliteratur* (1967–1975, *HKL*). Texts published after this date can be located in the annual "Register Assyriologie" of the periodical *Archiv für Orientforschung* and in the annual "Keilschriftbibliographie" of the journal *Orientalia*.

There are no comprehensive treatments of Eblaite. Studies of the major grammatical features and classification of Eblaite include Cagni 1981, 1984, 1987; Diakonoff 1990; Edzard 1984; Fronzaroli 1984, 1990, 1992, 1996; Gelb 1981; Krebernik 1992, 1996; and Lambert 1992.

Bibliography

Adler, H.-P. 1976. *Das Akkadische des Königs Tušratta von Mitanni.* Kevelaer: Butzon and Bercker.

Aro, J. 1955. *Studien zur mittelbabylonischen Grammatik.* Studia Orientalia 20. Helsinki: Societas Orientalis Fennica.

______. 1961. *Die akkadischen Infinitivskonstruktionen.* Studia Orientalia 26. Helsinki: Societas Orientalis Fennica.

Borger, R. 1988. *Assyrisch-babylonische Zeichenliste* (AOAT 33/33A, 4th edition; *ABZ*). Neukirchen: Butzon and Bercker.

Buccellati, G. 1996. *A Structural Grammar of Babylonian.* Wiesbaden: Otto Harrassowitz.

Cagni, L. (ed.). 1981. *La lingua di Ebla: atti del convegno internazionale (Napoli, 21–23 aprile 1980).* Istituto Universitario Orientale, Dipartimento di Studi Asiatici, Series Minor 14. Naples.

______. (ed.). 1984. *Il bilinguismo a Ebla: Atti del convegno internazionale (Napoli, 19–22 aprile 1982).* Istituto Universitario Orientale, Dipartimento di Studi Asiatici, Series Minor 22. Naples.

______. (ed.). 1987. *Ebla 1975–1985: Diece anni di studi linguistici e filologici. Atti del convegno internazionale (Napoli, 9–11 ottobre 1985).* Istituto Universitario Orientale, Dipartimento di Studi Asiatici, Series Minor 27. Naples.

Caplice, R. 1988. *Introduction to Akkadian* (3rd edition). Studia Pohl, Series Maior 9. Rome: Pontifical Biblical Institute.

Conti, G. 1996. "Thèmes 'assyriens' et thèmes 'babyloniens' Ebla." In P. Zemánek (ed.), *Studies in Near Eastern Languages and Literatures. Memorial Volume of Karel Petráček*, pp. 193–202. Prague: Oriental Institute, Academy of Sciences of the Czech Republic.

Deller, K. 1959. "Lautlehre des Assyrischen." Dissertation, Universität Wien.

Diakonoff, I. 1990. "The importance of Ebla for the history of linguistics." In C. Gordon (ed.), *Eblaitica: Essays on the Ebla Archives and Eblaite Language*, vol. 2, pp. 3–31. Winona Lake, IN: Eisenbrauns.

Edzard, D. 1970. Review of *The Chicago Assyrian Dictionary. Zeitschrift für Assyriologie* 60: 157–160.

______. 1984. "Zur Syntax der Ebla-Texte." *Quaderni di Semitistica* 13:101–116.

Fronzaroli, P. (ed.). 1984. *Studies on the Language of Ebla.* Quaderni di Semitistica 13. Florence: Università di Firenze, Istituto di Linguistica e di Lingue Orientali.

______. 1990. "La langue d'Ebla." *Les Annales Archéologiques Arabes Syriennes* 40:56–63.

______ (ed.). 1992. *Literature and Literary Language at Ebla.* Quaderni di Semitistica 18. Florence: Università di Firenze, Dipartimento di Linguistica.

______. 1996. "Notes sur la syntaxe éblaïte." In J.-M. Durand (ed.), *Amurru 1: Mari, Ébla et les hourrites – dix ans de travaux*, pp. 125–34. Paris: Editions Recherche sur les Civilisations.

Gelb, I. 1955. "Notes on von Soden's grammar of Akkadian." *Bibliotheca Orientalis* 12:93–111.

______. 1957. *Glossary of Old Akkadian.* Materials for the Assyrian Dictionary 3. Chicago: University of Chicago.

______. 1961. *Old Akkadian Writing and Grammar of Akkadian* (2nd edition). Materials for the Assyrian Dictionary 2. Chicago: University of Chicago.

______. 1969. *Sequential Reconstruction of Proto-Akkadian.* Assyriological Studies 18. Chicago: University of Chicago.

______. 1981. "Ebla and the Kish civilization." In Cagni 1981, pp. 9–73.

Gelb, I. *et al.* 1956–. *The Assyrian Dictionary of the Oriental Institute of the University of Chicago.* Chicago: University of Chicago.

Groneberg, B. 1987. *Syntax, Morphologie und Stil der jungbabylonischen "hymnischen" Literatur* (2 vols.). Freiburger Altorientalische Studien 14. Stuttgart: Steiner.

Haayer, G. 1986. "Languages in contact: the case of Akkadian and Sumerian." In H. Vanstiphout, K. Jongeling, F. Leemhuis, *et al.* (eds.), *Scripta signa vocis: Studies about Scripts, Scriptures, Scribes and Languages in the Near East, presented to J. H. Hospers*, pp. 71–84. Groningen: Forsten.

Harper, R. 1904. *The Code of Ḫammurabi King of Babylon about 2250 BC.* Chicago: University of Chicago.

Hecker, K. 1968. *Grammatik der Kültepe-Texte.* Analecta Orientalia 42. Rome: Pontifical Biblical Institute.

Hetzron, R. 1968. "Main verb markers in Northern Gurage." *Africa* 38:156–172.

Huehnergard, J. 1986. "On verbless clauses in Akkadian." *Zeitschrift für Assyriologie* 76:218–249.

______. 1987. "'Stative,' predicative, pseudo-verb." *Journal of Near Eastern Studies* 46:215–232.

______. 1989. *The Akkadian of Ugarit.* Harvard Semitic Studies 34. Atlanta: Scholars Press.

______. 1997a. *A Grammar of Akkadian.* Harvard Semitic Studies 45. Atlanta: Scholars Press.

______. 1997b. Review of *Grundriß der akkadischen Grammatik* (3rd edition), by W. von Soden and W. Mayer. *Orientalia* NS 66:434–444.

Hueter, G. 1996. "Grammatical studies in the Akkadian dialects of Babylon and Uruk 556–500 BC." Ph.D. dissertation, University of Oxford.

Izre'el, S. 1991. *The Akkadian Dialect of the Scribes of Amurru in the 14th–13th Centuries BC* (2 vols.). Harvard Semitic Studies 41. Atlanta: Scholars Press.

Knudsen, E. 1980. "Stress in Akkadian." *Journal of Cuneiform Studies* 32:3–16.

Kouwenberg, N. 1997. *Gemination in the Akkadian Verb.* Studies Semitica Neerlandica. Aasen: van Gorcum.

Kraus, F. 1987. *Sonderformen akkadischer Parataxe: Die Koppelungen.* Mededelingen der Koninklijke Nederlandse Akademie van Wetenschappen, Afd. Letterkunde, Nieuwe Reeks, 50/1. Amsterdam: North-Holland Publishing.

Krebernik, M. 1982–1983. "Zu Syllabar und Orthographie der lexikalischen Texte aus Ebla." *Zeitschrift für Assyriolgie* 72:178–236; 73:1–47.

_______. 1992. "Mesopotamian myths at Ebla: ARET 5, 6 and ARET 5, 7." In Fronzaroli 1992, pp. 41–62.

_______. 1996. "The linguistic classification of Eblaite: methods, problems, and results." In J. Cooper and G. Schwartz (eds.), *The Study of the Ancient Near East in the Twenty-First Century*, pp. 233–251. Winona Lake, IN: Eisenbrauns.

Labat, R. 1932. *L'Akkadian de Boghaz-köi. Étude sur langue des lettres, traités et vocabulaire trouvés à Boghaz-Köi.* Bordeaux: Librairie Delmas.

_______. 1988. *Manuel d'épigraphie akkadienne* (6th edition by F. Malbran-Labat; *MEA*). Paris: Paul Geuthner.

Lambert, W. 1992. "The language of ARET *V*, *6* and *7*." In Fronzaroli 1992, pp. 41–62.

Lieberman, S. 1977. *The Sumerian Loanwords in Old-Babylonian Akkadian. Volume 1: Prolegomena and Evidence.* Missoula, MT: Scholars Press.

_______. 1979. "The phoneme /o/ in Sumerian." In M. Powell, Jr. and R. Sack (eds.), *Studies in Honor of Tom B. Jones*, pp. 21–28. Neukirchen-Vluyn: Butzon and Bercker.

Marcus, D. 1978. *A Manual of Akkadian.* Washington, DC: University Press of America.

Mayer, W. 1971. *Untersuchungen zur Grammatik des Mittelassyrischen.* AOATS 2. Rome: Pontifical Biblical Institute.

Miller, D. and R. Shipp. 1996. *An Akkadian Handbook.* Winona Lake, IN: Eisenbrauns.

Patterson, R. 1970. "Old Babylonian parataxis as exhibited in the royal letters of the Middle Old Babylonian period and in the Code of Hammurapi." Ph.D. dissertation, University of California, Los Angeles.

Rainey, A. 1976. "Enclitic *-ma* and the logical predicate in Old Babylonian." *IOS* 6:51–58.

Reiner, E. 1966. *A Linguistic Analysis of Akkadian.* The Hague: Mouton.

Riemschneider, K. 1974. *An Akkadian Grammar.* Translated by T. Caldwell, J. N. Oswalt, J. F. Sheehan, *et al.* Milwaukee: Marquette University Press.

Soden, W. von. 1931, 1933. "Der hymnisch-epische Dialekt des Akkadischen." *Zeitschrift für Assyriologie* 40:163–227; 41:90–183.

_______. 1965–81. *Akkadisches Handwörterbuch* (3 vols.). Wiesbaden: Otto Harrassowitz.

_______. 1995. *Grundriss der akkadischen Grammatik* (3rd edition). Analecta Orientalia 33. Rome: Pontifical Biblical Institute.

Soden, W. von and W. Röllig. 1991. *Das akkadische Syllabar* (AnOr 42, 4th edition; *AS*). Rome: Pontifical Biblical Institute.

Streck, M. 1994. "Funktionsanalyse des akkadischen Št$_2$-Stamms." *Zeitschrift für Assyriologie* 84: 161–197.

_______. 1995. *Zahl und Zeit: Grammatik der Numeralia und des Verbal Systems im Spätbabylonischen.* Cuneiform Monographs 5. Groningen: Styx.

Ungnad, A. 1992. *Akkadian Grammar* (5th edition by L. Matouš). Translated by H. Hoffner, Jr. SBL Resources for Biblical Study 30. Atlanta: Scholars Press.

Vaan, J. de. 1995. *"Ich bin eine Schwertklinge des Königs": Die Sprache des Bēl-ibni.* AOAT 242. Neukirchen-Vluyn: Butzon and Berker.

Westenholz, A. 1991. "The phoneme /o/ in Akkadian." *Zeitschrift für Assyriologie* 81:10–19.

Wilhelm, G. 1970. *Untersuchungen zum Ḫurro-Akkadischen von Nuzi.* Kevelaer: Butzon and Bercker.

Woodington, N. 1982. "A Grammar of the Neo-Babylonian Letters of the Kuyunjik Collection." Ph.D. dissertation, Yale. Ann Arbor, MI: University Microfilms.

APPENDIX TO CHAPTER 4

The cuneiform script

Sign	Values	Sign	Values
	aš, dil, rum, rù		la
	ḫal		bin, pin; $^{(giš)}$APIN = *epennu* "plow"
	mug/k/q, b/puk		maḫ
	ba, pá		tu, ṭú
	zu, ṣú		li, le
	su, kuš; SU = *zumru* "body"; KUŠ = *mašku* "skin, hide"		kúr, bab/p, pap; KÚR =*aḫû* "strange, foreign, hostile," *nakāru* "to be hostile"
	rug/k/q, šin, šun		mu; MU = *nīšu* "life," *šattu* "year," *šumu* "name"
	bal, pal; BALA = *palû* "reign"		qa; SILA$_3$ = *qû* (unit of capacity)
	ád/t/ṭ, gír		kád/t, šíd
	búl, púl		kàd/t
	tar, ṭar, tír, ṭír, kud/t, qud/t, ḫaz/s/ṣ, ḫaš, sil, šil; SILA = *sūqu* "street"		gil, kíl, qíl
	an, ìl; AN = *šamû* "sky, heaven"; DINGIR = *ilu* "god" (also determinative before deities)		ru, šub/p
	ka, qà; KA =*pû* "mouth"		be, pè, bad/t/ṭ, til, mid/t/ṭ, ziz/s; BE = *šumma* "if"
	nag/k/q; NAG = *šatû* "to drink"		na
	KÚ = *akālu* "to eat"		šir
	rí, ré, iri$_4$; ere$_4$; URU = *ālu* "town, city"		k/qul; NUMUN = *zēru* "seed," "progeny"
	ÌR = *ardu* "slave"		ti, ṭì
	ITI = *arḫu* "mouth" (also determinative before names of months)		bar, pár, maš; MAŠ = *mišlum* "half, middle"; *šumma* "if"; MAŠ.GAG.EN or MAŠ.EN.GAG = *muškēnu* "dependent, commoner"
	šaḫ, šiḫ; ŠAḪ = *šaḫû* "pig"		nu

Tables © Ecological Linguistics 2002. All rights reserved. Used by permission.

MÁŠ = *ṣibtu* "interest," *puḫādu* "lamb"; $^{(lú)}$ MÁŠ.ŠU.GÌD = *bārû* "diviner, haruspex"	en; EN = *bēlu* "lord"
kun	ṭàr
ḫu, pag/k/q; MUŠEN = *iṣṣūru* "bird" (also determinative following names of birds)	šur
nam	suḫ
ig/k/q, eg/k/q	mùš; ^{d}INANA (deity, Sum. Inana, Akk. Ištar)
mud/t/ṭ	sa
rad/t/ṭ	gán, kán, gà; GANA$_2$ = *eqlu* "field"; IKU = *ikû* (surface measure)
zi, ze, sí, ṣé, ṣé	kár
gi, ge	gú, tik/q; GÚ = *kišādu* "neck"; GÚ.UN (or GUN) = *biltu* "weight, tribute, load"
ri, re, dal, tal ṭal	dur, ṭur
nun, zil, ṣil; NUN = *rubû* "prince"	GUN (or GÚ.UN) = *biltu* "weight, tribute, load"
gáb/p, kab/p, qáb/p ḫúb/p	làl; LÀL = *dišpu* "honey"
ḫub/p	gur, qur; GUR = *kurru* (measure of capacity)
kad/t/ṭ, qàd/t; GADA = *kitû* "linen"; NA.GADA "shepherd"	si, se
dim, tim	dar, tár, ṭár
mun	sag/k/q, šag/k/q, riš, ris, res; SAG = *rēšu*, "head"; SAG.ÌR = *ardu* "male slave"; SAG.GEME$_2$ = *amtu* "female slave"
ag/k/q	má; $^{(giš)}$MÁ = *eleppu* "boat"
MÈ = *tāḫāzu* "battle"	dir, ṭir
tab/p, ṭab/p, dáb/p; TAB.BA = *tappû* "business associate, partner"	in
šum, tag/k/q	rab/p
ab/p	šàr; LUGAL = *šarru* "king"
nab/p	šìr, ḫir, sar, šar; KIRI$_6$ = *kirû* "garden, orchard"
mul	bàt; BÀD = *dūru* "wall"
ug/k/q	sì, sè
az/s/ṣ	

URUDU = *erû* "copper, bronze"	kas, raš/s; KASKAL = *ḫarrānu* "road, path, journey"
ká; KÁ = *bābu* "gate, opening"	
um	gab/p, qab/p; GABA = *irtu* "chest, breast"
dub/p, tub/p, ṭup; DUB = *ṭuppu* "tablet"; DUB.SAR = *ṭupšarru* "scribe"	duḫ, taḫ, ṭuḫ
dá, ta ṭá	ru$_6$; EDIN = *ṣēru* "plain, steppe"
i	daḫ taḫ, ṭaḫ
ia	
gan, kan, kám (also determinative following numbers)	am; AM = *rīmu* "wild bull"
tur, ṭùr; DUMU = *māru* "son"; DUMU.MUNUŠ = *mārtu* "daughter"; TUR = *ṣeḫēru* "to be small, young"	šir$_4$; UZU = *šīru* "meat, flesh" (also determinative before body parts)
ad/t/ṭ; AD = *abu* "father"	ne, ṭè, bil, pil, kúm, bí; IZI = *išātu* "fire"
ṣi, ṣe, zí, zé	bíl, píl
šàm (variant of šám)	NA$_4$ = *abnu* "stone" (also determinative before stone objects)
ram	kak, qaq
šám; SA$_{10}$ = *šâmu* "to buy, purchase"	ni, né, zal, ṣal, lí, lé, ì; Ì (or Ì.GIŠ) = *šamnu* "oil fat"
zik/q	ir er
gum, kum, qum, qu	mal, gá, mà
gaz, gaṣ	DAGAL = *rapāšu* "to be wide, large"; AMA = *ummu* "mother"
SUḪUŠ = *išdu* "base, foundation"	SILA$_4$ = *puḫādu* "lamb"
kas$_4$; ^{lú}KAŠ$_4$ = *lasīmu* "courier"	ùr
úr; ÚR = *sūnu* "lap," *pēmu* "thigh"	dag/k/q, tág/k/q, ṭak
il, él	
du, ṭù, gub/p, kub/p, qub/p; DU = *alāku* "to go"; GUB = *uzuzzu* "to stand"	
dum, tum, ṭum, tu$_4$	pa, ḫad/t/ṭ; UGULA = *aklu* "overseer, inspector"
ANŠE = *imēru* "donkey"	šab/p, sab/p
EGIR = *arki* "behind, in back of, after"	síp; $^{\text{(lú)}}$SIPA = *rē'û* "shepherd"
GEŠTIN = *karānu* "wine"	

Sign	Values	Sign	Values
	uš, nid/t/ṭ		
	iš, íz/s/ṣ, mil; SAḪAR = *eperu* "earth, dust, soil"		giš, iz/s/ṣ, ez/s/ṣ; GIŠ = *iṣu* "wood" (also determinative before wooden objects)
	bi, bé, pí, kaš; KAŠ = *šikaru* "beer"		GUD = *alpu* "ox, bull"
	šim, rig/k/q		al
	kib/p, qib/p		ub/p, ár
	mar		gàr, qar
	e		id/t/ṭ; ed/t/ṭ; Á = *idu* "side, arm, strength"
	dug/k/q, lud/t/ṭ; DUG = *karpatu* "pot, container" (also determinative before vessels)		lil
	un; UN = *nišū* "people"; KALAM = *mātu* "land, country"		MURUB$_4$ = *qablu* "hip, waist, middle"
	gid/t/ṭ, kid/t/ṭ, qid/t, saḫ, líl		ṭe$_5$; $^{\text{(lú)}}$SIMUG = *nappāḫu* "smith, metal worker"
	šid/t/ṭ, lag/k/q		áš
	rid/t/ṭ, mis; KIŠIB = *kunukku* "cylinder seal"		ma
	ú, šam; Ú = *šammu* "grass, herb, plant" (also determinative before plants)		gal, qal; GAL = *rabû* "great"
	ga, kà, qá		BARAG = *parakku* "cult, dais, sanctuary"
	luḫ, làḫ, lìḫ, raḫ, riḫ		gir, kir, qir, biš, piš
	kal, dan, tan, rib/p, lab/p		mir; AGA = *agû* "crown"; NIMGIR = *nāgiru* "herald"
	bid/t/ṭ, pid/t; É = *bītu* "house, temple"		bur, pur
	nir		BALAG = *balaggu* "a musical instrument (drum)"
			ša
	gi$_4$, ge$_4$		šu, qad/t; ŠU = *qātu* "hand"
	ra		lul, lib/p, lup, nar
	LÚ = *awīlu* "man" (also determinative before male professions)		sa$_6$; GIŠIMMAR = *gišimmaru* "date-palm"
	šiš, sis, siš; ŠEŠ = *aḫu* "brother"		ALAN = *ṣalmu* "statue"
	zag/k/q; ZAG = *idu* "side, border"		URI = *Akkadû* "Akkadian"
	gam		zib/p, ṣib/p, sìp

Sign	Values	Sign	Values
	kur, mad/t/ṭ, nad/t, lad/t/ṭ, šad/t/ṭ, sad/t/ṭ; KUR = *šadû* "mountain," *mātu* "country, land"		
	še; ŠE = *ûm* "barley, grain" (also determinative before grains)		ḫi, ḫe
	bu, pu, sír, šir, gíd/t/ṭ, qíd/t, šúd		aʾ, iʾ, eʾ, uʾ, ʾa, ʾi, ʾe, ʾu
	uz/s/ṣ		aḫ, iḫ, eḫ, uḫ
	šud/t/ṭ, sir, sù		kam (also determinative following numbers)
	muš, ṣir		im, em
	tir		bir, pìr
	te, ṭe$_4$, de$_4$; TE = *ṭeḫû* "to approach"		ḫur, ḫar, mur; ^{giš}ḪUR = *uṣurtu* "design, plan"
	kar		ḫuš
	liš, lis		
	u$_4$, ud/t/ṭ, tam, tú, par, pir, liḫ, ḫiš; UD/U$_4$ = *ūmu* "day"; ^{d}UTU = Sum. Utu, Akk. Šamaš (deity)		
	pi, pe, tál; GEŠTU = *uznu* "ear, wisdom, understanding"		
	lìb, lìp; ŠAG$_4$ = *libbu* "heart, mind, thought, inside"		
	ṣab/p, zab/p; ERIN$_2$ = *ṣābu* "gang, army, troops"		
	u		ši, lim; IGI = *īnu* "eye"
	muḫ; UGU = *muḫḫu* "skull, top"; *eli* "on, upon, over, above"		ar
	lid/t/ṭ; ÁB = *arḫu* "cow"		SIG$_5$ = *damāqu* "to be good, favorable"
	kiš, kis, qiš, qis		ù
	mi, mé, ṣíl, gi$_6$; GI$_6$ = *mušītu* "night, nighttime"		ḫul
	gul, qúl, sún		di, de, ṭi, ṭe, sá; DI = *dīnu* "decision, judgment"; DI.KUD = *dânu* "to judge"
	nim, num, nù, tum$_4$		dul, tul
	lam		ki, ke, qí, qé; KI = *erṣetu* "earth, land, district" (also determinative following names of countries)
	zur, ṣur		din, tin

pan, ban	dun, šul
gim, kim, qim, ṭím	KUG = *ellu* "pure"; KUG.SIG$_{17}$ = *ḫurāṣu* "gold"; KUG.BABBAR = *kaspu* "silver"
ul	pad/t/ṭ, šug/k/q
GÌR = *šēpu* "foot"	man, mìn, niš
	eš, sin
	diš, tiš, ṭiš, tiz (also determinative before male proper names)
	lal, lá
kil, qil, rim, ḫab/p	šal, sal, rag/k/q, mán, mín; MUNUS = *sinništu* "woman" (also determinative before female proper names and occupations)
ENGUR = *apsû* "abyss, subterranean ocean"	zum, súm, ṣum, ṣu, ríg/k/q
(giš)GIGIR = *narkabtu* "chariot"	nin; NIN = *aḫātu* "sister," *bēltu* "lady, mistress"
zar, ṣar	dam, ṭam; DAM = *mutu* "husband," *aššatum* "wife"; DAM.GÀR = *tamkāru* "merchant"
ùʾ	GEME$_2$ = *amtu* "female slave"
bul, pul	gu, qù
sug/k/q	NAGAR = *nagāru* "carpenter"
NENNI = *annanna* "so-and-so, such-and-such"	nig/k/q
me, mì, šib/p, sib/p	el, il$_5$
meš (also a marker of plurality following logograms)	lum, ḫum
ib/p, eb/p	SIG$_4$ = *libittu* "(mud) brick"
ku, qú, dúr, tuš; TÚG = *ṣubātu* "garment" (also determinative before garments)	dúk, tug/k/q
lu; UDU = *immeru* "sheep"	ur, lig/k/q, daš, das, taš, tas, tíz, tís, tíš
dib/p, tib/p, ṭib/p, dab/p	a; A = *mû* "water"

	kin, qin, qi, qe; KIN = *šipru* "message, work, labor"		za, sà, ṣa
	šík, šíq; SÍG = *šīpātu* "wool" (also determinative before objects made of wool or types of wool)		ḫa, ku_6; KU_6 = *nūnu* "fish" (also determinative following names of fish)
	ERIN = *erēnu* "cedar"		sig/k/q, šik/q
	šú		ṭu
	ÉN = *šiptu* "incantation"		šá, níg/k/q, gar; NINDA = *akalu* "bread, food"

CHAPTER 5

Egyptian and Coptic

ANTONIO LOPRIENO

1. HISTORICAL AND CULTURAL CONTEXTS

1.1 Introduction

Ancient Egyptian and its latest historical stage, Coptic, represent a branch of the language family variously called Afro-Asiatic, Hamito-Semitic, or Semito-Hamitic (see *WAL* Ch. 6; also Diakonoff 1965; Hodge 1971; Zaborski 1992:36–37). The Afro-Asiatic family comprises, from antiquity to the present time, a number of languages spoken and written in the eastern Mediterranean world, in northern Africa, and in western Asia. These languages are characterized by the following linguistic features: (i) a preference for fusional or flectional morphology; (ii) the presence of bi- and triconsonantal lexical roots, capable of being variously inflected; (iii) a consonantal system displaying a series of pharyngealized or glottalized phonemes, called "emphatics," alongside the voiced and the voiceless series; (iv) a vocalic system originally limited to the three vowels *a*, *i*, *u*; (v) a nominal feminine suffix *-at*; (vi) a case system consisting of no more than two or three cases; (vii) a nominal prefix *m-*; (viii) an adjectival suffix *-ī* (called *nisba*, the Arabic word for "relation"); (ix) an opposition between prefix conjugation for verbal actions and suffix conjugation for verbal states; (x) a conjugation pattern singular first person *'a-*, second person *ta-*, third person masculine *ya-*, feminine *ta-*, first person plural *na-*, with additional suffixes in the other persons.

The individual branches of the Afro-Asiatic family are as follows:

1. *Egyptian*: Within Afro-Asiatic, Egyptian shows the closest relations to Semitic and Berber.
2. *Semitic*: The largest family of languages within Afro-Asiatic (Hetzron 1992:412–417).
3. *Berber*: A group of related languages and dialects currently spoken in competition with Arabic by a few million speakers in northern Africa from the Atlantic coast to the oasis of Siwa and from the Mediterranean Sea to Mali and Niger (Willms 1980). Modern Berber is most probably the descendant of the Libyan languages spoken in the same area in antiquity.
4. *Cushitic*: A group of languages spoken by 15 million people in eastern Africa, from the Egyptian border in northeast Sudan to Ethiopia, Djibouti, Somalia, Kenya, and northern Tanzania (Sasse 1992:326–330).
5. *Chadic*: A group which comprises about 140 languages spoken by more than 30 million speakers in sub-Saharan Africa around Lake Chad (Newman 1992:253–254).
6. *Omotic languages*: Spoken by approximately one million speakers along the Omo River and north of Lake Turkana in southwest Ethiopia, formerly thought to represent the western branch of Cushitic (Fleming 1976:34–53).

The productive history of Egyptian, which spans from 3000 BC to AD 1300, can be divided into two main stages, characterized by a major change from synthetic to analytic patterns in the nominal syntax and the verbal system (Junge 1985). Each of these two stages can be further subdivided into three different phases, which affect mainly the sphere of graphemics (Kammerzell 1995).

1.2 Earlier Egyptian

This is the language of all written texts from 3000 to 1300 BC, surviving in formal religious texts until the third century AD. Its main phases are as follows:

1. *Old Egyptian* (Edel 1955–1964): The language of the Old Kingdom and of the First Intermediate Period (3000–2000 BC). The main documents of this stage of the language are royal rituals such as the "Pyramid Texts," and funerary texts, especially "autobiographies" containing accounts of individual achievements inscribed in the rock tombs of the administrative elite.

2. *Middle Egyptian* (Gardiner 1957): Also termed *Classical Egyptian*, from the Middle Kingdom to the end of Dynasty XVIII (2000–1300 BC). Middle Egyptian is the language of classical Egyptian literature, which comprises ritual texts, for example the "Coffin Texts" inscribed on the sarcophagi of the administrative elite; wisdom texts that convey the educational and professional expectations of contemporary Egyptian society, for example the "Instructions of the Vizier Ptahhotep"; narratives relating adventures of a specific hero and representing the vehicle of individual, as opposed to societal, concerns (the most famous specimen of this genre is the "Tale of Sinuhe"); hymns and poetical texts with religious contents, written in praise of a god or of the king. Besides literary texts, the Middle Egyptian corpus comprises administrative documents, for example the Kahun papyri, and historical records.

3. *Traditional Egyptian*: The language of religious texts (rituals, mythology, hymns) from the New Kingdom to the end of Egyptian civilization. Late Middle Egyptian coexisted with later Egyptian for more than a millennium in a situation of diglossia (Vernus 1996:560–564). From a grammatical point of view, Late Middle Egyptian maintains the linguistic structures of the classical language, but on the graphemic side, especially in the Greco-Roman period, it shows an enormous expansion of the set of hieroglyphic signs.

Earlier Egyptian is characterized by a preference for synthetic grammatical structures: it displays a full set of morphological suffixes indicating gender and number; it exhibits no definite article; it maintains the VSO order in verbal formations:

(1)	sḏm	zẖꜣw	n	sbꜣ.t-j
	listen.PROSP.	scribe	to	teaching.FEM.-me

"May the scribe listen to my teaching"

1.3 Later Egyptian

Later Egyptian is documented from Dynasty XIX down to the Middle Ages (1300 BC–AD 1300). Its main phases are as follows:

1. *Late Egyptian* (1300–700 BC): The language of written records from the second part of the New Kingdom (Černý and Groll 1984; Junge 1996; Neveu 1996). It conveys the rich entertainment literature of Dynasty XIX, consisting of wisdom texts and tales, but also of new literary genres, such as mythology or love poetry. Late Egyptian was also the vehicle of Ramesside bureaucracy as documented by the archives of the Theban necropoleis or by school texts. Late Egyptian is not a wholly homogeneous linguistic reality; rather, the texts of this phase of the language show various degrees of interference with classical Middle Egyptian, with the tendency of older or more formal texts, such as historical records or literary tales, to display a higher number of borrowings from the classical language, as opposed to later or administrative texts, where Middle Egyptian forms are much rarer (Winand 1992:3–25).

2. *Demotic* (seventh century BC to fifth century AD): The language of administration and literature from the pharaonic Late Period to late antiquity (Johnson 1991). While grammatically close to Late Egyptian, it differs from it radically in its graphic system. Important texts in Demotic are narrative cycles and moral instructions.

3. *Coptic* (fourth to fourteenth century AD): The language of Christian Egypt, written in a variety of Greek alphabet with the addition of six or seven Demotic signs to indicate Egyptian phonemes absent from Greek (Lambdin 1983). As a spoken, and gradually also as a written language, Coptic was superseded by Arabic from the ninth century onward, but it survives to the present time as the liturgical language of the Christian church of Egypt and in a few linguistic traces it left in spoken Egyptian Arabic (Vittmann 1991).

Besides displaying a number of phonological evolutions, later Egyptian develops analytic features: suffixal markers of morphological oppositions are dropped and functionally replaced by prefixal indicators; the demonstrative "this" and the numeral "one" evolve into the definite and the indefinite article; periphrastic patterns in the order SVO supersede older verbal formations (Hintze 1950):

(2)	mare-p-sah	sôtm	e-ta-sbô
	OPT.-the-scribe	listen	to-the.FEM.my-teaching
	"May the scribe listen to my teaching"		

1.4 Dialects

Owing to the centralized nature of the political and cultural models underlying the evolution of Ancient Egyptian society, there is hardly any evidence of dialect differences in pre-Coptic Egyptian (Osing 1975; Lüddeckens 1975). However, while the writing system probably originated in the south of the country, the origins of the linguistic type represented by earlier Egyptian are to be seen in Lower (northern) Egypt, around the city of Memphis, which was the capital of the country during the Old Kingdom. The linguistic origins of Later Egyptian lie in Upper (southern) Egypt, in the region of Thebes, the cultural, religious, and political center of the New Kingdom (Zeidler 1992:208; Schenkel 1993:148).

Coptic is known through a variety of dialects differing mostly in the graphic rendition of Egyptian phonemes, and to a lesser extent also in morphology and lexicon. The most important dialect is *Sahidic* (from Arabic *al-ṣaʿīd* "Upper Egypt"), the written standard of the Theban area. Sahidic is the first dialect of Coptic literature. *Bohairic* (from Arabic *al-buḥayra* "Lower Egypt"), the dialect of Alexandria, eventually became the language of the liturgy of the Coptic church. Other important dialects of Coptic literature are *Akhmimic* from the city of Akhmim (Greek Panopolis) in Upper Egypt; *Subakhmimic*, also called *Lycopolitan*, spoken in the area of Asyut (Greek Lycopolis) in Middle Egypt; and *Fayyumic*, the variety of Coptic from the oasis of Fayyum, in the upper western corner of the Nile Valley (Kasser 1991b).

2. WRITING SYSTEMS

2.1 Principles

The basic graphic system of the Egyptian language from about 3000 BC to the first centuries of our era is composed of *hieroglyphs* (Fischer 1977). This term is the Greek counterpart to the Egyptian expression *mdw.w-nṯr* "god's words." Hieroglyphs were used primarily for monumental purposes, their main material support being stone or, less frequently, papyrus. For cursive uses the hieroglyphic system developed two handwritten varieties, called *Hieratic*, documented from the Old Kingdom through the third century AD, and *Demotic*, from the seventh century BC to the fifth century AD. Beginning in Hellenistic times, hieroglyphs and their manual varieties were gradually superseded by alphabetic transcriptions of words, and then of whole texts, inspired by the Greek alphabet with the addition of Demotic signs to render Egyptian phonemes unknown to Greek. The final result of this process is the emergence of *Coptic*. Unlike other writing systems of the Ancient Near East, for example Mesopotamian cuneiform, hieroglyphs were never used to write down any language other than Egyptian, except for their later adoption in Nubia for the writing of Meroitic (third century BC to fourth century AD; Wenig 1982). However, the Proto-Sinaitic inscriptions of the second millennium BC (Giveon 1982) show that hieratic signs may have inspired the shape of Northwest Semitic consonantal signs. As for Demotic, some of its sign groups were adopted and phonetically reinterpreted in Meroitic.

Because of the formal similarities with Egyptian hieroglyphs, the term "hieroglyph" has also been applied to the writing system of Luwian, an Anatolian language related to cuneiform Hittite, spoken and written during the Late Bronze and Iron Ages (between *c.* 1500–700 BC) in southern and southwestern Anatolia and northern Syria: hence the misleading designation "Hittite hieroglyphs" by which they are often referred to (Gelb 1963:81–84).

The Egyptian hieroglyphs constitute a variable set of graphemes, ranging from about 1000 in the Old Kingdom (third millennium BC) down to approximately 750 in the classical language (second millennium BC), then increasing to many thousands during the Ptolemaic and Roman rule in Egypt, from the third century BC to the second century AD. They are pictographic signs representing entities and objects, such as gods or categories of people, animals, parts of the human or animal body, plants, astronomical entities, buildings, furniture. But these pictograms are not organized within a purely ideographic system; rather, they represent a combination of phonological and semantic principles (Schenkel 1984). An Egyptian word usually consists of two components:

1. A sequence of phonograms, each of which represents a sequence of one, two, or three consonantal phonemes; hence their label as *monoconsonantal* (such as /m/), *biconsonantal* (such as /p-r/), or *triconsonantal* signs (such as /ḥ-t-p/). Phonograms convey a substantial portion of the phonological structure of the word: normally all the consonants, less regularly the (semiconsonantal) glides *j* and *w*. The vowels remain unexpressed in the writing. Bi- and triconsonantal signs may be accompanied by other phonograms, mostly monoconsonantal, which spell out one or two of their phonemes, allowing in this way a more immediate interpretation of the phonological sequence; these signs are called *phonetic complements*.

Egyptian writing displays a set of twenty-four signs of monoconsonantal value (see Table 5.1). Although these cover almost completely the inventory of consonants and glides – an exception being the liquid /l/, conveyed by the graphemes <n>, <r>, or <n+r> – the

Table 5.1 Monoconsonantal hieroglyphic signs

Sign	Entity depicted	Transliteration	Phonological value
𓄿	vulture	ꜣ (aleph)	earlier /ʀ/ > later /ʔ/
𓇋	flowering reed	*j* (yod)	earlier /y/ > later /ʔ/
𓇌	(1) two reed flowers	*jj* or *y*	/y/
𓏭	(2) two strokes		
𓂝	human forearm	ꜥ (ayin)	earlier /d/ > later /ʕ/ as in Arabic *kaʿba*
𓅱	quail chick	*w* (waw)	/w/
𓃀	foot	*b*	/b/
𓊪	stool	*p*	/p/
𓆑	horned viper	*f*	/f/
𓅓	owl	*m*	/m/
𓈖	water	*n*	/n/
𓂋	human mouth	*r*	/r/
𓉔	reed shelter	*h*	/h/ as in English *he*
𓎛	twisted wick	*ḥ*	/ħ/ as in Arabic *aḥmad*
𓐍	placenta	*ḫ*	/x/ as in German *Buch*
𓄡	animal's belly	*ẖ*	/ç/ as in German *ich*
𓊃	bolt	*z*	/θ/ as in English *think*
𓋴	folded cloth	s	/s/
𓈙	pool or lake	š	/š/ as in English *she*
𓈎	hill slope	*q*	/q/ as in Arabic *qurān*
𓎡	basket with handle	*k*	/k/
𓎼	stand for jar	*g*	/ḳ/
𓏏	bread loaf	*t*	/t/
𓍿	tethering rope	*ṯ*	/č/ as in English *choke*
𓂧	human hand	*d*	/ṭ/
𓆓	snake	*ḏ*	/č̣/

hieroglyphic system never became fully phonetic, but always maintained the original combination of logograms and phonograms.

The phonological value of the phonograms is derived from the name of the represented entity by means of the rebus principle, i.e., by applying the same phonological sequence to other entities semantically unrelated to them. For example, from the representation of water 𓈗 **maw* is derived the phonological value of this sign as /m-w/. In this process of derivation, called the *consonantal principle*, only a segment of the original sequence of phonemes of the represented entity, usually consisting of the strong consonants, is isolated to function as phonogram: thus, the sign for a house 𓉐 **pa:ruw*, is used for the sequence /p-r/. In later times, the consonantal principle was expanded by the so-called *acrophonic principle*, i.e., the derivation of a phonological value from the first consonantal sound of the represented entity.

2. The sequence of phonograms is usually followed by a *semagram*, called a *determinative*, which classifies a word according to its semantic sphere: for example, a sitting man 𓀀 expresses the lexical realm of "man, mankind"; a sitting man touching his mouth 𓀁 the domain of

Figure 5.1 From the cube statue of Senenmut, fifteenth century BC

"eating, speaking, thinking, sensing"; a scribe's equipment the area of "writing"; a stylized settlement identifies the word as a toponym.

Many items of the basic vocabulary of Egyptian are expressed by semagrams which indicate their own semantic meaning. They do this (i) iconically, by reproducing the object itself; (ii) indexically, by portraying an entity whose name displays a similar phonological structure; or (iii) symbolically, by depicting an item metaphorically or metonymically associated with the object. These signs are called *logograms* or *ideograms*: for example, the hieroglyph which represents the enclosure of a house is used to indicate iconically the concept "house" (*prw*); the sign representing a duck means "son" (*zꜣ*) by virtue of the phonetic similarity between the Egyptian words for "duck" and for "son"; the cloth wound on a pole, a sacred emblem placed on the pylons of Egyptian temples, through symbolic association denotes "god" (*nṯr*).

Unlike most other systems of pictographic origin, such as Mesopotamian cuneiform or Chinese logograms, Egyptian hieroglyphs kept their original iconicity throughout their entire history without developing stylized forms. From about 2150 BC, Egyptian developed a subsystem of hieroglyphic orthography to express a sequence of *consonant* + *vowel*. In this subsystem, dubbed "syllabic orthography" (Schneider 1992; Zeidler 1993; Hoch 1994:487–504) and mostly used for the writing of words of foreign origin, three consonantal symbols (/ʾ/, /y/, /w/) were used to express vowels, in a procedure similar to the use of *matres lectionis* in Northwest Semitic orthography.

The writing system also possessed a set of hieroglyphic signs used to convey logographically the numbers 10^0:10^6 and the fractions 1/2, 1/3, and 1/4 (Loprieno 1986). To indicate natural numbers, signs appear repeated and organized sequentially from the highest to the lowest (356 = 3 × 100, 5 × 10, 6 × 1).

The basic orientation of the Egyptian writing system, and the only one used in the cursive varieties, is from right to left, with signs facing to the right; in monumental texts, the order may be inverted to left to right for reasons of symmetry or artistic composition.

Hieroglyphic writing conventions could be modified by addressing the figurative content of the sign. First of all, signs could become the vehicle for the expression of a cultural attitude vis-à-vis the entity it represented. For example, signs referring to the divine or royal sphere preceded in the writing any other sign belonging to the same compound noun, regardless of their actual syntactic positions. Conversely, a sign referring to a negatively connotated entity (for example an enemy) could be modified by means of substitution or mutilation of one of its features, in order to neutralize its negative potential. Secondly, the array of functional values of a specific sign could be expanded beyond the limits of the fixed convention: a sign could be given a different phonological value from the traditionally established one, especially by using it to indicate only the first consonantal phoneme of the corresponding word according to the acrophonic principle. This type of connotational expansion of the hieroglyphic system is found sporadically from the Old Kingdom onward, but developed dramatically in Ptolemaic times, leading to a radical change in the laws regulating the use of hieroglyphs.

2.2 Historical evolution

While the principles described above basically apply to the entire history of Egyptian writing, their distribution varies somewhat in the course of time. In the *archaic period*, around 3000 BC, the emergence of writing in Egypt is associated with a gradual development of a centralized system of government covering the entire country. In the inscriptions from this period on seals, palettes, and other monuments pertaining to the royal or administrative sphere, phonological and semantic principles are already intertwined, with a high number of signs functioning as logograms (Kahl 1994). In the *Old Kingdom* (Dynasty III–VI, 2750–2150 BC), the quantity and the complexity of written documents expands dramatically. Phonetic complementation may precede or follow the main sign. In the *classical system* of the Middle Kingdom (2050–1750 BC), which remained in use until the end of Dynasty XVIII (*c.* 1300 BC), a developed school system for the education of the bureaucratic elite fixes Egyptian orthography by reducing the number of graphic renditions allowed for any given word. The conventional orthography of the word usually consists either of a logogram, for the most basic nouns of the lexicon, or of a sequence of phonograms, often complementized, followed by a determinative. The inventory of hieroglyphs now totals about 750 signs (Gardiner 1957:438–548). During Dynasty XIX (1310–1195 BC), major changes affect the writing conventions of hieroglyphs and especially of Hieratic. In monumental texts, the space units within which sequences of hieroglyphs are formally arranged undergo an aesthetic readjustment. Changes are even more significant in manual writing, with a constant interface between traditional historical writing and the evolved phonetic reality.

With the decay of a powerful centralized government in the first millennium BC, centrifugal tendencies affect writing conventions as well. During Dynasty XXVI (seventh century BC), cursive *Demotic* develops at first in the north of the country, where the royal residence was located, and is gradually extended to the southern regions. Unlike Hieratic, which has sign groups that mirror the shape of the original hieroglyphs rather closely, Demotic signs break away from this tradition and adopt a set of stylized, conventional forms, in which the connection to the hieroglyphic counterpart is hardly perceivable, and which are therefore more likely to be used in purely phonetic function. Determinatives have now lost to a large extent their function as lexical classifiers. The development of Demotic marks the beginning of a divorce between monumental and cursive writing which will have a dramatic impact on the evolution of the hieroglyphic system as well. Demotic remained in literary and administrative use until the end of the Roman period.

Table 5.2 The Coptic alphabet

Character	Transcription	Character	Transcription
ⲁ	a	ⲣ	r
ⲃ	b	ⲥ	s
ⲅ	g	ⲧ	t
ⲇ	d	ⲩ	u
ⲉ	e	ⲫ	ph
ⲍ	z	ⲭ	kh
ⲏ	ē	ⲯ	ps
ⲑ	th	ⲱ	ō
ⲓ	i	ϣ	š
ⲕ	k	ϥ	f
ⲗ	l	ϧ	ḫ
ⲙ	m	ϩ	h
ⲛ	n	ϫ	j
ⲝ	ks	ϭ	c
ⲟ	o	ϯ	ti
ⲡ	p		

In *Ptolemaic* and *Roman* times (fourth century BC to third century AD), an increasing consciousness of the symbolic potential inherent in the relation between hieroglyphic signs and semantic meanings led to the development of previously unknown phonetic values and also of so-called cryptographic solutions. This evolution, which originated in priestly circles and remained until the end the monopoly of a very restricted intellectual community, threatened the accessibility of the system, favoring a dramatic increase in the number of signs, which now reaches many thousands (Daumas 1988–1995) and exploiting the full array of potential meanings of the hieroglyphic sign. And it is exactly this radical change in the nature of the writing system in the Greco-Roman period which is at the origin of the view, held in the Western world from late antiquity to the emergence of modern Egyptology, of the symbolic, rather than phonological, character of the hieroglyphic writing (Fowden 1986:13–74). With few exceptions, the Ptolemaic system was applied only to monumental writing.

2.3 Coptic

The first two centuries of our era saw the development of a whole corpus of mostly magical Egyptian texts in Greek letters, with the addition of Demotic signs to supplement it when phonologically required, known in the literature as *Old Coptic*. The pressure to adopt an alphabetic system increased with the Christianization of the country, when religious reasons contributed to the divorce between Egyptian culture and its traditional writing systems. The last dated hieroglyphic inscription is from the year AD 394. Demotic texts substantially decrease in number, Egyptian being replaced by Greek as a written language (Bagnall 1993:235ff.). The last Demotic graffito is dated to AD 452. In the following century, the new convention, which we call *Coptic*, appears completely established: the Egyptian language is now written in a Greek-derived alphabet. By the fifth century, the Egyptian elite had already lost the knowledge of the nature of hieroglyphs: the *Hieroglyphiká* of Horapollo, a hellenized Egyptian, offer a "decipherment" of the hieroglyphs fully echoing the late antique symbolic speculations (Boas and Grafton 1993).

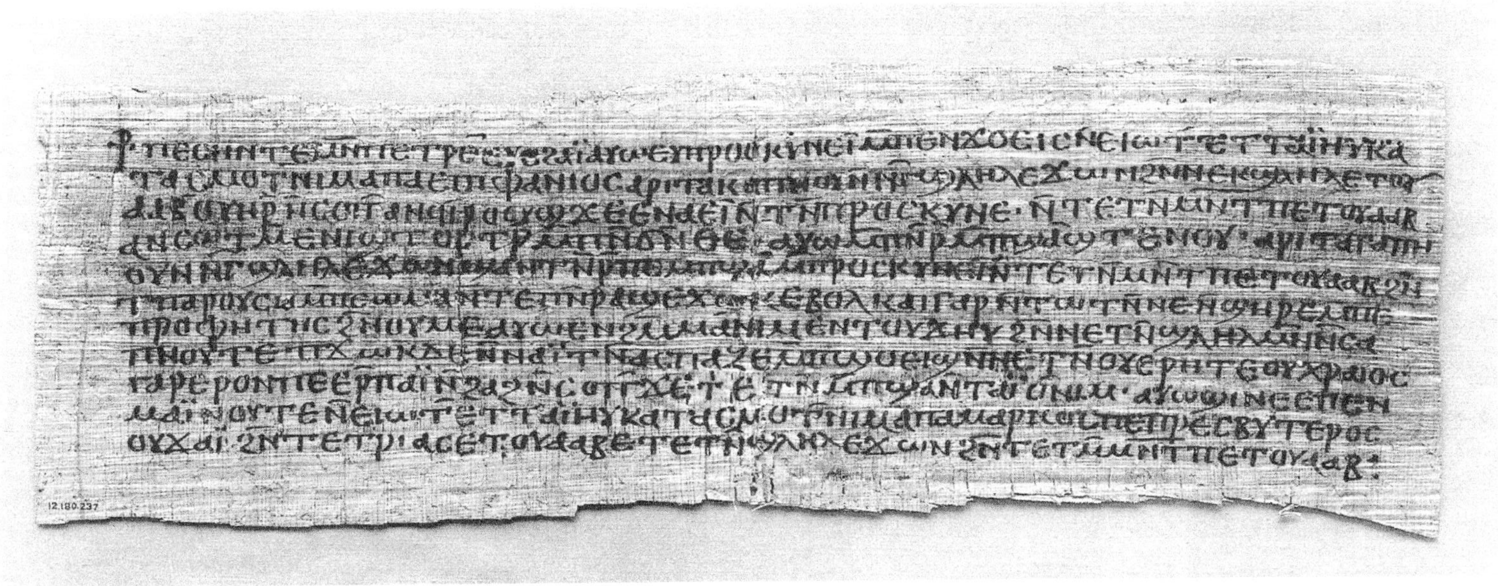

Figure 5.2 Photograph of Coptic text

2.4 Decipherment

The interest in matters Egyptian remained vivid in the West for the following centuries (Iversen 1961:57–123), but it was only in modern times that the understanding of the writing system was recovered. In the seventeenth century Athanasius Kircher recognized the linguistic derivation of Coptic from the language of the hieroglyphs (which he still took to be a symbolic writing), and in the eighteenth century Jean Barthélemy suggested that the cartouches which surround some hieroglyphic words contain divine and royal names. In 1799, during Napoleon's expedition to Egypt, the discovery of the so-called Rosetta Stone, a trilingual (Hieroglyphic, Demotic, and Greek) document from the Ptolemaic period found in the Egyptian town of Rosetta, in Arabic *Al-rašīd*, provided the possibility of comparing the same text in two unknown writing systems (Demotic and hieroglyphs) and in Greek; this event opened the way to the actual decipherment. First results were reached by the Swede Johan David Åkerblad for the Demotic section and especially by the English physician Thomas Young, who, however, did not progress beyond the royal names. The most decisive contribution to the decipherment was achieved by the French scholar Jean-François Champollion in his *Lettre à M. Dacier* (1822), and especially in the *Précis du système hiéroglyphique* (1824). On the basis of the writing of Greek names in the hieroglyphic text, Champollion was able to establish the presence of a phonetic component in the system, breaking away from the traditional symbolic approach (Iversen 1961:124–145).

3. PHONOLOGY

3.1 Phonemes and graphemes

The exact phonological value of many Egyptian phonemes is obscured by difficulties in establishing reliable Afro-Asiatic correspondences (Schenkel 1990:24–57). Vocalism and prosody can be partially reconstructed on the basis of (i) Akkadian transcriptions of Egyptian words and phrases from the second millennium BC, (ii) Greek transcriptions from the Late Period (corresponding roughly to spoken Demotic), and (iii) the Coptic evidence of the first millennium AD. In the sketch of Egyptian phonology presented below, Egyptological transliterations are given in italic, whereas underlying phonological realities are rendered between slashes and, since they are scholarly reconstructions, always preceded by an asterisk (note that by convention a dot is used to separate the root from morphological affixes; e.g., *sn.t* "sister" < root *sn* + feminine marker *t*). As for Coptic, in spite of a certain number of graphic idiosyncrasies, all dialects share a relatively uniform phonological system. For example, the graphic conventions of Sahidic – as opposed to those of Bohairic – do not distinguish between voiceless and ejective plosives (Sahidic *tôre*, Bohairic *thôri* = /tʰo:rə/ "willow" ~ Sahidic *tôre*, Bohairic *tôri* = /ṭo:rə/ "hand"); or between velar and glottal fricatives (Sahidic *hrai*, Bohairic *hrai* = /hraj/ "above" ~ Sahidic *hrai*, Bohairic *xrai* = /xraj/ "below"). Yet the presence of the corresponding oppositions in Sahidic can be established on the basis of comparative dialectology and of the different impact of these phonemes on their respective phonetic environment (Loprieno 1995:40–50).

3.2 Consonants

3.2.1 Stops and affricates

The stops and affricates of Earlier Egyptian are presented in (3):

(3) **Earlier Egyptian stops and affricates**

	Bilabial	*Dental*	*Palatal*	*Velar*	*Uvular*	*Glottal*
Voiced	b = /b/	(ʿ = /d/)	—	—	—	—
Voiceless	p = /pʰ/	t = /tʰ/	ṯ = /čʰ/	k = /kʰ/	—	—
Ejective	—	d = /ṭ/	ḏ = /č̣/	g = /ḳ/	q = /q/	ꜣ = /ʔ/

In the Egyptian phonological system, the opposition between voiceless and voiced phonemes (Schenkel 1993:138–146) appears limited to bilabial stops (4A), whereas in the other series the articulatory opposition – when present – is between voiceless and ejective stop or affricate (4B–C). The voiceless varieties displayed the optional feature of aspiration in pretonic and high-sonority environments:

(4) A. bilabial /b/ ~ /pʰ/: Bohairic *bôk* "servant" ~ *pʰôk* "yours.MASC.SG."
B. dental /tʰ/ ~ /ṭ/: Earlier Eg. *tm* "to complete" ~ *dm* "to sharpen"
C. palatal /čʰ/ ~ /č̣/: Earlier Eg. *ṯr.t* "willow" ~ *ḏr.t* "hand"

The dental series is typologically complex: while it probably exhibited a tripartite opposition *voiceless–voiced–ejective* in the earliest periods, the voiced stop */d/ evolved into a pharyngeal fricative */ʕ/ before the emergence of Middle Egyptian (Zeidler 1992:206–210), and then to a glottal stop (and eventually zero) in Coptic (5A). During the second millennium BC, the voiceless dental /t/ shows the tendency to be dropped in final position (5B):

(5) A. */d/ > */ʕ/ > /ʔ/ or /ø/:
Old Eg. *ʿš* */da:š/ > Late Eg. */ʕa:š/ > Coptic *ôš* /(ʔ)o:š/ "to call"
B. t > ø / __#:
Old Eg. *sn.t* */sa:nat/ > Late Eg. */sa:nə(t)/ > Coptic *sône* /so:nə/ "sister"

During the late second millennium BC, the place of articulation of stop consonants tends to be moved to the frontal region (Osing 1980:946): uvulars and velars are palatalized (6), palatals become dentals and dentals are dropped in final position (7):

(6) **Uvular and velar palatalization**

A. Late Eg. *kꜣm* */kʰaʔm/ > Coptic *côm* /kʸo:m/ "garden"
B. Old Eg. *gr* */ḳa:r/ > Coptic *cô* /kʸo:ʔ/ "to cease"
C. Old Eg. *qd* */qaṭ/ > Coptic *cot* /kʸot/ "form"

(7) **Palatal > dental; dental > ø/__#**

A. Old Eg. *ḏr.t* */č̣a:rat / > Late Eg. */ṭa:rə(t)/ > Coptic *tôre* /ṭo:rə/ "hand"
B. Old Eg. *rmṯ* */ra:mač/ > Late Eg */ra:mə(t)/ > Coptic *rôme* /ro:mə/ "man"

During the first millennium BC, the opposition between uvulars and velars is neutralized: Coptic exhibits a new tripartite opposition "palatalized : voiceless (with optional aspiration) : ejective" in the velar series:

(8) /kʰ/ ~ /ḳ/ ~ /q/ > /kʸ/ ~ /kʰ/ ~ /ḳ/

A. *kô* "shrine" (from Eg. */kʰ/) ~ *cô* "to cease" (from Eg. */ḳ/)
B. *côb* "weak" (from Eg. */ḳ/) ~ *kôb* "to double" (from Eg. */q/)
C. *cot* "form" ~ *kot* "wheel" (both from Eg. */q/)

(9) **Stops and affricates in Sahidic Coptic**

	Bilabial	*Dental*	*Palatal*	*Velar*	*Glottal*
Palatalized	—	—	—	c=/k^{y}/	—
Voiced	b = /b/	(d = /d/)	—	(g = /g/)	—
Voiceless	p = /p(^{h})/	t = /t(^{h})/	j = /č(^{h})/	k = /k(^{h})/	—
Ejective	—	t = /ṭ/	j = /č̣/	k = /ḳ/	/ˀ/

It should be noted that the opposition between voiceless and ejectives is neutralized as voiceless (unmarked) in posttonic position (10A), and that voiced dentals and velars are only found in Greek borrowings or as a result of assimilation of the corresponding voiceless in nasal environments (10B):

(10) A. *sôtm* /so:təm/ < /so:ṭəm/ "to hear" ~ *sôtp* /so:təp/ < /so:t(^{h})əp/ "to choose"
B. *tooun-g* < *tooun-k* "stand up!"

3.2.2 Fricatives

In Old Egyptian, all fricative consonants were voiceless; in Middle Egyptian, as we have just seen (in [5] above), a voiced pharyngeal /ʕ/ evolved from earlier /d/ via lateralization.

(11) **Fricatives in Earlier Egyptian**

	Labio-dental	*Inter-dental*	*Alveolar*	*Palato-alveolar*	*Palatal*	*Velar*	*Pharyngeal*	*Glottal*
Voiceless	f = /f/	z = /θ/)	s = /s/	š = /š/	ẖ = /ç/	ḫ = /x/	ḥ = /ħ/	h = /h/
Voiced	—	—	—	—	—	—	—	—

The interdental *z* merged very early with the alveolar *s* (/θ/ > /s/). In the first millennium BC, the tripartite opposition between fricatives in the palatal region (/š/ ~ /ç/ ~ /x/) was reduced to a bipartite one (/š/ ~ /x/), with a partial redistribution of the original articulation (Osing 1976:401–402; 503):

(12) A. */x/ > /š/:
Old Eg. *ꜥḫm* */da:xam/ > Late Eg. */ʕa:xəm/ > Coptic *ôšm* /ˀo:šəm/ "to extinguish"
B. */ç/ ~ /š/ > /x/:
Old Eg. *zẖꜣw* */θaçʀaw/ ~ /θašʀaw/ > Coptic *sah* /sax/ "scribe"
C. */ç/ > /x/:
Old Eg. *ꜥẖm* */daça:mv/ "falcon" > Late Eg. */ʕaça:m/ > Coptic *ahôm* /ˀaxo:m/ "eagle"

A similar neutralization affected in the first millennium BC the opposition between pharyngeal /ħ/ and glottal /h/ (Osing 1976:367–368):

(13) A. Old Eg. *ḥꜣ.t* */ħu:ʀit/ > Late Eg. */ħe:ˀə(t)/ > Coptic *hê* /he:ˀ/ "beginning"
B. Old Eg. *hꜣ.w* */haʀu:w/ > Late Eg. */həˀe:ˀ/ > Coptic *hê* /he:ˀ/ "season"

The distribution of fricative phonemes in Sahidic Coptic is thus as follows:

(14) **Fricatives in Sahidic Coptic**

	Labiodental	*Alveolar*	*Palato-alveolar*	*Velar*	*Glottal*
Voiceless	f = /f/	s = /s/	š = /š/	ḫ = /x/	h = /h/
Voiced	—	(z = /z/)	—	—	—

It should be noted that the voiced alveolar fricative *z* is only found in Greek borrowings or as a result of assimilation in nasal environments:

(15) Coptic *anzêbe* < *ansêbe* "school"

3.2.3 Sonorants

Historical evolutions affecting nasals, liquids, and glides during the second millennium BC (Loprieno 1995:38) involved (i) the loss of the uvular vibrant (i.e., nonlateral) /ʀ/ and its lenition to glottal stop /ʔ/ and eventually ø (16), and (ii) the loss of final vibrants and glides (17) in the same environments in which a final voiceless dental *t* was dropped (see [7]):

(16) /R/ > /ʔ/ > ø

Old Eg. *kꜣmw* */k^{h}aʀmaw/ > Late Eg. */k^{h}aʔm/ > Coptic *côm* /k^{y}o:m/ "garden"

(17) /r, y, w/ > ø / _#

A. Old Eg. *ḫpr* */xa:par/ > Late Eg. */xa:pə(r)/ > Coptic *šôpe* /šo:pə/ "to become"
B. Old Eg. *nṯr.w* */nac^{h}u:raw/ > Late Eg. */nət^{h}e:rə/ "gods" > Coptic *ntêr* /ənt^{h}e:r/ "idols"

(18) Sonorants in the Egyptian domain

	Labial	*Dental*	*Palatal*	*Uvular*
Nasal	m = /m/	n = /n/	š = /š/	
Vibrant	—	r = /r/	—	(ꜣ = /ʀ/)
Lateral	—	/l/	—	—
Glide	w = /w/	—	j = /y/	—

3.3 Vowels

The set of vowels posited for Earlier Egyptian (Osing 1976:10–30) is the same as for most Afro-Asiatic languages in their earliest stage of development (Diakonoff 1965:30–31):

(19) Vowels in Earlier Egyptian

	Short	*Long*
Front	/i/	/i:/
Central	/a/	/a:/
Back	/u/	/u:/

This system underwent a certain number of historical changes, only some of which can be discussed here. First and foremost, because of the presence of a strong expiratory stress, Egyptian unstressed vowels gradually lost phonological status, until in Coptic they are generally realized as *schwa*; only the short unstressed /a/ is maintained in pretonic position in specific phonetic environments (Schenkel 1990:91–93):

(20) A. Old Eg. *rmṯ nj km.t* */ramac-ni-k^{h}u:mat/ > Coptic *rmnkême* /rəmənk^{h}e:mə/ "Egyptian man"
B. Old Eg. *jnk* */janak/ > Coptic *anok* /ʔanok/ "I"

Stressed vowels underwent a global *Lautverschiebung*: during the second millennium BC, long /u:/ turned into /e:/, while short stressed /i/ and /u/ merged into /e/. In the main Coptic dialects and unless followed by glottal stop, this /e/ evolved into /a/:

(21) A. Old Eg. *rn* */rin/ > Late Eg. */ren/ > Coptic *ran* /ran/ "name"
B. Old Eg. *mꜣꜥ.t* */muʀdat/ > Late Eg. */meʔʕə(t)/ > Coptic *me* /meˀ/ "truth"
C. Old Eg. *km.t* */kʰu:mat/ > Late Eg. */kʰe:mə(t)/ > Coptic *kême* /kʰe:mə/ "Egypt"

Around 1000 BC, long /a:/ became /o:/ (/u:/ after nasals) and short /a/ became /o/, a change limited to the same portion of the Coptic linguistic domain to which /i/, /u/ > /e/ applies:

(22) A. Old Eg. *nṯr* */na:car/ > Coptic *noute* /nu:tə/ "God"
B. Old Eg. *sn* */san/ > Coptic *son* /son/ "brother"

(23) Vowels in Sahidic Coptic

	Unstressed	*Stressed*	
		Short	*Long*
Front			i, ei /i:/
		e /e/	ê /e:/
Central	e /ə/		
	a /a/	a /a/	
Back			ou /u:/
		o /o/	ô /o:/

3.4 Stress and syllabic patterns

In Earlier Egyptian, the stress lay on the ultimate (oxytone) or penultimate (paroxytone) syllable of a word (Schenkel 1990:63–86). Closed (CVC) and open (CV) syllables can be found in pretonic, tonic, and posttonic position. The stressed vowel of a penultimate open syllable is always long (CV:); according to some scholars, extrasyllabic additions under oxytone stress could generate syllables of the type CV:(C) or CVC(C) (Loprieno 1995: 36–37):

(24) Earlier Egyptian syllabic structures

	Pretonic	*Tonic*	*Posttonic*
Open	CV	$´CV:$	$CV#
Closed	CVC	$´CVC$	$CVC#
Doubly closed		$´CVCC#	
Long		$´CV:C$	

These syllabic structures were modified under the influence of the strong expiratory stress which always characterized the Egyptian domain (Fecht 1960) and prompted significant typological changes in morphology and syntax. The gradual loss of short unstressed vowels led to the emergence of complex consonantal clusters in syllable onset (i.e., word-initially) in Coptic (Loprieno 1995:48–50):

(25) Coptic syllabic structures

	Pretonic	*Tonic*	*Posttonic*
Open	\$CV\$	\$´CV:\$	\$CV#
	#CCV\$	#´CCV:\$	
Closed	\$CVC\$	\$´CVC\$	\$CVC#
	#CCVC\$	#´CCVC\$	
Doubly-closed		\$´CVCC#	
		#´CCVCC#	
Long		\$´CV:C#	
		#´CCV:C#	

Examples for the evolution of oxytone patterns follow:

(26) A. CV´CVC > CCVC
Old Eg. *wḏḥ* */wač̣aħ/ > Coptic *outah* /wəṭah/ "fruit"
B. CVC´CVC > CVC´CVC
Old Eg. *nmḥw* */numħiw/ "poor" > Coptic *rmhe* /rəmheʔ/ "free"

Examples for the evolution of paroxytone patterns:

(27) A. ′CVCCVC > CVCC
Old Eg. *ḫmtw* */xamtaw/ > Bohairic *šomt* /šomt/ "three"
B. CV′CVCCVC > CCVCC
Old Eg. *ḥjm.wt* */ħijamwat/ > Coptic *hiome* /hjomʔ/ "women"
C. CV′CV:CVC > CCV:C
Old Eg. *psḏw* */pisi:č̣aw/ > Coptic *psit* /psi:t/ "nine"

4. MORPHOLOGY

4.1 Word formation

Earlier Egyptian is a language of the flectional or fusional type, in which morphemes are unsegmentable units combining many grammatical functions. Morphological forms exhibit a number of correspondences with the patterns of word formation in other Afro-Asiatic languages (Schenkel 1990:94–121). In recent years, scholars have also emphasized the importance of prehistoric contact between Egyptian and Indo-European (Ray 1992:124–136; Kammerzell 1994:37–58).

The basic structure of an Egyptian word is a lexical *root*, an abstract phonological entity consisting of a sequence of consonants or semiconsonants which vary in number from one to four, with an overwhelming majority of biconsonantal, triconsonantal, and so-called weak roots, which display a vocalic or semivocalic last radical (i.e., phoneme) or a gemination of the second radical. Superimposed on the root as a separate morphological tier is a vocalic or semivocalic pattern, which together with the root forms the so-called *stem*, the surface form acquired by the root; the stem determines the functional class to which the word belongs. It is transformed into an actual *word* by means of inflectional affixes (in Egyptian for the most part suffixes), which convey deictic markers and other grammatical functions such as gender, number, tense and aspect, and voice (Reintges 1994).

Vocalic skeletons generally determine the structure of nominal patterns and of basic conjugational forms, whereas semivocalic suffixes convey the expression of the plural, of adjectival forms of the verb (participles and relative forms), and of some conjugational patterns. A *j*- or *w*- prefix can be added to biconsonantal roots to form triradical nominal stems; conversely, a triconsonantal root may lose a semivocalic glide and be reduced to a biradical stem. Examples of consonantal additions prefixed to a root are *s*- for causative stems, *n*- for singulative nouns and reflexive verbs, and *m*- for nouns of instrument, place, or agent. Egyptian stems resulting from the addition of a consonantal phoneme to a root tend to be lexicalized as new autonomous roots rather than treated as grammatical forms of the basic root: Egyptian, therefore, does not possess a full-fledged paradigm of verbal stems conveying semantic nuances of a verbal root similar to the ones known in Semitic.

Common modifications of the root are:

1. The reduplication of the entire root or of a segment thereof. This pattern affects the semantic sphere, creating new lexemes: from *sn* "brother," *snsn* "to befriend"; from *gmj* "to find," *ngmgm* "to be gathered" (with the *n*-prefix of reflexivity); from *snb* "to be healthy" *snbb* "to greet."
2. The gemination of the last radical, which affects the grammatical sphere: *ḏd* "to say" > *ḏdd.t* "what has been said"; *mrj* "to love" > *mrr-j* "that I love"; *sḏm* "to hear" > *sḏmm-f* "he will be heard" (Reintges 1994:230–240).

4.2 Nominal morphology

Both nouns and adjectives are included in this category.

4.2.1 Nouns

In Earlier Egyptian, nouns are built by adding to the stem a zero- or a non-zero-suffix, depending on whether the stem ends in a consonant, in which case the suffix is zero, or a vowel, in which case a *w*-suffix is added. The feminine marker is a *t*-suffix added to the masculine noun; the plural displays a *w*- or *ww*-suffix; the dual has a *j*-marker added to the stem of the plural in masculine, and to the stem of the singular in feminine, nouns:

(28) Nouns in Earlier Egyptian

	Masculine	*Feminine*
Singular	-ø, -w	-t
Dual	-w-j	-t-j
Plural	-ø, -w, -ww	-t, -j-t, -w-t

4.2.2 Adjectives

Adjectives are morphosyntactically treated like nouns. In a common derivational pattern, called *nisbation*, a morpheme masculine **ij*, feminine **it* is added to a stem, which may be different from the stem of the singular or plural noun, to form the corresponding adjective: *nṯr**/na:čar/ "god," *nṯr.w**/nač^{h}u:ra(w)/ "gods," *nṯrj**/nučriy/, *nṯrj.t**/nučrit/ "divine."

4.3 Pronouns

4.3.1 Personal pronouns

There are four sets of personal pronouns (Kammerzell 1991), including one reserved for the stative form of the verb (see §4.4.1). Stressed pronouns are used for the topicalized subject

Table 5.3 Personal pronouns in Earlier Egyptian

		Stressed	Unstressed	Suffix
SINGULAR	*1st com.*	jnk	wj	-j
	2nd masc.	ntk, ṯwt	ṯw	-k
	2nd fem.	ntṯ, ṯmt	ṯn	-ṯ
	3rd masc.	ntf, swt	sw	-f
	3rd fem.	nts, stt	sj, st	-s
(*ṯwt, ṯmt, swt* and *stt* are archaic forms found mainly in Old Kingdom religious texts)				
DUAL	*1st com.*		nj	-nj
	2nd com.	ntṯnj	ṯnj	-ṯnj
	3rd com.	ntsnj	snj	-snj
PLURAL	*1st com.*	jnn	n	-n
	2nd com.	ntṯn	ṯn	-ṯn
	3rd com.	ntsn	sn, st	-sn

of noun clauses in the first and second person (29A), and for the focalized subject of verbal cleft sentences (29B):

(29) A. jnk jt-k
I.TOPIC father-you
"I am your father"
B. nts s-ʿnḫ rn-j
she.FOCUS CAUS.-live.PART. name-me
"She is the one who makes my name live"

Unstressed pronouns are used for the object of verbal phrases (30A), for the subject of adjective clauses (30B) and of adverb clauses (30C):

(30) A. hꜣb-f wj
send.PERF.-he me
"He sent me"
B. nfr ṯw ḥnʿ-j
be.good.PART. you with-me
"You are happy with me"
C. mk wj m-bꜣḥ-k
behold me in-presence-you
"Look, I am in front of you"

Suffix pronouns are used as the subject of verb phrases, as possessive marker, and as the object of prepositions:

(31) ḏj-k r-k n-j ḫ.t-j
give.PROSP.-you toward-you to-me thing.FEM.-me
"You shall indeed (lit. 'toward-you') give me my possessions"

4.3.2 Demonstrative pronouns

Demonstratives are characterized by a deictic element preceded by the indicator of gender and number: masculine *pn, pf, pw*; feminine *tn, tf, tw* – for example, *rmṯ pf* "that man," *ḥjm.t* *tn* "this woman." They follow the noun they refer to. The plurals (originally neuter) *nw*, *nf*, *nn* are also used as pronouns in partitive constructions with the determinative pronoun *nj*: *nn nj srjw.w* "these officials" < *"this of officials." This determinative pronoun *nj*, feminine *n.t*, plural *n.w* is used primarily as a genitive marker: *rmṯ.w n.w km.t* "men of Egypt" > "Egyptians." On Egyptian articles, see §4.6.2.

4.3.3 Relative pronouns

The relative pronoun, masculine *ntj*, feminine *nt.t*, plural *ntj.w* "who, which, that," is morphologically derived from the determinative pronoun. In Earlier Egyptian, these pronouns agree in gender and number with the head noun, which must be semantically specific. Characteristic of Earlier Egyptian is the presence of a relative pronoun masculine *jwtj*, feminine *jwt.t*, plural *jwtj.w*, which semantically incorporates negation ("who/which/that not"):

(32)	jwtj	pẖr-f	ḏd.w	m	ẖ.t-f
	who.not	vent.AOR.-he	say.PART.IMPF.PASS.	in	belly.FEM.-him

"He who does not vent what is said in his belly"

4.3.4 Interrogative pronouns

Interrogative pronouns are *m* "who? what?," *jḫ* "what?," *jšst* "what?" They can be combined with prepositions or particles to form complex pronouns: *jn-m* "who?," *ḥr-m* "why?," literally "on-what?"

4.4 Verbal morphology

4.4.1 Finite verb-stems

Earlier Egyptian finite verb phrases display a limited number of stems (three or four) indicating tense, aspect, and voice followed by the pronominal suffix (33A) or nominal subject (33B):

(33) A. ʿnḫ-s
live.PROSP.-she
"She will live"

B.	h3b	ḥjm.t	z3-s
	send.PERF.	woman	son-her

"The woman sent her son"

Typical Egyptian verb "inflection"(utilizing the suffix pronouns) is illustrated in (34) with the verb-stem *sḏm* "hear":

(34)			
SINGULAR	*1st com.*	sḏm-j	"I hear"
	2nd masc.	sḏm-k	"you hear"
	2nd fem.	sḏm-ṯ	"you hear"
	3rd masc.	sḏm-f	"he hears"
	3rd fem.	sḏm-s	"she hears"
PLURAL	*1st com.*	sḏm-n	"we hear"
	2nd com.	sḏm-ṯn	"you hear"
	3rd com.	sḏm-sn	"they hear"

In addition to variations in the stem, a few verbal features are indicated by complementizers inserted between the stem and the subject. The most important of these indicators are *n* for the preterite tense, *t* for nonparadigmatic occurrences of the perfective aspect and for the prospective aspect of a few irregular verbs, *w* for prospective aspect and passive voice (in perfective stems), *tw* for passive (in nonperfective stems).

A particular verbal stem of nominal (probably relative) origin displays the tonic vowel between the second and the third radical, and in weak verbal classes the reduplication of the second radical: *stp-**/satap-/ (choose.REL.), *mrr-**/marar-/ (love.REL.). A similar verbal form indicates in Semitic languages the imperfective aspect; in Egyptian, its function is to mark the verb phrase as pragmatic theme of the sentence in which it appears (Polotsky 1976:4–25). In these sentences, the pragmatic rheme is usually a modifier or an adverb clause:

(35) jrr ḥm-k r mrj.t-f
do.IMPF. Majesty-your to desire.REL.FEM.-him
"Your Majesty acts as he desires"

The imperative has no suffix element in the singular, but sometimes, especially with weak verbs, a semivocalic suffix in the plural.

Egyptian also exhibits a verbal form, called Old Perfective, Stative, or Pseudoparticiple, which indicates the wide semantic range of "perfectivity," from perfect aspect (with intransitive verbs) to passive voice (with transitive verbs). This form is built with a special set of suffixes that are etymologically linked to the forms of the Semitic suffix conjugation (Schenkel 1990:104–108; Kammerzell 1991:165–199):

(36) mk wj jj-kw
behold me come.STATIVE-me
"Look, I have come," i.e., "I am here"

4.4.2 Nonfinite verbals

Nonfinite forms of the Egyptian verb are (i) the *participles*, with nominal stems derived from the verbal root (e.g., *sḏm* */sa:ç̌im/ "hearer"); and (ii) the *infinitives*, which display a suffix ø in the regular verbs (*sḏm* */sa:ç̌am/ "to hear"), *t* in some classes of weak verbs (*mrj.t* */mirjit/ "to love"), and *w* after verbs of negative predication, such as *tm* (*tm jr.w* */tam-ja:raw/ "not to do," lit. to complete-to do.NEG.INF.).

4.5 Particles

The basic negative particle is *n*, which is used for *contradictory negation* (37A); when combined with the adverb *js* "indeed," this morpheme expresses *contrariety* (37B; see Loprieno 1991):

(37) A. n rḏ-f n-j mw
not give.PERF.-he to-me water
"He did not give me water"

B. n-js jt-j rḏj n-j
not-indeed father-me give.PART. to-me
"It was not my father who gave [it] to me"

A morphological variant of *n*, conventionally transcribed *nn*, is used in noun clauses to negate the *existence* (37A) and in verb clauses to negate the *prospective* aspect (38B):

(38) A. nn m3ʿ.tjw
not.exist trust.ADJ.PL.
"There are no trustworthy people"
B. nn mwt-k
not.exist die.PROSP.-you
"You shall not die"

4.6 Morphological evolution

Under the pressure of a strong expiratory stress, which reduced the distinctive function of unstressed vowels, the flectional system underwent a profound crisis in Later Egyptian, requiring a reorganization of the morphological carriers of information.

4.6.1 Nominal lexicalization

The general trend was to replace synthetic structures by analytic constructions: for example, nominalized participles (39) or abstract nouns (40) were replaced by lexicalized compounds with nominal classifiers (Till 1970:71–75):

(39) PARTICIPLE > "MAN-WHO"-V
ṯ3w ref-jioue
steal.PART. "MAN-WHO"-steal.INF.
"Thief"

(40) ABSTRACT NOUN > "THING-OF"-N
r3 nj km.t mnt-rm-n-kême
mouth of Egypt "THING-OF"-man-of-Egypt
"Egyptian language"

4.6.2 Articles

Later Egyptian develops two sets of articles. The *indefinite article* comes from the numeral *wʿj* "one":

(41) N.[−SPEC] > INDEF.ART.-N.
Earlier Eg. *sn.t* "a.sister" > Late Eg. *wʿ(t)-sn(.t)* > Coptic *ou-sône* "a-sister"

whereas the *definite article* (Loprieno 1980) derives from a grammaticalized anaphoric pronoun:

(42) N.[+SPEC] > DEF.ART.-N.
Earlier Eg. *rmṯ* "the.man" > Late Eg. *p3-rm(t)* > Coptic *p-rôme* "the man"

The definite article also attracts the pronominal affix indicating the possessor, which in Earlier Egyptian followed the head noun (43A). Similarly, deictics now precede the noun they modify (43B):

(43) A. N.-SUFFIX > DEF.ART.-SUFFIX-N.
sn-f pe-f-son
brother-his the-his-brother
"His brother"

B. N.-DEICTIC	>	DEICTIC-N.
hjm.t tn		tei-shîme
woman this.FEM.		this.FEM.-woman
"This woman"		

4.6.3 Coptic morphological markers

Thus, because of the described loss of regular flectional patterns, the only device by which Coptic conveys the distinction between different patterns (masculine vs. feminine, nominal vs. verbal) is through the presence of morphological markers preceding the noun (44A–C; a zero-marker in the case of C):

(44) A. *rmṯ*: stem *ramač- + MASC.SG.ø = */ra:mač/ > Coptic *p-rôme* "the man"
B. *sn*: stem *san- + FEM.SG. *at*= */sa:nat/ > Coptic *t-sône* "the sister"
C. *ḫpr*: stem *xapar- + INF. ø = */xa:par/ > Coptic *šôpe* "to become"

4.6.4 Verbal lexicalization

The evolution towards a lexicalization of compound expressions also affected the verbal system (Winand 1992:20). In many instances, an earlier verbal lexeme is replaced in Later Egyptian, particularly in Coptic, by an auxiliary of generic meaning ("to do," "to give," "to take," etc.) followed by the verbal infinitive or by a noun object:

(45)	VERBAL LEXEME	>	AUXILIARY + NOUN
	wḏʿ		r-hap, ti-hap
	judge.INF.		do.INF.-law, give.INF.-law
	"to judge"		

Participles were superseded by analytic constructions with the relative pronouns (46A), while finite VSO forms were replaced by a paradigm of SVO-constructions, called "sentence conjugations" or "clause conjugations" (Polotsky 1960), resulting from the grammaticalization of a form of the verb "to do" followed by the infinitive (46B):

(46)					
A.	PARTICIPLE	>	RELATIVE CONSTRUCTION		
	Old Eg.	>	Late Eg.	>	Coptic
	sḏm		pꜣ-ntj (ḥr) sdm		p-et-sôtm
	hear.PART.IMPF.		the.one-who-(on-)hear.INF.		the.one-who-hear
	"the hearer"				
B.	VSO	>	SVO		
	Old Eg.	>	Late Eg.	>	Coptic
	sḏm.ḫr-f		ḫr-jr-f-sdm		ša-f-sôtm
	hear-AOR.-he		AOR.-do-he-hear.INF.		AOR.-he-hear
	"He usually hears"				

4.6.5 Coptic verb morphology

In this way, Coptic ultimately maintains only two flectional patterns from most verbal roots: (i) the infinitive for process predicates, and (ii) the so-called "qualitative," derived from the third masculine singular (rarely third feminine singular) form of the Old Perfective, for statives (Polotsky 1990:197–221):

(47) *f-kôt* ~ *f-kêt*
he-build.INF. it-build.STAT.
"He builds" "It is built"

Thus, with the productivity of root and stem variations massively reduced, Later Egyptian gradually moves toward the polysynthetic type which to a large extent characterizes Coptic:

(48) *Earlier Eg.*
jw sḏm.n-j ḫrw
"SITUATION" hear-PRET.-I voice
> *Late Eg.*
jr-j-sdm wꜥ-ḫrw
do.PRET.-I-hearing a-voice
> *Coptic*
ai-setm-ou-ḫroou
PRET.-I-hear-a-voice
"I heard a voice"

Nonfinite forms of the Coptic verb are the *infinitive*, which usually indicates (i) activities (*ei* "to come"), (ii) accomplishments (*ôô* "to conceive"), or (iii) achievements (*cine* "to find"); and the *qualitative*, which conveys states (*eet* "to be pregnant"). Although participial functions, as we saw above, are analytically conveyed by relative constructions, there are still few remnants of Ancient Egyptian synthetic participles (*mai-noute* "lover of god" > "pious"). Finite verbal forms now consist of a marker which conveys aspectual, temporal, or modal features, followed by the nominal or pronominal subject and by the infinitive (for actions) of the verb: *a-prôme sôtm* "the man heard," *a-i-hmoos* "I sat down." In the present and imperfect tense, which are treated as adverbial constructions, the infinitive can be replaced by the qualitative (for states): *ti-hkaeit* "I am hungry." The most important verbal markers are as follows (the double stroke indicates pronominal subjects, the simple stroke nominal subjects):

1. *e=, ere-*: circumstantial present (*e=i-hkaeit* "while I am hungry")
2. *ša=, šare-*: aorist of habit (*ša=i-ka pa-joi na=i* "I keep my ship for me")
3. *me=, mere-*: negative aorist (*me=f-sôtm* "he cannot hear")
4. *e=e, ere-e*: prospective of wish (*e=s-e-šôpe* "may it happen," "amen")
5. *nn(e)=, nne-*: negative prospective (*nne=f-eibe ša-eneh* "may he never be thirsty")
6. *mar(e)=, mare-*: optative (*mare-pe=k-ran ouop* "hallowed be your name")
7. *(n)tare=, (n)tare-*: final (*aitei tar=ou-ti nê=tn* "ask, that you may be given")
8. *šant(e)=, šante-*: completive (*šante-prê hôtp* "until the sun sets down")
9. *mpat(e)=, mpate-*: negative completive (*mpat=f-ei* "he has not yet come")
10. *a=, a-*: preterite (*a-ouša šôpe* "a festival took place")
11. *mp(e)=, mpe-*: negative preterite (*mpi-raše* "I did not rejoice")
12. *ne=, nere-*: imperfect (*nere-tmaau n-iêsous mmau* "Jesus' mother was there")
13. *nter(e)=, ntere-*: temporal (*ntere=f-je nai* "when he said these things")
14. *n=, nte-*: conjunctive (*e=k-e-nau n=g-eime* "may you see and understand")

In addition to these so-called sentence (or clause) conjugations, Coptic displays (i) an inflected form of the infinitive (*p-tre=f-sôtm* "the fact that he hears"); (ii) a special suffix conjugation for adjective verbs (*nanou=f* "he is good"); and (iii) a marker for the future of the present and imperfect tense (*ti-na-sôtm* "I shall hear").

4.7 Numerals

Numerals precede the noun to which they refer. The number 5 is etymologically derived from the word for "hand"; 20 is the dual of 10; 50 through 90 represent the plural forms of the respective units 5 through 9. Ordinals are derived from cardinals through the addition of a suffix *.nw* (from 2 to 9: *ḫmt.nw* "third"), later through the prefixation of the participle *mḥ* "filling" to the cardinal number: *mh-20* "twentieth").

(49) Egyptian numerals

Table 5.4 Earlier Egyptian numerals and their Sahidic Coptic outcome

1	*w ʿw* */wuʕʕuw/ > *oua* /waʔ/	10	*mḏw* */mu:ç̣aw/ > *mêt* /me:t/	100	**š(n).t** */š(iny)ut/ > *še*/šeʔ/
2	*sn.wj* */sinuwwaj/ > *snau* /snau/	20	*ḏwtj */ç̣awa:taj/ > *jouôt* /ç̣wo:t/	200	**š(n).tj** */š(iny)u:taj/ > *šêt* /še:t/
3	*ḫmtw* */xamtaw/ > *šomṇt* /šomn̥t/	30	*mʿbꜣ* */maʕbVʀ/ > *maab* /maʔb/	300–900	**ḫmtw-š(n.w)t*, etc.
4	*jfdw* */jifṭ aw/ > *ftoou* /fṭou/	40	**ḥm.w* */ħVmew/ > *hme* /hmeʔ/	1,000	*ḫꜣ* */xaʀ/ > *šo* /šoʔ/
5	*djw* */ṭ i:jaw/ > *tiou* /ṭ i:u/	50	**dj.w* */ṭ ijjaw/ > *taiou* /ṭajjəu/	10,000	*ḏbʿ* */ç̣Vbaʕ/ > *tba* /ṭbaʔ/
6	*sjsw* */saʔsaw/ > *soou* /sou/	60	**sjs.w* */saʔsew/ > *se* /seʔ/	100,000	*ḥfn*
7	*sf ḫw* */safxaw/ > *sašf* /sašf/	70	**sf ḫ.w* */safxew/ > *šfe* /šfeʔ/	1,000,000	*ḥḥ* */ħaħ/ > *hah* /hah/
8	*ḫmnw* */xama:naw/ > *šmoun* /šmu:n/	80	**ḫmn.w* */xamnew/ > *hmene* /xṃneʔ/		
9	*psḏw* */pisi:ç̣aw/ > *psit* /psi:t/	90	**psḏ j.w* */pisç̣ijjaw/ > *pestaiou* /pəsṭajjəw/		

5. SYNTAX

5.1 Sentence-types and word order

Egyptian syntax knows three types of sentences: the so-called noun clauses, adverb clauses, and verb clauses.

5.1.1 Noun clauses

In noun clauses, the predicate is a noun, whether substantive or adjective (Doret 1989–1992; Loprieno 1995:103–131). In categorical statements or qualifying adjectival sentences, the normal order of constituents is *Predicate–Subject* (50A); a demonstrative *pw* "this" functioning as copula may be inserted between the two phrases (50B):

(50) A. nfr mṯn-j
be.good.PART. path-me
"My path is good"

B. dmj.t pw jmn.t
city.FEM. COP. West.FEM.
"The West is a city"

The syntactic order Predicate(–Copula)–Subject is modified into a pragmatic order *Topic–Comment* in (i) classifying sentences when the subject is a first- or second-person pronoun (51A), (ii) identifying sentences when both the subject and the predicate are semantically determined or specified (51B), and (iii) in cleft sentences, in which the predicate is a participle and the subject is focalized (51C) (Loprieno 1988:41–52):

(51) A. ntk jtj n nmḥw
you father for orphan
"You are a father to the orphan"

B. zẖꜣw-f pw ḥrw
scribe-him COP. Horus
"His scribe is Horus"

C. jn sn.t-j s-ʿnḫ rn-j
FOCUS sister-me CAUS.-live.PART. name-me
"My sister is the one who makes my name live"

5.1.2 Adverb clauses

In adverb clauses, the predicate is an adverbial phrase or a prepositional phrase (Loprieno 1995:144–172). The word order is always Subject–Predicate. In Earlier Egyptian, main adverb clauses are often introduced by particles functioning as discourse markers (52A); in the absence of a discourse marker, the clause is to be understood as syntactically dependent (52B):

(52) A. jw nzw jr p.t
"SITUATION" king towards heaven.FEM.
"Now the king is [directed] towards heaven"

B. ẖr.t-k m pr-k
rations.FEM.-you in house-you
"[Because] your rations are in your house"

5.1.3 Verb clauses

In verb clauses, the predicate is a verbal phrase (Loprieno 1995:183–220); the word order is Predicate–Subject:

(53) jj.n-j m nw.t-j
come-PRET.-I from city.FEM.-me
"I came from my city"

As we observed in §4.4.1, a peculiarity of Egyptian syntax is that the predicate of verb clauses may function as the theme of the utterance. In general, Egyptian verbal syntax displays a comparatively high incidence of topicalization and focalization phenomena. The most common topicalization device is the extraposition of the topicalized argument through the particle *jr* "concerning" (54A); used as a conjunction, the same particle introduces the protasis of a hypothetical clause (54B):

(54) A.

jr	sf	wsjr	pw
concerning	yesterday	Osiris	COP.

"As for 'yesterday', it means 'Osiris' "

B.

jr	jqr-k	grg-k	pr-k
concerning	be.important.PROSP.-you	found.PROSP.-you	house-you

"If you become wealthy, you should found a household"

Unmarked VPs not introduced by discourse markers are less frequent than in related languages, mostly functioning as embedded or modal clauses:

(55) ḫꜥy-k
appear.PROSP.-you
"May you appear"

5.2 Prepositional phrases

The most frequent prepositions are *m* "in, with"; *n* "to, for"; *r* "toward"; *mj* "as, like"; *ḥr* "on"; *ẖr* "under"; *ḥnꜥ* "with"; *ḫft* "according to"; *ḫnt* "before." Prepositional phrases follow the noun or the verb they modify. Particularly noteworthy is the presence of the preposition *ḫr* "near"; its original semantic value "beneath" was applied to any situation in which the two participants A and B belong to different hierarchical levels:

(56) A.

ḏd-f	ḫr	ms.w-f
say.PROSP.-he	beneath	child.PL.-him

"He will say to his children"

B.

jmꜣḫy	ḫr	nṯr	ꜥꜣ
honor.PASS.PART.	beneath	god	great

"Honored by the great god"

5.3 Coordination and subordination

The presence or absence of morphemes indicating *paragraph initiality* is an important syntactic feature of adverb and verb clauses in Egyptian. The general rule is as follows: (i) adverbial and verbal patterns introduced by a discourse particle are *initial* main clauses; (ii) whereas bare patterns are *noninitial* clauses – either (a) paratactically juxtaposed to the initial predication as noninitial coordinate main clauses or (b) controlled by it as subordinate clauses. This flexibility in sentence patterns, which can appear as main sentence or as subordinate clause, depending on the syntactic environment, is a common feature of Egyptian syntax, being shared by the majority of patterns, whether nominal, adverbial, or verbal.

The dialectics between the initial main sentence introduced by a particle and the noninitial coordinate bare adverb clause is captured in the following example:

(57)

jw	ẖnw	m	sgr	jb.w	m	gmw	rw.tj
"SITUATION"	residence	in	silence	heart.PL.	in	mourning	portal.FEM.DUAL

wr.tj	ḫtm.w
great.FEM.DUAL	shut.STAT.

"The Residence was in silence, the hearts in mourning, the Two Great Portals shut"

An example of coordinate verb clause syntax is provided by the following passage, in which a series of noninitial main clauses is paratactically linked to the the initial verb form:

(58) jrj.t-j šm.t m ḫnt.yt nj kꜣ-j spr r ẖnw pn
make.INF.-I go.INF. in sail south not think.PERF.-I reach.INF. to residence this
ḫmt.n-j ḫpr ḥꜣꜥ.yt nj ḏd-j ꜥnḫ-j r-sꜣ-f
think.PRET.-I happen.PROSP. turmoil.FEM. not say.PERF.-I live.PROSP.-I after-it
nmj.n-j mꜣꜥ.tj m hꜣ.w nh.t zmꜣ.n-j m jw-snfrw
pass.PRET.-I Maaty in area sycamore arrive.PRET.-I in island-Snefru
"I made a journey southward, and I did not plan to reach the residence; I thought that there would be turmoil and I did not expect to survive after it; I crossed the lake Maaty in the Sycamore neighborhood, and I arrived at Snefru Island"

It is important to appreciate the difference between *initiality* as a property of discourse and *independence* versus *subordination* as syntactic features of the clause. In the examples of (57) and (58), there are only main clauses, in the sense that – if taken individually – all clauses represent well-formed Egyptian sentences paratactically organized within a chain of discourse (Collier 1992). In both cases, however, only the first sentence is initial: in the case of (57), it is introduced by an overt particle of initiality (*jw*), which indicates that the corresponding adverbial sentence (*ẖnw m sgr*) opens a new segment of discourse; in the example of (58), the initial verb form, a so-called *narrative infinitive*, provides the temporal and aspectual references for the chain of paratactically linked clauses.

We need, therefore, to draw a distinction between the level of *clause* and the level of *discourse.* Adverbial and verbal sentences introduced by a particle are always main clauses; noninitial patterns may be paratactically linked main clauses or embedded subordinate clauses. The difference between forms with and without introductory particle lies on the discourse level, in that the sentence introduced by an initial proclitic particle opens a segment of text. In this respect, rather than operating with the traditional two levels of clausal linkage (parataxis vs. hypotaxis, or coordination vs. subordination), it seems suitable to analyze Egyptian syntactic phenomena by positing three forms of linkage between sentences:

1. *Parataxis,* i.e., the linkage between main clauses: this linkage usually remains unexpressed in Egyptian syntax, as in the case of bare adverbial, pseudoverbal, or verbal sentences which follow an initial main clause within a chain of discourse. Specimens of paratactic chains were provided in (57)–(58).

2. *Hypotaxis,* i.e., a semantic, rather than syntactic, dependency of a sentence on the discourse nucleus: hypotactically linked clauses are usually introduced by particles such as *jsk, jḫr* or *js*; their semantic scope and their pragmatic setting can be properly understood only in reference to the message conveyed in the textual nucleus, as in example (59), which in the original text immediately follows the example of (57):

(59) jst r-f zbj.n ḥm-f mšꜥ r tꜣ-tmḥj.w zꜣ-f
meanwhile to-it send-PRET. Majesty-him army to land-Libyans son-him
smsw m ḥrj jry
elder in superior thereof
"Meanwhile, His Majesty had sent off to the land of the Libyans an army whose leader was his elder son"

3. *Subordination,* i.e., the syntactic dependency of a clause on a higher node, which itself can be a main or a subordinate clause: subordination is usually signaled by morphological markers such as prepositions (for example *m* "in" > "when") governing nominalized verbal phrases, conjunctions (such as *ḥr-ntt* "because"), or particles (*jr* "if"):

(60)

rḫ.n-j	qd-k	tw-j	m	zšj	m	wn-k	m	šms.wt
know.PRET.-I	character-you	indeed-I	in	nest	in	be.AOR.-you	in	following

jt-j
father-me

"I knew your character while still in the nest, when you were in my father's following"

In the absence of an overt marker of dependency, subordination can also be determined by syntactic control. In this case, one speaks of "embedding," as in the case of adverbial or verbal sentences functioning as virtual relative clauses or controlled by a verb of perception:

(61)

gmj.n-j	nb-j	ꜥnḫ.w	wḏꜣ.w	snb.w	ḫntj-f
find.PRET.-I	lord-me	live.STAT.	whole.STAT.	healthy.STAT.	sail south.AOR.-him

"I found my Lord (may he be alive, prosperous and healthy) travelling southward"

5.3.1 Relativization

As an example of the complex interface between overt and embedded subordination, let us consider relativization. Specific antecedents (Loprieno 1995:202–208) are resumed by an *overt marker of relativization,* such as (i) the relative pronoun masculine *ntj*, feminine *nt.t*, plural *ntj.w* "who, which, that" in adverb clauses (62A); or (ii) an agreement-marker inflected in the relative verb form – (a) a participle in the presence of coreferentiality of antecedent and subject of the relative clause (62B); (b) a finite relative form in its absence (62C):

(62) A.

mtr-n	wj	rmṯ.w	km.t	ntj.w	jm	ḥnꜥ-f
witness-PRET.	me	man.PL.	Egypt	who.PL.	there	with-him

"Egyptians who were there with him bore witness for me"

B.

ḏj-s	ḫ.t	nb.t	nfr.t	wꜥb.t
give.PROSP.-she	thing.FEM.	every.FEM.	be.good.PART.FEM.	be.pure.PART.FEM.

prr.t	ḥr	wḏḥ-s
exit.PART.FEM.	on	altar-her

"May she give every good and pure thing which goes up on her altar"

C.

ḫꜣs.t	nb.t	rwj.t-n-j	r-s
country.FEM.	every.FEM.	advance.REL.FEM.-PRET.-I	against-it

"Every country against which I advanced"

Nonspecific antecedents, on the other hand, are modified by relative clauses which lack overt agreement-markers (Collier 1991; Loprieno 1995:158–161). They are syntactically subordinated through embedding into the main clause:

(63)

k.t	n.t	msḏr	ḏj-f	mw
another.FEM.	that-of.FEM.	ear	give.AOR.-it	water

"Another (remedy) for an ear which gives off water"

5.4 Syntactic evolution

Syntactic patterns prove rather stable throughout the history of Egyptian. Late Egyptian (Satzinger 1981) and Coptic (Polotsky 1987:9–43) display the same variety of sentence-types as Earlier Egyptian:

1. *Noun clauses*: With an unmarked (syntactic) order Predicate–Subject when the subject is a noun (64A), and with a marked (pragmatic) order Topic–Comment in three environments: (i) when the subject is a pronoun (64B); (ii) when both the subject and the predicate are semantically specific (64C); and (iii) in cleft sentences, in which the predicate is a participle and the subject is focalized (64D):

(64) A. ou-me te te-f-mnt-mntre
a-truth COP. the-his-thing-witness
"His testimony is true"

B. anok ou-šôs
TOPIC-I a-shepherd
"I am a shepherd"

C. t-arkhê n-t-sophia te t-mnt-mai-nûte
the-beginning that.of-the-wisdom COP. the-thing-lover-god
"The beginning of wisdom is piety"

D. p-nûte p-et-sooun
the-god the.one-who-know.INF.
"God is the one who knows" (= "Only God knows")

2. *Adverb clauses* (Polotsky 1990:203–224): in which the predicate is an adverbial or a prepositional phrase; the order is Subject–Predicate:

(65) ti-hm-pa-eiôt
I-in-the-my-father
"I am in my father"

3. *Verb clauses* (Polotsky 1990:175–202): in which the predicate is a verbal phrase built according to the SVO-patterns described in §4.6.4; in these patterns, the subject can be extraposed to the right of the predicate and anticipated by a cataphoric pronoun in the regular syntactic slot:

(66) a-u-rîme nci-ne-snêu
PRET.-they-weep.INF. namely-the-brother.PL.
"The monks wept"

In Coptic verbal sentences, the tendency to have the verb phrase function as theme or rheme of the utterance reaches its full development: in the former case, the verb phrase is preceded by a relative marker *e-* or *nt-* and is described in Coptological literature as "second tense" (Polotsky 1987:129–140); in the latter, the form is preceded by the circumstantial marker *e-* and is described as "circumstantial" (Polotsky 1990:225–260):

(67) nt-a-n-jpo-f e-f-o n-blle
REL.-PRET.-we-beget-him "WHILE"-he-do.STAT. as-blind
"He was born to us blind" (lit. "That we begot him was while he is as blind")

6. LEXICON

Owing to Egypt's geographically protected location, Ancient Egyptian does not display in its earlier phase (from 3000 BC) detectable influences from other languages, although the neighboring languages certainly did contribute to the lexical development of historical Egyptian. The majority of the lexicon is of Afro-Asiatic origin and displays convergences especially with the Semitic and Libyan branches of this family (Schenkel 1990:49–57): for example, *sp.t* "lip," cf. Arabic *šafat-un*, *sfḫw* "seven," cf. Arabic *sabʿ-un*, *jnm* "skin," cf. Berber *a-glim*. There is also, however, some evidence for the impact of an Indo-European adstratum in the area of basic vocabulary (Kammerzell 1994:37–58): for example, Egyptian *jrṯ.t* */jala:čat/ "milk," compare Greek *gala*, *galak-tos*; or *ḫntj* */xant-ij/ "before," compare Latin *ante*. In some cases, for the same concept, for example "heart," Egyptian displays the coexistence of an Afro-Asiatic (*jb**/jib/, cf. Akkadian *lubb-um*) and of an Indo-European connection (*ḥ3tj* */ḥuʀtiy/, cf. Latin *cor*, *cord-is*), probably rooted in different dialectal areas of the country.

During the New Kingdom (*c.* 1500–1100 BC), contacts with the western Asiatic world led to the adoption of a considerable number of especially West Semitic loanwords (Hoch 1994), many of which remained confined to the scholarly and administrative sphere: for example *ṯpr* from Northwest Semitic *sôpēr* "scribe"; *mrkbt* (Coptic *berecôout*) from Northwest Semitic *merkābâ* "chariot"; *mryn* from Mitanni (Iranian) *maryannu* "chariot-fighter."

In the Late Period, after the seventh century BC, when the productive written language was Demotic, a limited number of (mostly technical) Greek words entered the Egyptian domain: *gawma* from *kauma* "fever"; *wynn* from *hoi Iōnes* "the Ionians" i.e., "the Greeks." The impact of Greek vocabulary became more dramatic with the Christianization of the country, Hellenistic Greek being the language in which the Christian Scriptures were transmitted in the Eastern Mediterranean world. The number of Greek loanwords in Coptic is therefore very high (Kasser 1991a) – depending on the nature of the text, up to one-third of the lexical items found in a Coptic text may be of Greek origin. Most of these words stem from the spheres of (i) religious practice and belief (*angelos* "angel," *diabolos* "devil," *ekklēsia* "church," *agios* "saint," *sōtēr* "savior," etc.); (ii) administration (*arkhōn* "governor," *oikonomei* "to administer," etc.); and (iii) high culture (*anagnōsis* "recitation," *logikos* "spiritual," etc.). In some texts translated from Greek, the influence of this language extends to the realm of syntax. A limited number of words from the military context are Latin (*douks* "general"), whereas documents from the end of the first millennium begin to display the adoption of loanwords from Arabic (*alpesour* from *al-bāsūr* "hemorrhoids"). The terms referring to the basic vocabulary, however, usually remained those of Egyptian origin: for example, "man" *rmṯ* > *rôme*; "woman" *ḥjm.t* > *shime*; "water" *mw* > *mau*; "two" *sn.wj* > *snau*.

7. READING LIST

The bibliography contains all the works referred to in this chapter. In the case of particularly important grammatical tools, I have added a short comment on their contents. In addition, some books have been listed which may prove valuable as further reading on a general topic on history or grammar of Ancient Egyptian or Coptic.

Bibliography

Allen, J. 1984. *The Inflection of the Verb in the Pyramid Texts.* Bibliotheca Aegyptia 2. Malibu: Undena. (A detailed morphological analysis of the earliest corpus of Egyptian texts.)

Bagnall, R. 1993. *Egypt in Late Antiquity.* Princeton: Princeton University Press.

Boas, G. and A. Grafton (eds.). 1993. *The Hieroglyphics of Horapollo.* Bollingen Series 23. Princeton: Princeton University Press.

Černý, J. and S. Groll. 1984. *A Late Egyptian Grammar* (3rd edition). Studia Pohl, Series Maior 4. Rome: Pontifical Biblical Institute. (A structural grammar of colloquial, i.e., scholastic and administrative, Late Egyptian.)

Comrie, B. 1981. *Language Universals and Linguistic Typology.* Chicago: University of Chicago Press.

Crum, W. 1939. *A Coptic Dictionary.* Oxford: Clarendon Press. (The standard dictionary of Coptic, with very detailed philological references.)

Collier, M. 1991. "The relative clause and the verb in Middle Egyptian." *Journal of Egyptian Archaeology* 77:23–42.

______. 1992. Predication and the circumstantial *sḏm(.f)/sḏm.n(.f)*. *Lingua Aegyptia* 2:17–65.

Daumas, F. (ed.). 1988–1995. *Valeurs phonétiques des signes hiéroglyphiques d'époque gréco-romaine* (4 vols.). Montpellier: University of Montpellier.

Davies, W. 1987. *Egyptian Hieroglyphs.* London: British Museum. (An introductory presentation of the writing system with many examples and references.)

Diakonoff, I. 1965. *Semito-Hamitic Languages. An Essay in Classification.* Moscow: Academy of Sciences of the USSR.

Doret, É. 1989–1992. "Phrase nominale, identité et substitution dans les Textes des Sarcophages." *Revue d'Égyptologie* 40:49–63; 41:39–56; 43:49–73.

Edel, E. 1955–1964. *Altägyptische Grammatik.* Analecta Orientalia 34–39. Rome: Pontifical Biblical Institute.

Erman, A. and H. Grapow. 1926–1953. *Wörterbuch der ägyptischen Sprache.* Berlin: Akademie-Verlag. (The fundamental dictionary for Old, Middle, and Late Egyptian.)

Faulkner, R. 1962. *A Concise Dictionary of Middle Egyptian.* Oxford: Oxford University Press. (A lexicographical aid for the translation of Middle Kingdom texts.)

Fecht, G. 1960. *Wortakzent und Silbenstruktur.* Ägyptologische Forschungen 21. Glückstadt: Verlag J. J. Augustin. (The standard analysis of the syllabic patterns of Egyptian.)

Fischer, H. 1977. "Hieroglyphen." In W. Helck and E. Otto (eds.), *Lexikon der Ägyptologie*, vol. II, pp. 1189–1199. Wiesbaden: Otto Harrassowitz.

Fleming H. 1976. "Cushitic and Omotic." In M. Bender, J. D. Bowen, R. L. Cooper, *et al.* (eds.), *Language in Ethiopia*, pp. 34–53. Oxford: Oxford University Press.

Fowden, G. 1986. *The Egyptian Hermes. A Historical Approach to the Late Pagan Mind.* Princeton: Princeton University Press.

Gardiner, A. 1957. *Egyptian Grammar, Being an Introduction to the Study of Hieroglyphs* (3rd edition). Oxford: Oxford University Press. (Still the most detailed tool for the philological study of the classical language.)

Gelb, I. 1963. *A Study of Writing* (revised edition). Chicago: University of Chicago Press.

Giveon, R. 1982. "Protosinaitische Inschriften." In W. Helck and W. Westendorf (eds.), *Lexikon der Ägyptologie*, vol. IV, pp. 1156–1159. Wiesbaden: Otto Harrassowitz.

Graefe, E. 1997. *Mittelägyptische Grammatik für Anfänger* (5th edition). Wiesbaden: Otto Harrassowitz. (A user-friendly manual for academic instruction in classical Egyptian.)

Hetzron, R. 1992. "Semitic languages." In W. Bright (ed.), *International Encyclopedia of Linguistics*, vol. III, pp. 412–417. Oxford: Oxford University Press.

Hintze, F. 1950. "Konversion und analytische Tendenz in der ägyptischen Sprachentwicklung." *Zeitschrift für Phonetik und Allgemeine Sprachwissenschaft* 4:41–56.

______. 1980. "Zur koptischen Phonologie." *Enchoria* 10:23–91. (A very influential generative analysis of Coptic phonology.)

Hoch, J. 1994. *Semitic Words in Egyptian Texts of the New Kingdom and Third Intermediate Period.* Princeton: Princeton University Press. (A companion for issues of comparative Egyptian–Semitic phonology and for Semitic vocabulary in Egyptian.)

Hodge, C. (ed.) 1971. *Afroasiatic. A Survey.* Janua Linguarum Series Practica 163. The Hague/Paris: Mouton.

Iversen, E. 1961. *The Myth of Egypt and its Hieroglyphs in European Tradition.* Princeton: Princeton University Press. (For the history and the cultural milieu of the decipherment of hieroglyphs.)

Johnson, J. 1991. *Thus Wrote 'Onchsheshonqy. An Introductory Grammar of Demotic* (2nd edition). Studies in Ancient Oriental Civilization 45. Chicago: Oriental Institute. (A short but comprehensive introduction to Demotic script and grammar.)

Junge, F. 1985. "Sprachstufen und Sprachgeschichte." In *Zeitschrift der Deutschen Morgenländischen Gesellschaft*, Supplement 6, pp. 17–34. Stuttgart: Steiner. (The most modern presentation of the history of Egyptian.)

______. 1996. *Einführung in die Grammatik des Neuägyptischen.* Wiesbaden: Otto Harrassowitz.

Kahl, J. 1994. *Das System der ägyptischen Hieroglyphenschrift in der 0.-3. Dynastie*. Göttinger Orientforschungen IV/29. Wiesbaden: Otto Harrassowitz.

Kammerzell, F. 1991. *Personalpronomina und Personalendungen im Altägyptischen. Ägypten im afro-orientalischen Kontext. Aufsätze zur Archäologie, Geschichte und Sprache eines unbegrenzten Raumes. Gedenkschrift Peter Behrens. Afrikanistische Arbeitspapiere*, pp. 177–203. Special issue edited by D. Mendel and U. Claudi. Cologne: University of Cologne. (The most thorough treatment of Egyptian pronouns, also important for comparative issues.)

———. 1994. *Panther, Löwe und Sprachentwicklung im Neolithikum*. Lingua Aegyptia Studia Monographica 1. Göttingen: Seminar für Ägyptologie und Koptologie.

———. 1995. "Zur Umschreibung und Lautung." In R. Hannig, *Großes Handwörterbuch Ägyptisch-Deutsch (2800-950 v.Chr.)*, xxiii–lix. Mainz: Philipp von Zabern.

Kasser, R. 1991a. "Vocabulary, Copto-Greek." In Aziz S. Atiya (ed.), *The Coptic Encyclopedia*, vol. VIII, pp. 215–222. New York: Macmillan.

———. 1991b. "Dialects; Dialects, Grouping and Major Groups of." In Aziz S. Atiya (ed.), *The Coptic Encyclopedia*, vol. VIII, pp. 87–88, 97–101. New York: Macmillan.

Lambdin, T. 1983. *Introduction to Sahidic Coptic*. Macon: Mercer University Press. (The standard academic handbook for teaching classical Coptic.)

Loprieno, A. 1980. "Osservazioni sullo sviluppo dell'articolo prepositivo in egiziano e nelle lingue semitiche." *Oriens Antiquus* 19:1–27.

———. 1986. "Zahlwort." In W. Helck and W. Westendorf (eds.), *Lexikon der Ägyptologie*, vol. VI, pp. 1306–1319. Wiesbaden: Otto Harrassowitz.

———. 1988. "On the typological order of constituents in Egyptian." *Journal of Afroasiatic Languages* 1:26–57.

———. 1991. *Topics in Egyptian Negations. Ägypten im afro-orientalischen Kontext. Aufsätze zur Archäologie, Geschichte und Sprache eines unbegrenzten Raumes. Gedenkschrift Peter Behrens. Afrikanistische Arbeitspapiere*, pp. 213–235. Special issue edited by D. Mendel and U. Claudi. Cologne: University of Cologne.

———. 1995. *Ancient Egyptian: A Linguistic Introduction*. Cambridge: Cambridge University Press. (A general presentation of linguistic features and historical grammar of Egyptian.)

Lüddeckens, E. 1975. "Demotisch." In W. Helck and E. Otto (eds.), *Lexikon der Ägyptologie*, vol. I, pp. 1052–1056. Wiesbaden: Otto Harrassowitz.

Neveu, F. 1996. *La langue des Ramsès. Grammaire du Néo-Égyptien*. Paris: Chéops.

Newman, P. 1992. "Chadic." In W. Bright (ed.), *International Encyclopedia of Linguistics*, vol. I, pp. 253–254. Oxford: Oxford University Press.

Osing, J. 1975. "Dialekte." In W. Helck and E. Otto (eds.), *Lexikon der Ägyptologie*, vol. I, pp. 1074–1075. Wiesbaden: Otto Harrassowitz.

———. 1976. *Die Nominalbildung des Ägyptischen* (2 vols.). Mainz: Philipp von Zabern. (The fundamental reference work on the vocalic patterns of the language from Middle Egyptian through Coptic.)

———. 1980. "Lautsystem." In W. Helck and W. Westendorf (eds.), *Lexikon der Ägyptologie*, vol. III, pp. 944–949. Wiesbaden: Otto Harrassowitz.

Polotsky, H. 1960. "The Coptic conjugation system." *Orientalia* 29:392–422.

———. 1971. Collected Papers. Jerusalem: Magnes Press. (For the development of the "Standard theory" of Egyptian syntax.)

———. 1976. "Les transpositions du verbe en égyptien classique." *Israel Oriental Studies* 6:1–50.

———. 1987–1990. *Grundlagen des koptischen Satzbaus*. Decatur, GA: Scholars Press.

Ray, J. 1992. "Are Egyptian and Hittite related?" In A. Lloyd (ed.), *Studies in Pharaonic Religion and Society in Honour of J. Gwyn Griffiths*, pp. 124–136. London: Egypt Exploration Society.

Reintges, C. 1994. "Egyptian root-and-pattern morphology." *Lingua Aegyptia* 4:213–244.

———. 1997. *Passive Voice in Older Egyptian. A Morpho-Syntactic Study*. Holland Institute of Generative Linguistics. Dissertations 28. The Hague: Holland Academic Graphics.

Sasse, H-J. 1992. "Cushitic languages." In W. Bright (ed.), *International Encyclopedia of Linguistics*, vol. I, pp. 326–330. Oxford: Oxford University Press.

Satzinger, H. 1981. "Nominalsatz und Cleft Sentence im Neuägyptischen." In D. Young (ed.), *Studies Presented to Hans Jakob Polotsky*, pp. 480–505. Beacon Hill: Pirtle and Polson.

Schenkel, W. 1990. *Einführung in die altägyptische Sprachwissenschaft. Orientalistische Einführungen.* Darmstadt: Wissenschaftliche Buchgesellschaft. (An essential companion for the study of the history of linguistic thinking in Egyptology and an indispensable tool for the study of the prehistory of Egyptian phonology and its comparative aspects.)

______. 1993. "Zu den Verschluß- und Reibelauten im Ägyptischen und (Hamito-)Semitischen. Ein Versuch zur Synthese der Lehrmeinungen." *Lingua Aegyptia* 3:137–149.

______. 1984. "Schrift." In W. Helck and W. Westendorf (eds.), *Lexikon der Ägyptologie*, vol. V, pp. 713–735. Wiesbaden: Otto Harrasowitz. (A systematic presentation of the features of the hieroglyphic system.)

Schneider, T. 1992. *Asiatische Personennamen in ägyptischen Quellen des Neuen Reiches.* Orbis Biblicus et Orientalis 114. Freiburg/Göttingen: Vandenhoeck and Ruprecht.

Shisha-Halevy, A. 1986. *Coptic Grammatical Categories.* Analecta Orientalia, 53. Rome: Pontifical Biblical Institute. (A complete grammatical study of Sahidic Coptic.)

Spiegelberg, W. 1925. *Demotische Grammatik.* Heidelberg: Carl Winter.

Till, W. 1970. *Koptische Grammatik* (2nd edition). Leipzig: Verlag Enzyklopädie.

Vernus, P. 1990. *Future at Issue. Tense, Mood and Aspect in Middle Egyptian: Studies in Syntax and Semantics.* Yale Egyptological Studies 4. New Haven: Yale Egyptological Seminar. (Especially important for the interface of aspect and mood in early Middle Egyptian.)

______. 1996. "Langue littéraire et diglossie." In A. Loprieno (ed.), *Ancient Egyptian Literature. History and Forms*, pp. 555–564. Probleme der Ägyptologie 10. Leiden: Brill.

Vittmann, G. 1991. "Zum koptischen Sprachgut im Ägyptisch-Arabisch." *Wiener Zeitschrift für die Kunde des Morgenlandes* 81:197–227.

Wenig, S. 1982. "Meroe, Schrift und Sprache." In W. Helck and W. Westendorf (eds.), *Lexikon der Ägyptologie*, vol. IV, pp. 104–107. Wiesbaden: Otto Harrassowitz.

Willms, A. 1980. *Die dialektale Differenzierung des Berberischen.* Afrika und Übersee Berlin: Reimer.

Winand, J. 1992. *Etudes de néo-égyptien, I. La morphologie verbale.* Aegyptiaca Leodiensia 2. Liège: CIPL. (A complete morphological and syntactic analysis of the verb in Late Egyptian.)

Zaborski, A. 1992. "Afroasiatic languages." In W. Bright (ed.), *International Encyclopedia of Linguistics*, vol. I, pp. 36–37. Oxford: Oxford University Press.

Zeidler, J. 1992. "Altägyptisch und Hamitosemitisch. Bemerkungen zu den Vergleichenden Studien von Karel Petráček." *Lingua Aegyptia* 2:189–222.

______. 1993. "A new approach to the Late Egyptian 'syllabic orthography'. " In *Sesto Congresso internazionale di Egittologia.* Atti, vol. II, pp. 579–590. Torino: Italgas.

Sign list

Listed below are the hieroglyphic signs most often found in Middle Egyptian texts, arranged into 27 groups on the basis of what they depict. The selection and order are those most commonly used by Egyptologists, based on the list in Gardiner's *Egyptian Grammar*, with some additional signs.[1] Each sign is identified as to what it depicts (as far as possible) and its uses, whether phonogram, ideogram, or determinative, arranged in order of frequency; words in SMALL CAPITALS indicate the class of words with which a sign is used as determinative. At the end of the sign list is a supplemental list of signs arranged by shape.

A. Human Beings, Male

No.	Description	Uses
1	seated man	Phonogram *j* (1s suffix pronoun). Determinative MAN; also in 1s pronouns *jnk*, *wj*, *.kw/kj*. Ideogram for *zj* "man" or *rḫw* "companion." With B1 and plural strokes, determinative PEOPLE and ideogram for *rmṯ* "people."
2	man with hand to mouth	Variants (A68), (A84). Determinative SPEAK, THINK, EAT, DRINK, and for emotions such as LOVE and HATE.
3	man sitting on heel	Determinative SIT.
4	man with hands raised	Determinative WORSHIP; also HIDE (for A5).
5	man hiding behind wall	Determinative HIDE.
6	A1 + W54	Variant of D60.
7	fatigued man	Determinative WEARY, WEAK, SOFT.
8	man performing *ḥnw*	Determinative in *ḥnw* "jubilation."
9	man with basket on head	Variant (A119) in *f3j*. Determinative LOAD, CARRY, WORK. Ideogram for *3tp* "load," *f3j* "carry, lift," *k3t* "work."
10	man with oar	Determinative SAIL, ROW.
11	man with scepter and crook	Determinative FRIEND.
12	soldier	Determinative SOLDIER. Ideogram with plural strokes for *mšʿ* "expeditionary force, army."
13	prisoner	Determinative ENEMY.

1 A number of signs that Gardiner placed in category Aa ("Unclassified") have since been identified. The sign R13 is included as a separate entry in G. The supplemental sign R61 is listed under I as well as R, and Y10 under M as well as Y. Additional signs are numbered, where possible, after the list in N. Grimal, J. Hallof, and D. van der Plas, eds., *Hieroglyphica* (Publications interuniversitaires de recherches égyptologiques informatisées, 1: Utrecht, Centre for Computer-aided Egyptological Research, Utrecht University, 1993). Such signs are placed where they belong in each group rather than in their numerical position: thus, for example, A359 after A28.

14	wounded man	Variant (A14a). Determinative DIE, ENEMY.
15	man falling	Variant (A97). Determinative FALL, DIE. Ideogram for *ḫr* "fall."
16	man bowing	Determinative BOW.
17	child	Variant (A17a). Determinative CHILD, YOUNG; in hieratic also SIT (for A3), DIGNITARY (for A21). Ideogram for *ẖrd* "child." Phonogram *nnj* "child" in *nnj-nswt* "Herakleopolis."
18	child with Red Crown	Determinative CHILD-KING.
19	old man with staff	Determinative OLD, DISTINGUISHED. Ideogram for *j3w* "old," *smsw* "eldest," *wr* "great, chief." Phonogram *jk* in *jky* "miner" (from *j3k* "age"). In hieratic sometimes for A25.
20	old man with forked staff	Variant of last. Determinative in *smsw* "elder," also ideogram for same.
21	dignitary	Determinative DIGNITARY. Ideogram for *srj* "official." Also as variant of A11 and A22. In hieroglyphic not always distinguishable from A19–20.
22	statue on base	Determinative STATUE. The form often varies.
23	king	Determinative KING.
24	man striking	Determinative FORCE, EFFORT. Ideogram for *nḫt* "victory."
25	man striking	Determinative in *ḥwj* "hit," often (striking the phonogram).
59	man threatening	Determinative DRIVE OFF.
26	man beckoning	Variant (A366). Determinative CALL. Ideogram for *j* "oh!" and *ꜥš* "call."
27	man running	Phonogram *jn* in *jn* "by" (from *jn* "messenger").
28	excited man	Determinative HIGH, JOY, MOURN, FRUSTRATION.
59	man with arms clasped	Determinative in *ḫsj* "freeze." Also rare variant of A1 (man pointing to himself).
29	man upside down	Determinative INVERT.
30	man worshipping	Determinative WORSHIP, RESPECT.
31	man shunning	Determinative TURN AWAY.
32	man dancing	Determinative DANCE.
33	man with stick and bundle	Variant (A166). Determinative in *mnjw* "herdsman," also ideogram for same. Determinative WANDER, STRANGER.
34	man pounding	Determinative in *ḫwsj* "pound, construct."
35	man building a wall	Determinative in *qd* "build," also ideogram for same.
37	man in vat	Variant (A36). Determinative in *ꜥftj* "brewer," also ideogram for same.
38	man with two animals	Variant (A39, with two giraffes). Ideogram for *qjs/qsj* "Qus" (town).

40	seated god	Determinative GOD, KING. Variant of A1 for 1s pronouns when the speaker is a god or the king.
41	seated king	Variant (A42). Determinative KING. Variant of A1 for 1s pronouns when the speaker is the king.
43	king with White Crown	Variant (A44). Determinative of *nswt* "king," also ideogram for same. Determinative of *wsjr* "Osiris."
45	king with Red Crown	Variant (A46). Determinative of *bjtj* "king of Lower Egypt," also ideogram for same.
47	shepherd seated	Determinative in *z3w* "guard," also ideogram for same. Ideogram for *mnjw* "herdsman." Sometimes variant of A48.
48	seated man with knife	Phonogram *jr* in the nisbe *jrj* "pertaining to."
49	foreigner with stick	Determinative FOREIGNER.
50	noble on chair	Determinative DIGNITARY, DECEASED. Variant of A1 for 1s pronouns when the speaker is deceased. Also variant of A51.
51	noble on chair, with flail	Determinative in *špsj/špss* "noble," also ideogram for same. Determinative DIGNITARY, DECEASED.
52	seated noble with flail	Determinative DIGNITARY, DECEASED.
53	mummy standing	Determinative MUMMY, STATUE, LIKENESS, FORM. Ideogram for *twt* "likeness, statue."
54	mummy recumbent	Determinative DEAD.
55	mummy on bed	Determinative LIE, DEAD. Ideogram for *sḏr* "lie down." The mummy is sometimes replaced by a man when used in/for *sḏr* "lie down."

B. Human Beings, Female

1	seated woman	Variant (B24). Determinative FEMALE. Rarely variant of A1 when the speaker is female.
2	pregnant woman	Determinative PREGNANT.
3	woman giving birth	Variant (B4). Determinative in *msj* "give birth," also ideogram for same.
5	woman nursing	Determinative in *mn*^{c}*t* "nurse."
6	nurse with child	Determinative in *rnn* "rear, foster."
7	seated queen	Determinative in queens' names.

C. Anthropomorphic Gods

1	god with sun-disk	Variant (falcon-headed, C2). Determinative in *r*^{c} "Re," also ideogram for same.
3	ibis-headed	Determinative in *ḏḥwtj* "Thoth," also ideogram for same.
4	ram-headed	Variant (C5). Determinative in *ḫnmw* "Khnum," also ideogram for same.

6	jackal-headed	Determinative in *jnpw* "Anubis" and *wp-w3wt* "Wepwawet," also ideogram for same.
7	Seth-animal-headed	Determinative in *stẖ/stš* "Seth," also ideogram for same.
8	Min figure	Determinative in *mnw* "Min," also ideogram for same.
9	goddess with horned disk	Determinative in *ḥwt-ḥrw* "Hathor," also ideogram for same.
10	goddess with feather	Variants (C10a), (C175a). Determinative in *m3ʿt* "Maat" (as goddess), also ideogram for same.
11	*ḥḥ*-figure	Ideogram for *ḥḥ* "million (§ 9.1)" and "Heh" (god supporting the sky).
12	Amun figure	Determinative in *jnmw* "Amun," also ideogram for same.
17	Montu figure	Determinative in *mnṯw* "Montu," also ideogram for same.
18	Tatjenen figure	Determinative in *t3-ṯnnj* "Ta-tjenen," also ideogram for same.
19	Ptah figure	Variant (C20). Determinative in *ptḥ* "Ptah," also ideogram for same.

D. Parts of the Human Body

1	head	Ideogram for *tp* and *ḏ3ḏ3* "head." Phonogram *tp* in *tpj* "first." Determinative HEAD.
2	face	Ideogram for *ḥr* "face." Phonogram *ḥr*.
3	hair	Determinative HAIR, SKIN, COLOR; also words associated with hair: BALD, MOURN, WIDOW. Ideogram for *wš* "missing."
4	eye	Phonogram *jr*. Determinative for actions associated with the eye. Ideogram for *jrt* "eye."
5	eye with paint	Variants (D6) and (D7a). Determinative for actions associated with the eye.
140	two eyes	Determinative in *ptr* "see, look," also ideogram for same.
7	eye with paint	Determinative ADORN. Also determinative in *ʿn* "beautiful" and *ʿnw* "Tura" (quarry near Cairo), from the Semitic root *ʿjn* "eye."
8	eye enclosed	Variant of D7 as determinative in *ʿn* "beautiful" and *ʿnw* "Tura."
9	eye weeping	Determinative in *rmj* "weep," also ideogram for same.
10	eye with falcon markings	Determinative in *wḏ3t* "Sound Eye (of Horus)," also ideogram for same.
11	part of D10	Ideogram for ½ heqat (§ 9.7.3).
12	part of D10	Ideogram for ¼ heqat (§ 9.7.3). Also determinative in *ḏfḏ* "pupil" and *m33* "see," the latter as variant of D4.
13	part of D10	Ideogram for ⅛ heqat (§ 9.7.3). Also determinative EYEBROW.
14	part of D10	Ideogram for 1/16 heqat (§ 9.7.3).
15	part of D10	Ideogram for 1/32 heqat (§ 9.7.3).
16	part of D10	Ideogram for 1/64 heqat (§ 9.7.3).
17	D15 + D16	Determinative of *tjt* "image," also ideogram for same.
18	ear	Determinative in *msḏr* "ear," also ideogram for same.
19	face in profile	Variant (D20). Determinative NOSE, FACE, and associated actions. Ideogram for *fnḏ* "nose." Phonogram *ḫnt*. In hieratic not always distinguishable from U31 or Aa32.

21	mouth	Phonogram *r*. Ideogram for *r* "mouth."
154	mouth plus water	Determinative in *j*^{c}*w-r* "breakfast," also ideogram for same.
22	mouth plus 2 strokes	Ideogram for *rwj* ⅔ (§ 9.6).
23	mouth plus 3 strokes	Ideogram for *ḫmt-rw* ¾ (§ 9.6).
24	lip with teeth	Variant (D24a). Determinative in *spt* "lip," also ideogram for same. Sometimes in error for F42.
25	two lips and teeth	Determinative in *sptj* "lips," also ideogram for same.
26	lips and water	Determinative SPIT, SPEW.
27	breast	Variant (D27a). Determinative BREAST, NURSE. Ideogram for *mnḏ* "breast."
28	two arms	Phonogram *k3*. Ideogram for *k3* "ka" (variant D29).
30	two arms and tail	Determinative in *nḥb-k3w* "Assigner of Kas" (a god).
32	two arms embracing	Variant in hieratic. Determinative EMBRACE, OPEN.
31	D32 plus U36	Variant. Ideogram for *ḥm-k3* "ka-servant" (mortuary priest).
33	arms and oar	Phonogram *ḥn* (from *ḥnj* "row").
34a	arms with shield and mace	Variant (D34). Ideogram for ^{c}*ḥ3* "fight."
35	gesture of negation	Ideogram for *nj* "not" and phonogram *nj* or *n* (§ 8.2.6), especially in *nn* "not"; *jw* or *jwt* in *jwt* "that not" and *jwtj* "which not" (§§ 12.9, 26.29.5). Determinative NEGATION.
36	forearm	Phonogram ^{c}. Ideogram for ^{c} "arm, hand." Often variant for D37–44.
36a	forearm	Ideogram for ^{c}*wj* "arms, hands."
12a	forearm with water	Determinative in *j*^{c}*j* "wash," also ideogram for same.
37	forearm with X8	Phonogram *dj* in forms of *rdj* "give." Also variant of D38.
38	forearm with bread	Phonogram *mj* or *m*. Determinative in *jmj* "give!" (§ 16.2.3).
39	forearm with pot	Determinative OFFER. Sometimes variant of D37–38.
18a	O43 + D36	Ideogram for *šzp* "receive."
40	forearm with stick	Determinative FORCE, EFFORT. Ideogram for *ḫ3j* "measure, evaluate." Rarely variant of D37.
41	forearm with palm down	Determinative ARM and actions associated with the arm or hand. Ideogram *rmn* "shoulder." Phonogram *nj*.
42	forearm with palm down	Determinative in *mḥ* "cubit" (§ 9.7.1), also ideogram for same.
43	forearm with flail	Phonogram *ḫw*.
44	forearm with scepter	Determinative in *ḫrp* "manage," also ideogram for same.
45	forearm with brush	Variant (D251). Determinative in *ḏsr* "sacred, clear away, raise the arm," also ideogram for same.
46	hand	Phonogram *d*. Ideogram for *drt* "hand."
46a	hand with water	Ideogram for *jdt* "fragrance."
47	hand	Determinative of *ḏrt* "hand" when spelled with phonograms.
48	hand without thumb	Ideogram for *šzp* "palm" (§ 9.7.1).
49	fist	Determinative GRASP.
50	finger	Ideogram for *ḏb*^{c} "finger" and *ḏb*^{c} "10,000" (§ 9.1). When doubled, determinative ACCURATE.

51	finger	Determinative for actions associated with the finger: *ḫ3j* "measure," *ṯ3j* "take," *dqr* "press." Determinative in *ʿnt* "fingernail," also ideogram for same. Determinative FRUIT, FLOWER, also ideogram for *dqrw* "fruit," *q3w* "flour."
52	penis	Determinative MALE. Phonogram *mt*. With E1, ideogram for *k3* "bull."
53	penis with fluid	Determinative PENIS and associated actions, also MALE. Determinative of *b3ḥ* in *m b3ḥ* "in the presence of," *ḏr b3ḥ* "since," *r b3ḥ* "before," also ideogram for same.
279	testicles	Determinative in *ḫrwj* "testicles," also ideogram for same.
280a	pelvis and vulva	Phonogram *ḥm*. Ideogram for *jdt* "vulva, cow."
54	walking legs	Determinative MOTION. Phonogram *jw* in forms of the verb *jwj* "come." Ideogram for *nmtt* "step."
55	legs walking backwards	Determinative REVERSE.
56	leg	Determinative FOOT and associated actions. Ideogram for *rd* "foot." Phonogram *pd* (from *p3d* "knee"). Ideogram for *wʿrt* "district" (from *wʿrt* "shin"), *sbq* "excellent" (from *sbq* "leg"), *gḥs* "gazelle."
57	leg with knife	Determinative MUTILATE. Ideogram for *j3ṯw* "place of execution" and *sj3tj* "cheater" (from *j3t* "short").
58	foot	Phonogram *b*. Ideogram for *bw* "place, thing."
59	D36 + D58	Phonogram *ʿb*.
60	D58 + W54	Ideogram for *wʿb* "clean, pure."
61	stylized toes	Variants (D62) and (D63). Determinative in *s3ḥ* "toe; kick, touch with the foot," also ideogram for same.

E. Mammals

1	bull	Determinative CATTLE. Ideogram for *k3* "bull, ox" *jḥw* "cattle."
166	bulls	Plural of E1.
177	two bulls joined	Determinative in *ḫns* "go back and forth."
176	bull tied for slaughter	Determinative *rḫs* "slaughter," also ideogram for same. Ideogram for *k3* "bull" as offering.
2	bull charging	Determinative in *sm3* "wild bull." Ideogram for *k3* in *k3 nḫt* "victorious bull" (epithet of the king).
3	calf	Determinative in *bḥz* "calf" and *wnḏw* "short-horned cattle."
4	sacred cow	Determinative in *ḥz3t* "sacred cow."
5	cow and calf	Determinative in *3ms* "solicitous."
6	horse	Determinative HORSE. Ideogram for *ssmt* "horse."
7	donkey	Determinative in *ʿ3* (originally *jʿ3*) "donkey."
8	kid	Variant (E8a). Phonogram *jb*. Determinative GOAT.
9	newborn bubalis	Phonogram *jw*.
10	ram	Variant (E11). Determinative SHEEP. Ideogram for *b3* "ram," *ḫnmw* "Khnum."
12	pig	Determinative PIG.
13	cat	Determinative in *mjw/mjt* "cat."

14 dog (saluki) — Determinative DOG.

15 jackal recumbent — Variant (D16). Determinative in *jnpw* "Anubis," also ideogram for same. Ideogram (D15) for title *ḥrj-sšt3* "master of secrets."

17 jackal — Determinative in *z3b* "jackal; dignitary," also ideogram for same.

18 jackal on standard — Variant (E19). Determinative in *wp-w3wt* "Parter of the Ways (Wepwawet)," also ideogram for same.

20 Seth animal — Variant (E21). Ideogram for *stẖ/stš* "Seth." Determinative TURMOIL, CHAOS. In hieratic often for E7 and E27.

22 lion — Determinative in *m3j* "lion," also ideogram for same.

23 lion recumbent — Phonogram *rw* (from *rw* "lion"). In hieratic often for U13.

128 two lions joined — Determinative in *3kr* "Horizon (god)," also ideogram for same.

24 panther or leopard — Determinative in *3by* "panther, leopard," also ideogram for same.

25 hippopotamus — Determinative HIPPOPOTAMUS.

26 elephant — Determinative in *3bw* "elephant." Ideogram for *3bw* "Elephantine" (in modern Aswan).

27 giraffe — Determinative in *sr* "foretell." Determinative in *mmj* "giraffe," also ideogram for same.

28 oryx — Determinative in *m3ḥḏ* "oryx."

29 gazelle — Determinative in *gḥs* "gazelle."

30 ibex — Determinative in *nj3w*, *nr3w*, *n3w* "ibex."

31 goat with collar — Determinative in *sʿḥ* "privilege," also ideogram for same.

32 baboon — Determinative BABOON, MONKEY, FURIOUS.

33 monkey — Determinative in *gjf* "monkey."

34 hare — Phonogram *wn*.

F. Parts of Mammals

1 head of ox — Variant (F63). Ideogram for *k3* "cattle" (in offering formulas).

2 head of charging bull — Determinative in *ḏnd* "rage."

3 head of hippopotamus — Determinative in *3t* "power," and *3t* "moment," also ideogram for latter.

4 forepart of lion — Ideogram for *ḥ3t* "front" and related words.

5 head of bubalis — Variant (F6). Determinative in *šs3* "skilled," and related words, also ideogram for same. Determinative in *sš3* "prayer" and *bẖnt* "pylon."

7 head of ram — Variant (F8). Determinative in *šfyt* "worth" (from *šft* "ram's head"), also ideogram for same.

9 head of leopard — Determinative in *pḥtj* "strength," also ideogram for same (often doubled).

11 head and neck of animal — Variant (F10). Determinative NECK, THROAT and related actions.

12 head and neck of jackal — Phonogram *wsr*.

13 horns — Phonogram *wp*. Ideogram for *wpt* "brow." For see O44.

No.	Sign	Description
14	F13 + M4	Variant (F15). Ideogram for *wpt-rnpt* "Opening of the Year" (New Year's Day).
16	horn	Phonogram *ꜥb*. Determinative HORN, also ideogram for same.
17	F16 + W54	Determinative in *ꜥbw* "purification," also ideogram for same.
18	tusk	Determinative TOOTH and associated actions. Phonograms *bḥ* and *ḥw*. Determinative in words with root *bj3*.
19	jawbone of ox	Determinative in *ꜥrt* "jaw."
20	tongue	Phonogram *ns*. Determinative for actions associated with the tongue. Ideogram for *ns* "tongue" and *jmj-r* "overseer" (§ 8.9). Sometimes for Z6.
21	ear of bovine	Phonograms *sḏm* and *jdn*. Determinative EAR and associated actions. Ideogram for *msḏr* "ear" and *ḏrḏ* "leaf."
22	hindquarters of feline	Phonogram *pḥ*. Determinative END, BOTTOM. Ideogram for *pḥwj* "end" and *kf3* "discreet" (from *kf3* "bottom").
23	foreleg of ox	Variant (F24). Determinative in *ḫpš* "strong arm; foreleg," also ideogram for same. Determinative in *msḫtjw* "Foreleg" (Ursa Major).
25	leg and hoof of ox	Phonogram *wḥm*. Ideogram for *wḥm/wḥmt* "hoof."
26	goatskin	Phonogram *ḥn*. Ideogram for *ḥnt* "hide, skin."
27	cowskin	Determinative HIDE, MAMMAL. Sometimes for N2.
28	cowskin	Phonogram *s3b* in *s3b* "dappled." Sometimes for U23.
29	cowskin with arrow	Determinative of *stj* "shoot," also ideogram for same. Phonogram *st*.
30	water-skin	Phonogram *šd*.
31	three fox-skins	Phonogram *ms*.
32	animal's belly and udder	Phonogram *ẖ*. Ideogram in *ẖt* "belly, body."
33	tail	Determinative in *sd* "tail," also ideogram for same.
34	heart	Ideogram for *jb* "heart." Determinative in *ḥ3tj* "heart."
35	heart and windpipe	Phonogram *nfr*.
36	lung and windpipe	Phonogram *zm3*.
37	spine and ribs	Variants (F38), (F37b). Determinative BACK. Ideogram for *j3t* "back." Sometimes for M21.
39	spine and spinal cord	Determinative in *jm3ḫ* "honor" (Essay 21), also ideogram for same. Determinative in *jm3ḫ* "spinal cord," also ideogram for same. Occasionally for F37 as determinative.
40	spine and spinal cord	Phonogram *3w*.
41	vertebrae	Variant of Y10. Determinative in *psḏ* "back."
42	rib	Phonogram *spr*. Determinative in *spr* "rib," also ideogram for same.
43	ribs	Determinative in *spḥt* "ribs."
44	joint of meat	Determinative in *jwꜥ* "inherit" and related words, also ideogram for same. Phonogram *jsw*. Determinative in *jwꜥ* "femur," *swt* "tibia."
45	cow uterus	Determinative in *jdt* "vulva, cow," also ideogram for same.
46	intestine	Variants (F47), (F48), (F49). Determinative MIDST, TURN, INTESTINE. Determinative in *wḏb* "shore" (from *wḏb* "turn").
50	S29 + F46	Phonogram *spẖr*.

51	piece of meat	Also , , . Determinative FLESH. Ideogram for *kns* "vagina" and (tripled) *ḫʿw* "body." Phonogram *js* in *jst* "Isis" and *ws* in *wsjr* "Osiris" in some Coffin Texts.
52	excrement	Determinative in *ḥs* "excrement."

G. Birds

1	Egyptian vulture	Phonogram *3*. Often distinguishable from G4 only by flatter head.
2	two vultures	Phonogram *33*.
3	U1 + G1	Phonogram *m3*.
4	buzzard	Variant (G4a). Phonogram *tjw*. G4 often distinguishable from G1 only by rounder head.
5	falcon	Ideogram for *ḥrw* "Horus."
6	falcon with flail	Determinative in *bjk* "falcon."
7	falcon on standard	Determinative DIVINE. Also variant of A1 when the speaker is a god or the king.
R13	falcon on standard	Ideogram for *jmnt* "West" (older form of R14).
7b	falcon in boat	Variant (G7a). Ideogram for *nmtj* "Nemti" (a god).
8	G5 + S12	Ideogram for *bjk nbw* "Gold Falçon" (title of the king: Essay 6).
9	falcon with sundisk	Ideogram in *rʿ-ḥrw-(3ḫtj)* "Re-Harakhti" (Essays 4, 12, 16).
10	falcon in Sokar bark	Determinative in *zkr* "Sokar" (a god) and *ḥnw* "Sokar-bark."
11	falcon image	Variant (G12). Determinative in *ʿḫm/ʿšm/ʿḫm* "idol" and *šnbt* "breast."
13	falcon image with plumes	Determinative in *spdw* "Sopdu" (a god). Ideogram for *ḥrw nḫnj* "Horus of Hierakonpolis."
14	vulture	Phonogram *mjwt/mjt/mwt/mt*, most common in *mwt* (*mjwt*) "mother." Determinative in *nrt* "vulture" and words with root *nr*.
14a	vulture on basket	Determinative in *nḫbt* "Nekhbet" (goddess).
15	vulture with flail	Determinative in *mwt* (*mjwt*) "Mut" (goddess), also ideogram for same.
16	G14a + I13	Ideogram for *nbtj* "Two Ladies" (title of the king: Essay 6).
17	owl	Phonogram *m*.
18	two owls	Phonogram *mm*.
20	G17 + D36	Variant (G19 = G17 + D37). Phonogram *mj*, *m*.
21	guinea-fowl	Phonogram *nḥ*. Ideogram for *nḥ* "guinea-fowl." Often with body like G1 or G43, but with "horns" and lappet of G21.
22	hoopoe	Phonogram *ḏb/db* in *ḏbt/dbt* "brick."
23	lapwing	Variant (G24). Determinative in *rḫwt/rḫyt* "subjects," also ideogram for same.
25	crested ibis	Phonogram *3ḫ*.

26	ibis on standard	Variant (G26a). Ideogram for *ḏḥwtj* "Thoth." Determinative in *hbj* "ibis."
27	flamingo	Phonogram *dšr* "red." Determinative in *dšr* "flamingo."
28	black ibis	Phonogram *gm*.
29	jabiru	Phonogram *b3*.
30	three jabirus	Ideogram for *b3w* "impressiveness."
31	heron	Determinative HERON.
32	heron on a perch	Determinative in *bꜥḥj* "inundate," also ideogram for same.
33	egret	Determinative in *sd3/sd3d3* "tremble."
34	ostrich	Determinative in *njw* "ostrich."
35	cormorant	Phonogram *ꜥq*.
36	forktailed swallow	Phonogram *wr*. Determinative in *mnt* "swallow."
37	sparrow	Determinative SMALL, BAD. Distinguished from G36 by the rounded tail.
38	goose	Phonogram *gb* in *gbb*, *gbw* "Geb." Determinative BIRD, INSECT. Variant of G39 as phonogram *z3*. Determinative in *wf3* "discuss," *wzf* "idle," *wdfj* "delay," *ḥtm* "perish, destroy."
39	pintail duck	Phonogram *z3*. Determinative in *zr/zrt/zj/zjt* "pintail duck." Often distinguishable from G38 only by more pointed tail.
40	pintail duck flying	Phonogram *p3*. Occasional variant of G41.
41	pintail duck landing	Phonogram *p3*, especially in hieratic. Determinative in *ḫnj* "land, alight" and other words with *ḫn*. Determinative in *sḥwj* "gather" and *qmyt* "gum." In combination with T14, determinative in *qm3* "throw," *qm3j* "create," and words with *ṯn/tn*.
42	fattened bird	Determinative in *wš3* "fatten," also ideogram in same. Determinative in *df3w* "food."
43	quail chick	Phonogram *w*. Ideogram for *w* "chick."
44	two quail chicks	Phonogram *ww*.
45	G43 + D36	Phonogram *wꜥ*.
46	G43 + U1	Phonogram *m3w*.
47	duckling	Phonogram *ṯ3*. Ideogram *ṯ3* "duckling."
48	ducklings in nest	Variants (G48a), (G49). Determinative in *zš* "nest," also ideogram for same.
50	two plovers	Ideogram for *rḫtj* "washerman."
51	bird and fish	Determinative in *ḥ3m/ḥjm* "catch fish."
52	bird picking up grain	Determinative in *snm* "feed."
53	human-headed bird	Ideogram for *b3* "ba."
54	plucked bird	Phonogram *snḏ/snd*. Determinative in *wšn* "wring the neck of birds."

H. Parts of Birds

No.	Sign	Description
1	head of duck	Ideogram for *ꜣpd* "bird" (in offering formulas). Determinative in *wšn* "wring the neck of birds." Variant of H2.
2	head of a crested bird	Determinative in *mꜣꜥ* "temple (of the head)," occasionally also *mꜣꜥ* "correct, true, real." Phonograms *pꜣq* (variant of H3), *wšm*.
3	head of spoonbill	Phonogram *pꜣq*.
4	head of vulture (G14)	For G14 as determinative in *nrt* "vulture" and words with root *nr*. Ideogram for *rmṯ* "people."
5	wing	Determinative WING and associated actions.
6	feather	Variants (H6a), (H6b). Phonogram *šw*. Ideogram for *šwt* "feather." Determinative in *mꜣꜥt* "Maat" (Essay 10), also ideogram for same.
7	claw	Phonogram *šꜣ* in *šꜣt* "Shat" (a place). Determinative in *jꜣft* "claw."
8	egg	Ideogram for *zꜣ* "son" in proper names. Determinative in *swḥt* "egg." Determinative in *pꜥt* "the elite."

I. Reptiles, Amphibians, and their Parts

No.	Sign	Description
1	gecko	Phonogram *ꜥšꜣ*. Determinative LIZARD.
2	turtle	Determinative in *štjw* "turtle," also ideogram for same.
3	crocodile	Determinative CROCODILE, AGGRESSION. When doubled, ideogram for *jty* "sovereign."
4	crocodile on shrine	Variant (I5a, crocodile image). Determinative in *sbkw* "Sobek," also ideogram for same.
5	crocodile with curved tail	Determinative in *sꜣq* "collect," also ideogram for same.
6	crocodile scales	Phonogram *km*.
7	frog	Determinative FROG. Ideogram for *wḥm ꜥnḫ* "repeating life" (epithet of deceased).
8	tadpole	Ideogram for *ḥfn* "100,000" (§ 9.2). Determinative TADPOLE.
9	horned viper	Phonogram *f*. Determinative in *jtj* "father."
10	cobra	Phonogram *ḏ*.
R61	emblematic cobra	Determinative in *ṯnjw* "desert border," also ideogram for same.
11	two cobras	Phonogram *ḏḏ*.
12	erect cobra	Variant (I64). Determinative in *jꜥrt* "uraeus" and names of goddesses.
13	cobra on basket	Determinative in *wꜣḏt* "Wadjet" (a goddess) and name of goddesses.
14	snake	Variant (I15). Determinative SNAKE, WORM.

K. Fish and Parts of Fish

No.	Sign	Description
1	bulti	Phonogram *jn*. Determinative in *jnt* "bulti."
2	barbel	Determinative in *bwt* "abomination."
3	mullet	Phonogram *ꜥḏ* in *ꜥḏ-mr* "district administrator." Determinative in *ꜥdw* "mullet."

4	oxyrhynchus	Phonogram *ḫ3*. Ideogram in *ḫ3t* "oxyrhynchus."
5	pike	Determinative in *bzj* "introduce." Determinative FISH, FISHY.
6	fish scale	Variant . Determinative in *nšmt* "fish scale," also ideogram for same.
7	blowfish	Determinative in *špt* "angry."

L. Insects and Invertebrates

1	scarab beetle	Phonogram *ḫpr*. Determinative in *ḫprr* "scarab beetle," also ideogram for same.
2	bee or wasp	Ideogram for *bjt* "bee; honey," and *bjtj* "King of Lower Egypt."
3	fly	Determinative in *ꜥff* "fly."
4	locust	Determinative in *znḥm* "locust."
5	centipede	Ideogram in *sp3* "Sepa" (place near Heliopolis). Determinative in *zp3* "centipede."
6	shell	Phonogram *ḫ3* in *ḫ3wt* "offering table."
7	emblematic scorpion	Variant (L7a). Determinative in *srqt* "Selket" (a goddess), also ideogram for same.

M. Vegetation

1	tree	Variant (M1a, with M3). Determinative TREE; also in *mꜥr* "fortunate." Phonogram *jm3*, often with only G17 *m* as complement = *jm(3)*.
2	plant	Determinative PLANT. Phonogram *ḥn*. Determinative in *jzj* "light," *jz* "tomb," *js* "old" (from *jzw* "reeds"). Rarely for A1 as determinative or in 1s pronouns (from *j* "reed"). Occasional variant of T24.
3	stick	Phonogram *ḫt*. Determinative WOOD. Ideogram for *ḫt* "wood, stick, tree, mast." Also vertically as determinative of *ḏꜥr* "seek."
4	rib of palm branch	Ideogram for *rnpt* "year" and *ḥsbt* "regnal year" (§ 9.9). Determinative in *rnpj* "young." Determinative TIME in *tr* "time, season." When doubled, ideogram for *snf* "last year."
5	M4 + X1	Determinative TIME in *tr* "time, season," also ideogram for same. Variant of M6.
6	M4 + D21	Determinative TIME in *tr* "time, season," also ideogram for same. Determinative of some roots ending in *tr* and *rj*.
7	M4 + Q3	Determinative in *rnpj* "young," also ideogram for same.
8	pool with lilies	Phonogram *š3*. Ideogram for *3ḫt* "Inundation (season)" (§ 9.8). Ideogram for *š3* "pool, marsh."
9	lily (lotus)	Determinative in *zššnj* "lily (lotus)," also ideogram for same.
10	lily (lotus) bud	Determinative in *nḥbt* "lily (lotus) bud."
11	flower on stem	Determinative in *wdn* "dedicate, offer," also ideogram for same. Occasional variant of F46 as determinative in *wḏb* "shore."
12	lily (lotus) plant	Phonogram *ḫ3*. Ideogram for *ḫ3* "1,000" (§ 9.1) and "lily (lotus)."
13	papyrus	Variant (M14, with I10). Phonogram *w3ḏ/w3d*, also *wḏ/wd*. Ideogram for *w3ḏ* "papyrus column."

15	clump of papyrus with buds	Determinative for *mḥw* "Delta," also ideogram for same. Determinative PAPYRUS, SWAMP. Phonogram *3ḫ* in *3ḫ-bjt* "Chemmis" (Delta town).
16	clump of papyrus	Phonogram *ḥ3*. Variant of M15 in *mḥw* "Delta."
17	reed	Phonogram *j*. When doubled, phonogram *y*. Occasional variant of A1. Ideogram for *j* "reed."
18	M17 + D54	Variant . Phonogram *j* in forms of *jj* "come."
19	emblem for offerings	Determinative in *ᶜ3b* "offer," also ideogram for same.
20	field of reeds	Determinative in *sḫt* "field" and *sḫtj* "peasant," also ideogram for same. Occasional variant of M21.
21	reeds with root	Determinative in *sm* "grass" and *sm* "help."
22	rush	Phonogram *nḫb*. When doubled, phonogram *nn*.
23	sedge	Phonogram *sw*. Ideogram for *nswt* "king." Ideogram for *swt* "sedge." Occasional variant of M24 and M26.
163	M23 + Aa1	Ideogram for *rḫ-nswt* "king's acquaintance."
24	M23 + D21	Variant (M25). Ideogram for *rsw* "south."
26	flowering sedge	Variant (M27, with D36). Phonogram *šmᶜ*. Ideogram for *šmᶜw* "Nile Valley" (Upper Egypt).
28	M26 + V20	Ideogram in title *wr mḏw-šmᶜw* "chief of the tens of the Nile Valley."
29	pod	Phonogram *nḏm* "pleasant."
30	root	Determinative in *bnr* "sweet," also ideogram for same.
31	rhizome	Variant (M32). Determinative in *rd* "grow," also in *rwḏ* "firm."
33	grain	Variants , . Ideogram for *jtj* "grain." Determinative GRAIN.
34	sheaf of emmer	Ideogram for *btj* (originally *bdt*) "emmer," also determinative for same.
35	heap of grain	Determinative HEAP.
36	bundle of flax	Variant (M37). Phonogram *ḏr*. Determinative in *dm3* "bundle."
38	bundle of flax	Determinative in *mḥᶜw* "flax" and *dm3* "bundle."
Y10	bundle of stems	Determinative in *šᶜt* "murderousness" (from *šᶜ* "cut").
39	basket of fruit or grain	Determinative VEGETABLES.
40	bundle of reeds	Phonogram *jz*.
41	piece of wood	Determinative WOOD.
42	rosette	Phonogram *wn*. In hieratic indistinguishable from Z11.
43	grapes on trellis	Variant (M43a). Determinative VINE, WINE, GARDENER, FRUIT. Ideogram for *jrp* "wine" and *k3ny* "gardener."
43b	wine or olive press	Determinative in *šzmw* "Shesmu" (god of the wine or olive press), also ideogram for same.
44	thorn	Determinative in *spd* "sharp," also ideogram for same. Determinative in *srt* "thorn." Determinative in *t-ḥḏ* "white-bread" (as bread of this form).

N. Sky, Earth, Water

1	sky	Determinative SKY, ABOVE. Ideogram for *ḥrj* "upper" (§ 8.6.7). Determinative in *rwt* "gate" and *h3yt* "ceiling, portal," also ideogram for latter.
2	sky with scepter	Variants (N3, with oar), (N46b, with star). Determinative NIGHT. Ideogram for *grḥ* "night."
4	sky with rain	Determinative DEW, RAIN. Ideogram for *j3dt* "dew."
5	sun	Determinative SUN, DAY, TIME. Ideogram for *r^c* "sun, Re," *hrw* "day," and *sw* "day" (in dates: § 9.8).
5a	sun with two strokes	Variant (N5 + N23). Determinative TIME.
6	sun with uraeus	Determinative in *r^c* "Re," also ideogram for same.
7	N5 + T28	Ideogram for *ẖrt-hrw* "daytime, course of the day."
8	sun with rays	Determinative SUNLIGHT. Phonogram *wbn* (from *wbn* "rise"). Ideogram for *ḥnmmt* "human beings."
9	moon	Variant (N10). Phonogram *psḏ* in *psḏt* "Ennead" and *psḏntjw* "new-moon festival." Variant of X6 in *p3t* "origin."
11	crescent moon	Variant as determinative. Determinative in *j^{c}ḥ* "moon," also ideogram for same. Ideogram for "month"(*3bd*) in dates (§ 9.8). Occasional variant of F42. Determinative in *w^{c}ḥ* "carob bean," also ideogram for same. Determinative in *šzp* "palm" (measure: § 9.7.1), also ideogram for same.
12	crescent moon	Variant as determinative. Determinative in *j^{c}ḥ* "moon," also ideogram for same. Occasional variant of F42.
64	N11 + N14	Ideogram for *3bd* "month."
13	half N11 + N14	Ideogram for *mḏdjwnt* "15th-day festival."
14	star	Determinative STAR, TIME. Phonogram *sb3* (from *sb3* "star"). Phonogram *dw3* (from *dw3* "morning"). Ideogram for *wnwt* "hour."
15	star in circle	Ideogram for *dw3t* "Duat" (Essay 2).
16	strip of land with sand	Variants (N16d), (N17). Ideogram for *t3* "land, earth, world." Phonogram *t3*. Determinative in *ḏt* "estate" and *ḏt* "eternity."
18	strip of sand	Ideogram for *jw* "island." Determinative DESERT, FOREIGN LAND. Ideogram for *sṯ3t* "aroura" (§ 9.7.2).
19	two strips of sand	Ideogram for *3ḫt* "Akhet" (Essay 2) in *ḥrw-3ḫtj* "Harakhti" (Essay 12).
20	tongue of land	Variant (N22). Phonogram *wḏb/wdb* in *wḏb* "turn." Determinative LAND, especially in *wḏb* "shore." Determinative in *ḥ3b-sd* "Sed Festival."
21	tongue of land	Determinative LAND. Ideogram for *jdb* "bank," when doubled *jdbwj* "Two Banks" (a term for Egypt).
23	irrigation canal	Variants , . Determinative LAND, especially IRRIGATED LAND. Also used in variant of N5a. Ideogram for *gbb/gbw* "Geb."
24	irrigation canal system	Determinative of *sp3t* "nome," also ideogram for same. Determinative in names of nomes and divisions of Egypt, also in *ḥzp* "garden." Ideogram for *ḏ3tt* "estate, farm."
25	mountain range	Ideogram for *ḫ3st* "desert cliffs, foreign land." Determinative DESERT, FOREIGN LAND.
76	N25 on standard	Ideogram for *ḥ3* "Ha" (desert god).

26	mountain	Phonogram *ḏw*. Ideogram for *ḏw* "mountain."
27	sun rising above mountain	Ideogram for *3ḫt* "Akhet" (Essay 2).
28	sun's rays above hill	Phonogram *ḫʿ*, especially in *ḫʿj* "appear."
29	sandy slope	Phonogram *q*.
30	hill with shrubs	Determinative in *j3t* "mound," also ideogram for same.
31	path with shrubs	Variant (N31e). Determinative for *w3t* "road," also ideogram for same. Determinative ROAD, DISTANCE, POSITION. Ideogram for *w3j* "tend, start" (from *w3t* "road"). Phonogram *ḥr* in *jn-ḥrt* "Onuris" (a god), *ḥrw* "Horus," and *ḥrw r* "except" (from *ḥrj* "go far away").
32	lump of clay	Variant of Aa2 and F52.
33	grain of sand	Variants (N33a), , . Determinative SAND, MINERAL, PELLET. When single, occasional substitute for signs with bad connotations, such as A14 and Z6. When triple, occasional substitute for plural strokes. Determinative in words with *qd* (from *qdj* "go around").
34	ingot of metal	Variant (N34a). Ideogram for *ḥmt* "copper, bronze." Determinative COPPER, BRONZE.
35	ripple of water	Phonogram *n*.
35a	three ripples of water	Ideogram for *mw* "water." Determinative WATER. Phonogram *mw*.
36	canal	Determinative BODY OF WATER. Phonogram *mr* and *mj*. Ideogram for *mr* "canal."
37	basin	Variants (N37a), (N38), (N39), etc. Phonogram *š*. Ideogram for *šj* "basin, pool, lake." Determinative of *sṯ3t* "aroura" (§ 9.7.2), also ideogram for same. Variant of X4 as determinative of *zn* "open" and *znj* "pass." Variant of O36.
40	N37 + D54	Phonogram *šm* in forms of *šmj* "go."
41	well with water	Variants (N42), (D280a). Determinative WELL. Determinative in *bj3* "cauldron, copper" and words with root *bj3*. Determinative in *pḥww* "outer limits," also ideogram for same (tripled). Often for D280a.

O. Structures and Parts of Structures

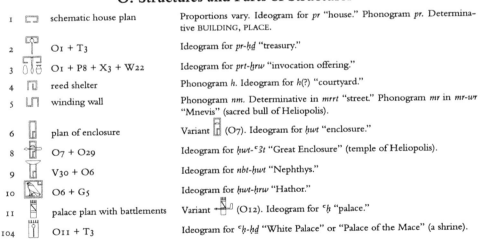

1	schematic house plan	Proportions vary. Ideogram for *pr* "house." Phonogram *pr*. Determinative BUILDING, PLACE.
2	O1 + T3	Ideogram for *pr-ḥḏ* "treasury."
3	O1 + P8 + X3 + W22	Ideogram for *prt-ḫrw* "invocation offering."
4	reed shelter	Phonogram *h*. Ideogram for *h*(?) "courtyard."
5	winding wall	Phonogram *nm*. Determinative in *mrrt* "street." Phonogram *mr* in *mr-wr* "Mnevis" (sacred bull of Heliopolis).
6	plan of enclosure	Variant (O7). Ideogram for *ḥwt* "enclosure."
8	O7 + O29	Ideogram for *ḥwt-ʿ3t* "Great Enclosure" (temple of Heliopolis).
9	V30 + O6	Ideogram for *nbt-ḥwt* "Nephthys."
10	O6 + G5	Ideogram for *ḥwt-ḥrw* "Hathor."
11	palace plan with battlements	Variant (O12). Ideogram for *ʿḥ* "palace."
104	O11 + T3	Ideogram for *ʿḥ-ḥḏ* "White Palace" or "Palace of the Mace" (a shrine).

13	enclosure with battlements	Variant (O14). Determinative in *sbḫ* "wall in" and related words.
15	enclosure + W10 + X1	Variant (O15a). Ideogram for *wsḫt* "broad hall."
16	cornice with cobras	Variant (O17). Determinative for *t3yt* "curtain," also ideogram for same and *t3jtj* "he of the curtain" (title of the vizier). O17 variant of S22 in *t3-wr* "port."
18	shrine in profile	Determinative in *k3r* "shrine," also ideogram for same.
19	shrine with poles	Determinative in *pr-wr* "Great House" (original shrine of Upper Egypt at Hierakonpolis), also in *jtrt šmꜥt* "Nile Valley Shrine" (same).
20	shrine	Determinative SHRINE.
21	shrine façade	Determinative in *zḥ* "booth," also ideogram for same.
22	booth with pole	Determinative in *zḥ* "counsel, advice" and *zḥ* "tent, booth," also ideogram for latter.
23	double platform	Determinative in *ḥ3b-sd* "Sed Festival," also ideogram for same.
24	pyramid and enclosure wall	Determinative PYRAMID.
25	obelisk	Determinative in *tḫn* "obelisk," also ideogram for same.
26	stela	Determinative STELA, also ideogram for *wḏ* "stela."
27	columned hall	Determinative HALL. Determinative of *ḫ3wj* "dusk" (from *ḫ3* "office"), also ideogram for same.
28	column with tenon	Phonogram *j(w)n*. Ideogram for *jwn* "column."
29	wood column	Variant . Phonogram *ꜥ3*.
30	support	Determinative SUPPORT, also ideogram for *zḫnt* "support."
31	door leaf	Variant (O31a). Variant in *ꜥ3wj* "door" (two door leaves). Determinative OPEN. Determinative in *ꜥ3* "door," also ideogram for same.
32	gateway	Determinative DOORWAY, also ideogram for *sb3* "doorway."
33	palace façade	Determinative in *srḫ* "serekh" (Essay 6).
34	doorbolt	Phonogram *z*. Ideogram for *z* "doorbolt." Variant of R22.
35	O34 + D54	Phonogram *z* in *zj* "go away, perish," *zy* "which?" (§ 5.11), *zbj* "send away, go away," and *mz* "bring."
36	wall	Determinative WALL. Ideogram for *jnb* "wall."
37	wall falling	Determinative TOPPLE, TILT.
38	corner	Determinative CORNER. Ideogram for *qnbt* "council." Determinative or ideogram for *tm* in the administrative title *ḥrj (n) tm* "chief of the *tm*."
39	stone block or brick	Determinative STONE, BRICK.
40	stairs	Determinative STAIRWAY, TERRACE. Ideogram for *rwd* "stairs" and *ḫtjw* "terrace."
41	double stairs	Determinative STAIRWAY, ASCEND.
43	fence	Variant (O42). Phonogram *šzp, sšp*.
44	emblem of Min	Variant (O44a) Determinative in *j3t* "office," also ideogram for same.

45	domed structure	Variant (O46). Determinative in *jp3t* "private quarters," also ideogram for same.
47	enclosed mound	Variant (O48). Ideogram for *nḫn* "Hierakonpolis" and *mḫnt* "jasper."
49	area with intersection	Variant (O49a). Ideogram for *nwt* "town." Determinative TOWN, SETTLEMENT.
50	threshing floor with grain	Phonogram *zp* in *zp* "occasion, event," *zpj* "be left over," and related words. Determinative in *zpt* "threshing floor."
51	pile of grain	Variant (O51b). Determinative in *šnwt* "granary," also ideogram for same.

P. Ships and Parts of Ships

1	boat on water	Variants (P1c), (P26). Determinative BOAT. Ideogram for "boat" (various readings: *dpt, ḥʿw, jmw, q3q3w*).
1a	boat capsized	Determinative in *pnʿ* "capsize."
2	boat under sail	Determinative in *ḫntj* "sail upstream."
3	sacred boat	Variants (P30), (P34). Determinative GOD'S BOAT. Ideogram for *wj3* "sacred bark."
3a	P3 + M23	Ideogram for *wj3-nswt* "king's bark."
4	boat with net	Variant (P4a). Phonogram *wḥʿ*.
5	mast with sail	Determinative WIND, AIR. Ideogram for *ṯ3w* "air" and *nfw* "sailor."
5f	sail	Determinative in *ḥt3w* "sail."
6	mast	Variant (P7). Phonogram *ʿḥʿ*.
8	oar	Variant in *m3ʿ ḫrw* "justified" (Essay 8). Phonogram *ḫrw*. Determinative OAR. Ideogram for *ḥjpt* "oar."
9	P8 + I9	Ideogram for *ḫr.fj* "says, said" (§ 22.18).
10	steering oar with rope	Determinative in *ḥmw* "rudder" and *ḥmy* "steerer."
11	mooring stake	Determinative in *mjnj* "moor, die" and related words. In hieratic often identical with T14.

Q. Domestic and Funerary Furniture

1	seat	Ideogram for *st* "seat, place." Phonogram *st*. Phonogram *ws* in *wsjr* "Osiris." Phonogram *ḥtm*.
2	portable seat	Phonogram *ws* in *wsjr* "Osiris." Ideogram for *st* "seat."
3	stool	Phonogram *p*.
4	headrest	Determinative in *wrsw* "headrest."
5	chest	Determinative CHEST, BOX.
6	coffin	Determinative in *qrs* "bury" and related words, also ideogram for same.
7	brazier with flame	Determinative FIRE. Ideogram for *srf* "temperature." When doubled, ideogram for *nsrsr* "flame" in *jw-nsrsr* "Island of Flame" (locality of creation and in the Duat).

R. Temple Furniture and Sacred Emblems

No.	Sign	Description
1	table with offerings	Variants (R2), (R36a). Determinative in *ẖ3wt/ẖ3yt* "altar," also ideogram for same.
3	low table with offerings	Determinative in *wḏḥw* "offering table," also ideogram for same.
4	bread loaf on mat	Phonogram *ḥtp*. Ideogram for *ḥtp* "offering slab."
5	censer	Variant (R6). Phonogram *k(3)p*. Determinative in *k3p* "fumigate," also ideogram for same.
7	bowl with smoke	Determinative of *snṯr* "incense," also ideogram for same. Variant of W10a/Aa4.
8	cloth wound on pole	Ideogram for *nṯr* "god." Phonogram *nṯr*. Determinative GOD.
9	R8 + V33	Determinative for *bd* "incense," also ideogram for same.
10	R8 + T28 + N29	Variants (R10e), (R50). Ideogram for *ẖrj-nṯr/ẖrt-nṯr* "necropolis."
11	reed column	Phonogram *ḏd*, also doubled with the same value. Ideogram for *ḏd* "*djed*-column/amulet."
12	carrying standard	Determinative in *j3t* "standard." Usually part of other signs.
14	feather on standard	Variant (R13). Ideogram for *jmnt* "West" and *wnmj* "right."
15	spear emblem	Variant (R15b). Ideogram for *j3b* "East, left." Variant of U23.
16	scepter with feathers	Determinative in *wẖ* (emblem of Qus), also ideogram for same.
17	wig with feathers on pole	Variants (R17b), (R18). Determinative in *t3-wr* "This" (nome of Abydos), also ideogram for same.
19	S40 with feather	Ideogram for *w3st* "Thebes" (town and nome).
20	Seshat emblem	Variant (R21). Ideogram for *sš3t* "Seshat" (a goddess).
22	Min emblem	Variants (R22a), (R23), (R23a). Ideogram for *mnw* "Min" (a god). Without standard, phonogram *ẖm* in *ẖm* "shrine" and *ẖm* "Letopolis" (town in the Delta).
24	Neith emblem	Variants , (R24a), (R24b), (R24c), (R25), (R25a), (R25b). Determinative in *njt* (originally *nrt*) "Neith," also ideogram for same.
61	emblematic cobra	Determinative in *ṯnjw* "desert border," also ideogram for same.

S. Regalia and Clothing

No.	Sign	Description
1	White Crown	Variant (S2). Determinative WHITE CROWN. Ideogram for *ḥḏt* "White Crown."
47a	S1 on standard with flail	Determinative in *b3b3y* "Babay" (a god), also ideogram for same.
3	Red Crown	Variant (S4). Determinative RED CROWN. Phonogram *n*. S3 variant of L2 as emblem of King of Lower Egypt.
5	Double Crown	Variant (S6). Determinative in *sẖmtj* "Double Crown," also ideogram for same. Determinative CROWN.

No.	Name	Use
7	Blue Crown	Determinative in *ḫprš* "Blue (War) Crown," also ideogram for same.
8	Atef Crown	Determinative in *3tf* "Atef Crown," also ideogram for same.
9	double plumes	Determinative in *šwtj* "double plumes," also ideogram for same.
10	headband	Phonogram *mḏḥ*. Determinative in *w3ḥw* "wreath" and *mḏḥ* "headband," also ideogram for latter.
11	broad collar	Determinative in *wsḫ* "broad collar," also ideogram for same. Phonogram *wsḫ*.
12	bead collar	Variant (S12a). Ideogram for *nbw* "gold" and related words. Determinative PRECIOUS METAL.
13	S12 + D58	Phonogram *nb*.
14	S12 + T3	Ideogram for *ḥḏ* "silver."
14a	S12 + S40	Ideogram for *ḏꜥm* "electrum."
15	faience pectoral	Variants (S16), (S17), (S17a). Determinative in *ṯḥn* "sparkle" and related words, also ideogram for same. Ideogram for *šzmt* "malachite" and related words.
18	bead necklace	Determinative in *mnjt* "bead necklace, counterweight," also ideogram for same.
19	seal on necklace	Ideogram for *ḫtm* "seal" and related words.
20	seal on necklace	Determinative SEAL. Ideogram for *ḫtm* "seal" and *š(n)ꜥtj* "ring" (§ 9.7.3). Variant of E31.
21	ring	Determinative RING.
22	shoulder knot	Phonogram *s(3)ṯ*. Determinative in *t3-wr* "port (of ship)," also ideogram for same.
23	knotted cloth	Phonogram *dmḏ/dmd*. Different from Aa6.
24	knotted belt	Phonogram *ṯ3z*. Ideogram for *ṯ3zt* "knot, vertebra."
25	garment with ties	Ideogram for *jꜥ3w* "guide, dragoman, interpreter."
26	kilt	Determinative in *šndyt* (originally *šnḏwt*) "kilt," also ideogram for same.
130a	strip of cloth	Determinative in *d3jw* "cloak," also ideogram for same.
27	cloth with two fringes	Determinative in *mnḫt* "cloth," also ideogram for same.
116	cloth with four fringes	Determinative in *jfdj* "four-ply linen," also ideogram for same.
118	cloth with six fringes	Determinative in *sjsj* "six-weave linen," also ideogram for same.
28	cloth with fringe + S29	Variant (V48). Determinative CLOTH.
29	folded cloth	Phonogram *s*. Abbreviation for *snb* in *ꜥnḫ.(w)-(w)ḏ3.(w)-s(nb.w)* (§ 17.20.2).
30	S29 + I9	Phonogram in *sf* "yesterday."
31	S29 + U2	Phonogram *sm3*.
32	cloth with fringe	Phonogram *sj3*. Ideogram for *sj3t* "fringed cloth."
33	sandal	Determinative SANDAL. Ideogram for *ṯbt* "sandal," *ṯbw* "sandalmaker."
34	sandal strap	Phonogram *ꜥnḫ*. Ideogram for *ꜥnḫ* "sandal strap" and "mirror."

35	sunshade or fan	Variant (S36). Ideogram for *šwt* "shadow, shade." Determinative in *sryt* "fan," also ideogram for same. Doubled (S36), ideogram for *ḥjpwj* "Hepwi" (a god).
37	fan	Determinative in *ḫw* "fan," also ideogram for same.
38	crook	Phonogram *ḥq3*. Determinative in *ḥq3t* "scepter," also ideogram for same. Variant of S39.
39	shepherd's crook	Phonogram *ꜥwt* in *ꜥwt* "flock" (from *ꜥwt* "crook").
40	animal-headed staff	Phonogram *w3s*. Ideogram for *w3s* "staff" of this shape. Ideogram for *j3tt* "milk, cream" and "Iatet" (milk goddess). Doubled, phonogram *w3b* in *w3bwj* "Wabwi" (name of a nome) and *w3bwt* "Wabut" (a town). Variant of S41 and R19.
40a	S40 on standard	Variant of S40 as ideogram for *j3tt* "milk, cream" and "Iatet."
41	animal-headed staff	Phonogram *ḏꜥm* in *ḏꜥmw* "fine gold" (from *ḏꜥm* "staff" of this shape).
42	scepter	Phonogram *sḫm*. Determinative in *ḫrp* "manage," also ideogram for same, especially in titles. Phonogram *ꜥb3*. Ideogram for *ꜥb3* "scepter" and "stela." Ideogram for *sḫm* "sistrum."
42a	lotus-bud scepter	Determinative in *nḥbt* "lotus-bud scepter," also ideogram for same.
43	staff	Phonogram *md*. Ideogram for *mdw* "staff."
44	staff with flail	Determinative for *3ms* "staff," also ideogram for same.
45	flail	Determinative in *nḫ3ḫ3w* "flail," also ideogram for same.

T. Warfare, Hunting, and Slaughter

1	mace with flat head	Phonogram *mn*.
2	T3 tilted	Determinative SMITE.
3	mace with round head	Variant (T4). Phonogram *ḥḏ*. Ideogram for *ḥḏ* "mace" of this shape.
5	T3 + I10	Phonogram *ḥḏ*.
6	T3 + I10 + I10	Phonogram *ḥḏḏ*.
7	axe	Determinative AXE and related words.
7a	axe	Determinative in *3qḫw* "axe" of this shape.
8	dagger	Phonogram *tp*. Determinative in *mṯpnt* "dagger" of this shape.
8a	dagger	Determinative in *b3gsw* "dagger" of this shape.
9	bow	Variants (T9a), (T10). Phonogram *pḏ/pd*. Determinative in *pḏt* "bow," also ideogram for same and words of the same root.
11	arrow	Phonogram *zwn*. Determinative ARROW.
12	bowstring	Phonogram *rwḏ/rwd*. Determinative in words with *3r* (*3j*, *3jr*, from *3r* "restrain"). Ideogram for *d3r* "subdue." Determinative for *rwḏ* "bowstring," also ideogram for same.
13	pieces of wood tied	Phonogram *rs* in *rs* "wake" and related words.

14		throw-stick	Variant (T15). Determinative with G41 in words with *ṯn/tn*. Determinative FOREIGN. Determinative in *qm3* "throw" and *qm3j* "create," also ideogram for same. Ideogram for *ᶜ3m* "Asiatic," *ṯḥnw* "Libya." Ideogram for *ḥq3t* "heqat" (§ 9.7.4). Variant of D50 as determinative ACCURATE; of M3 as determinative in *ḏᶜr* "seek"; of P11 as determinative in *mjnj* "moor, die"; of S39 as phonogram in *ᶜwt* "flock"; and of T13 and Aa6.
16		scimitar	Determinative in *ḫpš* "scimitar."
17		chariot	Determinative in *wrrt* "chariot," also ideogram for same.
18		crook with package attached	Phonogram *šms*.
19		bone harpoon head	Variant (T20). Phonogram *qs*. Determinative BONE, TUBE. Determinative in *qrs* "bury," *twr* "pure" (from *twr* "tube"). Ideogram for *gnwt* "annals" and *gnwtj* "sculptor" (often double in the latter).
21		harpoon	Variant . Phonogram *wᶜ* in *wᶜ* "one" and related words.
22		arrowhead	Variant (T23). Phonogram *sn*.
24		fishing net	Phonogram *ᶜḥ/jḥ*. Determinative NET.
25		reed float	Phonogram *ḏb3/db3*.
27		bird trap	Variant (T26). Determinative in *sḫt* "trap," also ideogram for same.
28		butcher's block	Phonogram *ḫr*.
29		T30 + T28	Determinative in *nmt* "slaughtering place," also ideogram for same.
30		knife or saw	Determinative KNIFE, SHARP. Ideogram for *dmt* "knife."
31		knife sharpener	Variants (T32), (T33). Phonogram *sšm* in *sšm* "guide" and related words.
35		butcher knife	Variant (T34). Phonogram *nm*. Determinative in *nm* "butcher knife."

U. Agriculture, Crafts, and Professions

1		sickle	Variant (U2). Phonogram *m3*. Determinative REAP, CROOKED.
3		U1 + D4	Phonogram *m3* in *m3* "see."
4		U1 + Aa11	Variant (U5). Phonogram *m3ᶜ* in *m3ᶜ* "true, correct," and related words.
6		hoe	Variants (U7), (U6a), (U7a). Phonogram *mr*. Determinative HACK. Variant of U8.
8		hoe	Phonogram *ḥn* (from *ḥnn* "hoe").
9		grain-measure with grain	Determinative GRAIN. Ideogram for *ḥq3t* "heqat" and *jpt* "oipe" (§ 9.7.4).
10		M33 + U9	Ideogram for *jtj* "barley, grain." Variant of U9 as determinative.
11		S38 + U9	Variant (U12). Ideogram for *ḥq3t* "heqat" (§ 9.7.4).
109		pitchfork	Variant (U109a). Determinative (U109) in *sḏb* "obstacle," also ideogram for same. Determinative in *ᶜbj* "collect" and *ᶜbt* "pitchfork."
13		plow	Variant (U14). Phonogram *šnᶜ*. Phonogram *hb*. Determinative PLOW. Ideogram for *prt* "seed."
15		sled	Phonogram *tm*.

16	loaded sled with jackal's head	Determinative in *bj3* "wonder" and related words, also ideogram for same. Determinative SLED.
17	pick and basin	Variant (U18). Phonogram *grg*.
19	adze	Variant (U20). Phonogram *nw*.
21	adze and block of wood	Phonogram *stp/sṯp*.
22	chisel	Determinative in *mnḫ* "functional." Determinative CARVE.
23	chisel	Phonograms *3b* and *mr*.
25	drill for stone	Variant (U24). Ideogram for *ḥmwt* "craft" and related words.
26	drill for beads	Variant (U27). Ideogram for *wb3* and related words. Occasional variant of U24–25.
29	fire-drill	Variant (U28). Phonogram *ḏ3*. Abbreviation for *wḏ3* in *ꜥnḫ.(w)-(w)ḏ3.(w)-s(nb.w)* (§ 17.20.2).
30	kiln	Phonogram *t3*.
31	baker's rake	Determinative in *ḫnr* "restrain" and related words, also ideogram for same. Determinative in *rtḥ/jtḥ* "restrain." Determinative in *rtḥtj* "baker," also ideogram for same. Variant of D19–20.
32	pestle and mortar	Determinative in *smn* "set, fix" (from *smn* "flatten dough"). Determinative POUND, HEAVY. Determinative in *ḥzmn* "natron; bronze," also ideogram for same.
33	pestle	Phonogram *tj/t*.
34	spindle	Variant (U35). Phonogram *ḫsf*. Determinative in *ḫsf* "spin."
36	launderer's club	Phonogram *ḥm*.
37	razor	Determinative in *ẖꜥq* "shave."
38	scale	Determinative in *mḫ3t* "scale," also ideogram for same.
39	upright of scale	Variants (U40), (U40a). Determinative in *wṯz* "hold up, carry, wear" and *ṯzj* "pick up."
41	plumb bob	Determinative in *tḫ* "plumb bob."

V. Rope, Baskets, and Cloth

1	coil of rope	Variant (V1a). Determinative ROPE, TIE, COIL. Ideogram for *št* "100" (§ 9.1). Phonogram *šn* in *šnt* "dispute." Different from Z7.
2	V1 + O34	Determinative in *sṯ3* "pull" and *3š* "hasten." Ideogram for *sṯ3t* "aroura" (§ 9.7.2).
3	three V1 + O34	Ideogram *sṯ3w* in *r-sṯ3w* "necropolis" (of Giza).
4	lasso	Phonogram *w3*.
5	looped rope	Determinative in *sntj* "lay out," also ideogram for same.
6	cord with ends up	Phonogram *šs* and *šsr*. Ideogram for *šsrw/šs* "linen." Variant of V33.
7	cord with ends down	Variant (V8). Phonogram *šn*.
9	round cartouche	Determinative in *šnw* "circuit" (of the sun), also ideogram for same. Determinative in *šnw* "cartouche."

10		cartouche	Surrounding names of kings, queens, and some gods. Determinative in *šnw* "cartouche" and *rn* "name."
11		end of cartouche	Determinative in *dnj* "dam" and *pḫ3* "split." Ideogram for *pḫ3*, a kind of grain. Ideogram for *djwt/dyt* "shriek."
12		string	Determinative in *fḫ* "loosen," *ᶜrq* "bind," *šfdw* "papyrus scroll," and other words associated with STRING. Determinative in *ᶜrq* "swear" and *ᶜrqy* "last day of the month" (§ 9.8) (from *ᶜrq* "bind"), also ideogram for latter. Ideogram for *fḫ* "loosen." Determinative in *fnḫw* "Phoenicians."
13		hobble	Variant (V14). Phonogram *ṯ/t*.
15		V13 + D54	Phonogram *jṯ* in forms of *jṯj* "take possession."
16		hobble for cattle	Variants (V16a), (V17, rolled-up tent), (V18). Phonogram *z3* in *z3* "protection" and related words.
19		hobble for cattle	Determinative SHRINE in *k3r* "shrine," *qnj* "palanquin" (also *qnj* "sheaf"), *štyt* "Sokar shrine." Determinative in *tm3* "mat" and *ṯm3* "cadaster," also ideogram for latter. Determinative in *ḫ3r* "sack" (§ 9.7.4), also ideogram for latter. Determinative in *mḏt* "stable, stall," also ideogram for latter.
20		V19 without horizontal	Ideogram for *mḏw* "10" (§ 9.7.1).
21		V20 + I10	Phonogram *mḏ*.
23		whip	Variant (V22). Phonogram *mḥ*.
24		cord wound on stick	Variant (V25). Phonogram *wḏ/wd*.
26		spool with thread	Variant (V25, without thread). Phonogram *ᶜḏ/ᶜd*. Determinative in *ᶜḏ* "reel," also ideogram for same.
28		wick	Phonogram *ḥ*.
29		swab	Phonograms *w3ḥ* and *sk*. Determinative in *ḫsr* "ward off." Variant of M1 in *mᶜr* "fortunate."
30		basket	Phonogram *nb*.
31		basket with handle	Variant (V31a) in hieroglyphic transcriptions of hieratic texts, where the handle always faces the front. Phonogram *k*.
32		wicker satchel	Variant (V96). Determinative in *g3wt* "bundle," hence also in *g3w* "absence, lack," hence also in *ḏ3rw* "need." Determinative in *msnw* "harpooner." Phonogram *msn* in *msn* "Mesen" (a Delta town).
33		bag	Variants (V34), (V35). Determinative in *ᶜrf* "pack, envelop," *stj* "perfume," and *šs(r)* "fine linen." Phonogram *g* in a few words. Ideogram for *sšrw* "grain." Determinative LINEN.
36		receptacle of cloth	Phonogram *ḥn*.
37		bandage	Determinative in *jdr* "herd," also ideogram for same. Determinative in *jdr* "bandage."
38		bandage	Determinative in *wt* "wrapping."
39		tie	Ideogram for *tjt* "Isis-knot" (amulet).

W. Stone and Ceramic Vessels

1		oil-jar	Determinative OIL. Ideogram for *mrḥt* "oil."

No.	Sign	Description
2	W1 without ties	Phonogram *b3s* in *b3stt* "Bastet" (goddess). Determinative in *b3s* "oil jar." Variant of W1.
3	alabaster basin	Variant (W4). Determinative FEAST. Ideogram for *ḥ3b* "feast."
5	T28 + W3	Ideogram for *ẖrj-ḥ3bt* "lector priest."
6	metal vessel	Determinative in *wḥ3t* "cauldron."
7	granite bowl	Variant (W8). Determinative in *m3ṯ* "granite" and *m3ṯ* "proclaim." Determinative in *3bw* "Elephantine," also ideogram for same. Determinative in *3bt* "family."
9	stone jug	Phonogram *ẖnm*.
10	cup	Determinative in words with *ʿb*. Determinative in *wsḫ* "wide" and related words, also ideogram for same. Phonogram *ḥnw* in *ḥnwt* "mistress" (from *ḥnt* "cup"). Determinative CUP. Variant of N41 in words with *bj3*.
10a	pot	Variant (Aa4). Phonogram *b3* in conjunction with E10 or G29.
12	jar stand	Variant (W11). Phonogram *g*. Determinative in *nst* "seat," also ideogram for same. Variant of W13 and O45.
13	pot	Determinative in *dšrt* "red-ware," also ideogram for same.
14	water jar	Phonogram *ḥz/ḥs*. Determinative in *ḥzt* "water jar" and *snbt* "jar," also ideogram for former.
15	water jar with water	Variant (W16). Determinative in *qbb* "cool" and *qbḥ* "cool, water," also ideogram for latter.
18	water jars in a rack	Variants (W17), (W18a), (W17a). Phonogram *ḫnt*. Ideogram for *ḫntw* "jar-rack."
19	milk jug with handle	Phonogram *mj* (originally *mr*). Determinative in *mhr* "milk jug."
20	milk jug with cover	Variant (W59). Determinative in *jrṯt* "milk."
21	wine jars	Determinative in *jrp* "wine."
22	beer jug	Variant (W23). Determinative POT. Ideogram for *ḥnqt* "beer" in offering formulas. Ideogram for *wdpw* "waiter."
24	pot	Phonogram *nw*. Phonogram *jn* in *jnk* (1S pronoun). Variant of N33 in words with *qd*. Determinative in *ḏ3ḏ3t* "council" and *nḫbt* "Nekhbet" (goddess), for unknown reasons. Often combined with Aa27 as phonogram *nḏ*. Variant of W22–23 as determinative.
24a	W24 + N35a	Ideogram for *m-ẖnw* "inside" = *m(w)-ẖ(r)-nw*.
25	W24 with legs	Phonogram *jn* in forms of *jnj* "get, fetch, bring."
54	pot pouring water	Variant of D60 and A6.

X. Bread

No.	Sign	Description
1	flat loaf of bread	Phonogram *t*. Ideogram for *t* "bread." Often phonogram for *(j)t(j)* "father," alone or in conjunction with I9.
2	tall loaf of bread	Variant (X3). Determinative BREAD, FOOD. Ideogram for *t* "bread" in offering formulas. Ideogram for *ḏḥwtj* "Thoth." Variant of X1 as phonogram for *(j)t(j)* "father."

4	bread roll	Variants , (X4a), and (X5). Determinative BREAD, FOOD. Determinative in words with *zn* (from *znw* "food offerings"). Variant of W3.
6	round loaf of bread	Determinative in *p3t* "origin" and related words; and in *p3t* "loaf."
7	half-loaf of bread	Determinative BREAD. Doubled, ideogram for *wnm* "eat."
8	bread mold	Phonogram *dj/d* (originally *ḏj*) in forms of *rdj* "give," rarely in other words.

Y. Writing, Games, and Music

1	papyrus scroll	Variants , (Y2), (Y1a). Determinative WRITING, ABSTRACT CONCEPTS. Ideogram for *dmḏ* "total." Ideogram for *mḏ3t* "scroll" and *mḏ3t* "chisel."
3	scribe's kit	Variant (Y4). Ideogram for *zẖ3* "write" and related words. Determinative in *nˁˁ* "smooth" and *ṯms* "ruddy" and related words, also ideogram for same. Determinative in *mnhd* "scribe's kit."
5	game board and pieces	Phonogram *mn*.
6	game piece	Determinative in *jb3* "game piece," also ideogram for same. Determinative in *jb3* "dance," also ideogram for same.
7	harp	Determinative in *bjnt* "harp."
8	sistrum	Determinative in *zšš t* "sistrum." Variant of S42.
10	bundle of stems	Determinative in *šˁt* "murderousness" (from *šˁ* "cut").

Z. Strokes and Figures

1	stroke	Used as ideogram of signs meant to be read as ideograms rather than phonograms (§ 3.3). Occasionally transferred to phonograms: for example, *ḥr* "face" but also preposition *ḥr* "upon." Determinative in *wˁ* "one," also ideogram for same. Written one to nine times as ideogram for numerals 1 to 9 (§ 9.1). Substitute for A1.
5	diagonal stroke	Replacement for complex or dangerous signs.
4	two strokes	Variant (Z49). Phonogram *j* as ending. Determinative DUAL.
2	three strokes	Variants , (Z2c), (Z3a), , (Z3), and (Z2a-b), , (N33a). Determinative PLURAL. Also used with words that are plural in meaning, such as collectives, food, and minerals, and with singular words ending in *w* or *wt* ("false plurals"): § 4.6. Determinative in *ḫmt* "think" (from *ḫmtw* "three").
6	hieratic variant of A13–14	Determinative DIE, ENEMY. Sometimes similar to F20.
7	from hieratic variant of G43	Phonogram *w*. Different from V1.
8	oval	Determinative ROUND, OVAL.
9	crossed sticks	Variant (Z10). Determinative BREAK, CROSS, NUMBER. Phonograms *sw3/zw3* in *sw3j* "pass" and *zw3* "cut off," *sḏ* in *sḏt* "flame," *šbn* in *šbn* "mix" and related words, *ḫbs* in *ḫbsw* "cultivation," *wp* in *wp-st* "detail, breakdown," and *wr* in a few words.
11	crossed planks	Phonogram *jm*. Variant of M42.

Aa. Unclassified

1	placenta?	Variant ○. Phoneme *ḫ*.
2	pustule or gland	Determinative SWELLING, UNHEALTHY. Variant of a number of older signs: F52 and N32 as determinative EXCREMENT, CLAY; M41 as determinative in *ʿš* "cedar"; V32 as determinative in *g3w* "absence, lack" and *g3wt* "bundle"; V38 as determinative in *wt* "bandage" and related words, and *srwḫ* "treat," also ideogram for former; W6 as determinative in *wḥ3t* "cauldron," also phonogram *wḥ3* in same and in *wḥ3t* "oasis"; W7 as determinative in *m3ṯ* "granite" and *3bw* "Elephantine"; Z10 as determinative in *ḥsb* "count," also ideogram for same.
3	Aa2 with liquid emerging	Variant of Aa2 as determinative SWELLING, UNHEALTHY.
4	pot	Variant of W10a.
5	part of a ship	Variant (Aa5a). Phonogram *ḥ(j)p*. Ideogram for *ḥjpt* "oar."
6	unknown	Determinative in *ṯm3* "cadaster" and *tm3* "mat." Different from S23.
7	unknown	Variant. Determinative in *sqr* "smash."
8	irrigation channel?	Phonogram *qn*. Determinative of *sp3t* "estate, farm," also ideogram for same. Determinative of *ḏ3ḏ3t* "council." Variant of N24 as ideogram in *sp3t* "nome"; O34 as phonogram *z* in *zmjt* "desert"; V26 as phonogram *ʿḏ*.
9	unknown	Determinative in *ḫwd* "rich."
10	unknown	Determinative in *drf* "writing."
11	platform	Variants , , (Aa12). Phonogram *m3ʿ*. Determinative in *ṯnt3t* "platform."
13	unknown	Variants (Aa14), (Aa15, with horizontals parallel). Phonograms *jm* and *m*. Variant of Aa16.
16	front half of Aa13	Ideogram for *gs* "side, half," phonogram *gs*.
17	lid	Variant (Aa18). Phonogram *s3*. Ideogram for *s3* "back."
19	unknown	Determinative in *ḥr* "prepare" and *ḥrj* "terrified" and related words. Determinative in *ṯ3r* "secure."
20	bag for clothing	Phonogram *ʿpr*.
21	unknown	Variant (Aa22). Phonogram *wḏʿ*. Ideogram for *wḏʿw* "judged one" (term used in place of *stẖ/stš* "Seth").
24	warp between stakes	Variant (Aa23). Determinative in *mḏd* "puncture, press, adhere" and related words, also ideogram for same.
25	unknown	Ideogram in *zm3* "stolist" (priest's title).
26	unknown	Determinative in *sbj* "rebel."
27	spindle	Phonogram *nḏ*. Often used in conjunction with W24.
28	builder's level	Variant (Aa29). Phonogram *qd*.
31	frieze element	Variant (Aa30). Determinative in *ḫkr* "adorn" and related words, also ideogram for same.
32	bow	Variant. Phonogram *sṯj/stj* in *t3-sṯj* "Nubia" and *stj* "ocher."

From James P. Allen, *Middle Egyptian: An Introduction to the Language and Culture of Hieroglyphs*, Cambridge, 1999, pp. 423–448.

CHAPTER 6

Ge'ez (Aksum)

GENE GRAGG

1. HISTORICAL AND CULTURAL CONTEXTS

There are four great kingdoms on earth: the first is the kingdom of Babylon and Persia; the second is the kingdom of Rome; the third is the kingdom of the Axumites; the fourth is the kingdom of the Chinese. Mani, *Kephalaia* LXXVII

1.1 Historical background

This third-century Manichaean text (cf. Kobishchanov 1979:59) shows the reputation enjoyed, at least sporadically, by the shadowy East African kingdom which was just over the horizon of the known classical universe, and which from time to time impinged on the consciousness of the world of late antiquity. Its capital city, Aksum, was located near the northern edge of the great Ethiopian plateau which rises abruptly behind the Red Sea coast, a mirror image to the coastal escarpment on the Yemeni side, and slopes down gently into East Africa, its steep southeast flank forming the northern wall of the Great Rift Valley in Africa.

The Kingdom of Aksum itself arose toward the end of the second century AD, and continued to play an important role in the region until the rise of Islam. But prior to that, the region of Aksum had been the site of a South Arabian colony, centered at Yeha, about 30 kilometers east of Aksum, paleographically dated to around 500 BC by monumental inscriptions of the classical Sabean type. Presumably, given the intensely commercial orientation of the South Arabian city-states and the geographical proximity (Arabia and the Horn of Africa are separated by only 40 kilometers in the Bab-el-Mandab straits at the southern end of the Red Sea), contacts based on trade relations go back even further. It is clear that many of the political and cultural traditions of the kingdom stemmed out of this colonization or its antecedents, and linguistically, as will be seen, Ethiopic Semitic is a close cousin of Old South Arabian. However, it is not possible to derive Ethiopic Semitic, or any of its constituent branches and languages, from any single attested form of Old South Arabian.

1.2 Linguistic history

Classical Ethiopic, the language of Aksum, whose self-designation is Ge'ez ([gəʕəz], etymology uncertain), is presumably derived from one or more forms of South Semitic brought from Yemen, probably in the first half of the first millennium BC. In all likelihood, Ethiopic Semitic evolved out of a South-Arabian-based trade lingua franca, perhaps passing through stages of piginization and creolization familiar from differentiation and development of language families elsewhere in the world (e.g., Romance). The substratum languages in this development presumably belonged to the Cushitic language family, and a number of important early loanwords from Cushitic are evident in Ge'ez – but at present it is not possible to reconstruct the mechanisms of this development. Ge'ez disappeared as a spoken language probably some time before the tenth century AD, but continued as the liturgical language of the Ethiopian Orthodox Church, and as the only official written language of Ethiopia practically up to the end of the nineteenth century.

As has been implied, Ge'ez is one of a number of Semitic languages spoken in Ethiopia. Although Ge'ez is the earliest attested Ethio-Semitic language, it cannot be taken as identical with Proto-Ethio-Semitic. One simple example – the word for "not" had to be **ʔal* in Proto-Ethio-Semitic (e.g., Amharic, *al* "not"), and does indeed have the form *ʔl* in Old South Arabian. In Ge'ez, however, it has become everywhere *i* (< **ay* by palatalization of the /l/), except for a fossilized remnant preserved in the word *albo* (< *al-bä-hu* "not in it") "not exist; not have." The other Ethio-Semitic languages could not have inherited this lexical item from Ge'ez in its present form.

Within the Ethio-Semitic subfamily, Ge'ez, together with Tigre and Tigrinya, falls into the Northern Ethio-Semitic branch. Here it is closely related to modern Tigre (northern highlands and Red Sea coastal plain), and perhaps stands in a more or less proximate ancestral relationship to Tigrinya (Northern Ethiopia and Eritrea), which probably started to emerge as a distinct entity on the home territory of Ge'ez from around the tenth century on. The remaining Ethio-Semitic languages (a dozen or so, including Amharic) belong to a separate (Southern) group, which cannot be derived from any attested Northern Ethio-Semitic language. Northern and Southern Ethio-Semitic, however, do seem to constitute a distinct genetic node in the Semitic family tree, a node which has thus the following structure:

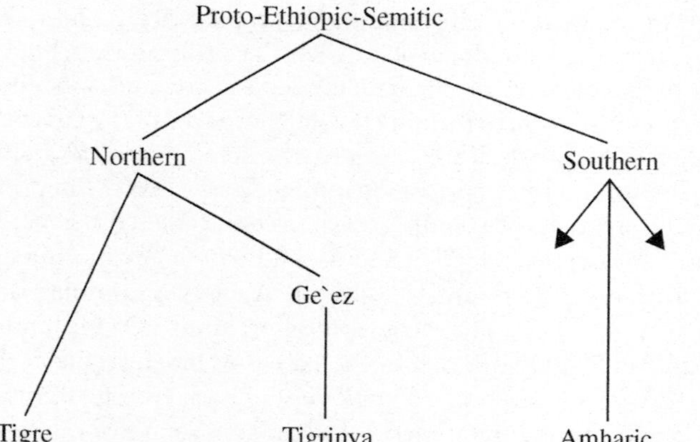

Figure 6.1 The Ethio-Semitic subfamily

On the level of Semitic as a whole, Ge'ez is most closely related to a Southern group of Semitic languages that includes Epigraphic and Modern South Arabian. The exact historical relationships among Epigraphic South Arabian (see *WAL* Ch. 15), Modern South Arabian, and Ethio-Semitic have been difficult to establish because of what was until quite recently insufficient data on the Modern South Arabian languages, and because of the phonological indeterminacy and morphological poverty of the textual evidence for Epigraphic South Arabian (an extensive corpus, but written in one of the more resolutely vowelless of the Semitic writing systems, and in a discourse format which, in spite of a respectable diversity of subject matter, managed to restrict itself almost entirely to third-person pronominal and verbal forms).

Even more difficult has been the relation of these three to the quite distinct Northern (Classical) Arabic, which we will henceforth refer to simply as "Arabic." At one time it had been common to group South Arabian, Ethiopic, and Arabic into one *South Semitic* subfamily, and to appeal to a small inventory of shared features:

1. On the level of phonology – the presence of a voiceless labial continuant /f/, instead of the stop /p/ as is the case in Canaanite, Aramaic (frequently grouped together in a subfamily referred to as *Northwest Semitic*), and Akkadian (usually considered to represent by itself a separate *East Semitic* branch).
2. On the level of morphology – the presence of a highly developed system of *internal* plurals, formed by changes in stem syllabicity and vocalism (a feature occurring only restrictedly in Canaanite, and apparently absent in Aramaic and Akkadian; see §4.1.1.2 for the patterns attested in Ge'ez).

More recently, however, there has been a tendency to give more weight to an innovation which Arabic shares with Northwest Semitic. Through this innovation, an ancestral *present stem* characterized by a bi-syllabic CVCVC pattern (and perhaps also by gemination of the middle consonant), found in Akkadian (*i-parras* "he decides") and Ethiopic (*yəqattəl* "he kills"), is dropped in favor of a CCVC (Arabic *ya-qtulu*, Hebrew *yi-qṭol* "he kills") pattern, which either coexisted with the bisyllabic pattern in Proto-Semitic, or was innovated on the basis of an inherited jussive stem pattern (Ethiopic *yəqtəl*, Arabic *ya-qtul*).

As opposed to this northern innovation, there is a genuinely southern feature, shared by Ethiopic and South Arabian, not present in Arabic. This has to do with the initial consonant of the first- and second-person subject suffixes of the past tense (the relevant forms for Arabic and Ge'ez, together with those of the Akkadian stative, are given in §4.3.1). In the (i) first-person singular and (ii) second-person singular and plural forms, Arabic, like Hebrew and Aramaic, has /t/, whereas Ge'ez, like Modern South Arabian, has /k/ (and we now know that Old South Arabian also had /k/, certainly in the second singular, and probably in the other forms also, see *WAL* Ch. 15, §4.3.1). Since 1969 many Semitists have subscribed to a theory first enunciated by Robert Hetzron: namely, that the earliest form of this paradigm can be seen in the Akkadian stative paradigm (where the consonant is preceded by a long /ā/). Here, as in the independent pronoun, the first person is marked by a /k/ and the second person by a /t/. In Western Semitic, the northern languages would have generalized the non-third-person consonant to /t/, whereas the southern languages would have generalized the /k/.

Giving a family tree interpretation to this line of argument, Arabic would be taken out of South Semitic, and either joined to Hebrew and Aramaic as a third branch of Northwest Semitic, or put into a separate Central (Western) branch – resulting in a Semitic family tree with a shape like that of Figure 6.2:

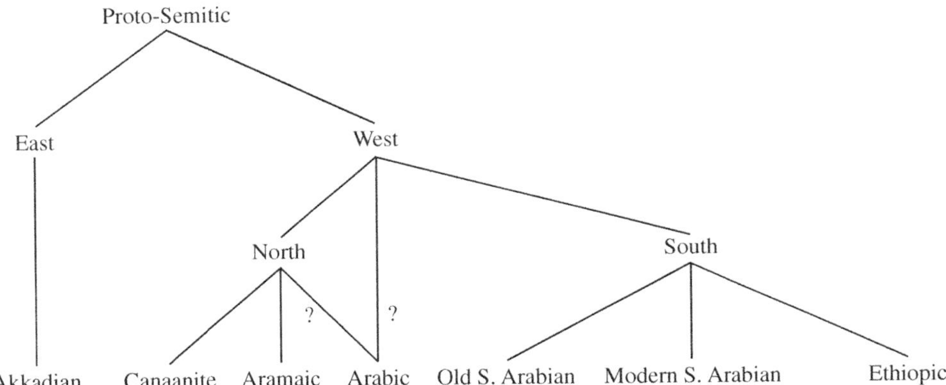

Figure 6.2 The Semitic language family

Using a more wave-like model of language differentiation, of course, one could simply observe the obvious correlation of geographical location and linguistic subgrouping and postulate that in the area (roughly noncoastal Syro-Palestinian) in which Semitic, having split from Afro-Asiatic, began to differentiate into various branches, different features were spreading from different centers of innovation. The central position of Arabic in this network of changes enabled it to share both in innovations originating from northern (reformation of the present tense, generalization of /t/ in the past) and in innovations from the south (*p > f, elaboration of internal plurals).

1.3 Ge'ez literature

The corpus of written Ge'ez material can be conveniently divided into three groups of texts.

1.3.1 Axumite and Pre-Axumite monumental inscriptions

The "prehistory" of this corpus is formed by about 160 Old South Arabian texts, many of them occurring in or near the core of the later Aksumite Ethiopian kingdom, and attested from around the sixth century BC. About 13 of these are "royal" in content. The Aksumite corpus itself is formed by about a dozen longish royal inscriptions in Ge'ez, the most important of which concern at least two kings called Ezana (perhaps mid-fourth century and late fifth century AD). Six of the Ge'ez inscriptions are written in the Old South Arabian script, 3 in nonvocalized Ethiopic, and 4 in the earliest attestation of vocalized Ethiopic script (see §2). The inscriptions of Ezana I are pagan, as are the first ones of Ezana II. The last ones of Ezana II attest to the introduction of monotheism (presumably Christian) to the court at Aksum, while those of his successors are explicitly Christian. The last few inscriptions may be as late as the ninth to eleventh century. There are also about 230 other short Aksumite inscriptions in vocalized and unvocalized Ethiopic – at least 9 of them from a period before Ezana I. Related to this corpus are 18 Greek inscriptions found on Aksumite territory, of which 6 are royal. At least 3 of the major royal inscriptions exist in three versions, Greek, Ge'ez written in Old South Arabian script, and Ge'ez written in Ethiopic script.

1.3.2 Early Christian texts

Although there are few, if any, extant manuscripts earlier than the twelfth century, scholars have isolated a corpus of texts which represent the earliest layer of Ge'ez literature – the first texts drawn up to define and propagate Chrisitianity in Ethiopia. The process of translation of these texts from Greek had begun by the fifth century, and later royal inscriptions contain explicit citations from the Book of Psalms. This body of texts includes the Ge'ez translation of the Bible and related apocrypha, liturgical texts, some lives of saints, some patristic fragments, and a version of the monastic Rules of Pachomius. Although the original translations date from a period when Ge'ez was still a spoken language, we know that many of the texts were revised in the light of standard Arabic redactions (particularly the Arabic "Vulgate" Bible). In view of this revision, especially given the lack of a long manuscript tradition, it is sometimes difficult to establish exact details of some aspects of this earliest manuscript corpus.

1.3.3 Ge'ez: post-1000 AD

After a very obscure period of isolation starting with the collapse of Byzantium in the Near East, and continuing during the first centuries of Islam, the Ethiopian church reestablished around the year 1000 an official contact with Egypt that would last until the end of World War II. There was a new flourishing of ecclesiastical literature of all genres (much of it translated from the Arabic, in turn translated from Greek, Coptic, Syriac, or other sources). In addition, an original secular or court literature arose in the form of royal chronicles, legal texts, even a sort of national epic (the *Kəbrä Nägäst* "Glory of Kings," an elaboration of the legend of Solomon and Sheba). A more popular magic literature also took shape, centered around the production of amulets and "magic scrolls" – a productivity that continued into the present century.

2. WRITING SYSTEMS

The Ethiopian consonantal script is derived more or less proximately from some version of the South Semitic writing system which also appears in the Epigraphic South Arabian inscriptions (see *WAL* Ch. 15, §2). The earliest Aksumite inscriptions are written without indication of vocalization. In a major innovation, introduced with apparent abruptness in the later inscriptions of Ezana II, an approach to vocalization appears which is unique among Semitic scripts. Alone among these scripts, Ethiopic represents vowels, not by a separate set of (superlinear or sublinear) vowel signs, but by means of a more or less uniform modification of the basic letter-shape. The base form of the consonant sign (the so-called *first-order* form) is taken to represent the consonant followed by the *unmarked* short vowel /ä/. Six other alterations of the basic shape are introduced to represent the consonant followed by the vowels /i, u, a, e, ə, o/ – the *second* through *seventh orders*. Note that the sixth order is used in addition to represent the consonant in isolation (with no following vowel). Each sign thus represents a CV sequence, and a 26-character consonantal script is thereby transformed into a 182-character syllabary. To this inventory are added five forms for each of the consonants *k*, *g*, *q*, and *h* to represent the labiovelars /k^w, g^w, q^w, $ḫ^w$/ plus the vowels /ä, i, a, e, ə/, for a grand total of 202 signs. The resulting basic syllabary, in the traditional Ethiopic order (which is also the order followed by dictionaries of Ethiopic languages which give head words in Ethiopic script), can be seen in Tables 6.1 and 6.2.

In fact, an influence from the Indian subcontinent cannot be excluded a priori in the development of this vocalized system – some of the first mentions of the Aksumite state are in itineraries of voyagers between the Mediterranean, the Red Sea and Indian Ocean spice coasts, India, and Ceylon. On the other hand it is not far-fetched to see some of the character modifications (note for example the *omicron*-like shape of many of the "seventh-order" character modifications) as vocalic subscripts influenced by the shape of the corresponding Greek vowel, as in Syriac vocalization. There is also a mystery concerning the historical origin of the order of consonants in the syllabary, which is quite different from that of the Hebrew, Aramaic, and Arabic scripts. However, there is some evidence that at least the beginning of this order – *h*, *l*, *ḥ*, *m* . . . – was known and used in ancient Ugarit, and also in Southern Arabia.

As an addition to the syllabary as such, Table 6.3 gives the Ethiopic number notation system. Although the general ductus and appearance of the numerals is influenced by those of the syllabary, the system is clearly borrowed from the Greek α, β, γ, δ, . . . = 1, 2, 3, 4, . . . and so forth.

Although the Ethiopic writing system provided a generally adequate representation of Ge'ez words (and continues to provide the same service for Amharic and Tigrinya), there are three aspects of phonological shape which are not directly represented: (i) stress, frequently not noted in practical orthographies in any case; (ii) lack of a way of indicating the phonologically prominent and morphologically important feature of gemination (a two-dot diacritic, introduced to represent gemination of consonants in European grammars and dictionaries of Ethiopic since the seventeenth century, never became part of the manuscript or printed Ethiopic orthographic tradition); and (iii) lack of an unambiguous

Table 6.1 The Ge'ez syllabary

	ä	*u*	*i*	*a*	*e*	*ə*	*o*
h	ሀ	ሁ	ሂ	ሃ	ሄ	ህ	ሆ
l	ለ	ሉ	ሊ	ላ	ሌ	ል	ሎ
ḥ	ሐ	ሑ	ሒ	ሓ	ሔ	ሕ	ሖ
m	መ	ሙ	ሚ	ማ	ሜ	ም	ሞ
ś	ሠ	ሡ	ሢ	ሣ	ሤ	ሥ	ሦ
r	ረ	ሩ	ሪ	ራ	ሬ	ር	ሮ
s	ሰ	ሱ	ሲ	ሳ	ሴ	ስ	ሶ
q	ቀ	ቁ	ቂ	ቃ	ቄ	ቅ	ቆ
b	በ	ቡ	ቢ	ባ	ቤ	ብ	ቦ
t	ተ	ቱ	ቲ	ታ	ቴ	ት	ቶ
ḫ	ኀ	ኁ	ኂ	ኃ	ኄ	ኅ	ኆ
n	ነ	ኑ	ኒ	ና	ኔ	ን	ኖ
ʔ	አ	ኡ	ኢ	ኣ	ኤ	እ	ኦ
k	ከ	ኩ	ኪ	ካ	ኬ	ክ	ኮ
w	ወ	ዉ	ዊ	ዋ	ዌ	ው	ዎ
ʕ	ዐ	ዑ	ዒ	ዓ	ዔ	ዕ	ዖ
z	ዘ	ዙ	ዚ	ዛ	ዜ	ዝ	ዞ
y	የ	ዩ	ዪ	ያ	ዬ	ይ	ዮ
d	ደ	ዱ	ዲ	ዳ	ዴ	ድ	ዶ
g	ገ	ጉ	ጊ	ጋ	ጌ	ግ	ጎ
ṭ	ጠ	ጡ	ጢ	ጣ	ጤ	ጥ	ጦ
p̣	ጰ	ጱ	ጲ	ጳ	ጴ	ጵ	ጶ
ṣ	ጸ	ጹ	ጺ	ጻ	ጼ	ጽ	ጾ
ḍ	ፀ	ፁ	ፂ	ፃ	ፄ	ፅ	ፆ
f	ፈ	ፉ	ፊ	ፋ	ፌ	ፍ	ፎ

Table 6.2 The labiovelar symbols

	ä	*i*	*a*	*e*	*ə*
q	ቈ	ቊ	ቋ	ቌ	ቍ
ḫ	ኈ	ኊ	ኋ	ኌ	ኍ
k	ኰ	ኲ	ኳ	ኴ	ኵ
g	ጐ	ጒ	ጓ	ጔ	ጕ

way of representing a consonant not followed by a vowel, i.e., in word- or syllable-final position (note the parallel ambiguity inherent in the Hebrew schwa symbol). As a consequence, an orthographic representation $k_1l_6b_6$ (where C_n is the nth-order shape of the consonant C) might conceivably stand for any of the following values:

(1) kälb käləb kälbə källəb
käləbb käləbbə källəbb källəbbə

(excluding many values such as those including /#kk.../ or /...llbb#/ or /...ləbə#/ on general phonotactic grounds).

Table 6.3 The Ethiopic numerals

1	፩	11	፲፩	20	፳
2	፪	12	፲፪	30	፴
3	፫	13	፲፫	40	፵
4	፬	14	፲፬	50	፶
5	፭	15	፲፭	60	፷
6	፮	16	፲፮	70	፸
7	፯	17	፲፯	80	፹
8	፰	18	፲፰	90	፺
9	፱	19	፲፱	100	፻
10	፲			200	፪፻
				1,000	፲፻
				10,000	፼
				100,000	፲፼

3. PHONOLOGY

Our principal source of explicit information for phonology is the living pronunciation tradition of ecclesiastical Ge'ez – a basically oral tradition which is only sporadically, and for the most part relatively recently, recorded in any written form. This tradition appears to be fairly uniform, and represents prestige pronunciation of Ge'ez in the central Ethiopian plateau (thus in a largely Amharic milieu) where royal residences and many centers of ecclesiastical influence have tended to be located since the decline of Aksum. This pronunciation tradition is thoroughly Amharicizing in its treatment of consonantal values, although more "Tigrinya-izing" pronunciation patterns seem to exist in the north. To the extent that the traditional pronunciation preserves stress, gemination, and syllable-structure patterns, which are at least in part distinct from those found either in Amharic or in Tigrinya, they may well reflect the state of affairs in an earlier stage of Ge'ez itself.

In any case, although the basic features of the pronunciation tradition are relatively clear, there is still much to be done by way of scholarly investigation and evaluation of this tradition. It must also be kept in mind that, apart from the relatively small corpus of Aksumite inscriptions, apparently from the early and formative period of classical Ge'ez, almost all Ge'ez texts were either produced in a period when Ge'ez was no longer a spoken language, or are preserved in a long, poorly studied manuscript tradition, with a gap of many centuries between the period of formation of the core classical corpus (Bible translation, key liturgical, hagiographic, and monastic texts – perhaps sixth century) and the oldest extant manuscripts (rarely older than the fourteenth century).

3.1 Consonants

In evaluating phonological representations of Ge'ez, it is important to keep a number of things distinct:

1. The conventional scholarly transliteration of the Ge'ez writing system. This is largely governed by conventional Semitist, largely Arabicizing notation under the constraint of providing one transliteration symbol for each consonant in the Ge'ez writing

system. Western scholarly pronunciations of Ge'ez tend to be unduly influenced by this transliteration notation. All Ge'ez citations in this chapter are in this traditional notation.

2. A largely Amharicizing traditional pronunciation that simply ignores consonantal distinctions which do not exist in Amharic.
3. The most completely preserved Ethiopian Semitic inventory of the original consonantal distinctions (not including, of course, new consonantal distinctions introduced since the disappearance of Ge'ez – for example, many new palatalized spirants and affricates). Here Tigrinya will serve.
4. The pronunciation of the corresponding consonants as reconstructed for South Arabian.
5. The corresponding Arabic consonants.
6. For control, the system as it appears in Hebrew.

A number of Ge'ez consonants will have the same representation in all five systems: *t, d, k, g, f, ʔ, m, n, r, l, w, y*. Another series of consonants, the labiovelars *k*^{w}, *q*^{w}, *g*^{w}, *ḫ*^{w}, are unique as such in Semitic, but correspond in cognates with the nonlabialized *k, q, g, ḫ*. For the others, the cognate sets yield the correspondence series of Table 6.4:

Table 6.4 Semitic consonantal correspondence series

South				Central	North
Ethio-Semitic					
Ge'ez (translit.)	Ge'ez (trad.)	Tigrinya	Old South Arabian	Arabic	Hebrew
P	P	P	—	—	—
Ṗ	P′	P′	—	—	—
f	f	f	f	f	p
ṭ	t′	t′	t′ <ṭ>	ṭ	ṭ
q	k′	k′	k′ <q>	q	q
s	s	s	s <s_3>	s	s
s	s	s	š <s_1>	s	š
s	s	s	θ	θ	š
ś	s	s	ɬ <s_2>	š	ś
ṣ	s′	s′	s′ <ṣ>	ṣ	ṣ
ḍ	s′	s′	ɬ′ <ḍ>	ḍ	ṣ
ḍ	s′	s′	θ′ <ẓ>	ẓ	ṣ
z	z	z	z	z	z
z	z	z	ð	ð	z
ḫ	h	ḥ	x	x	ḥ
ḥ	h	ḥ	ḥ	ḥ	ḥ
ʕ	ʔ	ʕ	ʕ	ʕ	ʕ
ʕ	ʔ	ʕ	γ	γ	ʕ

Details of interpretation are given below, but it is important to note the following regarding Table 6.4: the traditional pronunciation (column 2) gives consonantal signs essentially their Amharic value – pharyngeals ʕ and *ḥ* (/ħ/) merge with ʔ and *h* respectively; <ṣ> and <ḍ> are both pronounced ṣ, and <s> and <ś> are both pronounced *s*. Tigrinya (as well as Tigre) preserves the distinction between ʔ and ʕ and between *ḥ* and *h*. But *no Ethiopic language* and *no element of the pronunciation tradition* provides the least bit of information about the pronunciation of the Ge'ez graphemes <ś>, <ḍ>, and <ḫ>. Nevertheless, since the earliest pre-Aksumite writing system did adopt these consonant signs from the parent South Semitic alphabet, while excluding a large number of other signs representing consonants which had already merged in Ethiopic, they must have represented distinct consonants in early and classical Ge'ez. It is not clear when the mergers took place. The graphemes seem to be used consistently in the earlier monumental inscriptions, and in some strands of the manuscript tradition (recall, however, what was already said concerning the primitive state of the study of this tradition). However, variant writings of the same word with <ḥ> and <ḫ> begin to appear already in some late monumental inscriptions, and, in the low end of the manuscript tradition, <ḫ, ḥ> (and sometimes <h>), <ḍ, ṣ>, and <ś, s> are used as virtual allographs. In Table 6.5 the consonants corresponding to <ś>, <ḍ>, and <ḫ> are interpreted with the help of data from cognate languages (note especially the South Arabian correspondences in Table 6.4).

3.1.1 Voiceless labials (the graphemes < p, ṗ, f >)

Ge'ez is unique among the Semitic languages in having not only a voiceless labial stop and continuant, but an *emphatic* labial stop as well (see §3.1.2). Akkadian, Aramaic, and Canaanite have only a /p/, while Arabic and other South Semitic languages have only /f/. Ge'ez with /f/ thus patterns historically, as expected, with South Semitic and Arabic. A large number of the occurrences of /p/ and /p'/ occur in loanwords, mostly from or by way of Greek: for example, *piläs* "temple, gate" (from Greek πύλη (*pýlē*) "gate"); *ṗaṗṗ as* "metropolitan, patriarch" (from πάππας" (*páppās*) "father, title of priests"). However, there are a large number of other occurrences, fully integrated into the native grammar and vocabulary of Ge'ez, where the origin of the stop is much less clear: for example, *heṗä* "strike, throw, shoot with an arrow"; *häppälä* "wash clothes."

3.1.2 Emphatic consonants (the graphemes < ṗ, ṭ, q, q^{W}, ṣ, ḍ >)

As can be seen from Table 6.5, a coarticulatory feature usually called "emphasis" in Semitic is realized as *glottalization* in modern Ethiopian Semitic. Since the Arabic realization of this feature, *velarization* or *pharyngealization*, was once automatically imputed to early Semitic, glottalization in Ethio-Semitic was ascribed to the influence of language contact with earlier Cushitic languages in Ethiopia. However, the relatively recent discovery that emphatic consonants are also glottalized in the Modern South Arabian languages makes it possible that this might be a common South Semitic feature, and perhaps even, as some have argued, common Semitic. Note that /s'/ (ṣ), the glottalized version of /s/, in modern Ethio-Semitic languages, as in many languages worldwide, tends to be realized phonetically as an affricate $[t^{s}]$. The phonetic value of Ge'ez *ḍ* is uncertain; however, since it merged with the fricative *ṣ* (see §3.1.3), it had also become a continuant by the time of merger.

3.1.3 Sibilants (the graphemes < s, ś, ṣ, ḍ, z >)

The consonants represented by the graphemes <ś> and <ḍ> have merged respectively with *s* and *ṣ* in the phonological system represented by the traditional pronunciation – and, indeed, in all modern Ethiopic Semitic. These two consonants are reflexes of a lateralized series (voiceless and glottalized) in Proto-Semitic, also attested in South Arabian. There is, however, no evidence either in the tradition or in Ethiopic Semitic as to what value these consonants may have had in Ge'ez. For <ḍ> the transcription value *ḍ* comes from the conventional representation of the etymologically corresponding segment in Arabic and Old

South Arabian; while ș is an older conventional representation of the Proto-Semitic voiceless lateral, and also of the grapheme which represents its Hebrew reflex. In some grammars and dictionaries, Ge'ez <ś> is transcribed as š, since it corresponds etymologically to Arabic /š/. There are, however, some major problems with this practice. In the first place, it is not certain whether, or at what periods, Ge'ez <ś> might have been pronounced as [š]. More seriously, this transcription could lead to confusion, since a genuine /š/ did in time develop in Ethiopic Semitic (mostly from palatalization of /s/), and a new grapheme for it, properly transcribed as š, was created by adding a diacritic to the grapheme <s>. Moreover, this <š> grapheme *can* occur in late Ge'ez texts, usually in modern personal or place names.

3.1.4 Laryngeals (the graphemes < ʔ, ʕ, ḫ, ḥ, h >)

As can be seen from Table 6.4, in the pronunciation tradition the only accepted values for these consonants are [ʔ] for the first two, and [h] for the remainder. Moreover, as already noted, no Ethio-Semitic language has kept *ḫ* distinct from *ḥ*, Finally, in Ge'ez, as in many varieties of Semitic, there is no phonological distinction in word-initial position between simple vocalic (#[V-]) and glottal (#[ʔV-]) onset, even though the writing system has to use a glottal-stop symbol (<ʔ>) to "carry" the vowel.

3.1.5 Labiovelars (the graphemes < k^{w}, q^{w}, g^{w}, $ḫ^{w}$ >)

All of the velars of Ge'ez developed a corresponding labiovelar phoneme. In some cases, there is an unambiguous conditioning environment with a (long) rounded vowel: thus, the denominal verb *tärg*^{w}*ämä* "translate" comes ultimately from the Aramaic loanword *targūm* "translation"; *əḫ*^{w} "brother" shows the influence of the Proto-Ethiopic, and Proto-Semitic, long stem-vowel in *aḫū-. In other cases, derivation from a form with such an environment must be assumed.

3.1.6 Summary of consonantal features

With the foregoing reservations, the articulatory features of Ge'ez consonants will be interpreted as in Table 6.5:

Table 6.5 Consonants of Ge'ez

	Place of articulation						
Manner of articulation	Labial	Dental/ Alveolar	?	Velar	Labiovelar	Pharyngeal	Glottal
Stop							
Voiceless	p	t		k	k^{w}		ʔ
Glottalized	ṗ	ṭ		q	q^{w}		
Voiced	b	d		g	g^{w}		
Fricative							
Voiceless	f	s	ś	ḫ	$ḫ^{w}$	ḥ	h
Glottalized		ṣ		ḍ			
Voiced		z				ʕ	
Sonorant							
Nasals	m	n					
Liquids		r, l					
Glides		y			w		

3.2 Vowels

We can assume that Proto-Ethio-Semitic possessed the common Semitic vowel system, with three short vowels, three long, and two diphthongs:

(2)

Short		*Long*		*Diphthong*
i	u	ī	ū	
a		ā		ai au

The Ge'ez system then resulted from a series of changes:

(3) A. *i, *u → ə
B. *a → ä
C. *ai → e, *au → o

As a consequence of A and B, the quantity of the long vowels was made redundant, and they became simply the unmarked low, high-front, and high-back vowels of the system: in other words, **ā* > *a*, **ī* > *i*, **ū* > *u*. The monophthongizing of the diphthongs to /e, o/ rounded out the system, which is attested in the earliest vocalized texts, and remains remarkably stable even in many of the modern Ethiopian Semitic languages:

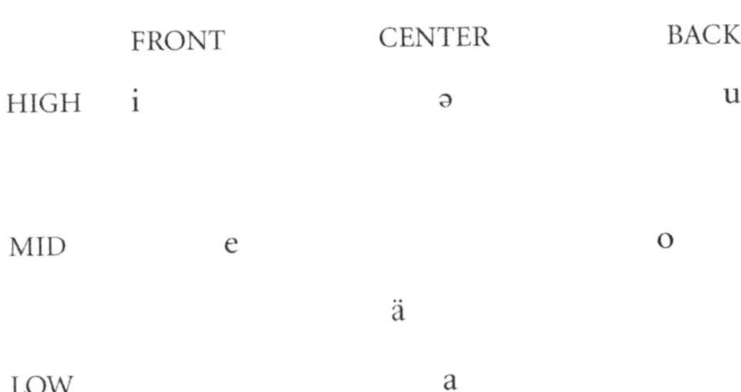

Figure 6.3 Vowels of Ge'ez

Here /ä/ is a low-central vowel, higher and more forward than /a/, secondarily perhaps also shorter. Note that in historicizing transliterations, what are here noted as the vowels /ä/ and /a/ are written as /a/ and /ā/ respectively.

3.3 Phonotaxis and syllable structure

The preferred syllable-type is (C)V(C), thus with no initial or final clusters; maximally, clusters of two consonants are allowed intervocalically.

3.3.1 Word-initial clusters

Word-initial clusters are resolved by epenthetic ə. Thus the imperative, whose systematic form for the simple stem of the verbs *ngr* "speak" and *lbs* "wear" would be /ngər/, /lbäs/, becomes *nəgər*, *ləbäs*. There is no productive rule for breaking up clusters with an initial vowel, but there are some isolated lexical patterns such as *əgziˀ* "lord" from the root *gzˀ* "rule"; note also the form of some common complementizers and conjunctions *əsmä* "because," *ənzä* "while," *əskä* "until" (of uncertain etymology, although the first may be connected to *səm* "name").

3.3.2 Word-final clusters

Word-final clusters are less clear. Most studies of traditional pronunciation seem to agree that word-final clusters of two consonants are not invariably broken up by an epenthetic vowel. Thus, Makonnen (1984) transcribes: *baḥrə* "sea"; *ṭäbbäbtə* "wise men" (masculine plural of *ṭäbib*); *yəblə* "he says, he will say" (irregular imperfective of *bəhlä*). The most common Western scholarly practice would be to pronounce the first two with a final cluster ([baḥr], [ṭäbbäbt]), and the last with epenthetic or reduced [ə], on the strength of the presumed underlying pattern: [yəbəl] reduced from **yəbəhhəl*, from **yəbahhəl* (by laryngeal rule [4B] below).

3.3.3 Gemination

Gemination is a widely employed inflectional and derivational process in Ge'ez, as in the rest of Ethio-Semitic. In the traditional pronunciation, all consonants can geminate except the laryngeals. In general, gemination seems to be limited to vowel-pattern environments in which the introduction of gemination will not give rise to problematic consonant clusters.

3.3.4 Laryngeal effects

A series of rules affect the vowels /ä, ə/ in the vicinity of laryngeals (ʾ, ʕ, ḫ, ḥ, h/), which find their most productive application in the conjugation of verbs containing a laryngeal as a radical (see §4.3.3). The following is simply a descriptive statement of the phenomena, with some illustrative examples (L = laryngeal):

(4) A. ə → ä / _ Lä
Ex.: yäḥärrəs "he plows" (cf. yənäggər "he speaks")
B. ä → ə / _ L [V, + high] ([V, + high] = /i, ə, u/)
Ex.: yəməḥər "he is merciful" (cf. yən**ä**ggər)
C. ä → ə / _ L_{final} V
Ex.: asməʕ-ä "he caused to hear" (cf. alb**ä**sä "he clothed")
D. ä → a / _ L {C, #}
Ex.: säm**a**ʕ-ku "I heard" (cf. läb**ä**sku "I wore")
E. ä → a / L _
Ex.: ḥaqäfä "he embraced" (cf. n**ä**gärä "he spoke")

3.3.5 Glide effects

There are a number of interactions of vowels and glides. As can be seen from the chart of labiovelar graphemes (Table 6.2), a labiovelar cannot be followed by a rounded vowel. On the other hand, there is a neutralization of the distinction between a labiovelar followed by /ə, ä/ and a velar followed by /u, o/: for example, *qwəl* ~ *qul* "bunch of grapes"; *qwäṭiṭ* ~ *qoṭiṭ* "slender." Most of the vowel-glide configurations which arise in the morphology can be handled by the following rules:

(5) A. äw → o (fätäwkä ~ fätokä "you loved")
B. äy → e (sätäykä [sätekä rare] "you drank")
C. *əw → u (*yəfättəw → yəfättu "he loves")
D. *əy → i (*yəsättəy → yəsätti "he drinks")

Of these rules, the first is optional, the second is rare, while the third and fourth are obligatory.

3.3.6 Consonant assimilation

This involves only the two consonants /t/ and /k/, widely utilized in affixation in Ge'ez. The velar /-k/, which occurs in suffixes marking first- and second-person subject in the verb, assimilates to a preceding (i.e., stem-final) velar stop: for example, *ädäg+kä* > *ädäggä* "you left"; *säräq+ku* > *säräqqu* "I stole." The dental /t-/ occurs as a prefix marking passive-reflexive derived stems in the imperfective tense (the shape of the prefix in the perfective is *tä-*). It assimilates fully to a following dental stop or sibilant: thus, *yəssämmä-* "he is heard"; cf. *yətqättäl* "he is killed." As a suffix /t-/ marks feminine (and also plural) forms of nouns and participles. Here it assimilates to a preceding dental stop: for example, *kəbud+t* > *kəbədd* "heavy" (fem.). Note, however, idiosyncratically "one" (fem.) *ahatti* < *ahad+ti*, "daughter"+t. wälätt < wäläd.

3.4 Stress

Our knowledge of stress depends completely on the still inadequately studied traditional pronunciation. At present some general patterns seem to hold:

1. Verbs are stressed on the penult except in the second-person plural feminine: *yə́ngər* "may he speak," *yənä́ggər* "he speaks," *nägä́rä* "he spoke," *yənäggə́ru* "they speak"; but *nägärkə́n* "you (2nd pl. fem.) spoke."
2. Nouns and pronouns have stem-final stress (i.e., not on the suffix vowel of the accusative; see §4.1.1.3): *nəgús* (nom.), *nəgúsä* (acc.) "king."
3. Personal pronouns as well as verbs and nouns with pronominal suffixes follow special patterns, giving rise to minimal pairs like *yənäggərá* (< yənäggər+ha) "he speaks to her" versus *yənäggə́ra* "they (fem.) speak."

4. MORPHOLOGY

4.1 Nominal morphology

Nominal morphology in Ge'ez expresses three morphosyntactic categories: gender (masculine, feminine), number (singular, plural), and case (absolute, accusative-construct). Under this heading will be treated nouns as well as adjectives and participles.

4.1.1 Nouns

4.1.1.1 Gender

In comparison with other classical Semitic languages, gender is less systematically marked in the morphology of the noun (see §4.1.2.1 for adjectives). There is a suffix *-t* that occasionally marks feminine nouns which are paired with a masculine noun using the same stem: for example, *bəˀsi* "man," *bəˀsit* "woman"; *əgziˀ* "lord," *əgziˀt* "lady"; *əḫ̮ʷ* "brother," *əḫ̮ət* "sister."

4.1.1.2 Number

Plural can be marked by suffixation or by internal vowel change. The common pluralizing process is by suffixation of *-at* (from common Semitic feminine plural, used in Ge'ez for both genders): thus, *may, mayat* (plural) "water"; *ṣəge, ṣəgeyat* (plural) "flower"; *ʕaśa, ʕaśat* (plural) "fish." Nouns with feminine formative *-t* may or may not drop this before the suffix: *śərəʕt, śərəʕ-t-at* (plural) "law," but *ʕäzäq-t, ʕäzäq-at* (plural) "well."

A great many Ge'ez nouns, however, form their plural according to one of the internal (so-called broken) plural patterns, if necessary using "underlying" glides or supplemental consonants to make up the canonical consonants of the pattern. The vast majority of triconsonantal internal plurals follow one of six patterns:

1. *CVCäC*: while probably the most archaic, this pattern is not the most productive, but does include some of the most basic lexical items. The pattern is probably to be connected with the one internal plural pattern that can be assigned to Proto-Semitic, exemplified in Hebrew by the so-called *shegolate plurals* (*melek* ~ *mlakim* < **malk-* ~ *malak-*), and indeed to Afro-Asiatic: for example, *əzn* ~ *əzän* "ear"; *əgr* ~ *əgär* "foot"; *əd* ~ *ədäw* "hand," *ab* ~ *abäw* "father," *əḫʷ* ~ *aḫäw* "brother."
2. *aCCaC*: this is the most productive pattern for triconsonantal nominal stems. Many biconsonantal stems that can be analyzed as *CwC* or *CyC* take this pattern, as well as a few *CC* stems that become *CCt* in the plural: for example, *ləbs* ~ *albas* "garment"; *färäs* ~ *afras* "horse"; *bet* ~ *abyat* "house"; *ṣom* ~ *aṣwam* "fast"; *səm* ~ *asmat* "name."
3. *aCCuC*: this pattern, a special Ethiopian development, seems to occur most frequently with initial laryngeal stems: for example, *adg* ~ *aʔdug* "ass"; *hägär* ~ *ahgur* "city."
4. *aCCəCt*: this pattern is a variant of the above, with the addition of a final *-t* and a reduction of *u* to ə, which originally had to be a shortening in closed syllable (i.e., **ū* → **u* / ___ CC: this is one of the few synchronic reflexes of the original length distinction between *u* < **ū* and ə < {**i*, **u*}): for example, *rəʔs* ~ *arʔəst* "head"; *gäbr* ~ *agbərt* "slave."
5. *CäCaCəC(t)*: this very productive (and common Semitic) quadriliteral pattern occurs on almost all noun stems with four consonants, as well as with a number of nouns having three consonants and at least one so-called "long" stem-vowel – *i, e, o*, or u (see §3.2). Consider the following examples: *dəngəl* ~ *dänagəl* "virgin"; *mäsfən* ~ *mäsafənt* "prince"; *kokäb* ~ *käwakəbt* "star"; *mäskot* ~ *mäsakut* (< *mäsakəwt*) "window"; *dorho* ~ *därawəh* "chicken"; *lelit* ~ *läyaləy* "night"; *bəḥer* ~ *bäḥawərt* "earth"; *wəḥiz* ~ *wäḥayəzt* "river"; *qäsis* ~ *qäsawəs* "priest."
6. *aCaCəC(t)*: this is another way of extending the quadriliteral pattern just discussed to triconsonantal stems: thus, *bägʔ* ~ *abagəʔ* "sheep"; *ganen* ~ *aganənt* "devil."

Note that the glide inserted to fill out the *triliteral* (CCC) or *quadriliteral* (CCCC) pattern is not generally predictable from the nature of the vowel. Although there are numerous exceptions, there is a tendency toward a polarity pattern in forms with optional *-t*: *-t* is added in the plural if it is absent in the singular (unless the noun is feminine), and absent in the plural if it is present in the singular.

Finally, an additional morphological plural marking occurs with all plural forms (suffix or internal) followed by possessive suffixes: an *-i-* is inserted between the noun and the suffix. Thus corresponding to *ṣəgeyat* "flowers," *abyat* "houses," we have *ṣəgeyatina* "our flowers," *abyatina* "our houses."

4.1.1.3 *Case*

Common Semitic had a three-case system: a nominative in *-u, a genitive in *-i, and an accusative in *-a (cf. Akkadian *kalb-u-m, kalb-i-m, kalb-a-m*; Arabic *kalb-u-n, kalb-i-n, kalb-a-n*). In Ethiopic the merger of short, high vowels ({*i, *u} → ə), plus the eventual disappearance of final ə (ə → φ / ___ #), automatically neutralized the distinction between nominative and genitive, and reduced the nominal case system to a single morphologically marked case form in Ge'ez, the *accusative-construct*, henceforth simply *accusative*. It is opposed to an unmarked *absolutive* form, identical with the stem, which we will refer to as *nominative*. The accusative is formed by suffixation of -ä to the unmarked form of the noun: thus, nominative *bet* "house," accusative *betä*. This form continues the inherited function of the direct object of a verb, as in: *särḥä nəgus betä* "The/a king built the/a house" (lit. "built king-NOM. house-ACC."). It is also used for the head (first) noun in the so-called *construct* configuration, as in: *betä nəgus* "the/a house of the/a king" (lit. "house-ACC. king-NOM.").

In both object and possessive constructions, morphological indication of case can be replaced by syntactic paraphrase. In the case of the direct object, the construction *Verb Noun*-ACC. can be replaced by *Verb+object suffix lä Noun*-NOM., where *lä* is the preposition "to." Thus, instead of *särḥä betä* "he made the/a house," one can have *särḥo* (< *särḥä+hu*) *lä bet* "he made the house" (note that the prepositional paraphrase tends to be preferred for definite direct objects). In lieu of the construct *Noun$_1$*-ACC. *Noun$_2$*-NOM., there are two possibilities: either *Noun$_1$ zä Noun$_2$*, where *zä* is the relative pronoun; or *Noun$_1$+ possessive suffix lä Noun$_2$*. Thus, instead of *betä nəgus* one can have either *bet zä nəgus* or *betu* (< *bet+hu*) *lä nəgus* (where the latter variant may be preferred for a definite head noun).

4.1.2 Adjectives and participles

The gender- and number-marking systems of this morphological class have undergone less simplification than was the case with the noun. The class includes the following:

1. General adjectives of many canonical shapes, of which we will use *śänay* "beautiful" as typical.
2. A special class of quality adjectives of the well-known Semitic form masculine singular *CäC(C)iC*: *ḥäddis* "new," *ʕäbiyy* "big."
3. The present or active participle of the verb, having the form *CäCaCi* (*qätali* "killer"). This replaces an older **CāCiC* common Semitic pattern with a compound reflex of **CaC(C)āC+ī* (a habitual agent nominalization, plus a relational – so-called *nisbe* – denominal adjective formation).
4. The passive or intransitive participle of the verb, of the form *CəCuC* (*qətul* "killed," Proto-Semitic **qutūl*).

4.1.2.1 *Gender*

Generally gender is marked in conjunction with the number category (see below for paradigms); most adjectives and participles form the feminine singular by suffixing *-t*, and keep the *-at* suffix for the feminine plural (as opposed to the noun, which generalizes the suffix to masculines). The masculine plural is marked by suffixing *-an*. Some masculine (and feminine) plurals are formed by internal vowel change, plus suffix *-t*; and adjectives of the *CäCCiC* form take a special *CäCCaC* shape.

4.1.2.2 *Number*

The paradigms for the classes of §4.1.2 are as follows:

(6)

	Singular	*Plural*
Masc.	śänay	śänayan
Fem.	śänayt	śänayat

The active participle has a special masculine plural form:

(7)

	Singular	*Plural*
Masc.	nägari	nägärt
Fem.	nägarit	nägariyat

The passive participle and the *CäCCiC* adjectives have a special feminine singular form:

(8)

	Singular	*Plural*
Masc.	nəgur	nəguran
Fem.	nəgərt	nəgurat
Masc.	ḥäddis	ḥäddisan
Fem.	ḥäddas	ḥäddisat

Some *CäCCiC* forms have a common plural like the active participle:

(9)

	Singular	*Plural*
Masc.	ʕäbiyy	ʕäbbäyt
Fem.	ʕäbbay	ʕäbbäyt

4.1.2.3 *Case*

Case is marked as on the noun.

4.2 Pronouns

Within Semitic, the personal pronouns of Ge'ez offer interesting pattern similarities and contrasts:

(10) **Independent pronouns**

	Akkadian		*Arabic*		*Ge'ez*	
	Sg.	*Pl.*	*Sg.*	*Pl.*	*Sg.*	*Pl.*
1st	anāku	nīnu	ʔana	naḥnu	anä	nəḥnä
2nd masc.	atta	attunu	ʔanta	ʔantum	antä	antəmu
2nd fem.	atti	attina	ʔanti	ʔantunna	anti	antən
3rd masc.	šū	šunu	huwa	hum	wəʔətu	wəʔətomu/əmuntu
3rd fem.	šī	šina	hiya	hunna	yəʔəti	wəʔəton/əmantu

As can be readily seen, the first- and second-person independent pronouns of Ge'ez are fairly straightforward representatives of Common Semitic, whereas a certain amount of idiosyncratic innovation has taken place in the third-person independent pronouns. The suffix pronouns, on the other hand, object and possessive, show predictable Semitic forms:

(11) Suffix pronouns

	Akkadian		*Arabic*		*Ge'ez*	
	Sg.	*Pl.*	*Sg.*	*Pl.*	*Sg.*	*Pl.*
1st	-ī, -nī	-ni	-ī, -nī	-nā	-Vyä/-Vni	-Vnä
2nd masc.	-ka	-kunu	-ka	-kum	-Vkä	-Vkəmu
2nd fem.	-ki	-kina	-ki	-kunna	-Vki	-Vkən
3rd masc.	-šu	-šunu	-hū	-hum	-hu~-u~-o	-homu~-omu
3rd fem.	-ši	-šina	-hā	-hunna	-ha~-a	-hon~-on

Note that the first singular suffix is *-Vyä* with nouns and *-Vni* with verbs. The stressed or unstressed vowel (V) with first- and second-person forms is, for nouns, the stem-final vowel, or vocalic suffix, if there is one, or ə if the noun form ends in a consonant. For verbs it is *ä* (except for second-person object suffixes with jussive verb forms, compare *yənäggərákkä* "he speaks to you" and *yəngə́rkä* "may he speak to you"). In the third person, in nouns and verbs *ä+hú/há/hómu/hón* gives *ó/á/ómu/ón* (as in *nägärä+hú* > *nägäró* "he spoke to him"; *betä+hú* > *betó* "his house" [acc.]) In nouns C+*h*V gives CV (as in *bet+hú* > *betú* "his house" [nom.]).

The deictic-relative paradigms are built on the stem-series *z-* (singular, mostly masculine), *ənt-* (most feminine singulars), *əll-* (plural), corresponding to *ð- (masculine), **t-* (feminine), and **l-* (plural) in Common Semitic. Far deixis adds the element *-ku*. Both near and far have a "long" form with suffix *-tu~ti~tä*. The paradigm of the whole deictic–relative–interrogative series is as follows:

(12)

		Singular		*Plural*	
		Nom.	*Acc.*	*Nom.*	*Acc.*
"this"	*Masc.*	zə-	zä	əllu	
	Fem.	za	za	əlla	
"this" (long)	*Masc.*	zəntu	zäntä	əllontu	əllontä
	Fem.	zati	zatä	əllantu	əllantä
"that"	*Masc.*	zəku	zəkʷä, zəku	alləku	
	Fem.	əntəku	əntəkʷä əntäku	əlləku	
"that" (long)	*Masc.*	zəktu	zəktä	əlləktu	əlləktä
	Fem.	əntakti	əntaktä	əllaktu	əllaktä
Relative	*Masc.*	zä-	əllä		
	Fem.	əntä		əllä	

The members of the interrogative series have the **mVn-* and *ˀ*ay-* shapes also known from Common Semitic:

(13)

	Singular		*Plural*	
	Nom.	*Acc.*	*Nom.*	*Acc.*
"who?"	männu	männä		
"what?"	mənt	məntä		
"which?"	ay		ayat	ayatä

4.3 Verbs

Although each Semitic language has its own elaboration and adaptation of the system of verbal inflection, there is a common core of categories and formal processes which is visible in the different systems, and which permits a fairly accurate approximation of the essential features of the proto-system. In all Semitic languages, finite verb paradigms can be analyzed into two "subparadigms": one marks *person* by the use of subject affixes; the other accounts for the *stem-form* – marks the combination of root, derived stem, and tense-mode.

4.3.1 Person morphology: subject affixes

As can be seen from (14), the prefixing subparadigms differ very little from one another within the major branches of Semitic, and presumably all continue fairly directly an ancestral Proto-Semitic system:

(14) Prefixing/Suffixing

	Akkadian		*Arabic*		*Ge'ez*	
	Sg.	*Pl.*	*Sg.*	*Pl.*	*Sg.*	*Pl.*
1st	a-	ni-	a-	na-	ʔə-	nə-
2nd masc.	ta-	ta- . . . -ā	ta-	ta- . . . -ū	tə-	tə- . . . -u
2nd fem.	ta- . . . -ī	ta- . . . -ā	ta- . . . -ī	ta- . . . -na	tə- . . . -i	tə- . . . -ā
3rd masc.	i-	i- . . . -ū	ya-	ta- . . . -ū	yə	yə- . . . -u
3rd fem.	ta-	i- . . . -ā	ta-	ta- . . . -na	tə-	yə- . . . -ā

The suffixing subparadigms, however, seem to have been subject to a certain amount of transformation (see §1.2):

(15) Suffixing

	Akkadian		*Arabic*		*Ge'ez*	
	Sg.	*Pl.*	*Sg.*	*Pl.*	*Sg.*	*Pl.*
1st	-āku	-ānu	-tu	-nā	-ku	-na
2nd masc.	-āta	-ātunu	-ta	-tum	-ka	-kəmmu
2nd fem.	-āti	-ātina	-ti	-tunna	-ki	-kən
3rd masc.	ϕ	-ū	-a	-ū	-a	-u
3rd fem.	-at	-ā	-at	-na	-at	-ā

On the one hand, the first- and second-person suffix forms, especially in the Akkadian, look very much like reduced enclitic forms of the independent pronouns given in (10) above, with the *-ā-* perhaps as some linking element. The third-person forms, on the other hand, look like elements from the nominal inflection – as a matter of fact, the Akkadian stative can be formed on the basis of any noun or adjective (e.g., *damq-at* "she is good," *šarr-āku* "I am king"). The major difference in the Arabic-like languages (Canaanite, Aramaic) is that the *-k-* ∼ *-t-* alternations in the paradigm have been leveled out in favor of *-t-*, whereas in Ge'ez and Modern South Arabian they have been leveled out in favor of *-k-*. As was pointed out by Hetzron 1972, this is important evidence in favor of the temporal priority of an Akkadian-like system over the other two. It is now usually supposed, therefore, that the Proto-Semitic system resembled the Akkadian one, and that the Western Semitic past tense evolved out of something like a verbal adjective with enclitic reduced pronouns.

4.3.2 Stem morphology

The second series of subparadigms governs the stem-form to which the subject markers are affixed. There are three basic morphological categories involved, which we will refer to as (i) *tense*, (ii) *derivational class*, and (iii) *lexical class*.

4.3.2.1 *Tense*

The primary "tense" categories are (i) past, (ii) non-past, (iii) jussive, and (iv) imperative. The imperative stem is identical with the jussive stem in Ge'ez, and hence will not be noted in the paradigms below. The infinitive is not a tense in any usual morphosyntactic sense of the term, but it will be useful to display infinitives in the paradigm as a fourth "tense" form.

4.3.2.2 *Derivational class*

The derivational classes are (i) *base* (zero-affix); (ii) *causative* (prefix ä-); (iii) *passive-reflexive* (prefix *tä-*, if not preceded by a subject prefix, otherwise *t-*); and (iv) *causative-passive* (prefix *ästä-*). The prefixes of (ii)–(iv) continue the common Semitic derivational stems: thus, (ii) causative **š*/*h* giving ʔ in Arabic and Ethiopic, with all three possibilities existing in Old and Modern South Arabian; (iii) prefix and infix *t(a)* in Akkadian, Cananite, Aramaic, Arabic, and South Arabian; (iv) the combination **š*+*t(a)* is attested as such in Arabic, South Arabian, and Akkadian, and as **h*+*t(a)* in Northern Semitic. As in all Semitic languages, these derivational classes are formed, with more or less idiosyncratic semantics, with all verbs in the lexicon, although not all verbs occur in all derivational classes.

4.3.2.3 *Lexical class*

Historically related to the various Semitic verbal derivation systems, but almost completely lexicalized in Ge'ez are the categories of lexical class, conventionally designated in Ge'ez with the letters *A*, *B*, and *C*. *A* is the unmarked class. In the base past and jussive there are two subclasses: *A1* has stem-vowel *ä* in the past and stem-vowel *ə* in the jussive; whereas *A2* has stem-vowel *ə* in the past and *ä* in the jussive. Recalling that Ge'ez *ə* represents Proto-Semitic **i* and **u*, this clearly corresponds to the common stem-vowel alternations (e.g., in Arabic): past *CaCaC* ~ present-jussive *CCuC*, past *CaCiC* ~ present-jussive *CCaC*. Note that some verbs can be A1 in the past and A2 in the jussive, and vice versa. B is the class of verbs with geminating middle radical (Piel in Hebrew, D-stem in Akkadian, Second Form in Arabic); C is the class of verbs with stem-vowel /ā/ after the first radical consonant (Third Form in Arabic). Unlike other Semitic languages, these do not occur in Ge'ez as derived forms of the unmarked base, but as a lexically determined class. A verbal root must be marked in the lexicon as class A, class B, or class C in Ge'ez, and if it occurs in one class, it will not occur in another (the few cases where this occurs are usually counted as homophonous). An exception to this general rule is the class of passive-reflexive C (*tänagärä*, cognate with the Sixth Form of Arabic) and causative-passive C (*astänagärä*) which occur with many verbs, the former frequently as a reciprocal, the latter with widely varying semantics.

Given the existence of this set of lexically determined categories, it is convenient to enter quadriradical verbs (verbs with four root consonants) under this general heading as lexical class *D*. These verbs are especially frequent in Ethiopic Semitic. There are only a few cases where they can be etymologically linked to triradical verbs, but phonologically most of them are either of the form $C_1RC_2C_3$ (R = /n, l, r/) or of the form $C_1C_2C_3C_3$, where C_1, C_2, C_3 otherwise follow the co-occurrence constraints of triconsonantal roots. As is often the case in Semitic, these D (quadriradical) verbs closely resemble B (middle-geminating) verbs in their morphological structure.

4.3.2.4 *Sample paradigms*

Table 6.6 gives the stem-paradigms for the so-called "strong" verbs (verbs with roots that do not have a glide or vocalic radical; see §4.3.3.1). The lexical items used are *ngr* "speak"

Table 6.6 Strong verb-stem paradigms

		Base	Causative	Pass.-refl.	Caus.-pass.
Past	*A1*	nägär-	angär-	tänägr-	astängär-
	A2	läbs-	albäs-	täläbs-	astälbäs-
	B	fäṣṣäm-	afäṣṣäm-	täfäṣṣäm-	astäfäṣṣäm-
	C	masän-	amasän-	tämasän-	astämasän-
	D	dängäṣ-	adängäṣ-	tädängäṣ-	astädängäṣ-
Pres.-fut.	*A*	-näggər(-)	-anäggər(-)	-tnäggär(-)	-astänäggər(-)
	B	-feṣṣəm(-)	-afeṣṣəm(-)	-tfeṣṣäm(-)	-astäfeṣṣəm(-)
	C	-masən(-)	-amasən(-)	-tmasän(-)	-astämasən(-)
	D	-dänäggəṣ(-)	-adänäggəṣ(-)	-tdänäggäṣ(-)	-astädänäggəṣ(-)
Jussive	*A1*	-ngər(-)	-angər(-)	-tnägär(-)	-astängər(-)
	A2	-lbäs(-)	-albəs(-)	-tläbäs(-)	-astälbəs(-)
	B	-fäṣṣəm(-)	-afäṣṣəm(-)	-tfäṣṣäm(-)	-astäfäṣṣəm(-)
	C	-masən(-)	-amasən(-)	-tmasän(-)	-astämasən(-)
	D	-dängəṣ(-)	-adängəṣ(-)	-tdängäṣ(-)	-astädängəṣ(-)
Infinitive	*A*	nägir(ot)	angəro(t)	tänägro(t)	astänägro(t)
	B	fäṣṣəmo(t)	afäṣṣəmo(t)	täfäṣṣəmo(t)	astäfäṣṣəmo(t)
	C	masno(t)	amasno(t)	tämasno(t)	astämasno(t)
	D	dängəṣo(t)	adängəṣo(t)	tädängəṣo(t)	astädängəṣo(t)
Gerund	*A*	nägir-	angir-	tänägir-	astänägir-
	B	fäṣṣim-	afäṣṣim-	täfäṣṣim-	astäfäṣṣim-
	C	masin-	amasin-	tämasin-	astämasin-
	D	dängiṣ-	adängiṣ-	tädängiṣ-	astädängiṣ-

(Class A1); *lbs* "wear" (Class A2); *fṣm* "finish" (Class B); *msn* "perish" (Class C): *dngṣ* "surprise" (Class D, quadriradical).

4.3.3 Strong and weak verbs

The distinction strong versus weak root is bound up with the fact that Semitic inflection and derivation typically involves a triconsonantal *strong* root, such as *lbs* "wear," into which are inserted different vowel patterns (combined with different prefixes, suffixes, and infixes): for example, *läbsä* "he wore"; *ləbs* "clothes"; *ləbsät* "dressing"; *mälbäs* "clothing"; *albas* "articles of clothing"; *albäsä* "he clothed"; *täläbsä* "get dressed"; *tälabäsä* "disguise oneself"; *astälabäsä* "clothe several persons"; and so forth. A number of words, however, do not have three true consonants, and the place of the "missing" consonant is occupied by a glide *w* or *y* (sometimes also *n* and ʾ), yielding *weak* roots of the form *wCC, yCC, CwC, CyC, CCw, CCy*, and so forth. Since some of the oldest and most widespread Semitic vocabulary (*wld* "bear child," *qwm* "stand," *bky* "cry") is of this form, it has been suggested that the unique phonological organization involved in triconsonantal strong roots is a tendency (already incipient in Afro-Asiatic) that only gradually overtook large portions of the Semitic lexicon and morphology, and that the weak roots are an attempt to fit older, nontriconsonantal lexical items onto the innovative triconsonantal patterns. Semitic languages differ in the extent to which weak verbs are assimilated to the strong patterns – in general, Akkadian tends to be the most conservative (i.e., least assimilating), and Ge'ez the most assimilating.

Arabic is somewhere in the middle, and Hebrew is somewhat more conservative than Arabic. Reflexes of the archaic weak root **mwt* "die" are illustrated in (16):

(16)

	Akkadian		*Arabic*		*Ge'ez*	
	Present	*Past*	*Present*	*Past*	*Present*	*Past*
3rd sg. masc.	i -mūat	i -mūt	ya -mūt- u	māt- a	yə -mawwət	mot-a
2nd sg. masc.	ta -mūat	ta -mūt	ta -mūt- u	mut- ta	tə -mawwət	mot- ka
3rd pl. masc.	i -mutt- ū	i -mūt- ū	ya -mūt- ū-na	māt- ū	yə -mawwət- u	mot- u

The finite base A form (see §§4.3.2.2; 4.3.2.3) of triconsonantal glide roots is illustrated in (17) using the lexical items *wrd* "descend," *wdq* "fall" (W1); *mwt* "die" (W2); *śym* "appoint" (Y2); *ftw* "love," *bdw* "be desert" (W3); *bky* "cry," and *sty* "drink" (Y3). The other lexical and derivational classes are straightforward extensions of the base A form. Note that for medial *w/y* verbs (W2/Y2) of the A class, there is no distinction between subclass A1 and A2, and that initial-*y* verbs (Y1) are very few in number, and have been largely regularized.

(17)

		Past	*Present*	*Jussive*
W1	*A1*	wäräd-	-wärrəd(-)	-räd(-)
	A2	wädq-	-wäddəq(-)	-däq(-)
W2	*A*	mot-	-mäwwət(-)	-mut(-)
Y2	*A*	śem-	-śäyyəm(-)	-śim(-)
W3	*A1*	fätäw/fäto-	-fättu(-)	-ftu(-)
	A2	bädw-	-bäddu(-)	-bdäw(-)
Y3	*A1*	bäkäy-	-bäkki(-)	-bki(-)
	A2	säty-	-sätti(-)	-stäy(-)

Verbs which have a laryngeal (*L*; i.e., ʔ, ʕ, ḫ, ḥ, *h*) as a radical largely follow the strong pattern, as modified by the special vowel–laryngeal sequence constraints noted above (see §3.3.4): thus for LCC, third masculine singular – past *ʕäqäbä* "he kept," present *yäʕäqqəb* (< **yəʕäqqəb*, by laryngeal vowel harmony). Many CLC verbs are also completely "regular," as *säḥäbä, säḥäbkä* "he, you (sg. masc.) pulled"; however, an important subclass of these verbs displays a past stem-vowel pattern with ə: *səḥtä, səḥətkä* "he, you (masc. sg.) erred." CCL verbs of the A class are idiosyncratic in that they are all of the A2 (*läbsä*) subclass: *wäḍʔä, wäḍakä* "he, you (masc. sg.) left." In addition, CCL verbs of the B, C, and D class have the unique property in the Ge'ez conjugation system of also having a "*läbsä*-like" pattern in the past: *läqqəḥä, läqqaḥkä* "he, you (masc. sg.) lent"; *baləḥä, balaḥkä* "he, you (masc. sg.) rescued," *zängəʕä, zängaʕkä* "he, you (masc. sg.) raved."

Finally, there are a dozen or so verbs, most with glide or laryngeal radicals, which show one or more idiosyncratic irregularities in stem-paradigm. An important one from the historical point of view is the unique (and archaic) conjugation pattern of the verb *bhl* "say" in its base form (the derived class forms are conjugated regularly). Instead of an expected past tense **bəhlä* (compare *kəhlä* from *khl* "be able"), this verb has a prefixing past tense, the only survival of this archaic form in Ethiopic Semitic, with stem *-be* in nonsuffixed forms, *-bel-* in suffixed: *yəbe, yəbelu* "he, they said." The present stem of this verb is *-bəl(-)*, and its jussive is *-bal(-)*: *yəbəl* "he says," *yəbal* "let him say" (compare *yəkəl* "can," *yekal* "let him be able").

4.4 Adverbs and prepositions

A number of adverbs are productively formed from accusatives (suffix *-ä*) of nouns and adjectives: for example, *lelitä* "by night"; *qədmä* "in front"; *rəḥuqä* "afar"; *märirä* "bitterly." Note that – although there is no direct etymological relation – an accusative-like form is also the norm for many conjunctions: thus, *əmä* "if"; *sobä* (earlier *sobe*) "when"; *ənbälä* "except"; *ənzä* "while"; *əskä* "until."

On the other hand, an adverbial (hence nominal) origin is clear for many prepositions: for example, *mängälä* "towards," *maʾkälä* "between." Most of the usual prepositions end in *-ä* before nouns, and *-e* before pronominal suffixes: thus, *ḫäbä* ~ *ḫabe-* "to, towards"; *dibä* ~ *dibe-* "on"; *məslä* ~ *məsle-* "with" (e.g., *məsläsäbʔ* "with (the) man," *məslehu* "with him"). Note the following special cases: *əmənnä* (proclitic form *əm-*) ~ *əmənne-* "from"; *kämä* ~ *käma-* "like"; *wəstä* ~ *wēstet-* "in"; *ʕäwdä* ~ *ʕäwdä-* "around"; *əskä* (does not occur with pronominal suffixes) "until, up to." The monosyllabic prepositions are proclitic: *bä-* "in" (*bə-* before first- and second-person pronouns, third-person singular *bo* ~ *bottu, ba* ~ *batti*); *lä-* "to" (except *litä* "to me," *lottu* "to him," *latti* "to her," *lon* ~ *latton* "to them" [fem. pl.]).

4.5 Numerals

The Ge'ez number system shows a number of archaisms. For one thing, even though gender marking is considerably reduced in the noun, the Ge'ez cardinal numbers show a faithful continuation of the common Semitic gender polarity switch, with a *t*-suffixed form in the masculine, and an unmarked form in the feminine. In addition to these forms, Ge'ez has a great variety of derived forms, the most important of which are the ordinals, chiefly of the pattern *CaCəC* (< **CāCiC*). There are also day-of-week/month forms (*CäCuC* pattern), and adverbial forms ("once," "twice," etc.; of the *CəCC* pattern). For the numbers 1 to 10, these forms are as follows:

(3)

	Cardinal		Ordinal	Day	Adverbial
	Masc.	Fem.			
1	aḫädu	aḥati	qädami	əḫud	məʕrä, aḥätä
2	kəlʔe, kəlʔetu	kəlʔeti	dagəm, kaləʔ, kaʕəb	sänuy	kaʕbä, dagmä
3	śälästu	śälas	śaləs	śälus	śəlsä
4	arbaʕtu	arbaʕ	rabəʕ	räbuʕ	rəbʕä
5	ḫäməstu	ḫäms	ḫaməs	ḫämus	ḫəmsä
6	sədəstu	səssu	sadəs	sädus	sədsä
7	säbʕätu	säbʕu	sabəʕ	säbuʕ	səbʕä
8	sämäntu	sämani	samən	sämun	səmnä
9	təsʕätu, täsʕätu	təsʕu, täsʕu	tasəʕ	täsuʕ	təsʕä
10	ʕäśərtu	ʕäśru	ʕaśər	ʕäśur	ʕəśrä

Except for the day nominalization, which uses the inherited Semitic root *sny* (< *θny), the inherited root of the numeral "two" has been replaced by **kilʔ-*, the Semitic word for "both." Other nominalizations involving "two" call upon the lexical items *dgm* "repeat" and *kʕb* "double." The ordinal for "one" uses the lexical item *qdm* "precede." The ordinals provide the only remnant in Ge'ez morphology of the common Semitic active participle of the form **CāCiC* > *CaCəC*, replaced by a new form in Ge'ez (see §4.1.2). The masculine cardinals have an accusative form in *-tä*, and have *-ti-* before suffix pronouns: *śälästä* "three" (acc.), *śälästihomu* "the three of them." Feminine cardinals are usually treated as invariants.

For numbers above ten the order is *Ten wä Unit*: thus, *ʕäśärtu wä śälästu*, *ʕäś ru wä śälas* "13" (masc. and fem.). The tens units are *ʕəśra* "20," *śälasa* "30," *arbʕa* "40," *ḫämsa* "50," *səssa* "60," *säbʕa* "70," *sämanya* "80," *təsʕa* or *täsʕa* "90"; while "100" is *mə*ʔ*ət*, "1,000" is *ʕäśärtu mə*ʔ*ət*, and "10,000" is *əlf*. The form cited for the ordinals in (18) is the masculine singular; there are alternate masculine forms in *-awi*, *-ay* (*ḫamsawi*, *ḫamsay* "fifth"), and feminine ordinals end in *-it* or *-awit* (*ḫamsit*, *ḫamsawit* "fifth").

5. SYNTAX

The standard grammars of Ge'ez usually represent that language's syntactic profile as somehow less prototypically Semitic than that of the so-called classical Semitic languages such as Hebrew or, even better, Arabic. Much remains to be learned about Proto-Semitic syntax, and the developments that led from it to what we find in the daughter languages. However, it is true that Ge'ez, on the one hand, underwent long centuries of interaction with the non-Semitic languages of the substrate population of the Aksumite empire; on the other hand, classic Ge'ez literature, as known from the literary-religious manuscript tradition, consists, until late in the middle ages, exclusively of translations, either directly from Greek, or, after the tenth century, from Arabic, translated in turn from Greek or other languages of the Christian Near East.

An excellent and extensive survey of the syntactic patterns of the Ge'ez of the literary texts can be found in Dillmann 1907 (see also a more concise characterization in Gragg 1997). That the sentence patterns of these texts are not mere "translationese" can be seen from a comparison with the major syntactic patterns of the Aksumite monumental texts (where, of course, the possibility of Greek influence cannot be entirely bracketed either, given the existence in this tradition of early monolingual and later bilingual Greek versions). The following brief syntactic illustrations will be drawn entirely from Aksumite monumental sources, text and line cited according to the edition of Bernard *et al.* 1991.

5.1 Word order

Although there are no sentences in this corpus with explicit nominal subject and nominal object (pronominal objects are encliticized to the verb), it seems clear that the unmarked main-clause word order in Aksumite Ge'ez is the standard Semitic verb–subject and verb–object:

(19) A. ḍäbʔu ʔägwezat (187, 4)
go to war [PAST, 3RD MASC. PL.] Agwezat
"The Agwezat went out to battle"

B. täkälu mänbärä bä-zəyä (188, 24)
set [PAST, 3RD MASC. PL.] throne [ACC.] in=there
"They set up a throne there"

For discourse and foregrounding purposes, of course, other pragmatically dictated word orders are possible, as in the following example of object–verb order:

(20) wä-lä-ʔäbäʔälkəʕo nəguśä ʔägwezat bäkä ḫädägnä-hu (187, 11)
and=to/=Abaʔalkəʕo king [ACC.] Agwezat naked [ACC.] leave [PAST, 1ST PL.]=him
"And Abaʔalkəʕo, king of the Agwezat, we left naked"

Nominal modifiers generally follow the head noun, as in the following illustrations of adjective, numeral, and relative constructions (and see *passim* for possessive):

(21) A. noba qäyḥ (189, 37)
Nubian red
"red Nubians"
B. mägäbtä kəlˀetä (189, 23)
leader [ACC. PL.] two [ACC.]
"two leaders"
C. ḥäwarya-nä zä-fänäwku l-ottu (189, 11)
messenger=our which=send [PAST, 1ST SG.] to=him
"our messenger which I sent to him"

However the order modifier–noun is also possible, and for numerals seems to be even more frequent:

(22) A. ärbäʕtu ˀängadä (188, 15)
four [MASC.] tribe [ACC. PL.]
"four tribes"
B. ʕəśra wä-sälusä mäwaʕəlä (189, 16)
twenty and=three day [ACC. PL.]
"twenty-three days"

The use of enclitics such as *-ssa* for fronting major sentence constituents, widely used in the standard translation literature to correspond to Greek constructions with μέν (*mén*) and δέ (*dé*), appears already in a sixth-century Ge'ez text from Marib, where it, in fact, is a citation of Psalm 19, 8:

(23) əmuntu-ssä bä-ˀäfras wä-bä-särägälat wä-nəḥnä-ssä näʕabi
they=indeed in=horses and=in=chariots and=we=indeed glory
bä-səmä əgziˀä bəḥer (195, 27)
in=name [ACC.] lord [ACC.] earth
"They indeed in horses and chariots, but we glory in the name of God"

5.2 Subordination

5.2.1 Relative clauses

As exemplified in (21), relative clauses are introduced by the relative pronoun *zä-* (singular and proclitic), *ˀəllä* (plural). Word order follows the general pattern of main clauses, although with more of a tendency for the verb to come at the end:

(24) ˀəgziˀä sämay zä-wähäbä-ni ˀəgziˀä kwəlu
lord [ACC.] heaven who=give [PAST, 3RD MASC. SG.]=me lord [ACC.] all
zä-b-ottu ˀämänku
who=in=him believe [PAST, 1ST. SG.]
"the Lord of Heaven who gave me (to be) lord of all, in whom I have believed"

5.2.2 Adverbial clauses

Adverbial clauses are introduced by the subordinating conjunctions mentioned in §4.4 and behave in general like relative clauses:

(25) ḍäbäʔku / noba / sobe / ʔäḍrärä / ʔəḥzabä
go to war [PAST, 1ST SG.] / Nubia / when / revolt [PAST, 3RD MASC. SG.] / people
noba (189, 8)
Nubia
"I went out to battle against Nubia when the peoples of Nubia revolted"

Note the use of *ʔənzä* and the past tense use of the imperfective (not present-future):

(26) baṣḥu / däwälä / ʔägädä / ʔə<n>zä
come [PAST, 3RD MASC. PL.] / region [ACC.] / Agada / while
yəqattəlu / wa-yəḍewwəwu
kill [IMPF., 3RD MASC. PL.] / and=take captive [IMPF., 3RD MASC. PL.]
wa-yəmähärrəku (187, 20)
and=plunder [IMPF., 3RD MASC. PL.]
"They came to the region of Agada killing and taking captives and plundering"

A subordinate clause expressing sequential action (*conjunctive*, i.e., "and then") is formed by the infinitive + suffix pronoun – the so-called *gerund* construction – before the main verb, found frequently in later Ge'ez, and indeed in all modern Ethiopic Semitic:

(27) wä-baṣiḥ-omu / ʔängäbo / bä-həyä / räkäbä-nä
and=come[INF.]=them / Angabo / in-there / find[PAST, 3RD MASC. SG.]=us
ʔäbäʔälkəʕo (187, 5)
Abaʔalkəʕo
"And they having come to Angabo, Abaʔalkəʕo found us there"

In the Aksumite texts this construction also occurs after the main verb:

(28) wä-däḫnä / ʔätäwu / ʔäfrih-omu / ḍar-omu
and=safe [ACC.] / return [PAST, 3RD MASC. PL.] / fear[CAUS., INF.]=them / enemy=their
wä-mäwiʔ-omu / bä-ḫaylä / ʔəgziʔä / bəḥer (189, 33)
and=conquer[INF.]=their / in=power [ACC.] / lord[ACC.] / earth
"And they returned safely having terrorized their enemy and conquered by the power of the Lord of the Earth (i.e., 'God')"

Simultaneity and adverbial modification can be expressed also paratactically (note the identity of tense in the *main* and *modifying* verbs):

(29) konäna-homu / ... kämä yəḥoru
order[PAST, 3RD MASC. SG.]=them ... that / go [JUSS., 3RD MASC. PL.]
wä-yəʕälu / wä-yəḥoru
and=spend day [JUSS., 3RD MASC. PL.] / and=go [JUSS., 3RD MASC. PL.]
wä-yəbitu (187, 13)
and=spend night [JUSS., 3RD MASC. PL.]
"He ordered them ... that they travel day and night"

In addition to its use in the so-called gerund construction – infinitive+pronominal suffix (see [27] and [28]) – the infinitive can also occur as a simple verbal complement:

(30) wä-ˀäbäyä ḫädigä (189, 13)
and=refuse [PAST, 3RD MASC. SG.] leave[INF., ACC.]
"And he refused to leave"

However, a much more frequent construction with verbs of commanding, willing, and so forth is the use of the conjunction *kämä* "that" followed by the jussive, as illustrated with the verb *konänä* "command" in (29). In this construction, it is also possible to use the simple jussive without the conjunction:

(31) wä-ˀäzäzu-omu yəḥoru
and=order[PAST, 3RD MASC. PL.]=them go[JUSS., 3RD MASC. PL.]
yəqtəlu (187, 15)
kill [JUSS., 3RD MASC. PL.]
"And they ordered them to go and kill"

The jussive can, of course, be used in the main clause in an optative sense, with or without an "asseverative" *lä* clitic (here translated conventionally as "indeed"). The following frequently used curse formula (here from 188, 26ff.) illustrates this, as well as the conditional and the existential "be" constructions:

(32) lä-ˀəmä b-o-zä näśät-o
indeed=if in=him=who destroy[PAST, 3RD MASC. SG.]=it
wä-näqäl-o wəˀətu wä-bəḥer-u wä-zämäd-u
and=uproot[PAST, 3RD MASC. SG.]=it he and=country=his and=family=his
lä-yətnäqäl wä-yətnäśät
indeed=uproot [JUSS., PASS., 3RD MASC. SG.] and=destroy [JUSS., PASS., 3RD MASC. SG.]
"If indeed there is anyone who destroys and uproots it [the stele], may he and his country and his family be uprooted and destroyed."

A final construction which occurs in these inscriptions, which is extensively used in later Ge'ez and in modern Ethiopic Semitic, is the specialization of the verb *bhl* "to say" as a quotative (i.e., as an introducer of direct speech), frequently in conjunction with other verbs of speaking (on the forms of this verb, see §4.3.3):

(33) sobe tämäkäḥä wä-ˀi-yəfalləs
when boast [PAST, 3RD MASC. SG.] and=not=cross [IMPF., 3RD MASC. SG.]
ˀəm-täkäze yəbe ˀəḥzabä noba (189, 8)
from=Takaze say [IMPF., 3RD MASC. SG.] people Nubia
"When the Nubian people boasted saying 'He will not cross the Takaze' "

Bibliography

Bernard, E., A. Drewes, and R. Schneider. 1991. *Recueil des inscriptions de l'Ethiopie des périodes pré-axoumites et axoumites.* Paris: Edition E. de Boccard.

Cohen, M. 1921. "La prononciation traditionnelle du guèze (éthiopien classique)." *Journal Asiatique*, Series 11, 17:217–269.

Daniels, P. 1997. "Scripts of Semitic languages." In Hetzron 1997, pp. 16–45.

Dillmann, A. 1857. *Grammatik der äthiopischen Sprache.* Leipzig: Tauchnitz.

______. 1907. *Ethiopic Grammar.* Translated by James Crichton. Second edition (enlarged and improved by Carl Bezold), 1899. London: Williams and Norgate.

Gragg, G. 1997. "Ge'ez (Ethiopic)." In Hetzron 1997, pp. 242–260.

Hetzron, R. 1972. *Ethiopian Semitic: Studies in Classification.* Journal of Semitic Studies Monograph 2. Manchester: Manchester University Press.

_______. 1997. *The Semitic Languages.* London: Routledge.

Kobishchanov, Y. 1979. *Axum.* Edited by Joseph Michels; translated by Lorraine Kapitanoff. University Park: Pennsylvania State University Press.

Lambdin, T. 1978. *Introduction to Classical Ethiopic (Ge'ez).* Missoula: Scholars Press.

Leslau, W. 1987. *Comparative Dictionary of Ge'ez.* Wiesbaden: Otto Harrassowitz.

Makonnen, A. 1984. *Matériaux pour l'étude de la prononciation traditionnelle du guèze.* Paris: Editions Recherche sur les Civilisations.

Mittwoch, E. 1926. *Die Traditionelle Aussprache des Äthiopischen.* Abessinische Studien, 1. Berlin/Leipzig: de Gruyter.

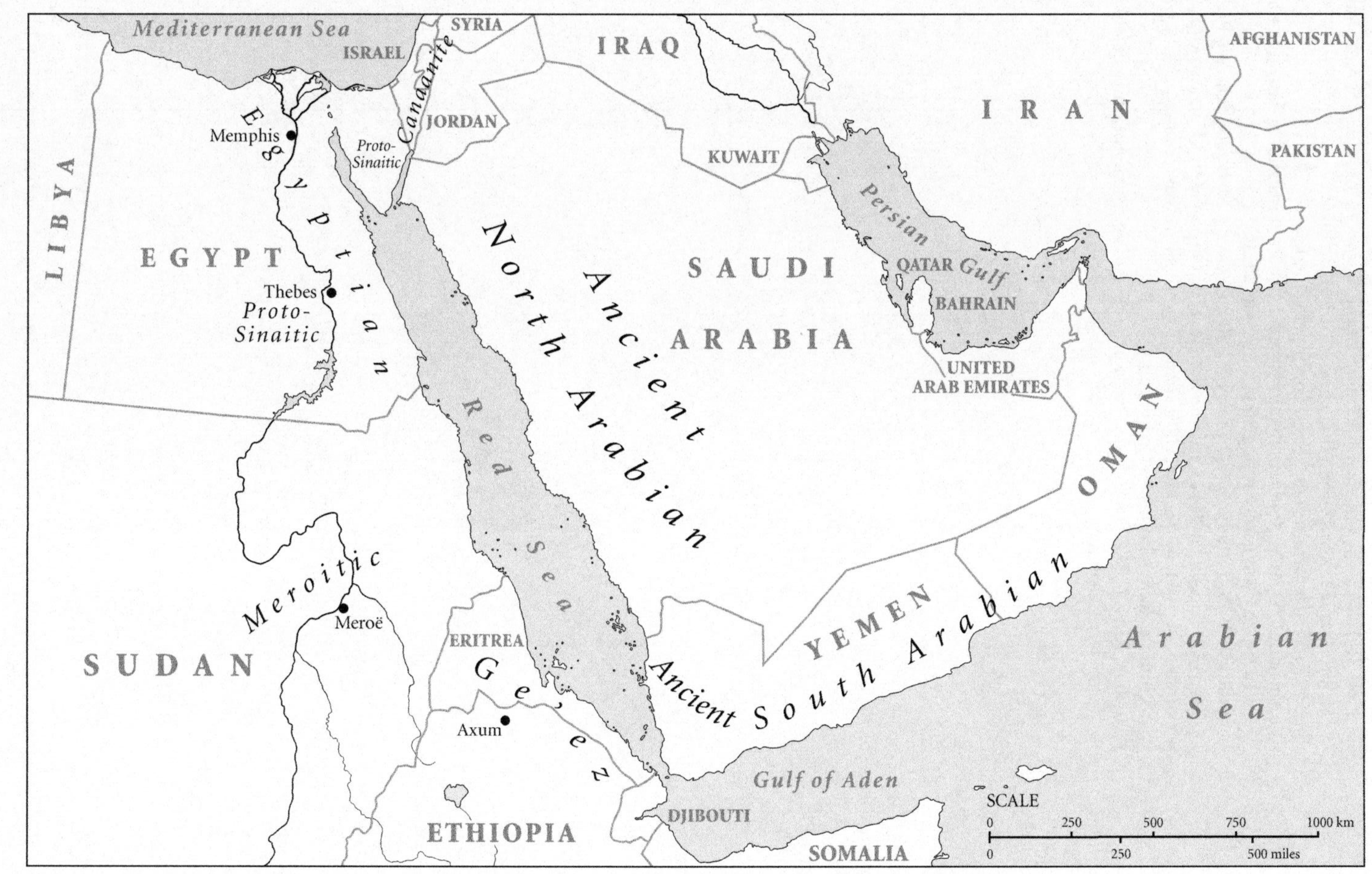

Map 1. The Ancient languages of Northeastern Africa and Arabia

Full tables of contents from *The Cambridge Encyclopedia of the World's Ancient Languages*, and from the other volumes in the paperback series

Table of contents of *WAL*

Table of contents of *The Ancient Languages of Asia and the Americas*

Table of contents of *The Ancient Languages of Asia Minor*

Table of contents for *The Ancient Languages of Europe*

Table of contents of *The Ancient Languages of Syria-Palestine and Arabia*

Index of general subjects

Index of grammar and linguistics

Index of languages

Index of named linguistic laws and principles

Printed in Great Britain
by Amazon